IN DEFENSE OF NATURAL LAW

IN DEFENSE OF
NATURAL LAW

ROBERT P. GEORGE

OXFORD
UNIVERSITY PRESS

OXFORD
UNIVERSITY PRESS

Great Clarendon Street, Oxford OX2 6DP

Oxford University Press is a department of the University of Oxford.
It furthers the University's objective of excellence in research, scholarship,
and education by publishing worldwide in

Oxford New York

Auckland Bangkok Buenos Aires Cape Town Chennai
Dar es Salaam Delhi Hong Kong Istanbul Karachi Kolkata
Kuala Lumpur Madrid Melbourne Mexico City Mumbai Nairobi
São Paulo Shanghai Singapore Taipei Tokyo Toronto

with an associated company in Berlin

Oxford is a registered trade mark of Oxford University Press
in the UK and in certain other countries

Published in the United States
by Oxford University Press Inc., New York

First published 1999
First published in paperback 2001

British Library Cataloguing in Publication Data
Data available

George, Robert P.
In defense of natural law / Robert P. George
p.   cm.
Includes bibliographical references (p.).
1. Natural law.   I. Title.
K474.G46I5   1998
340'112—dc21   98-30745
ISBN 0-19-826771-1
ISBN 0-19-924299-2 (Pbk)

5 7 9 10 8 6 4

Printed in Great Britain
on acid-free paper by
Bookcraft Ltd., Midsomer Norton, Somerset

For Cindy, David, and Rachel

ACKNOWLEDGEMENTS

The author would like to thank Micah Weinberg for his help in preparing this volume. He would also like to thank Joseph M. Boyle, Jr., Gerard V. Bradley, Greg Everts, John Finnis, Germain Grisez, Walter F. Murphy, William C. Porth, Dermot Quinn, Daniel N. Robinson, Adam Sloane and William L. Saunders for helpful comments on and critiques of these essays, and the Earhart Foundation for its support.

He would finally like to thank the following journals and publishing companies for permission to reprint the essays: Chapter 1, reprinted by permission from *The American Journal of Jurisprudence*, 41 (1996), 47–61; Chapter 2, reprinted by permission from *The University of Chicago Law Review*, 55 (Fall, 1988), 1371–1429; Chapter 3, reprinted by permission of Oxford University Press from *Natural Law Theory: Contemporary Essays*, Robert P. George, ed. (Oxford: Clarendon Press, 1992); Chapter 4, reprinted by permission from *The American Journal of Jurisprudence*, 37 (1992), 185–195; Chapter 5, reprinted by permission of Oxford University Press from *The Autonomy of Law: Essays on Legal Positivism*, Robert P. George, ed. (Oxford: Clarendon Press, 1996); Chapter 6, reprinted by permission of Academic Press, Inc. from *Social Discourse and Moral Judgement*, Daniel N. Robinson, ed. (San Diego, Cal.: Academic Press, 1992); Chapter 7, reprinted by permission of The Franciscan University of Steubenville Press from *We Hold These Truths and More: Reflections on the American Proposition*, Stephen Krason and Donald D'Elia, eds. (Steubenville, Ohio: Franciscan University Press, 1993); Chapter 9, reprinted by permission from *The American Journal of Jurisprudence*, 42 (1997); Chapter 10, reprinted by permission from *The Arizona State Law Journal*, 29 (1997), 569–580; Chapter 11, reprinted by permission of The Yale Law Journal Company and Fred B. Rothman & Company from *The Yale Law Journal*, Vol. 106 (1997), pp. 2475–2504; Chapter 12, reprinted by permission of Princeton University Press from *The Constitution of International Society: Diverse Ethical Perspectives*, Terry Nardin et al., eds. (Princeton, NJ: Princeton University Press, 1998); Chapter 13, reprinted by permission from *The Review of Metaphysics*, Vol. 42, No. 3 (March, 1989); Chapter 14, reprinted by permission from *Tulane Law Review*, 63 (1989), 1455–1474; Chapter 15, reprinted by permission of Georgetown University Press from *Natural Law and Contemporary Public Policy*, David Forte, ed. (Washington, D. C.: Georgetown University Press, 1998); Chapter 16, appearing originally as an article in the *Columbia Law Review*, Vol. 93 (1993), 783, reprinted by permission; Chapter 17, reprinted by permission from *The Michigan Law Review*, Vol. 88, pp. 1415–1429; Chapter 18, reprinted by permission from *The Harvard Law Review*, 110 (1997), 1388–1406.

TABLE OF CONTENTS

Law is nothing other than an ordinance of reason for the common good, promulgated by him who has the care of the community.

St Thomas Aquinas
Summa Theologiae I–II, q. 90, a. 4

Introduction

Earlier versions of the chapters that follow appeared as articles and re-view essays in journals of law, politics and philosophy, and as contribu-tions to edited volumes. They defend and apply a natural law theory of reasons for choice and action. That this theory is labeled a 'natural law' theory is not of great import, though the theory's rootedness in the tradi-tion of thought about practical reason and morality in which St Thomas Aquinas is so central a figure easily justifies such labeling. What matters is the validity—the truth—of the theory and its capacity to shed light on why we ought to do or refrain from doing certain things which it is in our power to do or refrain from doing, but which we have the effective freedom—the choice—to do or refrain from doing.

The natural law theory I defend and apply was originally adumbrated by Germain Grisez and has, over the past thirty-five years or so, been substantially developed by him, often in formal or informal collaboration with Joseph M. Boyle, Jr., John Finnis and others. Although I have perhaps been able to contribute to the development of some aspects of the theory, I can claim little credit for it. My main concern has been with the defense of the theory against criticism from various quarters and its application to problems at different levels of philosophical abstractness. My method is primarily dialectical, and in this, at least, I am a true Thomist. I proceed by engaging arguments against the positions I seek to defend. When possi-ble, I examine the arguments advanced by scholars who are critical of these positions. When that is not possible, I do my best as 'devil's advo-cate' to identify plausible arguments against my own view and then try to rebut these arguments. I leave it to the reader to judge the extent of my success or failure as a dialectician.[1]

I

Part One of this book comprises six essays that explain and defend central features of what is sometimes called the 'new natural law theory,' or the 'Grisez–Finnis theory.' It begins with 'A Defense of the New Natural Law Theory,' in which I try to meet the quite fundamental challenge to natural law theory (and other 'cognitivist' ethical theories) mounted by 'subjectivists' or 'non-cognitivists' who are deeply skeptical of reason's capacity to identify non-instrumental reasons for action and objective norms of morality. My principal interlocutor here is Jeffrey Goldsworthy, a contemporary philosopher who presents a sophisticated and vigorous critique of natural law ethical theory from a neo-Humean point of view. Against people like me who defend the proposition that there are objective moral truths, Goldsworthy maintains that moral norms and other basic practical principles are, in the end, mere projections of subjective feeling or emotion. Against the natural law theory I defend, he contends that, if moral principles are capable of motivating people and guiding their action, as I and others claim they are, these principles must be subjective, rather than objective, for only feeling or emotion can actually move people to act. If moral principles truly possessed the 'robust objectivity' I claim for them, Goldsworthy asserts, then they could not truly motivate people and guide their choices. Goldsworthy's criticisms provide an opportunity for me to flesh out the rather complex account of human action which is, I believe, required if we are to make sense of our own experience of practical thinking, and which, in any event, is presupposed by my natural law theory of practical rationality. Goldsworthy's mistake, I argue, is to suppose that truly rational, as opposed to merely emotional, motivation is impossible and that this is demonstrated by the fact that all human action *includes* emotional motivation. On the contrary, often our *rational* grasp of the *intelligible* point of certain possible actions (e.g., the exercise of our intellectual powers in an effort to understand whether morality is truly objective or necessarily merely subjective) is what stimulates the emotional support that is admittedly necessary for us to perform the actions. I also engage Goldsworthy's very capable re-presentation of John Mackie's argument 'from queerness' against belief in objective values, and his claim that non-cognitivism offers 'the best explanation' for our moral experience. I argue that objective values are no less 'queer' than many other non-material phenomena whose existence we all recognize (e.g., meaning, consciousness, causation), and that it is, in fact, cognitivism, rather than non-cognitivism, which best explains people's own understanding of the evaluative practices they engage in when they conclude, for example, that gratuitous cruelty is wrong.

The second and third essays in this Part concern what is probably the most common misunderstanding of the idea of natural law. This is the claim that it presupposes something that is logically impossible, namely, the inferring of 'values' from sheer 'facts.' It is true that some natural law theorists purport to deduce information about what human beings ought and ought not to do from knowledge of human nature considered in abstraction from any prescriptive principles. In other words, they propose to 'derive an "ought" from an "is." ' They view 'practical' (including 'moral') knowledge as entirely derivative of 'theoretical' or 'speculative' knowledge of human nature drawn from such fields as metaphysics, anthropology, sociology, political science, history and theology. It is also true, as critics maintain, that, strictly speaking, no such derivation is logically possible. It has been Germain Grisez's great achievement to show that natural law theory needn't, and, as practiced by its greatest exponents, hasn't, relied on what Finnis calls the 'illicit inference from facts to norms.' Grisez contends that 'practical reason' rests on its own first principles, and is not derived from methodologically prior purely theoretical knowledge (as indispensable as knowledge of the latter sort always is to sound moral judgment). These first principles direct human action toward more-than-merely-instrumental ends or purposes—'basic human goods'—that are our most fundamental reasons for choice and action. It is the integral directiveness of these goods that excludes certain options as practically unreasonable, even in circumstances in which they are, to a certain extent, rationally grounded, and thus distinguishes what is morally right (or, at least, morally acceptable) from what is morally wrong.

Grisez's critics, including Russell Hittinger, Ralph McInerny, and, from a very different perspective, Lloyd Weinreb, have argued that the 'new natural law theory' is effectively Kantian or even Humean in its acceptance of the 'modern' idea of a logical gulf between 'is' and 'ought.' In Chapter Two, 'Recent Criticism of Natural Law Theory,' and Chapter Three, 'Natural Law and Human Nature,' I offer a reply to these critics. My goal is to show that objective practical knowledge (including moral knowledge) is in fact possible, and it is possible precisely because of our intellective grasp of truly basic, underived, practical principles. In fact, the error of Kantian—and *a fortiori* of Humean—ethical theory is to leave these principles and their objectivity out of account. This is an error, which the 'new' natural law theorists manifestly do not commit.

Among the most controversial features of the 'new natural law theory' is its understanding of the basic human goods to which practical reason's first, underived principles direct choice and action as, in an important sense, 'incommensurable.' If so, people ask, how is it possible to deliberate and adjudicate among competing possibilities for action in circumstances of morally significant choice? Indeed, R. George Wright has asked whether the 'incommensurability thesis' imperils certain common sense moral judgments—such as the judgment that one ought, ordinarily, to interrupt recreational activities to save a drowning child. In Chapter Four, 'Does the "Incommensurability Thesis" Imperil Common Sense Moral Judgments?,' I try to show that it does not. Rather, as Grisez, Finnis and others have rightly maintained, the integral directiveness of basic practical principles makes it possible for us to identify methodological principles of practical reasonableness (what Grisez calls 'modes of responsibility') whose concrete application often enables us to identify morally right and wrong answers even in circumstances requiring us to choose between or among rationally-grounded possibilities. Among these principles is the Golden Rule of fairness demanding a certain impartiality among persons where one has no reason (whatever one's emotional inclinations) to prefer one person (including oneself) to others. I try to show that application of the Golden Rule to a hypothetical case which Professor Wright proposes as a challenge enables us to see that the incommensurability thesis is fully compatible with what common sense tells us ought to be done.

The concluding chapters of Part One apply the theory of natural law I favor to some central questions in contemporary jurisprudence. Chapter Five, 'Natural Law and Positive Law,' explores the implications of the theory for the scope and limits of judicial authority. It is often supposed that belief in an objective moral law entails the proposition that judges should enjoy a more or less free wheeling authority to, in effect, nullify positive laws that they believe to be incompatible with it. After all, was it not the teaching of not only Augustine and Aquinas, but also of Cicero, Plato and others figures of importance in the natural law tradition, that 'an unjust law is not a law?' Here it is important to avoid misunderstanding. Although it is true that the positive law is to be derived (in different ways, depending, as I explain, on the subject matter) from the natural law, that does not by itself imply anything about the proper scope of judicial, as opposed to legislative and executive, power. Indeed, the allocation of political authority as between the judiciary and other branches of government is settled for any particular political system not by the natural law, but rather by the positive law of the polity's formal or informal constitution. Natural law principles neither require nor forbid schemes of allocating authority under which judges enjoy a broad power of judicial review and, thus, play a significant legislative role. What is important as a matter of natural law is that judges and other actors in a political system should not exceed the constitutionally established limits of their own authority. The usurpation of political authority, particularly by judges, violates the moral–political ideal of the rule of law—an ideal central to natural law thinking regarding political morality.

The final chapter of Part One, 'Free Choice, Practical Reason and Fitness for the Rule of Law,' offers an account of why, under natural law principles, the ideal of the rule of law is so central. Although the specific content of the rule of law—its demand for clarity, nonretroactivity, promulgation, etc.—is largely procedural, I agree with the late Lon L. Fuller that there are important *moral* reasons for rulers to respect its requirements. In particular, the human ability to understand and act on reasons, which itself both presupposes and is presupposed by the capacity for free choice, entails, as Neil MacCormick suggests, that people are due the respect they are shown when rulers govern according to the principles of the rule of law. Although respect for the rule of law is not all that justice requires of those exercising political authority, it is nevertheless a requirement of justice.

II

In the Introduction to my book *Making Men Moral: Civil Liberties and Public Morality*, which was published by Oxford University Press in 1993, I promised in future writings to turn my attention to some of the practical implications of my rejection of 'neutralist' or 'anti-perfectionist' liberalism, and to apply to certain concrete political issues my general theory of the place of moral judgment in political decisionmaking. The six chapters in Part Two attempt to fulfill that promise, or at least to begin doing so, by considering a range of morally-charged contemporary political disputes, including those over abortion, pornography, religious freedom, homosexuality, marriage and the international order. One of my central aims in this Part is to show that the sort of natural law theory I defend provides a credible alternative to the liberalism currently dominant in the academy and among American and European elites generally. Defenders of liberalism justly complain that its critics often are content to point out liberalism's flaws without proposing an alternative way of thinking about problems of law and liberty. I want to offer a concrete alternative to liberalism—one that, I believe, takes on board the key insights and achievements of the liberal tradition, including, notably, its concern to protect the basic rights and liberties of individuals.

Religious liberty was, as Joseph Raz has observed, at the cradle of liberalism and surely stands as the liberal tradition's premier achievement. But what are its grounds? Does principled belief in freedom of religion presuppose or entail religious indifferentism or even the nonexistence of religious truth? Does it require the 'privatization' of religion and the exclusion of religiously informed moral judgment from public life? I think not. In Chapter Seven, 'Religious Liberty and Political Morality,' I defend a conception of religious liberty that is rooted in an appreciation of the nature of religion as a basic human good. I offer a natural law theory of religious freedom as an alternative to the more familiar liberal conceptions. I note, however, an important similarity between my natural law argument for religious freedom and the Lockean liberal approach to the subject. Central to both approaches is a recognition of the fact that religious faith, by its nature, cannot be coerced. If the good of religion is to be realized in the life of the believer, it must be by his free assent of mind and will to the truths of faith. It is not so much wrong to coerce faith as it is impossible. The price of attempted coercion is religious inauthenticity, at best. I argue, however, that from this fact it is a mistake to conclude, as many contemporary liberals do, that political authority must, in effect, profess agnosticism and concern itself not at all with people's religious or spiritual well-being. It is an even worse mistake to suppose, as some liberals do, that it is illegitimate for people to act on religious motivations in the creation of law and formulation of public policy with respect to important issues of justice and human rights.

The next two chapters address questions of sexuality, marriage and public policy. Chapter Eight, 'Marriage and the Liberal Imagination,' written with Gerard V. Bradley, responds to Stephen Macedo's important critique of natural law thinking on these issues. According to Macedo, traditional sexual morality, inasmuch as it condemns sodomitical and other intrinsically non-marital sex acts and conceives marriage as an inherently heterosexual institution, takes an unreasonably narrow view of the value of sex. Alternatively, he suggests, if the natural law view is sound, it is nevertheless ineligible to serve as a legitimate ground for public policy making because the complexity of the arguments needed to support it places the natural law position on sex and marriage beyond the bounds of 'public reason.' Chapter Eight explicates and defends two related propositions: (1) that marital sexual intercourse, whether or not procreation is desired or even possible, unites spouses in a one-flesh personal union that is intrinsically, and not merely instrumentally, valuable; and (2) that in choosing to engage in non-marital orgasmic acts, including sodomitical acts, persons necessarily reduce their bodies to the status of mere means or extrinsic instruments in ways that damage their personal and interpersonal integrity. The arguments for these propositions are, as Macedo says, complex, but, we argue, only an unreasonably narrow conception of public reason—one rigged in advance to generate liberal conclusions—could exclude them as illegitimate. Moreover, we argue that Macedo's attempt to find a 'middle ground' between the 'conservative' position we espouse and the utterly permissive view held by so-called sexual 'liberationists' (a view which Macedo also rejects) necessarily fails. There is no possible principled basis for such a 'middle ground.'

The argument advanced in Chapter Eight is further developed and refined in Chapter Nine, 'What Sex Can Be: Alienation, Illusion or One-Flesh Union,' written with Patrick Lee. It spells out the senses in which non-marital sexual acts necessarily, and wrongfully, create a mere illusion of marital intimacy, and/or involve treating the body as an extrinsic instrument whose role is to generate satisfactions for the benefit of the conscious and desiring aspects of the 'self.' The focus of the chapter is on the practical dualism implicit in the ideologies that license the pursuit of sexual satisfaction outside the one-flesh communion of marriage or by way of sodomitical or other intrinsically non-marital sex acts. We argue that any such dualism is philosophically indefensible and morally degrading. Taken together, Chapters Eight and Nine defend the view that marital sex truly unites persons in a way that is uniquely and profoundly good; non-marital sex, by contrast, alienates persons from themselves and others and is for that reason morally bad.

Nowhere are the self-alienating and illusory qualities of non-marital sex more manifest than in the culture of pornography. Still, many people believe that the legal prohibition or restriction of pornography constitutes a form of 'censorship' which is simply incompatible with a due regard for freedom of expression. In Chapter Ten, 'Making Children Moral: Pornography, Parents and the Public Interest,' I challenge this belief. In my view, a social milieu in which pornography circulates freely constitutes a genuine threat to the moral well-being of children. It also imposes an intolerable burden on parents who take seriously their responsibility to inculcate in their children the virtues of modesty, chastity and respect for self and others in matters of sexuality. A society that truly cared for its children would utterly reject what Ronald Dworkin has approvingly called the 'right to pornography,' and would, within the limits of prudence, put in place firm measures to discourage its use and restrict its availability.

Obviously, views like those I hold and defend in these chapters are out of line with the dominant liberal understandings of morality and civil liberties. Most academics, apparently, do not share them. Still, many ordinary people do. Sometimes, or in some communities, majorities can be gotten together to, say, ban the sale of pornographic materials. A familiar liberal response to this sort of event is to claim that the action of the majority is wrong, not because its views about the immorality of pornography are false, but because people who do not share these views have the right to enjoy pornographic images if they care to do so—the immorality of their doing so notwithstanding. There are various justifications for this response. In *Making Men Moral*, I canvassed and criticized some of the most influential and important ones. Since I completed that book, John Rawls and some of his followers have proposed a new and highly sophisticated justification for the liberal view. I have already referred to this justification in my account of Stephen Macedo's critique of natural law thinking on sexual morality. It is the view that excludes certain moral understandings as illegitimate grounds for public policy making because they allegedly fail to meet the standards of 'public reason.' I address Rawls's argument directly, and state my reasons for rejecting it, in Chapter Eleven, 'Public Reason and Political Conflict: Abortion and Homosexuality.' I argue that Rawls's 'political' liberalism is simply arbitrary in its exclusion of those non-liberal views that appeal, as do natural law views, to publicly accessible reasons. Moreover, Rawls's narrow conception of 'public reason' consistently and unjustifiably 'loads

the dice' in favor of 'comprehensive' liberal conclusions in important
public policy debates such as those over abortion and homosexuality.

Liberals often suppose that natural law thinking, though not overtly
'religious,' is unavoidably 'absolutist' and 'doctrinaire.' It is true that the
natural law tradition (to its credit!) has always resisted moral relativism
and defended certain moral absolutes. At the same time, however, sound
natural law thinking recognizes a legitimate relativity across a fairly wide
range of morally significant human affairs. One area in which this is
particularly clear is the question of how we ought to order relations
between political communities. Certainly we should not treat as optional
the need for international cooperation for the sake of a great many important human goods that cannot be effectively protected or advanced by
national communities operating on their own. We should not, however,
suppose that there is a single, uniquely correct way of ordering international affairs to achieve the morally required cooperation. In Chapter
Twelve, 'Natural Law and International Order,' I focus on the diverse
ways in which contingent facts, historical circumstances and other factors
create the need for what Aquinas referred to as 'determinationes' in structuring the international order. A determinatio is the opposite of a 'time-
less' principle that properly governs choice and action from the moral
point of view in all times and places. It is, rather, an authoritative judgment selecting for a community (or the international community) one
among a number of possible and morally legitimate schemes of cooperation or coordination for the sake of the overall common good. I argue that
when it comes to the structuring of the international order, we should
beware of false absolutes. Moral principles take us only so far. Beyond
that, choices must be made among a range of morally acceptable options.

III

The six chapters in Part Three engage the thought of some leading
contemporary moral, political and legal philosophers. The first three of
these chapters concern work by Catholic thinkers who draw, in various
ways, on the tradition of natural law theorizing. Chapter Thirteen, 'Moral
Particularism, Thomism and Traditions,' considers Alasdair MacIntyre's
critique, from a Thomistic–Aristotelian perspective (which I largely
share), of the mainstream of the liberal tradition in moral and political
philosophy in his important book *Whose Justice? Which Rationality?* I find
much that is persuasive and valuable in MacIntyre's analysis; still, I am
concerned that his strong 'particularism,' (viz., his view of moral inquiry
as not only 'tradition-constitutive,' but also 'tradition-constituted')
renders the idea of objective moral truth highly and unnecessarily

problematic and risks collapsing into a form of moral relativism. So I suggest certain modifications of the view MacIntyre defends that would, I believe, give 'tradition' its due in moral analysis, yet avoid any strong relativist implications.

Chapter Fourteen, 'Human Flourishing as a Criterion of Morality: A Critique of Perry's Naturalism,' explores and criticizes a view of the nature of practical reasoning and moral judgment that profoundly differs from, yet is easily confused with, the natural law view I hold. The former view is ably set forth and defended by Michael Perry in his book, *Morality, Politics, and Law*. Like the latter view, it understands 'human flourishing' as, in some sense, a criterion of morality. Unlike the view I defend, however, it rejects the 'incommensurability' of the basic practical principles which direct choice and action toward those intelligible purposes ('basic human goods') that constitute the most fundamental aspects of human flourishing. The adoption of what I call a 'psychologistic' conception of value makes it possible for Perry and other 'naturalists' of this school to propose a consequentialist (or 'proportionalist') approach to moral decision-making that purports to distinguish morally upright from wrongful choosing on the basis of a direct comparison of values. I argue, however, that the psychologistic conception of value is false and that the reality of the incommensurability of basic practical principles renders any direct comparison of basic human values, and, thus, the consequentialist method of moral judgment, hopelessly unworkable.

Something very much like Perry's psychologistic conception of value is at work in Andrew Sullivan's critique of natural law thinking regarding homosexuality in his book *Virtually Normal: An Argument About Homosexuality*. Although Sullivan recognizes that the natural law tradition, particularly in its Catholic expressions, 'tells a coherent and at times beautiful story of the meaning of our natural selves,' he contends that its contemporary exponents who continue to condemn homosexual acts as immoral are caught in a contradiction. On the one hand, they recognize that genuine homosexual 'orientation' exists; homosexuals are not merely heterosexuals who, for whatever reason, choose to pervert their sexuality by engaging in homosexual acts. Some people are, Sullivan says, homosexual 'by nature.' On the other hand, and inconsistently, Sullivan claims, natural law theorists continue to insist that homosexual acts are 'unnatural' in some morally normative sense. In Chapter Fifteen, 'Nature, Morality and Homosexuality,' I argue that Sullivan's critique of natural law thinking about homosexuality and other questions of sexual morality ignores a distinction that is crucial to understanding in this area, namely, that between *reasons* for action and restraint, and *desires*, which may, rightly or wrongly, also motivate people. The basic goods of human nature which provide *reasons* for action should not be reduced, as in

Sullivan's essentially neo-Humean account of value, to *desires*, even of the
deep and more or less stable sort which Sullivan describes as 'yearnings.'
Once we bring this distinction into focus, it is clear that there is no
inconsistency in the natural law position. That position is that: (a) the
intrinsic good of marriage as a one-flesh union of persons consummated
and actualized by sex acts that are reproductive in type, whether or not
they are intended to be, or even can be, reproductive in effect, provides
spouses with a non-instrumental reason to unite in acts of genital intercourse; and (b) the evil of personal and interpersonal dis-integration
provides persons, irrespective of 'sexual orientation' or marital status,
with conclusive moral reasons to refrain from sodomitical and other non-
marital sex acts.

Chapter Sixteen, 'Can Sex Be Reasonable?,' offers a critique from the
natural law viewpoint of Richard Posner's 'economic analysis' of sex in
his book *Sex and Reason*. Unlike many contemporary writers on sexuality,
Posner recognizes the intellectual integrity and force of natural law teaching on sexuality and strives sincerely to make his critique of that teaching
an informed one. Nevertheless, I argue, he does not come fully to terms
with the natural law view because he fails adequately to understand the
arguments advanced by its proponents. By the same token, this failure
of understanding obscures his awareness of the profound respects in
which the work of natural law theorists undermines the purely instrumental conception of practical reason which is presupposed by Posner's
economic analyses, not only of sex, but of law, and other activities
and socially constituted phenomena that are, at least in part, the fruit of
practical deliberation and human choosing.

Surely there is no greater blessing for a philosopher, especially one
whose method is essentially dialectical, than to have the benefit of
thoughtful, fair-minded and analytically rigorous opponents. For this
reason, I am grateful for the work of Joel Feinberg—particularly his four-
volume masterwork entitled *The Moral Limits of the Criminal Law*.
Nowhere, to my knowledge, is the liberal view that the law ought to
refrain from enforcing putatively private moral obligations set forth with
greater clarity and skill. My goal in Chapter Seventeen, 'Moralistic Liberalism and Legal Moralism,' is to meet the challenge Feinberg presents
(especially in *Harmless Wrongdoing*, the fourth and final volume of *The
Moral Limits of the Criminal Law*) to those of us who reject the liberal view.
I try to show that Feinberg's argument begs key questions against proponents of 'the legal enforcement of morals' by presupposing the truth of
certain moral judgments which, however widely shared by liberals, non-
liberals typically (and for good reasons) reject. I also respond to an important and highly original argument Feinberg advances in an effort to
show that natural law theorists and other traditional moralists, who

typically subscribe to retributive justifications for punishing criminals, cannot square their retributivism with the punishment of 'victimless' immoralities. The nerve of Feinberg's argument is that retributivism seeks to restore an order of justice violated by wrongful acts; but injustice cannot be said to be present in the case of actions which do not violate the rights of others. So retributive justifications of punishment would seem to presuppose something like J. S. Mill's 'harm principle' in establishing the just limits of criminal prohibition. I argue in reply, however, that the injustice which justifies criminal punishment on the retributive view need not inhere in the underlying immoralities of the acts that are prohibited under the criminal law. If, as natural law theorists, Kantians, and other retributivists tend to believe, there is a prima facie moral obligation to obey the laws of a basically just society, and if, as they also tend to believe, this obligation is itself an obligation in justice to one's fellow citizens, then the breach of a duty to obey a law that is not in itself unjust—even a law prohibiting putatively victimless wrongdoing—constitutes an injustice, and may justly be punished under the retributive view.

Disputes between liberals and conservatives over abortion, homosexuality, and many other morally-charged political issues raise important questions of how a democratic republic should go about setting its policies in the face of deep and apparently intractable disagreement. Of course, some liberals treat the sheer existence of moral disagreement as a ground for resolving controversial issues their way. To some extent, this seems to be the burden of Rawls's argument in *Political Liberalism*. That is why Rawls's critics accuse him—justly, in my view—of 'stacking the deck' in favor of policies favored by liberals. Other legal and political theorists, however, including some whose work is broadly within the liberal tradition, decline to endorse Rawlsian or other principles that would rule non-liberal views out of the bounds of legitimate political discourse. They seek terms of political deliberation and debate that are truly fair to liberal and non-liberal citizens alike. Chapter Eighteen, 'Law, Democracy and Moral Disagreement,' considers two particularly noteworthy recent efforts in this regard: Amy Gutmann and Dennis Thompson's *Democracy and Disagreement: Why Moral Conflict Cannot Be Avoided in Politics, and What Should Be Done About It*, and Cass Sunstein's *Legal Reasoning and Political Conflict*. These books are, in my judgment, exemplary in their willingness to take the problem of moral disagreement seriously and treat it in an ideologically non-partisan manner.

Gutmann and Thompson helpfully develop a theory of 'deliberative democracy' which appeals to citizens' obligations to each other to provide rational arguments in support of the policies they favor. It is important to see that this requirement of reason-giving, which itself follows from the political ideal of reciprocity between citizens (an ideal that Gutmann and

Thompson valuably explicate), is far less exclusionary—and, thus, I believe, far more reasonable—than the narrow doctrine of liberal 'public reason' by which Rawlsians propose to rule out certain policies that many liberals find unpalatable. By examining some aspects of the debate over slavery in antebellum America, I try to refine and extend Gutmann and Thompson's analysis of the stance citizens should take toward each other when they find themselves in profound moral disagreement over issues of justice and basic human rights. The case of slavery, I suggest, teaches us some lessons about how people on both sides of the contemporary debate over abortion ought to understand and deal with each other.

Late-twentieth century American liberals have often turned to courts to accomplish their policy objectives when established democratic processes have failed to generate the results they favor. The most dramatic and controversial instance, of course, was the creation of a right to abortion by the Supreme Court of the United States in the 1973 case of *Roe* v. *Wade*. From the viewpoint of liberals such as Ronald Dworkin, the judiciary, in cases of this sort, provides citizens with a 'forum of principle' which contrasts with the messy and apparently unprincipled business of legislative politics. Critics, however, contend that these cases amount to the judicial usurpation of democratic political authority in the cause of elite liberal political hegemony. Cass Sunstein does not join Robert Bork, Antonin Scalia, and others in the wholesale condemnation of judicial intervention into morally-charged political disputes. Like Jeremy Waldron, however, he does criticize Dworkin and other proponents of 'judicial activism' for taking too optimistic a view of the wisdom, foresight and moral sensitivity of judges, and too pessimistic a view of the capacity of people in democracies to make sound public policy regarding issues of moral importance. Indeed, Sunstein joins deliberative democrats such as Gutmann and Thompson in stressing the need to build and maintain a political culture in which politics is itself a 'forum of high principle.' Astutely recognizing the fact that judicial overreaching, even in the best of causes, tends to erode the capacity of democratic institutions to function in morally principled ways, Sunstein calls on judges to resist the temptation to intervene decisively or comprehensively in large-scale disputes over abortion, affirmative action, euthanasia, homosexuality and other morally-charged questions. To the extent that courts have a constructive role to play in the resolution of disputes of this sort, they fulfill that role, Sunstein argues, by proceeding in limited, incremental, and, for the most part, tangential ways, offering what he calls 'incompletely theorized agreements,' rather than grand, completely theorized resolutions.

Ronald Dworkin once claimed that his theory of legal interpretation and understanding of the judicial role qualified him as a natural law theorist. By the same token, one might suppose, someone like Sunstein would count as a 'legal positivist.' But if the analysis I propose in Chapter Six, 'Natural Law and Positive Law' is correct, then I am on firm natural law ground in preferring Sunstein's understanding of the need for judicial self-restraint to Dworkin's expansive view of judicial power. That Sunstein and I, despite our normative theoretical differences, find ourselves occupying much common ground on the question of the proper role of courts in democratic republican politics, shows, perhaps, that 'incompletely theorized agreements' are possible in scholarly discourse as well as in judicial politics.

NOTES

1 Some of the chapters that follow repeat points made or examples used in other chapters. I have not deleted every instance of repetition, lest the individual chapters lose their capacity to function as free-standing essays. Where possible I direct readers familiar with material I am repeating forward to new material.

Part One
THEORETICAL ISSUES

1

A Defense of the New Natural Law Theory

In 'Fact and Value in the New Natural Law Theory,'[1] Jeffrey Goldsworthy offers a vigorous critique of the natural law theory of practical reason and morality advanced by Germain Grisez, John Finnis and Joseph M. Boyle, Jr. Goldsworthy argues that Grisez, Finnis and Boyle's putatively cognitivist account of the objective prescriptivity of moral principles and the motivational force of non-instrumental reasons for action fails either because it is: (1) ultimately indistinguishable from Humean non-cognitivism, according to which morality is subjective and practical reasoning is purely instrumental; or (2) vulnerable to decisive objections based on John Mackie's argument from 'queerness' as reinforced by the argument from 'the best explanation.'

As Goldsworthy points out, Grisez, Finnis and Boyle disavow the claim of neo-scholastic natural law theorists that practical principles, including moral norms, can be deduced from purely theoretical truths ('facts') about (human) nature.[2] In this respect, they share common ground with non-cognitivists. Grisez, Finnis and Boyle reject, however, the non-cognitivist claim that 'since norms cannot be deduced from facts they must be projections of our feelings and desires rather than objects of our reason' (p. 2). They maintain that moral norms and other basic practical principles are rational principles whose directiveness and prescriptivity are independent of people's feelings or desires. The most basic practical principles, according to Grisez, Finnis and Boyle, prescribe actions which people have reasons to perform because they constitute opportunities to realize for themselves and/or others benefits whose intelligible value is not merely instrumental. As grasped in intellective acts, these and more proximate practical principles, including moral principles, are, or state, truths about what ought to be done which are analogous to, however different they are in their adequation from, truths about what is the case.[3]

Goldsworthy agrees with Grisez, Finnis and Boyle that moral norms are practical principles; he denies, however, that such principles can possess the 'robust objectivity' necessary to qualify them as 'truths.' He argues, in fact, that Grisez, Finnis and Boyle are caught in a dilemma: If moral norms are practical, and, as such, motivating, then they cannot be objective; for what moves people to act are feelings and desires, not reasons. Reasons, as such, he seems to suppose, lack motivating power. He contends that Grisez, Finnis and Boyle have, in any event, failed to demonstrate the possibility of rationally motivated action. The simpler, and therefore preferable, account of human action, he suggests, is non-cognitivism, according to which people's ends are necessarily given by their feelings and desires, and reason's role is limited to identifying efficient means to these ends. Against the more-than-merely-instrumental conception of practical reason advanced by Grisez, Finnis and Boyle, Goldsworthy asserts the Humean conception of reason as 'the slave of the passions.'[4]

Grisez, Finnis and Boyle explicitly hold that all human acts, including rationally motivated acts, involve feelings, emotions, imagination and other factors which are not, strictly speaking, reasons. But this suggests to Goldsworthy the possibility that They fail to distinguish their putatively cognitivist conception of practical reason and its motivational force from Humean non-cognitivism. To explain why, he usefully analogizes human action to a guided missile. As non-cognitivists understand human action, 'desire determines the target and supplies the propulsion, while reason locates the target and guides action toward it.' Goldsworthy asks: 'How does the role of reason in Grisez, Finnis and Boyle's theory differ from this, if it can only motivate action with the assistance of emotional motivation?'

The answer is that Grisez, Finnis, Boyle and other natural law theorists affirm, and non-cognitivists deny, that practical reason can 'determine the target.' This is the upshot of their view that people can have, and be aware of, non-instrumental reasons for action. What distinguishes rationally motivated actions is precisely that people perform them for non-instrumental reasons. Someone who acts for a non-instrumental reason acts ultimately not on the basis of a brute desire, as non-cognitivists believe people always and inevitably act, but, rather, because of his intelligent grasp of the intelligible point of performing the action. Such a person does not merely want, or want to do, something; he wants it, or wants to do it, *for a (non-instrumental) reason*. Were it not for the practical judgment of the acting person that the end he has in view is (intrinsically) valuable, he might very well have no desire to pursue it. In other words, his desire to pursue it may be, not a brute desire, but, rather, 'reason-dependent.'[5]

Grasping the (not-merely-instrumental) point and value of pursuing knowledge of a certain sort, for example, or of having or being a friend, or of maintaining one's personal integrity is, according to natural law theory, an act of the practical intellect—a cognitive achievement. Now, by itself, abstracted from other factors which figure in the genesis of human action including, notably, desires which may themselves be generated by practical insight, such an achievement cannot generate human action. As Grisez, Finnis, Boyle and other sophisticated cognitivists fully recognize, even acts that people perform for non-instrumental reasons involve, in addition to people's grasp of those reasons, a variety of other factors, including imagination, various natural tendencies and inclinations, emotions, and acts of the will.[6] Grisez, Finnis and Boyle's differences with non-cognitivists cannot be summed up by the idea that they simply replace desire as a motivator with bare beliefs, thoughts or judgments. What sets Grisez, Finnis and Boyle and other cognitivists apart from non-cognitivists is the claim that people can have, and be aware of, non-instrumental reasons for acting, and that their grasp of these reasons figures decisively in some actions. If cognitivists are correct, then sometimes people's desires are consequent and dependent on their (practical) judgments of value. In these cases, reason, rather than desire, 'determines the target.' In grasping the intelligible point of possible actions, practical reason functions as something more than 'passion's slave.'

In their work in fundamental moral theory, Grisez, Finnis and Boyle are primarily concerned with the normativity or prescriptivity of practical reasons (including moral norms). In his account of this normativity or prescriptivity, Finnis has referred to reasons for action as 'rational motives,' which are to be distinguished from feelings, desires and other sub-rational motives. Finnis's discussions of motivation to which Goldsworthy refers stress his claim that reasons for action give people positive guidance and do not merely provide constraints on action generated by non-rationally based desires. Neither Finnis nor his collaborators, however, have been concerned with the question of motivation apart from the prescriptivity of practical reasons. They have not offered anything approaching a complete account of the psychology of human motivation.

Central to Goldsworthy's critique, however, is his claim that Grisez, Finnis and Boyle must either deny any connection between prescriptivity and motivation or discredit the Humean theory of motivation which denies the possibility of non-instrumental reasons for action. This is a false dilemma. Grisez, Finnis and Boyle and other cognitivists hold that people can have, and be aware of, and act on non-instrumental reasons. Unless non-cognitivists can discredit this position, by showing that there are no non-instrumental reasons for action, cognitivists are perfectly entitled to believe that people sometimes want to do things, not as a brute matter of psychological fact, but precisely because they grasp the non-instrumental point, and thus, the intelligible intrinsic value, of doing them.

As for the connection between prescriptivity and motivation, Goldsworthy's critique succeeds only if he can show that people's desires are always sufficient to generate their actions, so that what natural law theorists and other cognitivists take to be non-instrumental reasons would be superfluous in accounting for what people do. It is not enough for Goldsworthy to show that reasons cannot motivate all by themselves.

Grisez, Finnis and Boyle assume that desires and other non-rational factors are essential ingredients even in rationally motivated actions. Their
claim is simply that people sometimes desire to pursue certain ends or
purposes precisely because of the reasons constituted and supplied by
these ends or purposes themselves. So, for example, someone might want
to know more about the causes of the First World War, or the origin of
species, or the truth of the question about cognitivism in ethics, not as a
matter of brute desire, but precisely because of his practical judgment
that such knowledge is humanly enriching and therefore worth pursuing,
quite apart from any instrumental value it might have. Were it not for his
intelligent grasp of the non-instrumental reasons for acting provided by
the intrinsic value of knowledge of these matters, someone might well
consider inquiry into them to be pointless and therefore have no desire to
conduct the study.

In attacking Grisez, Finnis and Boyle's theory of practical reasoning,
Goldsworthy introduces a distinction between the idea of something's
being 'good for somebody' and that of something's being 'good
(*simpliciter*).' He argues that Grisez, Finnis and Boyle's claims about
the objectivity of moral norms and other basic practical principles trades
on a confusion of these two senses of 'good,' the former possibly objective
but, if so, not genuinely practical, the latter genuinely practical but not
objective.

He correctly notes that, according to Grisez, Finnis and Boyle, nothing
can provide a non-instrumental reason for action unless it is good *for*
somebody. He asserts, however, that Grisez, Finnis and Boyle's conception of 'good' is 'double-headed': 'To believe that something is good is to
believe *both* that it is something that people have reason to seek *and* that
it is good *for* people' (p. 5). He says that non-cognitivists can accept
this 'double-headed' conception of good because it is not inconsistent
with their claim that people's ultimate motives must be non-rational
factors, such as feelings, and cannot be reasons as such. The decisive issue,
as Goldsworthy sees it, is whether or not motivation depends on desire.

He quickly adds, however, that non-cognitivists *need not* accept a conception of value according to which something's being good means that
it is good *for* somebody: 'To act for a reason is to act in order to achieve
something believed to be worthwhile, or good (*simpliciter*), but not necessarily in order to achieve something believed to be good *for* someone
(whether oneself or others)' (p. 8).

Grisez, Finnis and Boyle are entirely right, however, to resist
Goldsworthy's claim that: (1) something could be 'good (*simpliciter*)' yet
provide a reason for acting; and (2) be 'good *for* someone' yet not provide
such a reason. If there are any non-instrumental reasons for acting, then
the intrinsic goods which provide those reasons must have an intelligible

aspect. Only a benefit, that is to say, something which contributes in some way to someone's well-being or fulfillment, could be the intelligible aspect of a purpose whose achievement will instantiate an intrinsic good. (This is why Grisez, Finnis and Boyle refer to the intrinsic goods which provide non-instrumental reasons for action as 'basic *human* goods.') Thus, I see no reason to accept Goldsworthy's distinction between 'good (*simpliciter*)' and 'good *for* someone.' On the contrary, it strikes me as sounder to hold, as Grisez, Finnis and Boyle hold, that people have a reason to seek something if, and only if, it provides some intelligible benefit for someone, and thus has an intelligible point. Ends or purposes which provide basic reasons for action (i.e., basic human goods) are known in acts of understanding by which the practical intellect grasps the intelligible point of possible actions, judging them to be not *mere possibilities* (i.e., things that could be done, however pointlessly), but, rather, *opportunities* (i.e., things that are worth doing precisely inasmuch as they promise some intelligible benefit).

Goldsworthy wishes to show that cognitivists cannot successfully resist his distinction. He argues that, notwithstanding the fact that Grisez, Finnis and Boyle use the terms 'good' and 'good for' interchangeably, the concepts of 'good *for* someone' and 'good (*simpliciter*)' differ because the former concept 'is always attached to particular people, while [the latter] is not' (p. 8). He contends that only the latter concept 'is necessarily connected with [the concept] of reasons for action. Thus, for people to believe that something is 'good,' and therefore a reason for action, it is neither necessary nor sufficient for them to believe that it is good *for* someone.

To show that it is not *necessary*, Goldsworthy cites the example of environmentalists who value nature for its own sake, independently of its value for people and other creatures. For them, nature is 'good (*simpliciter*).' To show that it is not *sufficient*, he argues that someone could believe that something would be good for Hitler, but not believe that one has any reason to help him get it.

In claiming that the concept of 'good *for* someone' is always attached to 'particular' people, while the concept of 'good (*simpliciter*)' is not, Goldsworthy fails to notice that he is trading on a equivocation. In one sense, 'particular' just means individuals—some members of a class, but any member of that class. In another sense, it means designated individuals—certain members of a class and not other members of that class. When Grisez, Finnis and Boyle refer to the basic human goods which provide non-instrumental reasons for action as the goods of 'particular' persons, they employ the term in the former sense; their point is that these goods cannot be mere abstractions ('Platonic forms'), but must be aspects of the genuine well-being and fulfillment of particular (i.e., members of the class of) human beings. Goldsworthy's suggestion that they mean 'particular' in the latter sense simply is incorrect.

Let us now turn to Goldsworthy's claim that something's being 'good *for* someone' is neither necessary nor sufficient for it to be 'good (*simpliciter*).' If successful, according to Goldsworthy, 'the most plausible explanation of the distinction is that reasons for action depend on desires which the [latter] concept helps to express' (p. 16). I shall argue, however, that Goldsworthy's claim is unsuccessful, and that people, in truth, never have reasons (though they may have sub-rational motives) to do things which promise no intelligible benefit to anyone, and always have reasons (though not always conclusive ones, and, indeed, sometimes merely defeated ones) to do whatever provides an intelligible benefit for themselves or others.

It is apparently psychologically possible for people to value nature apart from its value to human beings. This does not, however, mean that action to preserve the non-human world other than for the sake of human values has an intelligible point. On the contrary, valuing nature in this way can only be accounted for as expressive of a purely emotional attachment or some sort of non-rational faith or ideology. Environmentalism has its rational appeal because people grasp the value for themselves and others (including members of future generations) of preserving nature. Unsurprisingly, environmentalists' arguments characteristically appeal to human values: possible damage to human health, the potential loss for science and aesthetic experience, injustice to future generations, and so forth. In any event, I do not see how anyone who, laying these considerations aside, fails to see the value of environmental preservation as good-in-itself and, thus, providing a non-instrumental reason for action, could justly be accused of a failure of practical *reason*. More to the point, the fact that some people, whatever their subjective motivation, value nature apart from its value to human beings does not entail that specifically human values lack an intelligible point and must similarly be accounted for as merely expressive of feelings or desires.

As for the example of Hitler, someone who knew that something would be genuinely good for him (and not something wicked that nevertheless he desired, such as harming innocent people) would have *a* reason to help him obtain it, even if there were competing reasons not to help him (for example, to prevent his crimes or his evasion of just punishment) and even if these competing reasons were conclusive. And, to be sure, one might have powerful emotional motives not to help Hitler where one nevertheless had reasons—even conclusive reasons—to help him. In any event, someone's decision to help Hitler obtain some good for him, however controversial, would not be utterly pointless or baffling; nor would it be explicable only as motivated by a non-rationally-based emotion or ideology. Even people who would not themselves agree to help him (indeed, even those who would oppose others helping him) could grasp the intelligible point of someone's helping him.

Let us suppose that Hitler were captured, convicted after a fair trial for crimes against humanity and sentenced to life in prison. While there, he suffers a rupture of the appendix. The prison surgeon, however much he detests Hitler, and notwithstanding his powerful emotional aversion to helping him in any way, plainly has a reason to perform the surgery necessary to save his life (and this reason is not merely that saving Hitler's life will lengthen his just punishment). A decent surgeon would act on this reason unless he had a competing reason which would justify not performing the operation. He would, that is to say, resist any temptation he might feel, based on his aversion to Hitler, to let him die when he could, by exercising ordinary surgical skills, save his life. Moreover, even someone who would himself be inclined to 'let Hitler die,' and who would be willing to make a moral argument to justify that choice, could nevertheless 'see the point' of the surgeon's decision to help him. His argument against the surgeon, if he were rational, would not be that the surgeon has *no* reason to save Hitler; it would rather be that he has *a better reason* to let him die. He would not claim that saving Hitler is irrational, the way the hording of money by an already fabulously wealthy miser is irrational. Even if he believes that the surgeon in saving Hitler does wrong (because he believes, let us say, that Hitler deserves to die), he does not, or at least need not, maintain that the surgeon's decision is pointless, or baffling, or explicable only as an expression of non-rationally-grounded emotion. (After all, the surgeon may himself be resisting a powerful emotional aversion to saving Hitler.)

Goldsworthy's claim about Hitler overlooks the fact that reasons for action can be defeated or undefeated, conclusive or nonconclusive. It does not follow that because someone: (i) reasonably does not wish to help Hitler; (ii) reasonably does not consider himself to be under an obligation to help Hitler; or (iii) reasonably considers himself to be under an obligation not to help Hitler, he never has *a* reason to help him. The truth of the matter, I think, is that action to help even Hitler achieve or obtain something that is genuinely good for him has a point—is not irrational—even when it is wrong (because, for example, it is unfair to others). Someone has *a* reason to help him, *even if there is a morally better reason to deny him help.*[7]

Anticipating objections of the sort I have been raising, Goldsworthy asserts that natural law theorists must show that the beliefs that: (i) people can have reasons to act when human values are not at stake; and (ii) people sometimes don't have reasons to act when human well-being is at stake, are not merely unjustified, but conceptually incoherent. 'It is this that is implausible, which is why not only the existence but the mere possibility of these beliefs confirms that there is a difference between "good (*simpliciter*)" and "good for"' (pp. 11–12).

I do not see how Goldsworthy can justify the standard he sets for his opponents to meet. A proposition can be linguistically coherent and intelligible up to a point but unsound and even indefensible (for example, self-referentially inconsistent or just baseless). So I do not see the warrant for Goldsworthy's insistence that natural law theorists show, for example, that valuing nature apart from any judgment of its value for human beings is not only unjustified but 'conceptually incoherent.' It should be enough to show that such valuing is the fruit of emotion or ideology, rather than reason, or that the claim that nature is valuable apart from its value to human beings trades on a covert appeal to certain aspects of human well-being served by a healthy natural environment. After all, natural law theorists and other cognitivists do not deny the possibility of purely emotionally motivated action; they merely affirm the possibility that people can have, be aware of, and act on non-instrumental reasons. They have no interest in showing, nor need they show, that valuing nature apart from its value for human beings is psychologically impossible or 'conceptually incoherent.' Their proposition is, and need only be, that there are goods that are intrinsically valuable for human beings ('basic human goods') and, precisely as such, provide intelligible (non-instrumental) *reasons* for action, and not merely emotional motives.

Goldsworthy's central claim against natural law theory, and cognitivism generally, is John Mackie's proposal that belief in objective values requires us to postulate the existence of 'qualities or relations of a very strange sort, utterly different from anything else in the universe,' and, correspondingly, 'a faculty of moral perception or intuition, utterly different from our ordinary ways of knowing everything else' (p. 23).[8] Allowing that we might be justified in postulating such odd qualities and faculties if this were required to explain some observed phenomenon, Goldsworthy reinforces Mackie's 'argument from queerness' with the 'argument from the best explanation.' According to this argument, the non-cognitivist account of human motivation and practical reason is preferable because, unlike the cognitivist account, it can explain these realities without postulating anything as queer as the idea of objective values.

As Finnis has shown,[9] and as Goldsworthy appears to concede (p. 25), various phenomena, including consciousness, meaning and causation, are no less 'queer' than the idea of objective values. This is why the argument from the best explanation is required to reinforce Mackie's argument from queerness. Goldsworthy contends that, however singular and puzzling we find a phenomenon such as meaning, 'our best explanation still includes the postulate that [it] exist[s]' (p. 25). Given, however, the option of accounting for all human behavior as a matter of desire providing the motives and reason finding the means to satisfy desire, it is unnecessary, Goldsworthy argues, to postulate objective values which 'would somehow have to exist in the world around us rather than our own minds; they would have to be part of the "fabric" or the "furniture" of the universe' (p. 23).

Now, objective values 'exist' just in case ends or purposes have an intelligible point and thus provide non-instrumental reasons for action. Are such values and reasons parts of the 'furniture of the universe,' which 'somehow exist in the world around us rather than our own minds?' Mackie and Goldsworthy accept, at least implicitly, the objective prescriptivity of truth and of validity in argumentation. But are 'truth' and 'validity' things that exist 'in the world around us' rather than 'in our own minds?' The 'queerness' dialectic, which demands that everything be placed in one or the other of these categories, falls silent when we ask whether such realities as the validity of arguments and truths of conclusions are or are not 'in the world around us.' Equally, it offers no reason for admitting the objective prescriptivity of truth and sound argumentation despite having no serious account of either as 'furniture of the universe.' The argument from queerness, even as reinforced by the argument from the best explanation, fails to impress in large measure because it assumes the validity of categories (e.g., 'furniture of the universe') which cognitivists such as Grisez, Finnis and Boyle, for perfectly sound reasons, reject as inappropriate for classifying realities such as meaning, validity, truth, and, to be sure, practical reasons.

People accustomed to thinking of theoretical truth ('facts') as the model of all truth tend to find the idea of practical truth incorrigibly queer. At the end of the day, however, even non-cognitivists cannot do without at least one principle of practical reason which is neither theoretical nor reducible to desire or some other subrational factor. One might call this principle 'the first principle of technical reasoning' and formulate it as follows: Available means are to be used efficiently to satisfy desires. Under a non-cognitivist account, someone who failed to act on this principle would be acting unreasonably (though not necessarily immorally); yet the principle is irreducibly practical. Without it one cannot generate a hypothetical imperative, since the mere facts that: (1) someone wants something; and (2) performing a certain action would most efficiently secure it, do not logically entail the practical conclusion that the action is to be done. Hence, non-cognitivists do not differ from natural law theorists as if they could get along without practical principles which cannot be reduced to desires and are not factual, yet express truths. Rather, the disagreement is about the content and number of such principles. Non-cognitivists propose to get along with one or, perhaps, a few. Natural law theorists, such as Grisez, Finnis and Boyle, think that there are many basic practical principles which refer to the various basic human goods providing non-instrumental reasons for action.

So it seems to me that the argument from queerness fails to place the cognitivism of natural law theory in any real jeopardy. In the end, the objectivity of values understood as providing non-instrumental reasons for action is not all that peculiar. Still, Goldsworthy might insist, non-cognitivism supplies a simpler, and therefore preferable, account of how people actually behave. It is still 'the best explanation.' Finnis, however, has argued that non-cognitivism is inferior to cognitivism in accounting for aspects of people's evaluative practices as they are understood from the 'internal viewpoint' of the people whose practices they are. One of the many commendable features of Goldsworthy's argument is that it forthrightly and carefully addresses this often overlooked criticism of ethical non-cognitivism. I think his counter-argument fails, however, leaving the argument from the best explanation in the cognitivist, rather than non-cognitivist, armory.

As Finnis has observed, people who believe or say that certain forms of knowledge, for example, are intrinsically good, and therefore treat these forms of knowledge as providing non-instrumental reasons for action, think that they desire the knowledge in question because it is valuable. They do not, according to their own self-understanding, treat the knowledge as valuable only because, or insofar as, they happen to desire it. For example, I and (I assume) Professor Goldsworthy are expending time and intellectual effort in exploring the question whether cognitivism is defensible, and even true, because we believe that it would be worthwhile to know. We do not understand ourselves to be treating knowledge of this matter as valuable only, or insofar as, we happen to desire it. Rather, we think we see the point, and thus grasp the value, of conducting the inquiry in pursuit of the knowledge. To say that we are inquiring because we desire the knowledge the inquiry promises to yield is not to tell the whole story as we ourselves understand what we are doing. According to our self-understanding, there is something behind our desire for the knowledge, namely, the practical judgment that the knowledge is worthwhile and, under that description, desirable.

Now, as Goldsworthy apparently acknowledges (pp. 29–30), there is no obvious reason to regard the internal viewpoint as delusory. How, then, without denying the validity of this viewpoint, can non-cognitivism account for people's self-understanding of their evaluative practices?

The non-cognitivist says that 'we find knowledge valuable because we desire it.' This statement, according to Goldsworthy, is a 'second-order' statement about the causality of our evaluative beliefs, which must be distinguished from 'first-order' statements of those beliefs themselves. Yet from the 'internal standpoint' of someone participating in evaluative practices, the non-cognitivist 'can accept or reject any first order statement whatsoever' (p. 29). But we must ask: If the truth of the matter, as judged from the external viewpoint, is that people value things because they desire them, how can it be 'perfectly legitimate' for someone who knows this to shift to the internal viewpoint and declare that he desires knowledge precisely because and insofar as it is good?

To answer this question, Goldsworthy appeals to Simon Blackburn's analogy between practical evaluation and vision: 'Just as the eye is not part of the visual scene it inspects, the sensibility responsible for the emotional impact of things is not part of the scene it takes for material' (p. 30).[10] Blackburn argues that someone can legitimately reject, as an offensive ethical opinion, the proposition that 'cruelty is wrong because we don't like it,' while at the same time accepting, from the external standpoint, the non-cognitivist proposition that causally it is only because we have feelings and desires that we dislike cruelty and therefore deem it to be wrong. In defending Blackburn's position, Goldsworthy explains that 'The difference is that when adopting the external standpoint, the non-cognitivist reflects upon her feelings and desires, and their causal role in the shaping of her evaluative judgments. But when adopting the internal standpoint, she does not reflect on her own feelings and judgments—she expresses them in reflecting on other things' (p. 30).

The fatal problem with this defense of non-cognitivism is that people's judgment that, say, cruelty is wrong, like their judgment that certain forms of knowledge are valuable, is either rationally-based or it is not. If there is no reason for such judgments, then it cannot be rationally legitimate for people to deny that 'cruelty is wrong only because I don't like it,' or for them to affirm that 'cruelty is wrong irrespective of whether I, or anyone else, happens to like or dislike it.' These judgments can only be legitimate, from any standpoint, if people are correct in supposing that they have some *reason* not to like cruelty. And, of course, if they do, then non-cognitivism is not only inadequate to explain our evaluative practices, it is false.

Blackburn's analogy is flawed precisely in its assimilation of reason and understanding to the senses and sensing. The eye can shift its viewpoint and can see only what is visible from its present viewpoint; but the understanding which knows 'externally' or 'in the causal order' that there is no *reason* to judge, say, cruelty to be wrong, or knowledge to be valuable, cannot shake off that knowledge by adopting an 'internal viewpoint.' The same understanding controls all the judgments it makes. What one understands (e.g., that there is no *reason* to dislike cruelty), one understands (whether or not one happens to dislike it)—and not 'from a viewpoint.'

Of course, even if my argument is successful in discrediting the attempts of Blackburn and Goldsworthy to show that non-cognitivism can accommodate our common sense evaluative practices, that does not mean that non-cognitivism is certainly false. Perhaps there really are no non-instrumental reasons for action. Perhaps people really are deluded to suppose that they grasp the point of certain possible actions, understand the ends of those possible actions to be humanly valuable, and therefore have reasons to desire and act for these ends. Perhaps we deceive ourselves into denying the unedifying truth that all of our moral beliefs and actions really are ultimately motivated by brute desires. Goldsworthy's critique of natural law theory, however, despite its admirable lucidity and sophistication, gives us no compelling reasons to suppose that we really are deluded and self-deceived. Indeed, Goldsworthy himself struggled to come up with a way of affirming non-cognitivism without supposing such a thing. His failure in this regard, if I am correct, leaves non-cognitivism in the position of a possible account of practical reasoning and human action in search of data which would make it plausible. When it comes to the data of ordinary human moral evaluation and experience, by contrast, the alternative account proposed by natural law theorists and other cognitivists strikes me as 'the best explanation.'

NOTES

1 Jeffrey Goldsworthy, 'Fact and Value in the New Natural Law Theory,' *American Journal of Jurisprudence*, 41 (1996).
2 Thus, according to Goldsworthy, Grisez, Finnis and Boyle 'affirm the Humean principle that one cannot logically deduce . . . an "ought" from an "is"' (p. 1). Grisez, Finnis and Boyle, however, would not concede that the logical distinction between 'what is the case' and 'what ought to be done,' which Goldsworthy refers to as 'the Humean dichotomy' (p. 2), is properly labeled 'Humean.' Finnis, for example, argues that the distinction is one that Hume himself muddled and sometimes ignored, and the great classical philosophers for the most part strictly respected. See John Finnis, *Natural Law and Natural Rights* (NY: Oxford University Press, 1980), esp. 37, n. 43.
3 On practical truth and the difference in its adequation from theoretical truth, see Germain Grisez, Joseph Boyle and John Finnis, 'Practical Principles, Moral Truth, and Ultimate Ends,' *American Journal of Jurisprudence*, 32 (1987), 99–151, 115–117.
4 'Reason is, and ought only to be, the slave of the passions, and can never pretend to any office, other than to serve and obey them.' David Hume, *A Treatise of Human Nature* (1740), bk. 2, pt. 3, iii. Hume's conception of practical reason as purely instrumental is fully in line with Thomas Hobbes's conception: 'The Thoughts are to the Desires as Scouts and Spies to range abroad, and find the way to the things desired.' *Leviathan* (1651), pt. 1, ch. 8.
5 On the reason-dependent character of desires, see Joseph Raz, *The Morality of Freedom* (Oxford: Clarendon Press, 1986).

6 Under the cognitivist account of practical reasoning offered by Grisez, Finnis and Boyle, a variety of factors figure in the genesis of acts people perform for non-instrumental reasons. These include acts of the will, which in GFB's understanding (as in Aquinas's) is a 'rational appetite,' i.e., an appetite for intelligibilities which is satisfied precisely by understanding reasons for acting.

First of all, there are underlying natural inclinations (which are various sorts of dynamic tendencies) that provide much of the experiential content in which people gain insight into first practical principles. Secondly, there is what Grisez, Finnis and Boyle call 'aliveness' to basic goods, or 'simple volition,' which is a sort of appetite, but which is not a free choice. Thirdly, there is what Grisez, Finnis and Boyle refer to as 'interest,' which at its first stage presupposes nondeliberate, non-free behaviors and experiences of satisfaction, which themselves depend on contingent factors and both natural appetites and emotions. At the first stage, interests, while limiting the field of possible action, do not differentiate good and bad; hence their subjectivity does not poison the truth value of the normative conclusions of the practical reasoning which nevertheless depends on them as a necessary condition and is, as I say, limited by them. But later stages of interests depend on earlier choices and actions, and to the extent that these are immoral, our interests (which are a sort of habitual desire) can shape and motivate action, even so much that without choice people sometimes do morally bad things (by what Grisez, Finnis and Boyle call 'executive willing'). Fourthly, there are emotions bearing on what Grisez, Finnis and Boyle call 'goals,' which we imagine and which engage our feelings whenever we act. These are needed, together with reason bearing on what they refer to as 'benefits,' which appeal to our rationality by promising to instantiate, either immediately or down the road, some basic human good. Without emotion bearing on goals, it would be impossible for human beings to engage in purposive action; this view is the counterpart of the common Aristotelian view that there can be no human understanding or insight in any field, however intellectually refined, without some imaginative representations ('phantasms'). (As Goldsworthy points out, Grisez, Finnis and Boyle do say that one's rational grasp of a benefit can precede and stimulate the emotion that one needs to pursue a goal in an effort to realize that benefit; they do not, however, maintain that one's grasp of a benefit could come about independently of one's interest in, say, knowledge, friendship, integrity, or some other value.) Fifthly, and finally, there is the central appetitive act without which reason could not motivate morally significant conduct: the act of 'free choice.' In the end, according to Grisez, Finnis and Boyle, it is not the judgment or belief that something would be good (or bad), or is morally required (or forbidden), that gets it done (or blocks its being done); it is, rather, the choice which endorses the judgment by decisively preferring this option to alternative possibilities, and which leads to the executive resolve and self-direction to carry out the act (or to resist even powerfully contrary desire and refrain from carrying it out.) For the complete account, see Grisez, Boyle and Finnis, 'Practical Principles.'

7 One can have a reason to perform an action despite the moral truth that performing it is wrong. In such a case, the moral norm forbidding the action provides a conclusive reason not to perform it. The moral norm defeats one's reason to perform it. However, even when defeated, a reason remains a reason. Should one, in defiance of the moral norm forbidding it, perform the action, one's behavior is not pointless or baffling; the intelligibility of the end or good which provides the reason remains even if acting for it in the manner under consideration (which may be the only possible way of acting for it here and

now) is excluded by a conclusive moral reason. So one's action in this event, though practically unreasonable (i.e., immoral), is by no means irrational.

8 John Leslie Mackie, *Ethics: Inventing Right and Wrong* (NY: Penguin, 1977), 38.
9 John Finnis, *Fundamentals of Ethics* (Oxford: Clarendon Press, 1983), 58–60.
10 Quoted from Simon Blackburn, 'How to be an Ethical Anti-Realist,' *Midwest Studies in Philosophy*, vol. 12 ('Realism and Anti-Realism'), P. French, T. Uehling, Jr. and H. Wettstein, eds. (Minneapolis, Minn.: University of Minnesota Press, 1988), 361, 371.

2

Recent Criticism of Natural Law Theory

A noteworthy feature of contemporary philosophy in the English-speaking world and beyond is a reawakening of interest in practical reason. The willingness to take reasons for action seriously in descriptive and prescriptive jurisprudence, as well as in political philosophy and ethics, has been a mark of many notable philosophical achievements over the past few decades. In jurisprudence, the works of H. L. A. Hart, Joseph Raz and Ronald Dworkin certainly come to mind. In political philosophy, one immediately thinks of the competing theories of justice developed by John Rawls and Robert Nozick. In ethics, a long list of contributions would only begin with those of Alan Donagan, Alan Gewirth, Philippa Foot, David Wiggins and John McDowell.

The revival of interest in practical reason has brought in its wake renewed philosophical attention to theories of natural law. Long relegated to merely historical interest (at least outside of Roman Catholic intellectual circles), natural law theory is once again a competitor in contemporary philosophical debates about law, politics, and morals. What this means, for one thing, is that the writings of St Thomas Aquinas, Hugo Grotius, Francisco Suarez and leading neo-scholastic natural law theorists such as Jacques Maritain and Yves Simon have again found an audience in the secular academy. Moreover, a number of contemporary authors have developed modern theories of natural law. While certain of these theories remain more or less within the scholastic tradition, not all do. The natural law theory recently advanced by Michael S. Moore, for example, breaks sharply with the scholastic tradition on various points.

Two significant books on the subject of natural law theory have recently been published. The first, Lloyd Weinreb's *Natural Law and Justice*,[1] is a profoundly ambitious study. It not only charts the history of natural law theory through the ages, but also presents a sophisticated philosophical argument that, if valid, makes practical philosophy a largely meaningless exercise. He argues that all efforts to develop a credible theory of natural law are doomed and yet, that it is impossible to devise an alternative to conceiving of problems in moral and political philosophy as problems of natural law. The second book, Russell Hittinger's *A Critique of the New Natural Law Theory*,[2] presents a detailed case against a particularly influential modern theory. Hittinger's target is the theory of natural law originally developed by Germain Grisez, and widely publicized in John

Finnis's influential book *Natural Law and Natural Rights*.[3] Weinreb also singles out this theory for detailed criticism, citing it as an especially significant example of contemporary 'deontological' natural law theories.

In what follows, I shall largely, though not exclusively, focus on this recent criticism of what, following Hittinger's convention, I shall refer to as 'the Grisez–Finnis natural law theory.' My claims are that neither Weinreb nor Hittinger represents the theory accurately or presents compelling arguments against it. Before taking up criticisms of the Grisez–Finnis theory in particular, however, I shall describe Weinreb's general argument and criticize his treatment of Aquinas's theory of natural law.

I. WEINREB'S *NATURAL LAW AND JUSTICE*

A. *'Ontological' Natural Law and the 'Normative Natural Order'*

Among Lloyd Weinreb's goals in *Natural Law and Justice* is to 'restore[ ] the original understanding of natural law as a theory about the nature of being, the human condition in particular.'[4] Weinreb claims that contemporary natural law theorists, among whom he counts not only Finnis, but Lon L. Fuller, David A. J. Richards and Ronald M. Dworkin, have abandoned this understanding, which he labels 'ontological.' These theorists, as he reads them, seek to replace ontological understandings of natural law with 'deontological' understandings. A natural law theory is deontological, as Weinreb uses the term, when it purports to identify principles of moral rectitude independently of inquiries into the nature of (human) being(s). Whereas yesterday's natural law theorists derived basic principles of natural law from knowledge of (human) nature, today's natural law theorists eschew the strategy of deriving the moral 'ought' from the 'is' of (human) nature.

According to Weinreb, the *quaestio vexata* of ancient and medieval natural law theory concerned human freedom in a causally determined universe. He asserts flatly that '[t]he question that Thomas Aquinas and others answered was, "How can human beings be part of the natural order and still be free and morally responsible?" '[5] This is a problem, Weinreb supposes, because:

[f]ull moral responsibility seems to require that an act be both free and determinate. Unless a person's act is free, that is, self-determined, he is not morally responsible for it. But unless the circumstances of his act and the personal qualities that make him act as he does are determinate, the act seems to be the product of arbitrary occurrences as far as he is concerned and not something for which he individually is responsible. Yet if the circumstances and his personal qualities are determinate and determine his act, then once again the act is not self-

determined and he is not morally responsible. In order for a person to act freely in the relevant moral sense, his act must be determined; but if it is determined, he is not free.[6]

Moral responsibility, as Weinreb understands it, both requires, and is inconsistent with, causal determinacy. We experience ourselves as self-determining choosers, and this experience of freedom grounds our very notion of moral responsibility. Yet, on reflection, we must acknowledge a causally determinate background order without which human acts would seem arbitrary (only a causally determinate background can provide reasons for action) and, thus, lacking in moral significance.

The great natural law theorists of the past, as Weinreb reads them, proposed to solve the problem by positing a 'normative natural order': 'The contradiction in the idea of freedom is overcome by the supposition that the conditions and circumstances of a person's act compose a determinate background order that is itself normatively ordered: personal responsibility extends not only to what a person does but also to what he is and all the circumstances of his life.'[7]

For Weinreb, '[t]hat solution . . . was the core of the old natural law.'[8] But, if he understands Aquinas and his predecessors correctly, then Weinreb surely is right in saying that their solution, from our vantage point at least, 'seems hopeless.'[9] Belief in the sort of normative natural order he describes would apparently require us to conclude that natural evils such as deadly childhood illnesses 'and all the other "accidents" of our lives are not misfortunes but are deserved.'[10] This, as Weinreb observes, 'is not only incomprehensible but morally outrageous.'[11] The modern insight is that laws of nature, which produce, among other things, deadly childhood illnesses, are not normative. Children stricken with meningitis, for example, do not 'deserve' the disease.[12] What 'is' is not necessarily what 'ought to be.' The ontological and moral orders can (and often enough apparently do) diverge.

Having rejected belief in a normative natural order as a solution to the problem squarely faced by their predecessors, modern natural law theorists, according to Weinreb, have attempted to change the subject. They simply ignore the problem of causal determinacy, and are thus able to present 'natural law . . . as a response to the problem of freedom in a morally indeterminate . . . universe.'[13] In short, they separate ontology from morality. While prescinding from the former, they reduce the latter to political theory and, ultimately, jurisprudence. 'The question now is simply, "How can we be obligated to obey the law?" '[14] The dispute is no longer one with skeptics over the grand question of the nature of reality; it is with legal positivists over the comparatively mundane question of obligation. But, according to Weinreb, neither natural law theorists nor legal positivists can avoid the problem of freedom and cause. It lurks in the background, informing the terms of the debate over obligation, and rendering that controversy ultimately unresolvable. 'Beneath the surface of an apparently inconsequential dispute,' says Weinreb, 'there lingers the central puzzle of the human situation.'[15]

B. An Overview of Weinreb's Account of Natural Law and Justice

Weinreb's book is divided into two parts. In the first, entitled 'Natural Law,' he presents a largely historical account of what he views as the failures of traditional natural law theorists to come up with a satisfactory answer to the ontological question. He then provides a brisk review of what he sees as the unsuccessful strategy of early modern and Enlightenment thinkers, from Hobbes to Kant, to transfer the problem of 'the normative basis of human existence'[16] from nature to the civil state. Finally, he offers a critical philosophical analysis of the efforts of modern natural law theorists to come up with a credible deontological alternative to the ontological question. His considered judgment is that the traditional authors failed because their question is unanswerable, and their successors fail because there is simply no avoiding that question: '[T]he puzzle of human freedom in a determinate, causally ordered universe persists for ordinary persons and philosophers alike. The vocabulary and the conceptual context have changed; but we endorse answers to the problem in our daily lives and in our philosophizing, because we must. We could not carry on either otherwise.'[17]

In the second part, entitled 'Justice,' Weinreb broadens his analysis by examining the attempts of certain contemporary thinkers to treat the problems of moral and political philosophy as problems about 'the nature of justice' rather than about whether nature is just.[18] In the thought of liberal political theorists such as John Rawls and Robert Nozick, and in the work of their communitarian critics, among whom Weinreb includes Alasdair MacIntyre, Michael Sandel and Michael Walzer, the separation of ethics from ontology obscures the antinomy of freedom and cause. Yet, this antinomy undercuts the efforts of deontological natural law theorists no less thoroughly than it did those of their ontological predecessors. To obscure the antinomy is not to eliminate it. It reemerges in the form of analogous antinomies of desert and entitlement (in respect of individual justice) and liberty and equality (in respect of justice in the social order) within the concept of justice. Such antinomies are ultimately rooted in the antinomy of freedom and cause (in respect of a putatively normative natural order).

Desert, Weinreb says, is an implication of moral responsibility, which in turn presupposes freedom. The upshot of this connection with moral responsibility and freedom is that desert is 'insistently individual.'[19] Entitlement, by contrast, 'is based on the application of a rule according to its terms, without regard to individual qualities that the rule ignores.'[20] The fulfillment of individual justice, as Weinreb understands it, would require a perfect harmony of desert and entitlement. Unfortunately, however, conflict between these elements of justice 'is not an occasional, regrettable lapse but is inherent and unavoidable.'[21]

The very concept of desert requires a background order of entitlement. For example, we regard persons as entitled to natural assets. When people successfully make use of their natural assets, we treat them as deserving (e.g., a prize in a foot race). However, the ground of that initial entitlement cannot itself be desert. As Weinreb puts it, 'if every one of a person's qualities has itself to be deserved, the idea of a person as the subject of desert loses meaning.'[22] But where the ultimate ground of desert is (undeserved) entitlement, in what serious sense can persons be understood as deserving? A way out of the dilemma could, of course, be a notion of free choice that would provide, at least in some respects, an ultimate ground of desert not reducible to sheer entitlement. But to appeal to such a notion, according to Weinreb, is precisely to confront the antinomy of freedom and cause that exercised the ancient and medieval natural law theorists. So, as Weinreb sees it, inquiry into the nature of justice ultimately reintroduces the 'ontological' problem of the justice of nature.

Similarly, liberty and equality—the elements, for Weinreb, of a just social order—inherently contradict each other. Just as freedom requires a determinate causal background with which it is ultimately inconsistent, and just as desert requires a background order of entitlement with which it is ultimately inconsistent, liberty (the social analogue of desert and freedom) requires a background of equality with which it is ultimately inconsistent. According to Weinreb, '[l]iberty and inequality, equality and restriction of liberty, are the same, except that we ordinarily use the former member of each pair to indicate our approval and the latter to indicate disapproval.'[23] Hence, every attempt to advance liberty comes at a cost in terms of equality. But to the extent that inequalities are tolerated, the conditions of liberty are erased. Inasmuch as one is 'less' equal, one is unfree. Yet enforced equality would destroy liberty.

Weinreb maintains that attempts to overcome this antinomy by reference to a principle of 'equality of opportunity' fail for reasons familiar to those acquainted with the current debate about justice. There seems to be no principled way to avoid either broadening the meaning of equality of opportunity to the point of requiring equality of results (thereby directly eliminating liberty) or narrowing it to a mere formalism (thereby sacrificing the substantive equality that serves as a condition of liberty). So, under Weinreb's analysis, Nozick rightly charges Rawls with throwing over liberty for the sake of equality. But, by the same token, Nozick must plead guilty to jilting equality for the sake of liberty. And since liberty presupposes a background order of equality—an order which the concept of equality of opportunity cannot provide—liberty itself cannot survive under Nozick's scheme. Unfortunately for egalitarian and libertarian theorists of justice alike, the very concept of justice is 'antinomic.'

If Weinreb's arguments are telling, moral and political philosophy are doomed to frustration. The antinomy of freedom and cause that, according to Weinreb, eventually undid ontological theories of natural law reemerges to undo every modern alternative, whether they be deontological natural law theories or theories of justice. Contrary to what the older natural law theorists supposed, Weinreb insists, '[w]e cannot be part of nature and at the same time apart from it.'[24] Yet it is ultimately untenable to hold that we are merely part of nature or that we are apart from it. We cannot hold that we have free will (which would set us apart from nature) because this would, he says, require us to deny the determinate background of causality upon which the concept of free will depends. We cannot hold that we are determined (which would make us merely a part of nature) because 'whether we explain it or not, [our] experience of freedom remains.'[25] And we cannot hold that we have free will and are at the same time determined (which would make us part of nature and at the same time apart from it) because 'every compatibilist solution depends on a confusion of the manner in which we experience freedom and cause with the propositions that are necessary to sustain either.'[26]

C. Weinreb on Aquinas's Natural Law Theory

For Weinreb, as for most commentators, Aquinas occupies a central place in the history of natural law theorizing:

Aquinas stated the theory that has defined natural law as a school of thought. It is because they can be perceived as precursors or anticipations of his theory that earlier statements of Cicero and others . . . are regarded as part of the natural law tradition, even when they do not use that term. And it is their association with his theory, however abstract, that qualifies subsequent theories as within the tradition.[27]

Sympathetic interpreters of Aquinas differ on the question of whether he supposed that 'nature is normative.' Neo-scholastic natural law theorists understand Aquinas as saying that the standard of moral uprightness for human actions is conformity to (human) nature. In this sense, norms of human action, including moral norms, are implicit in the natural order. Ethics begins with a speculative inquiry: What is human nature like? This question concerns the human telos, viz., it intends knowledge of the natural ends constitutive of human fulfillment. Once we acquire such knowledge, we can judge proposed actions according to their conformity, or lack of conformity, to these ends.

It is at this point that what Aquinas, following Aristotle, calls the practical intellect takes over.[28] Aquinas formulates the first principle of practical reason as 'good is to be done and pursued, and evil is to be avoided.'[29] According to neo-scholastic interpreters, 'good,' in this formulation, simply refers to those actions that conform to properly human ends; 'evil' refers to those actions that fail so to conform. Hence, the human intellect operating in its practical mode directs us according to its first principle to act in a morally upright fashion. But thus understood, the first principle of practical reason presupposes knowledge of what is morally upright and what is not. Such knowledge is acquired by the intellect operating in its speculative mode. The crucial point is that under this interpretation sound practical thinking depends upon a methodologically prior speculative (e.g., metaphysical—or 'ontological'—and theological) inquiry. Such an inquiry yields the philosophy of (human) nature upon which moral philosophy rests. Inasmuch as we derive moral norms from speculative knowledge of (human) nature, nature is indeed normative.[30]

The neo-scholastic interpretation of Aquinas's moral philosophy has been challenged precisely on the question of the normativity of (human) nature. In an influential article published in 1965, Germain Grisez attacked the claim that Aquinas identified moral norms by reference to speculative knowledge of human nature.[31] Aquinas, Grisez argues, did not propose his first principle of practical reason as a moral imperative. Rather, Aquinas supposed that such a principle controls all coherent practical thinking—whether morally good or evil. 'Good,' as Grisez understands Aquinas's formulation, refers not only to what is morally good, but to whatever within human power can be understood as intelligibly worthwhile; 'evil' refers to any privation of intelligible goods. Interpreted in this way, the principle neither presupposes a knowledge of right and wrong nor, *a fortiori*, enjoins us to choose the morally upright course of action. The work done by the first principle is more primitive. It states a condition of any coherent practical thinking, viz., that one's reasoning be directed toward some end that is pursuable by human action. Even morally wicked choices, to the extent that they are intelligible, meet this condition (although, as we shall see, not so well as morally upright choices). Consider, for example, a choice that treats another person unfairly. To the extent that such a choice has an intelligible point, it will be consistent with the first principle of practical reason, despite its immorality. Understood as a directive, the first principle is weak: It requires only coherence, not full moral rectitude.

Under Grisez's interpretation, Aquinas believed that ultimately any choice has its intelligibility by reference to the intelligible end(s) for the sake of which one terminates one's deliberation and acts. Our initial intelligent grasp of these ends requires no knowledge of metaphysical anthropology or any other speculative discipline, although various sorts of speculative knowledge (including sound metaphysics) can help one to pursue these ends more intelligently. The most basic knowledge of these ends is, rather, the fruit of practical insights. The practical intellect itself grasps certain ends as reasons for action that require no further reasons. They are intelligible as ends-in-themselves. As such, their intrinsic choiceworthiness is, as Aquinas says, *per se nota* (self-evident). It is by reference to such an end-in-itself, as the ultimate term in a more or less complex chain of practical reasoning culminating in a choice, that a non-baffling account of that choice can be given. Once one brings such an end into focus, no further questions relevant to the choice necessarily arise for someone seeking such an account.

For Aquinas, as Grisez reads him, the ends that the practical intellect grasps as ultimate reasons for action are properly understood as intrinsic human goods and, as such, aspects of human fulfillment. As goods 'to be done and pursued' they are fundamental determinations of the first principle of practical reason, and, thus, basic precepts of natural law. They are not, however, singly and directly criteria of moral rectitude. Knowledge of human goods does not by itself resolve moral questions because it does not exclude some choices which, while intelligible, are morally wrongful. Rather, our intelligent grasp of human goods is what makes moral questions possible.

For example, is it morally wrongful for a scientist to kidnap a child and subject her to deadly experiments—not, let us suppose, out of any malice, but in a sincere quest to identify the causes and cure for a ravaging communicable disease? The question arises by virtue of our grasp of the genuine human goods at stake in a decision either way. Let us suppose that a moral norm does in fact forbid the kidnapping and experimentation. As Grisez understands Aquinas, the first principle of practical reason could not have generated this moral norm because a choice to go through with the kidnapping and experimentation would not be incoherent. The wrongfulness of such a choice would not consist in its being unintelligible. To the contrary, the goods of knowledge (here, scientific knowledge) and life and health (here, the lives and the health of victims and potential victims of the disease) provide the intelligible ends by reference to which even the morally wrongful choice would be intelligible.

But in view of the goods that the scientist could realize by carrying out the kidnapping and experimentation, it is worth asking whether a moral norm forbidding the decision to do so would itself come into conflict with the first principle of practical reason. The answer is that it does not; for the choice not to kidnap and experiment is also intelligible. The life and health of the child, among other goods, are the ends that provide the intelligibility of this alternate choice. The moral norm provides a decisive reason for choosing between two courses of action, both of which are consistent with Aquinas's first principle. It excludes as wrongful one of the intelligible choices. As a moral norm, it does not identify the 'good[s] to be done and pursued'; rather, it guides and structures human choice and action respecting such goods.[32]

According to Grisez, Aquinas did not bequeath us a systematic account of moral norms. Nor did he establish the link between the specific moral rules he did articulate and the self-evident first principles (i.e., the determinations of the first principle of practical reason) specifying the goods 'to be done and pursued.' In his own natural law theory of morality, Grisez has sought to remedy these inadequacies. In so doing, he freely departs from Aquinas at a number of points, while retaining Aquinas's fundamental theory of practical rationality as he understands it. Later, I shall discuss Grisez's revisions and development of Aquinas's moral theory. For the moment, however, I simply want to highlight the implications of Grisez's interpretation of Aquinas's theory of practical reason.

Grisez's Aquinas does not propose to judge the morality of acts by their conformity to human nature. The knowledge of human goods that sets practical inquiry in motion and ultimately accounts for the intelligibility of human choices is not the fruit of metaphysical anthropology or any other speculative discipline. Nor can speculative inquiry generate moral norms by reference to which human beings can uprightly guide and structure their choosing in respect of human goods. Such norms are needed, but they cannot be derived from (human) nature. Thus, under Grisez's interpretation of Aquinas, nature is 'normative' neither in Weinreb's sense nor in the neo-scholastic sense.

While Weinreb cites Grisez's article in a footnote to his own discussion of Aquinas's first principle of practical reason, he makes no reference to the interpretative dispute in which it figures as a central text. Indeed, almost immediately after stating Aquinas's principle, he baldly asserts that 'natural law thus directs us to fulfill our natural inclinations.'[33] Weinreb does not even consider Grisez's alternative account. He states that natural law 'is a reflection of human nature, the natural human inclinations toward appropriate human ends.'[34] The role of reason, he says, is 'to translate the natural inclinations into practical decisions and actions.'[35]

If one accepts Grisez's interpretation of Aquinas's first principle of practical reason, then the idea of a normative natural order has no place in

Aquinas's ethics. If one rejects Grisez's interpretation in favor of something like the neo-scholastic reading of Aquinas, an idea of what might be called a normative natural order is, indeed, required. But Weinreb's idea of such an order is nothing like what neo-scholastics (whose interpretation of Aquinas's first principle Weinreb seems to share) have in mind. When neo-scholastics claim that, for Aquinas, natural law theory hinges on matters of ontology (or metaphysics), they do not mean that the central problem that must be addressed is that of human freedom in the face of causal determinism. Rather, they mean that moral norms must be derived from speculative knowledge of (human) nature.

According to the neo-scholastics, Aquinas's idea of a normative natural order does not purport to account for the putative responsibility of individuals for conditions and events in their lives over which they apparently exercise no control. As they interpret him, Aquinas saw no need for any such account because, contrary to what Weinreb says, he simply did not identify the problem of freedom and cause as one that inquiry into the principles of natural law was meant to solve.

It is not that Aquinas failed to recognize that moral norms, if they exist, are norms for free choice. Nor is it that he was unaware that free choice was a philosophical problem. Indeed, he considered the matter of free choice directly in several of his works.[36] But having satisfied himself that some free choice exists in human affairs (i.e., that some events in the world are brought about by human choosing that, while conditioned in various ways by causes beyond the control of the chooser, remains in important respects free), Aquinas aimed in his moral philosophy, and thus in his theory of natural law, at clarifying the intelligibility (rather than the possibility) of human choices and identifying norms by reference to which reason could guide such choices reliably.

That the neo-scholastic reading of Aquinas is on this crucial point superior to Weinreb's is evident, I think, from the first sentence of the Prologue to the second main part of the *Summa Theologiae*—the part principally concerned with morals and containing Aquinas's fullest statement of his theory of natural law:

[M]an is said to be made to God's image, in so far as the image implies an intelligent being endowed with free-will and self-movement: now that we have treated of the exemplar, i.e., God, and of those things which come forth from the power of God in accordance with his will; it remains for us to treat of His image, i.e., man, inasmuch as he too is the principle of his actions, as having free-will and control of his actions.[37]

Under the neo-scholastic reading of Aquinas, moral norms are, as I have noted, implicit in, and derivable from human nature. Knowledge of that nature—what is intended by the inquiring intellect in the (speculative) discipline of metaphysical anthropology—is, therefore, under this reading, the key to moral philosophy. But this sort of knowledge is not knowledge of some supposed 'justice of nature.' The 'natural order' is normative precisely inasmuch as it provides moral norms for free human choosing. The normativity of that order has nothing to do with the ascription of moral responsibility 'to what [a person] is and all the circumstances of his life.'[38]

Weinreb seems to assume that Aquinas's theory of nature included something like the empiricist notion of causality that dominates modern understandings of the natural order. It is only in light of some such notion that the problem of freedom and cause, as Weinreb describes it, becomes an issue (in moral and political philosophy or anywhere else). But Aquinas's theory of nature was Aristotelian rather than modern. It allowed ample room for chance events. Aquinas understood the basic mode of causality to be the causality of the end—i.e., that for the sake of which the event happens. (This is commonly described as the 'teleological' view of nature.) Under this understanding of the world, the belief that intelligent agents act freely for ends is not an anomaly, but rather a paradigm case of the way people behave. We correctly judge this to be defective physics. (We do not believe, for example, that love moves the sun and the other stars.) But, defective or not, it does not give rise to the problem of freedom and cause that Weinreb supposes Aquinas appealed to natural law to solve.

Under Aquinas's theory, the whole of creation (everything other than God) can be divided into two parts: that which does not presuppose human thinking and free choice to be as it is, and that which does. It is the former that is 'natural'; the latter is not. While both parts, inasmuch as they depend ultimately on God's free action, are suffused with meaning and value, the latter part is also suffused with humanly given meaning and value (by virtue of the contributions of human intelligence and free action). The meaning and value of nature is provided by divine intelligence and free choice alone.

Weinreb says of Aquinas that 'He started from the unquestioned propositions that the universe is the creation of a providential God and that it displays its Creator's purpose in all its aspects; hence, it is orderly throughout, and its order is normative.'[39] While Aquinas left very little 'unquestioned,' there is not much else to quibble about in this particular statement until the final clause, with which various sorts of Thomists would not only quibble but quarrel—at least if it is understood as Weinreb suggests we understand it. As I have observed, the whole of creation is, for Aquinas, suffused with meaning and value by divine intelligence and free choice. The universe is, indeed, ordered to the purposes of a providential Creator. But as Aquinas saw it, this does not rule out the proposition that some aspects of creation also are suffused with meaning and value by human intelligence and free choice. The natural (moral) law concerns meaning and value insofar as it is within the ambit of human intelligence and free choice. The natural law is a participation in the eternal law because even that part of creation subject to the norms of the natural law ultimately depends upon divine intelligence and free choice. Nothing that exists or obtains lies outside of the divine plan. But, contrary to what Weinreb implies, personal responsibility, for Aquinas, extends only to a person's free choices. Such responsibility extends 'to what [a person] is and all the circumstances of his life' only insofar as these depend on his prior free choices. Whatever does not depend on free choices is the responsibility of someone else—ultimately God.

Since Aquinas perfectly well understood that persons are often victims of evils for which they bear no responsibility, he recognized the need for a theodicy. But even here Aquinas made no appeal to a normative natural order under which 'nature does justice.' His theodicy was not designed to get God off the hook by showing that persons somehow deserve all they receive. As a Christian philosopher, Aquinas wanted to show that the evil to be found in the world is not chosen by God. God accepts the evil for the sake of the good, otherwise unattainable, that God will in His wisdom bring out of situations involving evil. As with any theodicy, there is ultimately a mystery about this, for the norms (if any) governing divine causality (if it exists) cannot be known by the human intellect. But this mystery has nothing to do with an alleged contradiction at the core of the idea of human freedom and responsibility. Weinreb misreads Aquinas's theory of natural law in supposing that that theory was proposed in an effort to overcome any such contradiction.

D. Weinreb on Finnis and 'Deontological' Natural Law

Among those whom Weinreb classifies as contemporary 'deontological' natural law theorists, John Finnis alone works self-consciously within the tradition of Aquinas. Weinreb singles out Finnis's work for special praise. 'In his book *Natural Law and Natural Rights*, John Finnis has developed the most substantial and serious contemporary theory to which the label of natural law attaches.'[40] As Finnis himself observes, however, there is 'not . . . much that is original' in his arguments.[41] The natural law theory of morality Finnis proposes as a foundation for the political theory and jurisprudence he defends is, as he says, 'squarely based' on the work of Germain Grisez.[42] And, as we have already seen, Grisez's approach to ethics builds upon his own understanding of Aquinas's theory of practical rationality. In the years since Finnis's book was published, Grisez and Finnis have collaborated on a number of projects (usually along with Joseph M. Boyle, Jr.), and have developed their ethical theory in important respects. I will deal with what is perhaps the most significant of these developments in the present section.

Weinreb's basic criticism of Finnis's natural law theory is that it is based on the mistaken 'belief that, if one reflects carefully about the human condition, the principles of moral action are a self-evident basis for the determination of concrete obligations.'[43] Weinreb supposes that Finnis '[r]eject[s] explicitly any proof for his claims except the self-evident truth of the claims themselves.'[44] In one instance, Weinreb refers (dismissively) to 'Finnis' apparent claim that his position on [the subject of abortion] is a self-evident truth.'[45] More generally, Weinreb suggests that 'even those who agree with [Finnis] on the merits may suppose that he has confused self-evidence with personal conviction.'[46] And, while allowing that '[t]he conclusions that Finnis reaches may be correct,' Weinreb flatly accuses Finnis of 'repeatedly [suggesting that] arguments opposed to his own are . . . accepted only by persons who have not thought carefully or are blinded by bias or self-interest or convention.'[47]

On this last point, Weinreb offers no citation to Finnis's writings, nor could he have done so. He has simply misunderstood the implications of Finnis's account of the reality of immoral choosing.[48] This account does not imply that arguments opposed to Finnis's own are only accepted by those who are thoughtless, biased, or self-interested. What Finnis, like most moralists, does suppose is that persons (and whole cultures) can, in their practical thinking, be led astray by factors such as bias, self-interest, convention and emotion. It is hardly fantastic to think, for example, that such factors had something to do with the blindness of many Americans of another age to the immorality of slavery. But, while virtually no one today is unimpressed (or admits to being unimpressed) by arguments against slavery, it is worth noting that even certain arguments directly in support of slavery were accepted by some people who were not simply 'careless in their thinking or blinded by bias, self-interest, or convention.' Nothing in Finnis's account requires him to deny this in order to hold both that pro-slavery arguments were wrong, and that those who accepted them were wrong in so doing.

Weinreb's substantive objections to Finnis's theory have mainly to do with Finnis's appeals to self-evidence. Since putatively self-evident propositions do figure crucially in the moral theory Finnis defends and deploys, it is worth attending closely to these objections. I shall argue that Weinreb has seriously misunderstood the place of propositions claimed to be self-evident in the Grisez–Finnis theory of morality. Contrary to what Weinreb supposes, those subscribing to the theory do not hold conclusions in normative ethics to be self-evident. Once I have cleared away this interpretative mistake, I shall explain what sorts of principles they do suppose to be self-evident and offer a defense of the plausibility of such principles.

Weinreb makes a basic interpretive error in supposing that Finnis thinks that his conclusions (whether about abortion or any other issue in normative ethics or political theory) are self-evident. Specific moral norms (like a norm about abortion or its legal regulation) are, under the Grisez–Finnis theory, derived from more general moral norms that guide human choice and action in respect of intrinsic human goods. Any such derivation requires an argument. One must argue one's way to a conclusion. If, as Grisez and Finnis suppose, a general moral norm forbids direct attacks on such intrinsic goods, then abortion, if it destroys the human life of a person directly (i.e., either as an end or, what is more likely, as a means to another end, rather than as a foreseen and accepted side-effect of an otherwise morally acceptable choice) is immoral. But if a specific moral norm does forbid abortion, that norm is not, for Finnis and Grisez, self-evident.

As it happens, both Grisez and Finnis accept the argument that a specific moral norm forbids abortion. It will be still more illuminating for the present purpose, however, if we consider a question of the justifiability of killing on which they have disagreed. Their dispute has to do with whether a specific moral norm forbids the killing involved in capital punishment. Finnis has defended the position that capital punishment does not (necessarily) involve direct killing. His argument is that the action of public authorities in executing someone guilty of a sufficiently grievous crime may immediately and in itself instantiate an intrinsic good, viz., the good of justice, thus enabling the killing accurately to be characterized as something other than the taking of life as a means to an ulterior end.[49] Capital punishment may, therefore, be morally permissible. Grisez disagrees. In his view, the intentional structure of any choice to kill as a punishment is such that executing even those guilty of the most heinous crimes cannot but be characterized as the choice of an evil means to a good end.[50] What is important to notice for our purposes about this dispute is that neither Finnis nor Grisez supposes that the other is failing to grasp a self-evident point. Each, to be sure, believes his own position to be correct and, therefore, by logical entailment, his interlocutor's position to be mistaken. But both understand the question as one to be resolved by argument, not by an appeal to self-evidence. The intentional structure of the choice to kill as a punishment—the decisive issue in the debate for Finnis and Grisez—requires, as they explicitly acknowledge, analysis.[51] It is not self-evident.

So, if specific moral norms are not supposed to be self-evident, what sorts of principles are supposed to be? The answer is: the first principle of practical reason, and, in a sense, its determinations; and what Grisez and Finnis call the first principle of morality. These are the (underived) foundational principles that provide the ultimate premises of moral arguments.[52] While they may be defended by dialectical arguments designed either to rebut arguments against them, or show up the defects or inadequacies of ethical theories that attempt to do without them, they cannot themselves be deduced or inferred or otherwise derived from more fundamental premises. One cannot argue one's way to them (the way one can, on the basis of more fundamental premises, argue one's way to a conclusion). The claim that they are self-evident does not imply that they are undeniable or, still less, that no one denies them. What it does imply is that the practical intellect may grasp them, and practical judgment can affirm them without the need for a derivation (which is not to say that they can be grasped without an understanding of the realities to which they refer).

The reader will recall that the determinations of the first principle of practical reason refer to the intrinsic goods that render human choices intelligible, according to Grisez's interpretation of Aquinas, by providing ultimate reasons for action. These determinations thus serve as first practical principles—the most basic precepts of natural law. The goods to which they refer are, in the Grisez–Finnis parlance, 'basic human goods.' Included under this rubric is anything an instantiation of which can be intelligibly chosen as an end-in-itself. According to the Grisez–Finnis theory, the basic goods are not extrinsic to the persons by and in whom they are instantiated, but, are, rather, intrinsic aspects of human well-being and fulfillment.[53] While they are capable of being 'participated in'[54] by limitless numbers of persons on limitless numbers of occasions in virtually limitless forms, they can be grouped, according to Grisez and Finnis, under a small number of categories.[55] In *Natural Law and Natural Rights*, Finnis categorizes them as: life (and health); knowledge; play; aesthetic experience; sociability (friendship); practical reasonableness; and 'religion.'[56]

Are these, as some (including Russell Hittinger) have charged, mere intuitions? Is the claim that they are 'self-evident' nothing more than a piece of rhetoric masking naked conviction? Or, as Grisez and Finnis claim, does the practical intellect grasp the basic human goods in non-inferential acts of understanding by picking out intelligibilities in the data that human experience presents? Well, let me tell a little story designed to demonstrate how Grisez and Finnis suppose we can grasp first practical principles that refer to basic human goods.

E. The Identification of a First Practical Principle

I have employed as a teaching assistant a graduate student named Adam. He has been remarkably successful as a teacher because he combines extraordinary intellectual curiosity and ability with genuine dedication to the education of his students. Indeed, he sometimes devotes himself so fully to his teaching that he is left with but little time for his own projects. Now, let us suppose that I discover that Adam has taken a part-time job on the late-night shift (9 p.m.–3 a.m.) flipping hamburgers at the local Burger King. Naturally, my curiosity is aroused. I wonder why, in view of all the other demands on his time and energy, he has made a choice to spend time that he could, after all, devote to reading, writing, relaxing, being with friends, enjoying himself, getting some sleep, and the like, sweating over a hot grill in a noisy fast-food restaurant. I know that Adam is not irrational, so I assume, of course, that there must be some coherent explanation.

So, let us suppose that I ask him about it. Now, if he responds to my inquiry by saying that he took the job to earn some extra money, I would hardly find his explanation baffling. I am well aware of the utility of money. One can, after all, spend it on things one needs or wants. One can save it for a rainy day, enjoying the peace of mind that comes, I am told, with financial security. One can even collect and study money, in the form of bills or coins, as a hobby or amusement. Of course, I would suppose that if Adam took the job to earn money, he sought the extra income for some such reason. But if, contrary to my supposition, Adam should inform me that he wants the money just for its own sake, I would find his decision to take the job simply unintelligible.

Let us suppose I press him on the matter: 'Surely, Adam, you want the extra money for a reason. Are there things you want to purchase with it?' 'No, I already have enough money to buy anything I'll ever want.' 'Then, do you want it for the power or prestige available to those known to be wealthy?' 'No, I am a Gandhian; I have no interest in such things.' 'Do you want it in order to give it away to a friend, or to a cause, or to the poor?' 'No.' 'Then perhaps it is not the money you want, after all. Perhaps your reason for taking the job is that you enjoy that sort of work.' 'Are you kidding? Only a fool would work as a short order cook except to make money. As I said, the money is what I'm after. But I'm not after it for any ulterior reason. It is an end-in-itself.'

Well, this conversation would leave me baffled. The curiosity aroused in the first instance when I learned of Adam's decision to take the part-time job would remain unsatisfied. A question that the inquiring intellect cannot but consider relevant—why do you want the money?—would remain unanswered. The putative desirability of money for its own sake just 'does not compute.' So, Adam's account would leave me scratching my head in bewilderment. I would remain unable to make sense of his decision to take the job. It is not that I would view Adam's choice as somehow immoral or even imprudent. Questions of moral rectitude or prudence would simply not be reached. I would be stuck contemplating the (ir)rationality of the choice. Under Adam's account, his decision to take the job would seem utterly pointless, and therefore irrational. It would seem to violate Aquinas's first principle of practical reason (as Grisez interprets it).

The general lesson to be drawn from reflection on the matter thus far is that money can only have (important) instrumental value. It cannot serve as a reason for action that requires reference to no further reason in order to ground the action's intelligibility. If we trace a chain of practical reasoning culminating in a choice back to its ultimate term, and find that that term is money sought as an end-in-itself, the data provide no intelligibilities for the inquiring intellect to pick out.

But let us now suppose that Adam's account of his decision to take the job does not end with his desire to earn some additional money. In reply to my inquiry, he says that he wants the extra money for a reason—to buy an expensive medicine. Of course, I immediately suppose that he, or someone close to him, is ill. But, again, what if my supposition is incorrect? When I ask after his health, he says, 'Oh no; it is kind of you to ask, but I'm not sick. No one I know is sick. I'm not buying the medicine to administer it to anyone. Medicine is worth having just for its own sake.' 'Have you become interested in pharmacology?' 'Nope.' 'You haven't started a medicine collection, have you?' 'Of course not.' This conversation leaves me no less baffled than the one about money. Inasmuch as medicine, like money, is something of instrumental value rather than intrinsic value, it fares no better than money as an intelligible ultimate reason for action. It is not an 'explanation stopper.'

Of course, since Adam is a rational person, his account of his decision would not stop with the reference to medicine. He would give a reason for wanting the medicine. Let us suppose that his reason is that his sister has been afflicted with a serious illness that only a costly medicine can cure; so he has decided to take the job in order to earn the money to buy the medicine needed to restore his sister's health. If Adam's explanation stops here, has he left me baffled? Not at all. I now have the data I need to make sense of Adam's decision, and, thus, to understand it as, at least, rational. I can now see the point of his decision to take the part-time job. Acting for the sake of (his sister's) health as an end-in-itself is perfectly intelligible. The intelligibility of health as a reason for action need not be supplied, as in the case of money or medicine, by some more fundamental reason.

Of course, there is nothing to stop me from asking Adam why health is something he wants his sister to have. But there would be nothing baffling about the straightforward reply that, beyond any instrumental value health might have for his sister, health is one of those things worth having just for its own sake. Adam's decision, and the chain of practical reason culminating in that decision, are completely intelligible simply by reference to (his sister's) health as something intrinsically valuable. And this intelligibility is available to anyone inquiring into the matter—regardless of whether the inquirer himself would have acted as Adam did had a loved one of his own been ill.[57]

Grisez and Finnis notice that we do not grasp the intelligibility of health as something intrinsically valuable in the same way we come to understand the purely instrumental value of things like money or medicine. Instrumental values can (only) be established by way of deductions or inferences from still more fundamental premises. But intrinsic values, as ultimate reasons for action, cannot be deduced or inferred. We do not, for example, infer the intrinsic goodness of health from the fact, if it is a fact, that people everywhere seem to desire it (although this sort of anthropological information can figure usefully in dialectical arguments—especially those meant to rebut claims that our belief in the intrinsic goodness of health is merely culturally induced). We see the point of acting for the sake of health, in ourselves or in others, just for its own sake, without the benefit of any such inference. Acts performed for the sake of health (even where we do not approve of them—e.g., when the scientist kidnaps the child in order to find a cure for the ravaging disease) do not strike us as utterly pointless. It is in this light that Grisez and Finnis claim that principles such as 'health is a good to be promoted and protected' are 'self-evident.'[58]

Once we have traced a chain of practical reasoning back to its ultimate term (e.g., health), if that term provides for its own intelligibility, it enables us to make sense of those terms in the chain of reasoning that do not supply their own intelligibility (e.g., medicine and money). The principle that we grasp in (at least implicitly) affirming the intrinsic value of the end indicated by the ultimate term is self-evident. Generalizing from our inquiry into Adam's practical reasoning, we can affirm, as a self-evident practical truth, the proposition that 'health is a good to be done and pursued' (i.e., preserved, protected, restored). Thus, we have identified a basic precept of natural law.

It must be emphasized that this is no more than a general prescription to act for the sake of health. As such, it is weak. It does not, for example, say anything about when, if ever, it is wrong not to act for the sake of health. Nor does it indicate whether it is ever right to sacrifice health ultimately for the sake of some other intelligible end.[59] While it grounds the intelligibility and, thus, our judgment of the rationality of Adam's decision, it says nothing about whether that decision was morally required or even permissible.

F. From First Practical Principles to Moral Norms

Under the Grisez–Finnis theory, first practical principles and basic precepts of natural law (i.e., those concerning the basic goods) do not state moral propositions. As determinations of the first principle of practical reason, they are, in a sense, 'pre-moral.' They identify as self-evidently choiceworthy not only moral goods, but also non-moral goods (e.g., health, friendship, knowledge and play). Taken together, they exclude as unchoiceworthy only pointless activity. They are action-guiding in the sense that they are principles by which reason directs human choices toward intelligible ends. But if these were the only action-guiding principles, then there would never be a reason to choose (as distinct from an explanation for choosing—e.g., one's tastes, desires, sheer preferences) one intelligible course of action over another. For example, there may be an intelligible reason to play Russian roulette ('play') and an intelligible reason not to play it ('life' and the other goods attainable by the living). Are there reasons on the basis of which we can judge the choice to play, despite its intelligibility, less than fully reasonable? If there are such reasons, principles that are analytically distinct from the first practical principles must supply them. If these principles of full practical reasonableness could be identified, they would provide standards for distinguishing merely rational choices from morally upright ones. By prescribing some choices as morally required and proscribing others as immoral, such principles would accomplish what the determinations of the first principle of practical reason by themselves cannot do.

The Grisez–Finnis theory presents a set of general moral principles that, while analytically distinct from the basic practical principles and derived from a still more abstract foundational moral principle, in effect, put the ensemble of basic practical principles to work in concert. The role of these moral principles is to structure and guide human choosing between intelligible human goods. In *Natural Law and Natural Rights*, Finnis labeled these principles 'requirements of practical reasonableness.' In their collaborative work, however, Grisez and Finnis follow the former author's usual practice of referring to them as 'modes of responsibility.' I shall do so here as well.

Insofar (but only insofar) as the Grisez–Finnis theory understands the intelligibility of human choices as grounded ultimately in human goods (understood as constitutive aspects of human fulfillment), it is 'teleological.'[60] Weinreb's labeling notwithstanding, Finnis's natural law theory is by no means purely deontological.[61] In its teleological dimension (but only in this dimension), it resembles consequentialist ethical theories as well as certain neo-Aristotelian and neo-scholastic natural law theories.

Any teleological theory of practical reasoning that identifies more than one human good will need, if it is to ground a theory of morality, a principle or set of principles capable of guiding human choice and action in respect of the various goods. For consequentialists, the master principle of ethics directs the chooser to act in the way most likely to produce the best net proportion of good to bad consequences, overall and in the long run. Grisez and Finnis reject this principle on the ground, among others, that it assumes what is false, viz., that the instantiations of human goods (and bads) are commensurable in such a way as to make possible the intelligent weighing or measuring of 'value' necessary to consequentialist calculations. As ultimate reasons for action, the human goods, and their instantiations, must be irreducible to one another or to any more fundamental category. Thus, they are incommensurable.[62]

Grisez and Finnis maintain that the principle proposed by many neo-Aristotelian and neo-scholastic moralists as an alternative to consequentialism is no more plausible. This principle supposes that speculative inquiry can identify an objective hierarchy among the goods. It directs the chooser, at least in certain conflict situations, to act for the sake of the superior good. Grisez and Finnis deny that anything in our grasp of fundamental practical principles warrants the conclusion that there is an objective hierarchy among the basic goods to which these principles refer—at least in any sense of 'hierarchy' relevant to choice. Indeed, they suspect that any claim that such a hierarchy exists supposes the false thesis about commensurability that renders consequentialism untenable. It supposes, that is, that some goods have 'more' good in them than others.

Having rejected consequentialist and neo-scholastic principles, Grisez and Finnis propose their 'modes of responsibility.' These are put forward as a set of general norms by reference to which various forms of unreasonableness in choosing in respect of human goods can be identified. But what do Grisez and Finnis take to be the standard of (un)reasonableness? The answer to this question remained obscure in Finnis's book and in Grisez's early work. As presented, the modes of responsibility, while intuitively appealing to many readers and defensible dialectically against various criticisms, appeared to pop out of nowhere. Especially perplexing to some readers was the mode that forbids acting directly against a basic good, i.e., 'doing evil that good might come of it.' Even some readers who found Grisez's and Finnis's criticisms of consequentialism and neo-scholasticism compelling felt uncomfortable with an apparently ungrounded moral norm capable of generating moral absolutes (e.g., no direct killing, no torture).

Perhaps the most important development in this theory since the publication of Finnis's book is the formal identification of what Grisez and Finnis call the 'first principle of morality.' As formulated in their most recent collaborative work, this principle enjoins persons to 'choose and otherwise will those and only those possibilities whose willing is compatible with integral human fulfillment.'[63] If sound, this principle provides an intelligible grounding for the various modes of responsibility. The modes themselves are, in effect, specifications of this first principle. They exclude as practically unreasonable (i.e., immoral) various types of willing inconsistent with a will that is well-disposed toward all of the human goods.

The concept of integral human fulfillment, as it figures in the Grisez–Finnis statement of the first principle of morality, is easily misunderstood. It is not meant to indicate a supreme good above or apart from the basic goods. The basic human goods are reasons for action in a sense that integral fulfillment cannot be. But the fulfillments offered by basic goods, while genuine, are incorrigibly partial. No choice, or set of humanly possible choices, can bring about overall fulfillment. In none can one realize every humanly fulfilling possibility. The very open-endedness of the basic goods precludes this. The possibilities realized in and by human choices and actions are aspects, but only aspects, of complete human well-being. Inasmuch as no human choice, or set of choices, can realize anything more than aspects of complete human well-being, integral fulfillment cannot be a grand operational objective (whether of an individual, a community or the whole human race). As Finnis and Grisez put it, '[e]thics cannot be an architectonic art in that way; there can be no plan to bring about integral human fulfillment.'[64]

Thus, for Grisez and Finnis, the principle of integral human fulfillment is an ideal: not in the sense of a Platonic form of the good existing in a realm transcending this world, but in the sense of something that, while not a direct object of choices or attainable by and in them, can nevertheless be imagined (if imperfectly) and even wished for, and so can provide the standards by which choices may reasonably be guided.[65] The first principle of morality, in making reference to this ideal, does not direct us to choose in such a way as to bring about (or contribute to a project of bringing about) integral human fulfillment, for any such principle would be worse than utopian. It would direct us to do what in principle cannot be done. Any such principle would itself be an ideal—and a useless one at that; it would be both too general to actually guide choices and incapable (in view of incommensurability and the lack of an objective hierarchy of basic goods) of rational specification. But the first principle of morality, though it makes reference to an ideal (which is not a principle), is itself not an ideal. It directs us to do something that can be done. It says that in choosing partial fulfillments, as we inevitably must, we should treat every possible human fulfillment for what it is; i.e., an essential aspect of integral human fulfillment.

This treatment has implications, for we often have incentives, and therefore confront temptations, to treat integral human fulfillment in some of its aspects (i.e., to treat some types of fulfillments or the fulfillments of some human beings) as expendable for the sake of others. When we act on these incentives, we opt for possibilities the willing of which is simply incompatible with the guiding ideal. We choose with a bad will, and hence, immorally.

Under the Grisez–Finnis theory, the modes of responsibility are derived from the first principle of morality.[66] They identify the various incentives to choose incompatibly with a will to integral human fulfillment, and they direct the chooser not to act on these incentives.[67] The modes thus provide premises for the often complex moral analysis by which persons can reason their way to specific moral norms. While our grasp of the modes gets moral argument off the ground, it does not always make such argument easy. Often, extremely careful and insightful analysis is required to determine whether a proposed act of, say, killing is direct and therefore impermissible; or, where an act of killing is clearly indirect, it sometimes takes equally subtle analysis to establish the fairness or unfairness (forbidding unfairness is one of the modes) of the act.

Under the Grisez–Finnis theory, the identification of the modes is necessary because the first principle of morality, if left unspecified, is too general to make possible the derivation of specific moral norms. In the absence of modal specifications, one could not begin to derive norms about, say, abortion or capital punishment (not to mention economic justice or political participation) from an injunction to choose with a will toward integral human fulfillment. Such norms cannot be derived immediately from so abstract a principle. Thus, Grisez and Finnis sometimes describe the modes as 'intermediate' moral principles; they occupy a place between the very abstract first principle and the most concrete and specific moral injunctions.[68] Inasmuch as the modal specifications of the first principle of morality are derived from that principle, they, unlike the determinations of the first principle of practical reason, are not self-evident.[69] But the first principle of morality itself, as an underived principle, is self-evident.

Is this a case in which Grisez and Finnis have, to recall Weinreb's charge, 'confused self-evidence with personal conviction?' I think not. Of course, the charge cannot be rebutted by presenting a derivation of the first principle of morality; a successful derivation would prove that the principle is not self-evident, but rather dependent upon premises still more fundamental. So any defense of the claim that it (or any other principle) is self-evident will have to be a dialectical defense, rather than a derivation.[70]

The principal dialectical arguments for the first principle of morality demonstrate the failures or inadequacies of proposals that would deny the principle or leave it out of account. Especially powerful in this regard are arguments that reveal crucial flaws in the general moral principles put forward in theories that share with the Grisez–Finnis theory a concern for directing choice and action respecting human goods. If, for example, consequentialist principles go awry in treating basic human goods as commensurable, then an adequate alternative will have to treat basic goods as incommensurable. But to do so, a general moral principle would have to direct choosing in a way respectful of each basic human good and each human individual as an ultimate locus of incommensurable values.[71] This, of course, is exactly what the first principle of morality, as formulated in the Grisez–Finnis theory, is designed to do.

In the absence of some understanding of human goods, knowledge of the first principle of morality would not be possible. Does this confute the alleged self-evidence of this principle? No. If anything, it establishes that our grasp of the principle is not, as some have charged, a mere intuition. Rather, it, like our grasp of first practical principles, is accomplished by intelligent reflection on data. Our practical intellects pick out intelligibilities in the data provided by our grasp of first practical principles, thus making possible additional practical—in this case moral—judgments.

Here, I think, it is worth spelling out briefly the relationship between the first principle of practical reason, its determinations, and the first principle of morality. We have already seen that, under the Grisez–Finnis theory, practical knowledge in its 'pre-moral' aspect is directive (although not fully normative). It directs action toward intelligible ends and, thus, away from pointlessness. It identifies goods as 'to be done and pursued.' Thus, immoral choices are not irrational. (Indeed, purely irrational acts are not 'chosen' in any morally significant sense.) One chooses immorally for a reason. The intelligibility of immoral choices, like that of all rational acts, is grounded ultimately in the goods for the sake of which they are made. These goods are, as we have seen, the subjects of first practical principles. Any immoral choice is, thus, consistent with at least one such principle. The immoral choice responds to the directiveness of that (or those) principle(s). The good available in such a choice can be sought as a genuine benefit. But it is a benefit that comes only at the cost of ignoring the directiveness of other practical principles.

The goods that are treated as something other than irreducible, incommensurable aspects of integral human fulfillment in an immoral choice are themselves, of course, the subjects of practical principles. Thus, the responsiveness of immoral choices to the first principles taken as a whole (i.e., to the first principle of practical reason) is imperfect. Indeed, they are imperfect in a sense in which morally upright choices cannot be judged imperfect. Let me explain.

In any morally upright choice, there will be 'goods to be done and pursued' that are not done and pursued. No choice can bring about integral human fulfillment by perfectly realizing every possible human good. But the directiveness of first practical principles does more than identify goods as 'to be done and pursued.' It identifies the damaging of these goods as 'to be avoided.' A choice that is rational inasmuch as it responds to a practical principle, can still be less than fully reasonable in its failure to respect a different practical principle. To choose with a will toward realizing a certain good is to choose rationally. Both morally upright and immoral choices embody this sort of willing. But to choose with a will that another good be sacrificed or damaged is to seek a goal 'at the expense of reason, part of whose directiveness will have been ignored by choice.'[72] Such choosing is the mark of immorality—not because it contradicts the first principle of practical reason, but inasmuch as it responds to it imperfectly.

Does this imply that the first principle of morality is unnecessary because the determinations of the first principle of practical reason themselves are sufficient to forbid immoral choices? No. By making knowledge of the ideal of integral human fulfillment (and what is inconsistent with that ideal) possible, first practical principles provide the occasion (i.e., the data) for judging that a principle of complete reasonableness would direct action by reference to that ideal. Unless the judgment is made, and the principle formulated, however, there is no ultimate ground for full moral normativity, as distinguished from practical directiveness. Does this imply, then, that the first principle of morality is deduced or inferred from pre-moral practical principles? Again, the answer is no. The judgment is made in light of the data provided by the first practical principles, but it is not the fruit of a derivation from those principles. Such principles do not provide the grounds of the epistemic legitimacy of an affirmation of the first principle of morality. Those grounds are provided by the proposition stated in the principle itself. There is, for example, no relationship of entailment between the first principle of practical reason, and/or its determinations, and the first principle of morality.

G. Free Choice, Causality and Moral Responsibility

I presented the foregoing lengthy exposition and defense of the Grisez–Finnis theory to correct Weinreb's account of the role of self-evident principles in the Grisez–Finnis natural law theory and to answer his criticism of Finnis's appeals to such principles in *Natural Law and Natural Rights*. This, as I understand it, is the heart of Weinreb's case against 'deontological' natural law theory of the Grisez–Finnis sort. Having assumed that Finnis's work confuses self-evidence with personal conviction, Weinreb does not develop a detailed case against the Grisez–Finnis theory for failing to solve what Weinreb himself takes to be the central puzzle of moral and political philosophy (and, indeed, human existence itself), namely, the 'ontological' problem of human freedom in a causally determinate universe. I shall conclude my discussion of Weinreb by remarking on how the question of freedom and cause can be handled under the Grisez–Finnis theory.

Weinreb is correct to suppose that the problem of human freedom, i.e., self-determined action, is crucial in moral and political philosophy. In the absence of some free choice in human affairs, there could be no moral norms because such norms govern only free choices. Anyone who proposes a moral norm presupposes some free choice. But this presupposition does not establish that free choices are possible. It might be the case, after all, that no human actions are self-determined and, therefore, that there are no moral norms. If it is more reasonable to believe in complete determinism than in some free choice, then it is more reasonable to disbelieve than to believe in any moral norms. If, as Weinreb argues, the issue is inherently unresolvable, then no moral theory (and no moral norm) can be secure. Indeed, if Weinreb's argument succeeds, there would appear to be no practical point to moral theorizing.

Recognizing the relevance of free choice to moral theory, Grisez, together with Joseph M. Boyle, Jr. and Olaf Tollefsen, took up the problem directly in a book published in 1976 entitled *Free Choice: A Self-Referential Argument*. Therein, the authors presented an argument for the proposition that someone can make a free choice. The argument is self-referential in the sense that it proposes to establish the falsity of the proposition that nobody can make a free choice by reference to the very act of asserting that proposition as true. Reducing a very lengthy and dense argument to its central propositions, here is a summary: The arguments made by those who deny free choice will, like any other arguments purporting to ground rational affirmations, presuppose both the existence of norms of rationality which prescribe unconditionally, and the physical and psychological possibility of one's refusing to adhere to such norms. Rational affirmation of the proposition that there are no free choices is possible only for one who chooses between the alternatives of, on the one hand, adhering to the prescriptions of the norms of rationality appealed to by those who argue against free choice, or, on the other hand, refusing to adhere to those prescriptions. But this choosing is itself an instance of free choice. So any argument that there cannot be free choices is ultimately self-refuting.

Retorsive arguments against complete determinism are familiar to contemporary philosophers. Determinists commonly defend themselves against such arguments by accusing their interlocutors of begging the question of whether reasons are anything other than causes (of behavior).

The argument developed by Grisez and his co-authors is an especially compelling version of the retorsive argument for free choice inasmuch as its focus on the role of norms of rationality denies determinists this escape route. But Weinreb's case is not, the reader will recall, an argument for determinism as such. So, even if successful, the self-referential argument for free choice is not sufficient to meet Weinreb's challenge to theorists of natural law and justice. It is certainly the case, as Weinreb argues, that free choice is possible only against a background order of causality. Otherwise, the immediate consequences (if any) of self-determined human actions would be utterly random and unpredictable. Such actions would be merely arbitrary insofar as they would lack a rational ground. There would be no intelligible point to performing some action rather than another (or no action at all). Where there are no reasons for action, choice is pointless. In the absence of reasons, there could be no intelligent self-determined action, but merely arbitrary human behavior.

Determinists have long attempted to establish that unless human actions are caused, they are arbitrary. Defenders of free choice have countered with the proposal that free choice need only suppose the existence of reasons for action in order to avoid the implication of arbitrariness. Determinists reply that reasons, if they exist, are merely causes by another name. But among the problems with this reply is the fact that reasons differ from causes in that the former, unlike the latter, can exist without bringing about effects. One can have reasons to perform an act, yet not perform it. This is because one can, at the same time, have reasons not to perform the act. All questions of morality aside, either way one will act (or not act) on the basis of reasons. One's action (or inaction) will be rationally grounded and, thus, intelligible. Despite its being the fruit of choice, rather than causation, the rational grounding of one's action (or inaction) prevents it from being 'arbitrary' in the strong sense alleged by determinists.

But Weinreb could argue, as critics of free choice have argued, that even if a choice between two live alternatives is 'not arbitrary' in the sense that either alternative has an intelligible point, such a choice is in itself arbitrary in the sense that it lacks sufficient conditions apart from the person's choosing itself. There may be a 'reason' grounding—and thus making intelligibly choiceworthy—each of the options, but in the absence of a reason to choose between them, the choice of one over the other is either determined (by desire, taste, etc.) or unintelligible—in other words, the intelligibility of an event depends upon its cause. But this is precisely what the proponent of (some) free choice denies in the first place: His whole point in claiming that someone can make a free choice is that the categories of 'causally determined' and 'random' do not exhaust the possibilities.

To assert that someone can make a free choice is precisely to claim that a class of actions (viz., free choices) have their own intelligibility without reference to something else (e.g., causes). If the critic of free choice (or one who holds free choice to be antinomic) responds by invoking a 'principle of sufficient reason' (which, in Leibniz's famous formulation, holds that 'there can be no fact real or existing, no statement true, unless there be a sufficient reason why it should be so and not otherwise'), he opens himself up to a different retorsive argument because there is no sufficient epistemic reason to accept the principle of sufficient reason itself.[73]

Moreover, one may admit a qualified principle of sufficient reason under the terms of which there must be a reason for everything except those things (e.g., free choices) by reference to which other things are ultimately explained. Adoption of a principle of sufficient reason qualified in this way comports with the view that there are boundaries of explanation (i.e., that explanation does not go on ad infinitum). At the boundaries, the intellect picks out intelligibilities in realities that are intelligible in themselves, and can therefore be understood without further explanation. Someone arguing on the basis of a principle of sufficient reason is hardly in a position to deny this supposition, for he himself implicitly relies on it in appealing to a principle of sufficient reason. Any such principle is either at the boundaries of explanation, and intelligible in itself, or else unintelligible. There is no sufficient reason for it (which is by no means to say that it is false).

Much earlier I quoted Weinreb's assertion that unless the circumstances of a person's act, together with the qualities that make him act as he does, are determinate, his act seems to be 'the product of arbitrary occurrences as far as he is concerned and not something for which he individually is responsible.'[74] This claim grounds the alleged antinomy of freedom and cause that Weinreb thinks is the central, unavoidable, yet unresolvable, question of moral and political philosophy. I think that his claim is confused. 'Arbitrary' refers to human action, while 'occurrence' refers to what happens apart from action. To the person choosing, the choice he is making seems 'arbitrary' only in the trivial sense that he perceives nothing forcing him to make it. It does not seem 'arbitrary' in the sense of irrational or non-rational, because whatever he opts for does not seem to him pointless. The choice does not, however, seem like an 'occurrence.' It seems like something he is doing, not like something that is happening to him. From his own point of view, at least, he is determining the action.

Of course, the particular options a person faces may have little or nothing to do with that person's (or, for that matter, anyone else's) free choices. The sheer givenness of a set of options does not mean that the choice between them is not free, nor does it mean that one cannot be responsible for choosing one way rather than another. Free choice does presuppose causality—otherwise there could be no determinate options for choice—but it does not presuppose a measure of causality with which it is incompatible. When we have a free choice to make, lots of things that are already determined, including everything that brings us to that point, provide the open alternatives among which we must choose and which make our choosing possible. All that it means to say that this is a free choice is that nothing causes us to make the choice one way rather than another.

Implicit in many arguments that actions must either be caused or are random is the so-called phenomenalist conception of the self.[75] Under this conception, the self is a collection of discrete experiences bundled together only by various regularities. Any event, then, that is not integrated into these regularities by a cause, must be the product of mere chance. A 'free choice' made by such a self would be a random event. And, as Alasdair MacIntyre argued many years ago, '[w]hat is random is no more free than what is caused.'[76]

Were the phenomenalist conception of the self compelling, it would provide profound support for Weinreb's alleged antinomy. But a great many arguments can be marshaled against the phenomenalist conception, and Weinreb does not argue for it.

Implicit in the free choice position is an alternative conception of the self as substantially, but not completely, integrated. For a person to make a free choice that is not merely random but truly his, he must have a character and personality. Without these, there is no self capable of understanding the intelligible goods promised by the options, deliberating about them, and acting.[77] But, at the same time, his character and personality must be sufficiently open that these causal factors do not determine the choice. The conception of the self as substantially, but incompletely, integrated comports well with our common sense understanding of human agency. Under this conception, persons partially determine their characters and personalities by their own free choices. Heredity, environment and free choice together account for a person's character.[78] Free choice accounts for the possibility of self-determined changes (for better or worse) in character, and hence for the possibility of, for example, repentance and reform.

The more or less determinate self that makes a free choice determines itself further in that choice. The choice, in a sense, then, 'lasts' in the character and personality of the chooser—at least until the chooser makes another choice incompatible with it (thus re-orienting his character and personality by his own free choice).[79] The upshot of this self-constituting quality of choices is that subsequent acts performed in accord with a character established by one's free choices are acts for which one can reasonably be held (and hold oneself) morally responsible. Weinreb is correct to say that '[f]ull moral responsibility seems to require that an act be both free and determinate.'[80] But he is wrong to suppose, if indeed he does suppose, that any self that is determinate enough to enable a person's act to be his own is completely determinate, and therefore incapable of doing anything other than whatever it does.

As we have seen, a central feature of the Grisez–Finnis moral theory is its account of ultimate reasons for action. The first principle of practical reason and its determinations guide action by reference to these reasons. Thus, they make free choice possible without implying 'arbitrariness' in any sense that would undercut moral responsibility for one's actions. If these principles are sound, we need not account for every aspect of non-arbitrary human action by reference to causality. Causal factors will bear on human choice and action in a wide variety of ways, but some free choice can exist against the background causal order without contradiction. Moral norms, if they can be identified, provide the standards for fully reasonable (free) choosing where free choice exists. Moral and political philosophy are not, then, as Weinreb's arguments would lead us to conclude, doomed to frustration by an antinomy at their core. A theory of natural law, including a natural law theory of justice, need not adopt the implausible proposal that the causal natural order parcels out illness and health, plenty and privation according to the desert of the recipients in a desperate effort to dissolve the alleged antinomy.

II. RUSSELL HITTINGER'S *A CRITIQUE OF THE NEW NATURAL LAW THEORY*

Russell Hittinger's *A Critique of the New Natural Law Theory* is both narrower in its scope and less ambitious in its claims than Weinreb's book. Hittinger's work is a critical examination of the Grisez–Finnis natural law theory—a theory Hittinger identifies as a product of the movement abroad in contemporary moral philosophy to recover a credible 'pre-modern' tradition of ethics. This movement, which he labels 'the recoverist project,'[81] is generated, in his view, by widespread disillusionment with what appears to be a stalemate between utilitarianism and deontology in modern discourse about ethics. It was in reaction to this apparent stalemate, according to Hittinger, that Alasdair MacIntyre, perhaps the most prominent 'recoverist,' set about diagnosing what he called the 'interminability' of contemporary moral debates in his influential treatise, *After Virtue*.[82] Other 'recoverists,' as Hittinger reads them, include Alan Donagan, Stanley Hauerwas, Elizabeth Anscombe and, from a distinctively Marxist perspective, Ernst Bloch.

Hittinger justifies his focus on the Grisez–Finnis theory, which '[f]or lack of a better term' he labels 'the new natural law theory,'[83] on three grounds. First, Grisez and Finnis claim to have recovered Aquinas's theory of natural law in a way that both avoids the standard Enlightenment and post-Enlightenment criticisms of Aquinas's theory, and (according to Hittinger) 'rescue[s] [that theory] from the problems inherent in the rest of Aquinas's work;'[84] Second, 'they contend to have retrieved the systematic core of natural law theory in a way that is congruent with the older tradition and in a way that is persuasive to contemporary ethicians;'[85] Third, Grisez has recently undertaken to apply his natural law ethical theory to Roman Catholic moral theology in a massive multi-volume project.[86] The adequacy of the Grisez–Finnis theory for moral theology is an important focus of Hittinger's criticisms of the theory, but I will refrain from addressing these criticisms here. I shall concentrate instead upon Hittinger's critique of the Grisez–Finnis theory as a philosophical theory of morality.

Hittinger's thesis is that the Grisez–Finnis 'project' fails, in the end, because it does not 'interrelate systematically practical reason with a philosophy of nature.'[87] The 'reclamation of natural law,' Hittinger declares, 'obviously requires a commitment to law as in some way "natural," and nature as in some way normative.'[88] This is a commitment which, as we have already seen, Grisez and Finnis steadfastly decline to make. They reject not only the rather perplexing idea of a normative natural order that Weinreb identifies as 'the core of the old natural law,' but also the neo-scholastic position that nature is normative in a way that enables us to derive moral norms from speculative knowledge of human nature acquired prior to the achievement of practical knowledge. Thus, they deny any rational basis of an identification of 'the natural' with 'the morally good' (and therefore deny the presupposition that the most basic moral norm is the imperative: 'follow nature'). One cannot derive the moral 'ought,' according to Grisez and Finnis, from the 'is' of human nature (or the human condition, or human being).

A. Practical Reason as Autonomous

Hittinger's book brings together a range of criticisms of the Grisez–Finnis theory marshaled over the years by neo-scholastic and neo-Aristotelian commentators, including Ralph McInerny, Vernon Bourke and Henry Veatch. The chief criticism, perhaps, is the charge that relates to the proposition that practical reason operates autonomously. In other words, Grisez and Finnis contend that practical reason operates on its own first principles without dependence upon methodologically antecedent knowledge drawn from speculative disciplines such as anthropology, metaphysics or theology. Critics contend that this theory embraces

Kantian deontologism and borrows all of its problems. As Veatch has put it, 'though the hands are those of Germain Grisez, the voice is that of Immanuel Kant.'[89] Hittinger, it seems, agrees.

The fundamental problem with Kantian moral theory, according to neo-scholastics (and others), is that, in refusing to ground morality in a concern for human well-being, it renders moral rules ultimately pointless. But if human well-being is identified as, in some sense, the ultimate ground of the intelligibility of moral norms, then some substantial knowledge of 'the (human) good' becomes necessary if we are to discern 'the (morally) right.' Yet, the glaring teleological dimension of the Grisez–Finnis theory marks an obvious difference with Kantian ethics. As we have seen, the first practical principles and the basic precepts of natural law refer, under the Grisez–Finnis theory, to basic human goods. In this respect, at least, the theory is radically unlike Kantian deontology. So, we must ask, in what sense do neo-scholastic critics of the Grisez–Finnis theory suppose that theory to be Kantian?

Hittinger suggests the answer. In maintaining that the axiological knowledge needed to get moral theory off the ground comes as the product of practical reflection, rather than a speculative inquiry into human nature, Grisez and Finnis, in effect, accept Kant's supposition that ethics can dispense with the philosophy of nature. The Grisez–Finnis theory resembles Kantianism above all in its declaration of the methodological independence of ethics from metaphysics (or ontology). In Weinreb's pithy formulation, it represents a theory of 'natural law without nature.' Such an approach, in Hittinger's judgment, attempts 'to recover natural law theory by way of shortcuts.'[90] And, for him, no less than for Weinreb (although for a different reason), shortcuts will not do.

Hittinger's critique of the Grisez–Finnis theory begins with a set of arguments purporting to show that the attempt to identify human goods without appeal to a speculative philosophy of nature falls into a sort of intuitionism that leaves the basic goods vulnerable to skeptical attacks. Indeed, he implies that Grisez and Finnis themselves seem to perceive this inasmuch as they regularly marshal evidence acquired by various sorts of speculative inquiry (e.g., anthropological data) in support of the putatively self-evident basic goods. Arguments based on evidence of this sort ought to be unnecessary, Hittinger suggests, if the practical intellect can grasp the first principles that refer to basic goods without inferring anything from speculative knowledge of the goods as natural human ends.[91]

In criticizing Weinreb's account of Finnis's appeals to self-evidence, I discussed the familiar charge that the Grisez–Finnis theory of first practical principles is based on intuitions. Here I wish to say a word about the use of dialectical arguments in defense of propositions claimed to be self-evident. Dialectical argumentation focuses on the relationships between propositions (including putatively self-evident propositions) to be defended and other knowledge. The point of such argumentation is to highlight the unacceptable implications of denying the propositions to be defended, or the inappropriateness of relying on certain evidence (shown to be inapt or defective) to deny or cast doubt on those propositions.

Now, speculative arguments can be useful in casting doubt upon propositions alleged to be self-evident practical truths. For example, the presentation of anthropological evidence tending to show that no form of friendship existed in certain non-Western cultures prior to their contact with the West, while not itself a disproof of the self-evident value of friendship, would cast substantial doubt on the proposition that friendship is intrinsically valuable. It would provide an occasion for anyone who judged friendship to be objectively good to at least rethink the matter. One would be surprised to learn that a self-evidently worthwhile human end was unknown (or known but unvalued) by a substantial part of mankind.

In carefully rethinking the matter, perhaps one would discover a mistake in one's practical judgment about friendship. Perhaps it would transpire that, while friendship is not intrinsically valuable, its historically contingent, but very close, links with certain more fundamental goods in one's own culture deflected one's understanding of the matter, leading one falsely to conclude that the value of friendship is intrinsic (rather than, say, merely instrumental). On the other hand, perhaps, even after a searching reconsideration, one's judgment of the intrinsic worth of friendship would not change. In this event, one would likely find the anthropological evidence perplexing in light of one's considered practical judgment. The phenomenon of a widespread failure to grasp what one judges to be a self-evident practical truth would itself demand an explanation; it would set a substantial question for further speculative inquiry.

Just as speculative arguments can cast doubt on propositions claimed to be self-evident practical truths, speculative arguments can be effective in rebuttal. An effective speculative argument of this sort does not establish the self-evidence of a self-evident practical truth. It simply removes a particular doubt about that truth. For example, an argument that established that the apparent non-existence of friendships in certain non-Western cultures can be accounted for by the failure of Western anthropologists to appreciate the distinctive forms and expressions of friendship in such cultures, would itself remove the doubts raised by the disturbing anthropological evidence. But, one might ask, can there be doubts about self-evident truths? Yes—precisely because such truths are not mere intuitions or innate ideas. They are grasped by intelligent reflection on data presented by experience (e.g., one's own direct or indirect experiences of friendships). And any such grasp involves an act of understanding. Many factors capable of derailing understanding respecting non-self-evident propositions, whether practical or speculative, are equally capable of impeding sound judgment in respect of self-evident propositions. Thus, we would do well to follow Aquinas in distinguishing propositions that are self-evident to everyone, from propositions that are self-evident only to the wise.[92] It is possible for anyone to fail to grasp a self-evident truth; just as it is possible for anyone to mistakenly suppose that what is in reality a derived proposition (or even a false proposition) is a self-evident truth.

Dialectical arguments are, I think, especially powerful in rebuttal. However, they may be employed affirmatively in support of a self-evident practical truth, often with persuasive force. For example, the considerable anthropological evidence tending to show that various form of friendship, knowledge and religion are to be found in virtually all cultures, while not evidence of the self-evidence of the value of these realities (for there can be no 'evidence' of 'self-evidence'), does show that a practical judgment of their intrinsic worth comports well with the data. It places something of a burden on anyone who would deny the proposition stating this practical judgment to account for the universality of phenomena such as friendship, intellectual inquiry and worship. Any theory that proffers an explanation proposing a sociologically deterministic or psychologically reductionistic account will be subject to the increasingly familiar criticisms of all forms of determinism and reductionism. Perhaps someone skeptical about basic goods could meet these criticisms. But here the skeptic would, in any event, be the party attempting to rebut dialectical arguments supporting self-evident practical truths (but not, of course, establishing their self-evidence).

In view of the foregoing analysis, I see no warrant for Hittinger's suspicion of Grisez's or Finnis's use of evidence procured by way of speculative inquiry in support of propositions they hold to be self-evident practical truths. But Hittinger has another, more substantial, argument against the proposal that first practical principles are not derived from speculative knowledge. He argues that there are respects in which at least a certain minimum amount of speculative knowledge is indispensable to our practical judgments. For example, a basic understanding of the integral organic functioning of the human body (i.e., of being alive) is a condition of any judgment, including any practical judgment, about the status of life and health as basic goods. Grisez himself has implicitly acknowledged this, as Hittinger points out, especially in his early work on contraception.[93] There, as Hittinger reports, Grisez argued, for example:

that the good of life must be judged as a whole rather than in relation to the end of each faculty or physiological power. Accordingly, respiration and nutrition cannot be said to be basic human goods. However, from a biological point of view, the 'work of reproduction is the fullest organic realization of the living substance.' [Citation omitted.] In other words, it differs from respiration in the sense that it bestows the good of life as a whole, and therefore ought to be included within the basic good of life.[94]

Hittinger assumes that Grisez's use of this sort of argument shows that he 'does in fact directly rely upon anthropological, if not metaphysical, evidence for including procreation in the list of basic goods.'[95] Grisez indeed judges that the generation of a new human life is not merely an instrumental end, but is intelligibly worthwhile just for the sake of the new life generated. Hittinger's claim is that the above-quoted passage shows that Grisez himself relies 'upon a theoretical [i.e., speculative] argument concerning what is essential or accidental to human organicity'[96] in reaching this judgment. As Hittinger sees it, then, Grisez's own analysis of at least one basic human good is 'not consistent with his understanding of the inferential and deductive underivability of the basic practical principles.'[97]

Is Hittinger's allegation of inconsistency telling? No. His argument rests on a misunderstanding of what Grisez expects to get out of arguments like the one Hittinger cites. Grisez need not, and, in fact, does not, deny that a certain minimum amount of speculative knowledge is needed as a condition of practical judgment. (Nor does he deny that additional speculative knowledge has any place in moral reasoning.) While practical knowledge is not derived from propositions about the realities judged to be intelligibly choiceworthy, practical judgments (i.e., that something is a 'good to be done and pursued') are not, according to Grisez, made in the complete absence of data for reflection. Without a basic understanding of the realities one is supposed to be making practical judgments about (e.g., life, friendship, religion), one simply could not judge. In the complete absence of speculative knowledge of what Hittinger calls human organicity, for example, no practical judgment of the intelligibility of life or health as an ultimate reason for action would be possible. Can we make sense of someone's choice to act just for the sake of preserving, or protecting, or transmitting human life? It will be impossible to answer that question unless we first have some basic idea of what 'human life' is; thus, some speculative (i.e., biological) knowledge is a condition of our practical knowledge of the goods of life and health. But to acknowledge the need for a minimum of biological knowledge as a condition for reaching axiological judgments of this sort is not to imply that such judgments are inferred, deduced or otherwise derived from the biological knowledge.

Even perfect knowledge of human organicity, including perfect knowledge of what is essential and what is merely accidental to it, could not provide a warrant for judgments about the intelligibility of choosing life or health as ends in themselves (although such knowledge would profoundly enhance our capacity to preserve and promote these goods). The intelligibility of such choices, to the extent that they are intelligible, will be picked out of the data by insights that, while not unconditioned by speculative knowledge, are not logically entailed by it. Any such insight will therefore be not only fundamental, but fundamentally practical.

In arguing that Grisez smuggles speculative knowledge illicitly (on his own terms) into judgments about basic goods, Hittinger claims that among the terms Grisez variously employs 'for the "goods" . . . [are] "tendencies" [and] "basic inclinations." '[98] This report comes after, and seems to support, Hittinger's claim that '[a]ll of Grisez's goods have content derived from inclination.'[99] Now, the fact that something is a 'tendency' or 'basic inclination' is straightforwardly an item of speculative knowledge. To treat the fact that humans 'tend' or are 'basically inclined' toward something as a logical warrant for a judgment of the intrinsic value of whatever the tendency or inclination is toward, is to suppose that knowledge of basic practical principles can be derived from speculative knowledge. Were Hittinger's report accurate, Grisez would be guilty of an inconsistency in his treatment of first practical principles. But Grisez never implies, much less says, that basic goods are 'tendencies' or 'basic inclinations.' Hittinger's claim that Grisez 'employs' these terms for the goods has no basis in anything Grisez has written.

Hittinger's misunderstanding of Grisez's theory of basic goods is further evident in his assertion (again without citation) that, for Grisez, 'goods are defined as actions which are attractive to the agent.'[100] Not only does Grisez carefully distinguish goods from the actions by which persons may participate in goods, he never defines the goods by reference to their attractiveness to the persons who participate in them. Any theory of value that does define 'good' as what is 'attractive to the agent' flirts (at a minimum) with subjectivism. But Hittinger does the Grisez–Finnis theory an injustice by implying that a derivation of value from a speculative philosophy of nature is necessary to rescue that theory from subjectivism. Nowhere in the theory is the intelligibility of first practical principles made to depend upon the attractiveness of the basic goods to the acting person (which is to deny neither that basic goods can be attractive nor that their attractiveness can motivate action).

At one point, Hittinger accuses Grisez of holding an axiology in which the basic goods 'are curiously Platonic-like forms.'[101] The charge is untenable. Repeatedly, and in virtually all of their works on ethics, Grisez and Finnis make the point that goods do not exist in some transcendent realm, but are constitutive aspects of persons. To cite perhaps the most forceful statement, Finnis says in *Natural Law and Natural Rights* that 'the basic

aspects of human well-being are . . . not abstract forms, they are analytically distinguishable aspects of the well-being, actual or possible, of you
and me—of flesh-and-blood individuals.'[102]

Hittinger seems to assume that the Grisez–Finnis theory must rely on
some mysterious Platonic notion of the good because it does not propose
to derive basic goods from speculative knowledge of human nature. But,
as a critique of the Grisez–Finnis theory of practical knowledge, this
assumption simply begs the question. Grisez and Finnis claim that first
practical principles are self-evident truths grasped in non-inferential acts
of understanding. It is this claim that Hittinger set out to prove false. But
this proof cannot be accomplished by a gratuitous assertion—directly
contrary to what Grisez and Finnis actually say—that basic goods are
'curiously Platonic-like forms.'

B. *Goods and Persons*

Near the end of a discussion of Grisez's stated opinion that 'Kant's view
of moral principles is not so much false as grossly inadequate,'[103] Hittinger
raises some questions about 'the meaning and implications of shifting
one's focus from persons to goods.'[104] Hittinger asks:

Does this not assume, or suggest, that goods and persons are strictly co-extensive
both ontologically and in terms of actions which bear upon them? Is moral agency,
for instance, something more than the sum of the parts of the goods with which
practical reason is interested? In other words, is there something of value in
personhood that needs to be affirmed in terms quite different from merely our
concern for goods which fulfill persons?[105]

Alan Donagan shared Grisez's interpretation of Aquinas's theory of practical reasoning and has, in his own Kantian 'respect for persons' ethics,
defended many of the specific moral norms defended by Grisez and
Finnis.[106] Still, Donagan criticized the Grisez–Finnis theory along the lines
Hittinger's questions imply. Here it must be recalled that, under this
theory, basic human goods, while analytically distinguishable from the
persons whom they fulfill, are not extrinsic purposes of human action, but
rather intrinsic aspects of persons. In the earliest statement of the theory,
Grisez held that persons 'actualize and receive the human goods into
personal existence.'[107] But, from the point of view of action in respect of a
person, the person is not a value standing alongside the values that are
constitutive aspects of the person. To act for the sake of a person, for
example, is to favor some constitutive aspect(s) of that person's well-
being—i.e., to promote or preserve or protect basic goods as instantiated
in that person.

Of course, one respects or loves the person for the sake of whom one acts as a unity, not as an amalgam of distinct parts.[108] But the good that is sought in a choice made for the sake of the person is, in the end, only that which one supposes can be attained in the choice. There can be no act for the sake of the person considered apart from the various aspects of his well-being and fulfillment. Specific actions undertaken for the sake of a person are directed toward these aspects. But it is, as I have said, regard for the person as a unity that motivates specific actions. In view of the complex relationship between goods and persons, Hittinger's questions are far from trivial; but they are hardly embarrassing ones for the Grisez–Finnis theory.[109]

Elsewhere, in accusing Grisez of an equivocation on the question of whether 'the emphasis or focus of morality [is] given to the goods, or to my own fulfillment,'[110] Hittinger ignores an important feature of the Grisez–Finnis account of the relationship between basic goods and the persons whom they fulfill. The problem of whose flourishing, or whose good, is the ultimate point of moral norms is a perennial issue in discussions of eudaimonistic ethical theories. Is the rational basis of one's obligation to choose in a morally upright fashion ultimately a concern for one's own flourishing (which would be somehow profoundly damaged by one's own immoral choice)? Or, is it a concern for the flourishing of others, one's own well-being aside? In the Grisez–Finnis theory, it is, as we have seen, a regard for the ideal of integral human fulfillment, which would include, in principle, one's own flourishing as well as everyone else's. Thus, the theory excludes, again in principle, an essentially egoistic account of moral obligation.

Hittinger generates this alleged equivocation by interpreting in a strictly individualistic sense a reference to 'human self-limitation' in Grisez's formulation of what one avoids in morally good choices. Not only is there no warrant for such a reading in Grisez's work, but specific passages in Grisez's writings specifically exclude this sort of individualism. For example, Grisez says that '[basic human] goods do not have anyone's proper name attached to them.'[111] And in his formal discussion of the ideal of integral human fulfillment, Grisez states that the ideal 'is that of a single system in which all the goods of human persons would contribute to the fulfillment of the whole community of persons.'[112] This is a point that Grisez and Finnis have repeated many times.[113]

I have identified a variety of respects in which Hittinger has misunderstood the Grisez–Finnis theory at the level of first practical principles. His misinterpretations lend apparent plausibility to his basic claim that the Grisez–Finnis theory cannot succeed without drawing on a speculative philosophy of nature from which knowledge of fundamental goods is derived. Once these misinterpretations are brought to light, the credibility of this claim vanishes. I shall now turn to Hittinger's critique of the

Grisez–Finnis theory of moral principles. Again, basic interpretative errors ground Hittinger's most powerful criticisms.

C. *Moral Norms and the Ideal of Integral Human Fulfillment*

The reader will recall that, under the Grisez–Finnis theory, the first principle of morality refers to the ideal of integral human fulfillment. Our knowledge of this ideal comes from our understanding of the complete set of first practical principles—the self-evident determinations of the first principle of practical reason. While specific moral norms cannot be directly derived from the first principle of morality, they can be derived from intermediate moral norms—the modes of responsibility—that are themselves directly derived from the first principle of morality. These norms identify and forbid various forms of unreasonableness in human willing.

Hittinger erroneously interprets Grisez in particular as maintaining that the first principle of morality is an ideal. This misinterpretation is important for Hittinger's analysis of the adequacy of the Grisez–Finnis theory for moral theology: 'In his transition from moral principles to moral theology, Grisez regards Jesus as the concrete good that annuls the ideality of the Fpm [first principle of morality]. Its ideality, therefore, makes room for (even requires) a move into moral theology.'[114]

But the implications of this misinterpretation for the Grisez–Finnis theory when it is considered solely as philosophical ethics are profound. As I noted in the previous section, if the first principle of morality were itself merely an ideal, then it would be both too general to guide concrete human choices, and incapable of rational specification. Although our grasp of first practical principles gives us some knowledge of integral human fulfillment, it is nevertheless an ideal in the sense that it cannot be realized in human choices.[115] But the first principle of morality is anything but an ideal. It is capable of specification, and the norms thereby derived direct us to do things that can be done.

The point is critical: We cannot choose to bring about integral human fulfillment, but we can choose compatibly with a will to integral human fulfillment. The standard of practical reasonableness is not how close we come to bringing about integral fulfillment in our choices (nor is it how 'much' fulfillment, in some aggregative sense, we bring about); rather, it is whether our choices are compatible with a will to integral fulfillment. Hittinger seems to miss this point altogether. Indeed, in the course of his theological discussion, he accuses Grisez of 'taking away with one hand what was just given with other' because Grisez, as Hittinger understands him, holds that '[t]he achievement of the state of integral human fulfillment (the goal of the moral life for ethics and moral theology) is not a human act.'[116] Hittinger judges this to be 'a contradiction in terms, or at least a paradox of some sort,'[117] and he is correct. But the contradiction or paradox is generated not by Grisez's first principle of morality, but by Hittinger's own fundamental misunderstanding of it; Grisez never proposes integral human fulfillment as a 'state' (or state of affairs); nor does he imagine that it can serve as a 'goal' to be sought in human choosing.

D. The Question of a Hierarchy of Basic Goods

The centerpiece of Hittinger's case against the Grisez–Finnis theory of moral principles features the claim that unless an objective hierarchical ordering of the goods is built into ethics at the axiological level, moral problems raised by the plurality of goods and opportunities for their instantiation will render many moral problems unresolvable. His proposal is, of course, that a speculative philosophy of human nature is needed to provide the hierarchical ordering.

As discussed earlier, the Grisez–Finnis theory relies not on a principle of hierarchy to govern choice and action in respect of basic goods, but, rather, on the modes of responsibility. Hittinger does not allege that the modes are incapable of resolving any moral problems, but only that there are many important moral problems that they cannot resolve. He does not suppose, as do some critics of the Grisez–Finnis theory, that the modes cannot rule out any rational choices as practically unreasonable inasmuch as any choice, qua rational, will ultimately have its intelligibility by reference to some intelligible good(s) sought in the choice. (These critics, overlooking the force of the modes altogether, argue, for example, that, inasmuch as aesthetic appreciation is as much a fundamental good as life is, a healthy adult may reasonably (i.e., morally) stand by the side of a wading pool appreciating the beauty of the sunshine and not raise a finger to help a drowning infant easily within reach. Indeed, some might argue that nothing in the Grisez–Finnis theory forbids the adult from tossing the infant into the pool in order to appreciate the beautiful nobility of its struggling.) But Hittinger does claim that reliance on the modes to rule out immoral actions done for the sake of intelligible goods is rather odd. I shall present Hittinger's argument in his own words:

Grisez has reserved moral grounds for objecting to[, for example, Aztec religious practices involving human sacrifice]. For instance, he might argue that these practices violate some other human good, such as life; but this moral judgment does not disqualify the rituals as the good of religion; it only indicates that this particular religious observance violates the good of morality by failing to respect other basic goods. In other words, the Aztecs, according to nature, participate in the good of religion, for they find their religious practices attractive and gratifying; yet the practices, according to natural moral norms, violate [the mode of responsibility that forbids doing evil for the sake of good]. Nature appears to speak with a forked tongue.[118]

My first task here is to clear away some, by now familiar, interpretative mistakes. First, religious rituals, practices and observances are not, under the Grisez–Finnis theory, the good of religion. Hittinger's statement to the contrary reflects his failure to notice Grisez's distinction between goods and the actions by which persons may realize and participate in goods. Second, what rationally excludes the Aztec rituals, under the Grisez–Finnis theory, is not 'the good of morality,' but a specific moral norm forbidding direct killing (which is itself derived from the mode of responsibility Hittinger cites). Third, the fact that the Aztecs find their religious practices 'attractive and gratifying' is not, for Grisez (or Finnis), a ground of the goodness of the practices. Here again Hittinger imports into Grisez's axiology a conception of the basic goods as mere subjective motives. Such a conception has no foundation in Grisez's writings.

The Grisez–Finnis theory of natural law recognizes (and gives an account of the fact) that the Aztec rituals were not unintelligible acts. To the extent that they were sincerely performed (and so far as I know there is no reason to doubt the sincerity of those who performed them), the intelligible point of the rituals was harmony with the divine, or 'religion.' That someone would choose ultimately for the sake of such an end is hardly baffling. Even if one's own considered judgment is that there is nothing beyond the material world—no divine realities with whom to seek harmony—one may still understand the religious acts of those who have reached different conclusions. Inasmuch as the Grisez–Finnis theory understands 'good' as that which provides an ultimate reason for action, it is hardly an occasion for puzzlement that the murderous Aztec rituals can be said to have been performed for the sake of a good. This understanding in no way implies that such rituals were morally good—not even 'a little bit.' In truth, they were evil—not because they were pointless (for they were not) but because they violated moral norms (e.g., those derived from the modes forbidding the moral evils of direct killing and injustice). They were, then, objectively immoral (although this need imply no subjective guilt on the parts of those individuals who performed the murderous rituals). But notice this: Any theory of basic practical principles that excluded an understanding of the rituals as acts performed for the sake of the good of religion would undercut the possibility of judging the murderous acts by standards of morality. Lacking an intelligible point, the acts would have to be judged irrational and, as such, not susceptible to moral evaluation.

But let us get back to the issue of hierarchy. What if one finds oneself in a situation in which the modes of responsibility do not narrow one's morally acceptable alternatives down to one? Don't we need to know which good is the superior in order to choose correctly? It is here that the Grisez–Finnis theory is bound to disappoint absolutists. The theory seems incapable of providing norms that would generate a single, uniquely correct answer to every practical dilemma. It will not, for example, provide an answer for a gifted, morally serious undergraduate facing a choice of careers between law and medicine, who would like to know whether life and health are, in the great scheme of things, objectively more or less important than justice. Both options offer fulfillments (for the student and others), but no mode of responsibility will in principle rule out one or the other. The choice of either option, then, can be made compatibly with a will to integral human fulfillment. And the choice of neither option can bring it about (or somehow bring mankind nearer to bringing it about).

Of course, one's moral obligations can, sometimes, be affected by choices one has already made. For example, if I promise to do something, certain modes of responsibility ordinarily require me to do it, even where, but for my promise, no mode would generate such a requirement. Even aside from promises, prior commitments can give rise to moral obligations where, but for those commitments, none would exist. And the modes do forbid choosing in dilettantish, uncommitted ways. Self-integration is itself an intelligible good. Anyone who chooses with an utter disregard for it chooses some possibilities incompatible with a will to integral human fulfillment. So a morally serious and upright person will, *inter alia*, take care in his choosing to integrate his choices and harmonize them with one another. In *Natural Law and Natural Rights*, Finnis analyzed this mode under the rubric of 'a coherent plan of life.' Quoting John Rawls, Finnis said that:

we should 'see our life as one whole, the activities of one rational subject spread out in time. Mere temporal position, or distance from the present, is not a reason for favoring one moment over another.' But since human life is in fact subject to all manner of unforeseeable contingencies, this effort to 'see' our life as one whole is a rational effort only if it remains on the level of general commitments, and the harmonizing of them. Still, generality is not emptiness . . .[119]

Despite Finnis's explicit warning not to 'confuse the adoption of a set of basic personal or social commitments with the process, imagined by some contemporary philosophers, of "choosing basic values," ' his references to 'life-plans' (and his citation of Rawls) confirmed the worst fears of certain neo-scholastics. They perceived Finnis here as implicitly endorsing value (and therefore moral) relativism. After all, they reasoned, does not the idea that one can choose—free of the constraints of moral norms—'basic personal and social commitments,' reek of the modernist conception of human liberty against which the natural law tradition has long held out?

There are, certainly, modern ideas of moral liberty that are radically inconsistent with anything that can plausibly be claimed to be within the tradition of natural law theorizing. But the Grisez–Finnis theory of natural law allows no place for any such ideas. It emphatically rejects subjectivist conceptions of value (which make the value of an end depend on someone's choosing it or, at least, desiring it). And the modes of responsibility provide abundant guidance (many critics say that they provide far too much 'guidance') in choosing with respect to human goods—including choices of basic personal or social commitments. Although a great many options remain, the modes rule out more than a few live options for individuals and societies. Still, Henry Veatch, in a slightly different context, has warned Grisez and Finnis about supping with the devil: In the words of the old saw, 'one needs a very long spoon.'[120] But, recognizing that fundamentally important choices are often choices among morally acceptable options hardly places one at the dinner table with the devil—even if the devil is a moral relativist (which I doubt).

Hittinger seems to share the suspicions of some neo-scholastics. In an article published just before his book, he sought to establish the need for a hierarchical ordering of basic goods by seizing on a hypothetical case Grisez once employed to illustrate the implications of his view on the question of hierarchy:

[I]n *Beyond the New Morality* Grisez states that on Sunday morning one can either participate in the basic good of play (a round of golf perhaps), read the Sunday paper (the good of knowledge), or attend church. Since there is no objective hierarchy prior to choice, one can do any of these, so long as one chooses 'inclusively'—that is, so long as one remains open to the goods which are not chosen.[121]

The lesson Hittinger invites us to draw from this is that religion and other ends cannot be judged to be good 'without an antecedent justification of their rationality.'[122] This justification, of course, must be the fruit of speculative inquiries: 'Whether God exists, or in any event, whether human desires which are identifiably "religious" are good, are,' he declares, 'crucial questions.'[123]

Now, whether God exists is a very important question. (I am not quite sure what Hittinger means by identifiably 'religious' human desires.) If one judges that God exists (a speculative judgment), one will base one's understanding of the good of religion (i.e., that end by reference to which human religious acts have their intelligibility) on one's (further speculative) judgments about God and what He reveals and commands. But nothing in these judgments need alter one's grasp of foundational practical and moral principles, nor one's basic understanding of how to employ these principles in one's practical thinking. Let us suppose that one believes that God has authorized certain human authorities to establish rituals and set rules for worship. Among the rules, there is a requirement that one attend a certain ritual on Sunday. In view of these (speculative) religious judgments, one would, as far as one's own understanding of the good of religion is concerned, be acting directly contrary to that good in failing in what one judges to be one's obligation to attend church. The genuine goods to be realized by reading the paper or playing golf would not excuse one from one's responsibilities under the moral norm.

The subject in Grisez's hypothetical case will not be able to reach the judgment that he is under a moral obligation to choose to go to church on Sunday over reading the paper or playing golf, without some speculative knowledge (here, religious knowledge). But the knowledge that he needs is not knowledge of the hierarchical ordering of religion in relation to the other possible goods. Rather, it is the sort of speculative knowledge (whether of religion, or health, or any other good) whose relevance to morally upright choosing the Grisez–Finnis theory never denies. Indeed, in the most recent statement of the theory, Grisez, Finnis and Boyle explicitly acknowledge the bearing of speculative knowledge on particular moral judgments:

Just as [speculative] knowledge, true opinion, and experience enhance the initial insight into the substantive goods [e.g., life and health, knowledge, and aesthetic appreciation], so they deepen understanding of the reflexive goods [e.g., friendship, self-integration, authenticity, and religion]. For example, both sound metaphysics and experience in practicing authentic religious faith contribute to one's understanding of the good of religion. In doing so, they enhance the power of the principle underlying the religious quest.[124]

Attending to Grisez's hypothetical case shows that speculative knowledge can enrich one's understanding of human goods, and even affect thereby one's judgments about moral responsibilities. This is by no means uniquely true for the good of religion. Speculative knowledge of various types can also, as Grisez and Finnis observe, enrich one's understanding of the goods of health, friendship, aesthetic appreciation and, certainly, knowledge itself. But the hypothetical case does not show that a hierarchy of basic goods must be posited if the religious believer is to judge himself to be under a moral obligation to observe his sabbatarian requirements. Nor does it show that speculative knowledge is needed (or able) to ground an inference that religion, health, friendship, aesthetic appreciation or knowledge is 'a good to be done and pursued.' It leaves untouched the Grisez–Finnis claim that any such judgment must be a non-inferential practical judgment.

In other words, speculative knowledge of this sort cannot be a substitute for foundational practical knowledge (e.g., knowledge of the basic practical principle that harmony with the divine—if there is a divine—is a 'good to be done and pursued,' and the intermediate moral principle that one ought never to act directly against a basic human good). It can only supplement it (albeit in ways that can make critical differences for one's judgment in specific situations of choice).

Here again it is evident that the Grisez–Finnis theory erects no wall of separation between practical and speculative knowledge. But it does try to sort out the specific contributions of practical and speculative knowledge in understanding specific moral norms. And it eschews what I now hope to show is the ultimately hopeless strategy of trying to make decisions by reference to an alleged objective hierarchy of basic values.

Let us suppose, for a moment, that such a hierarchy does exist, and let us further suppose that religion ranks higher than knowledge or play. We are, to be sure, likely to conclude that Grisez's newspaper-reading golfer ought to go to church on Sunday. (As we have seen, the Grisez–Finnis theory can reach the same conclusion on the basis of different principles.) But we are likely to have trouble figuring out what he ought to do on Monday morning when he faces the option of going to a morning church service or getting to work on time. Does the supposed hierarchical priority of religion release him from the moral obligation (to be at work promptly) entailed by his prior commitment to his employer? Perhaps the principle of hierarchy does not control this particular choice; perhaps we can conclude that, despite the priority of religion, our subject ought to go to work in this case rather than to church. But what if he can manage to attend the service and still make it to work on time, thus avoiding any violations of moral norms? Does the priority of religion entail that he behaves immorally if he opts instead to spend his time before work reading the paper, or listening to some jazz recordings, or playing with his children? Suppose he does forgo all these possibilities in favor of the morning church service. Is he also morally required to forgo a pleasant walk in the park after lunch in order to attend a noontime religious observance? Does the priority of religion over the other human goods mean that in every situation of choice in which one is under no moral obligation to do something else, one must, if possible, act specifically for the sake of religion? If not, then when must one so act? The hierarchical ordering does not seem to indicate.[125]

Under the Grisez–Finnis theory, to fail to meet what one understands to be one's religious obligations, where one could meet them, is to violate a moral norm. But it is not the case that every choice not made for the sake of religion, even where a choice for religion could uprightly be made, implicates one in such a violation. Speculative knowledge will be required in order to judge what one's religious obligations in fact are, but, as we have seen, the Grisez–Finnis theory frankly acknowledges the relevance of such knowledge to one's practical judgments. The attempt to resolve choices involving religion (or anything else) by reference to an alleged principle of objective hierarchy, by contrast, seems hopeless inasmuch as it either requires us virtually always to choose for the sake of religion, or fails to provide a principle on the basis of which to decide when choices for religion are required and when they are not.

Hittinger's argument that a principle of hierarchy is necessary for morally upright choosing is no more successful than his other arguments purporting to establish that the Grisez–Finnis theory of natural law fails. Once we dispense with his interpretative mistakes, and his misguided criticisms of the proposition that knowledge of the foundational principles of natural law is the fruit of practical insights, all that remains of Hittinger's case is the gratuitous assertion that a speculative philosophy of nature is 'obviously' required to ground axiological and moral first principles. Hittinger's critique, for all its pugnacity, leaves the Grisez–Finnis natural law theory unscarred.

III. CONCLUDING REMARKS

Whether or not Aquinas himself supposed that sound practical philosophy necessarily depends upon a methodologically antecedent speculative philosophy of nature, this supposition has long prevailed among those who have understood themselves to be working within the Thomistic tradition of natural law theorizing. It is hardly surprising therefore that the Grisez–Finnis theory, inasmuch as it dispenses with this supposition, strikes many thinkers who are sympathetic to natural law theory as woefully inadequate. It seems 'obvious' to them that natural law theory must be about deriving norms of conduct from nature. To deny that moral norms can be so derived is, they assume, to embrace Kantian formalism, at best, and moral relativism or even skepticism at worst.

The attacks on the Grisez–Finnis theory that Weinreb and Hittinger mount represent attempts to identify with precision the inadequacies that they and others suppose must attend any theory of natural law that appeals other than to the normativity of nature in identifying fundamental moral principles. Both authors take the Grisez–Finnis theory seriously; but, unfortunately, neither manages to understand it adequately. Each proposes a set of criticisms based on fundamental misunderstandings of important claims and arguments Grisez and Finnis make in their elaborations and defenses of the theory. Perhaps the theory is vulnerable to damning criticisms. If so, the basic flaws in the theory are unlikely to be brought to light by critics who have not first achieved an accurate grasp of what is and is not being claimed by those advancing it.

NOTES

1 Lloyd L. Weinreb, *Natural Law and Justice* (Cambridge, Mass.: Harvard University Press, 1987).
2 Russell Hittinger, *A Critique of the New Natural Law Theory* (Notre Dame, Ind.: University of Notre Dame Press, 1987).
3 John Finnis, *Natural Law and Natural Rights* (NY: Oxford University Press, 1980).
4 Weinreb, *Natural Law and Justice*, 7.
5 Ibid., 3.
6 Ibid., 6.
7 Ibid., 6–7.
8 Ibid., 7.
9 Ibid.
10 Ibid.
11 Ibid.
12 Ibid., 4–5.
13 Ibid., 63.
14 Ibid., 3.
15 Ibid., 12.
16 Ibid., 67.
17 Ibid., 4.
18 Ibid., 126.
19 Ibid., 10.
20 Ibid.
21 Ibid.
22 Ibid., 205.
23 Ibid., 225.
24 Ibid., 263.
25 Ibid., 126.
26 Ibid., 201, n.*.
27 Ibid., 53–4.
28 The distinction between the speculative (or what Aristotle called the 'theoretical') intellect and the practical intellect does not imply two different intellectual faculties. For Aquinas, there is but one human reason. Speculative and practical reason use the same intellectual operations but aim at different objectives. While Aquinas allows for what might be called paradigm cases of purely speculative or purely practical reasoning, he understands most actual reasoning to be both speculative and practical.
29 Thomas Aquinas, *Summa Theologiae*, 1–2, q. 94, a. 2, in William P. Baumgarth and Richard J. Regan, eds., *Saint Thomas Aquinas on Law, Morality, and Politics* (Indianapolis, Ind.: Hackett Press, 1988).
30 See, e.g., Thomas J. Higgins, *Man as Man: The Science and Art of Ethics* (Milwaukee, Wis.: 1958), 49–69, 88–100, 120–6.
31 Germain Grisez, 'The First Principle of Practical Reason: A Commentary on the Summa Theologiae,' *Natural Law Forum*, 10 (1965), 168.
32 Of course, nothing changes if the correct moral norm requires a different result. Let us suppose not only that the scientist may kidnap the child and experiment on her but also that a moral norm commands this course of action. Either choice in the face of the putative moral norm in control of this situation would remain intelligible. The goods of life and health (here, the life and

health of the child) would provide the intelligible determinants by reference to which the putatively immoral choice of not going through with the kidnapping and experimentation would be intelligible. Reference to these goods would provide a non-baffling answer to the question 'why didn't you do it?' His choice not to do it, while, we are supposing, immoral, would be perfectly consistent with the first principle of practical reason.

33 Weinreb, *Natural Law and Justice*, 58.

34 Ibid., 59.

35 Ibid.

36 Thomas Aquinas, *Summa Contra Gentiles*, Book II, ch. 47 (Burns, Oates, and Washbourne, 1923); Thomas Aquinas, *Summa Theologiae*, 1, q. 82, a. 2 (Christian Classics, 1981); ibid., 1–2, q. 10, a. 2; Thomas Aquinas, *De Veritate*, q. 22, a. 6 (Henry Regnery, 1954).

37 Thomas Aquinas, *Summa Theologiae*, 1–2, Prologue (Benzinger, 1947) (emphasis in the original).

38 Weinreb, *Natural Law and Justice*, 6–7.

39 Ibid., 63.

40 Ibid., 108.

41 Finnis, *Natural Law and Natural Rights*, vi.

42 Ibid., vii.

43 Weinreb, *Natural Law and Justice*, 115.

44 Ibid., 109.

45 Ibid., 296, n. 32.

46 Ibid., 113.

47 Ibid., 112.

48 Finnis offers this account as part of his reply to moral skeptics who cite the diversity of moral opinion and, especially, cultural relativity, as part of their case against natural law. See Finnis, *Natural Law and Natural Rights*, 127.

49 See John Finnis, *Fundamentals of Ethics* (Washington, DC: Georgetown University Press, 1983), 130.

50 See Germain Grisez and Joseph M. Boyle, Jr., *Life and Death With Liberty and Justice* (Notre Dame, Ind.: University of Notre Dame Press, 1979), 400. For what it is worth, I agree with Grisez.

51 John Finnis, Joseph M. Boyle, Jr. and Germain Grisez, *Nuclear Deterrence, Morality and Realism* (Oxford: Clarendon Press, 1987), 317–18.

52 The theory of morality Finnis defends and deploys in his book is foundationalist. And any foundationalist theory will rest ultimately upon principles that are themselves thought not to be deducible or derivable from still more fundamental premises. Various foundationalists argue that their first principles are basic intuitions, or necessary truths, or self-evident precepts.

53 Finnis, Boyle and Grisez, *Nuclear Deterrence*, 277.

54 On this locution, see Finnis, *Natural Law and Natural Rights*, 64.

55 Grisez and Finnis, both individually and in their collaborative works, categorize the basic goods differently at different times. Not much turns on the differences.

56 Finnis, *Natural Law and Natural Rights*, 85–90.

57 Of course, affirming the intrinsic value of health does not preclude acknowledging that health, like other intrinsic goods, has tremendous instrumental value as well.

58 Adam or his sister might value her health, in part, because it enables her to participate in a sport which she enjoys and for which she has a special talent.

They might be interested in restoring her health, in part, to enable her to finish her own studies, or find her own job, or care for an aged aunt. But besides all the respects in which they may value health instrumentally, Adam's acting to restore his sister's health—or *a fortiori*, his own—just for its own sake is perfectly intelligible.

59 People make such sacrifices all the time, sometimes for profound reasons, other times for trivial ones. But if someone chooses to do something at a cost to his health, we shall only be able to understand that choice as rationally grounded (regardless of how we evaluate it morally) if it is made for the sake of some other ultimate end, the self-evident point of which we can grasp. Health is certainly not the only basic human good. Indeed, someone who, while enjoying perfect health, never had occasions to participate in other intrinsic goods—no opportunities for friendship, or recreation, or inquiry or any other activity by which one participates in basic goods other than health—would hardly find his life satisfactory. The variety of basic goods reflects the range of respects in which human persons can flourish (and decline).

   While I am on the subject of the diversity of ultimate reasons for choice and action, I should point out that reason is not the sole human attribute capable of projecting goals and motivating behavior. The fact that passion shares this capability with reason raises interesting questions for the Grisez–Finnis theory. Why, for example, do 'emotional satisfaction' or 'pleasure' not count as basic goods? They are after all, 'explanation stoppers' in the sense that they often provide the ultimate term in accounts of human behavior. 'Why did Joe have a drink?' 'Because he was thirsty.' Is any additional information needed to ground the intelligibility of Joe's action? No. It is perfectly understandable that someone would seek to quench his thirst for no other reason. But if this is so, are we not forced under the Grisez–Finnis theory to recognize the satisfaction of desire as a basic good? Weinreb does not raise this sort of skeptical challenge to Finnis's theory, so I will not respond to it here. A full defense of the Grisez–Finnis theory would, however, include such a response, which would work out in detail the relationships among emotion, motivation and basic practical principles.

60 The theory is not 'teleological' in any sense that implies a commitment to a consequentialist principle of moral judgment, on the one hand, or a teleological view of nature, on the other.

61 Under pure deontological theories, practical reason identifies moral norms without reference to human goods.

62 On the damning implications of incommensurability for all forms of consequentialism, see Germain Grisez, 'Against Consequentialism,' *American Journal of Jurisprudence*, 23 (1978), 21; Finnis, *Fundamentals of Ethics*, 86–93; and Finnis, Boyle and Grisez, *Nuclear Deterrence*, ch. 9. See also Joseph Raz, 'Value Incommensurability: Some Preliminiaries,' *Proceedings of the Aristotelian Society*, 86 (1985–86), 117–134; and Joseph Raz, *The Morality of Freedom* (NY: Oxford University Press, 1986), ch. 13; Anselm W. Muller, 'Radical Subjectivity: Morality Versus Utilitarianism,' *Ratio*, 19 (1977), 115–132; Philippa Foot, 'Utilitarianism and the Virtues,' *Mind*, 94 (1985), 196–209; and Philippa Foot, 'Morality, Action, and Outcome,' in Ted Honderich, ed., *Morality and Objectivity* (Boston, Mass.: Routledge and Kegan Paul, 1985), 23–38; Alasdair MacIntyre, *After Virtue* (Notre Dame, Ind.: University of Notre Dame Press, 1981), 61–2, 67–8; Charles Taylor, 'The Diversity of Goods,' in Amartya Sen

and Bernard Williams, eds., *Utilitarianism and Beyond* (Cambridge, Mass.: Harvard University Press, 1982), 129–144; and David Wiggins, 'Weakness of Will Commensurability and the Objects of Deliberation and Desire,' in Amelie Oksenberg Rorty, ed., *Essays on Aristotle's Ethics* (Berkeley, Cal.: University of California Press, 1980), 241–65.

63 Finnis et al., *Nuclear Deterrence*, 283 (emphasis removed).

64 Ibid.

65 The possibility of there being possibilities for choice the willing of which is compatible with integral human fulfillment depends on a particular (and controversial) theory of human action. Under this theory, the commonly accepted model of action—that under which an agent: (1) wants to bring about a certain state of affairs; (2) makes plans to bring it about by causal factors within his power; and (3) carries out a set of performances to bring it about—must be rejected as inadequate. The theory proposes a more complex model under which persons choose not just for extrinsic purposes, but for ends which are intrinsic to themselves as persons—goods, in other words, in which they participate. A person's actions have moral significance as voluntary syntheses of the person with human goods in three ways: when one chooses something for its intrinsic value; when one chooses something as a means; and when one voluntarily accepts side-effects (good or bad) brought about incidentally to acting in the other two ways. All of this is rejected by consequentialists, for example, who deny that voluntarily accepted side-effects can be outside of the scope of an intelligent agent's intention in any morally significant way. Finnis, Boyle and Grisez formally set out and defend their theory of action (against consequentialist and other criticisms) in *Nuclear Deterrence*, especially 288–91.

66 Grisez and Finnis (both individually and in collaborative works) have formulated the modes in various ways. Finnis's list of the modes, as set out in chapter 5 of *Natural Law and Natural Rights* is reported in Weinreb, *Natural Law and Justice*, 110. Grisez's most detailed presentation of the modes is in his massive theological work, *The Way of the Lord Jesus*, Vol. I, *Christian Moral Principles* (Chicago, Ill.: Franciscan Herald, 1983), ch. 8.

67 In addition to the mode that rules out doing evil for the sake of good, thus generating some absolute specific moral norms, Grisez and/or Finnis have identified modes forbidding, among other moral evils, unfairness, fanaticism, laxity and dilettantism. The specific moral norms derived from these latter modes, unlike those derived from the one prohibiting the doing of evil for the sake of good, are, according to the Grisez–Finnis theory, rarely absolutes. For example, the specific norm requiring promise-keeping, derived ultimately from the mode forbidding unfairness, while ordinarily in force when one has made a promise, is non-absolute. This is because there are circumstances in which it is not unfair to break a promise. There are no circumstances, however, in which the norm against direct killing, e.g., of non-combatants (even as a means of winning a just war), is not in force. Inasmuch as this norm is derived from the mode against doing evil for the sake of good, it is absolute.

68 See, for example, Grisez, *Christian Moral Principles*, 189; Finnis, *Fundamentals of Ethics*, 70; and Finnis et al., *Nuclear Deterrence*, 284.

69 The status of the intermediate moral principles as derived principles was, in *Natural Law and Natural Rights*, unclear. Some critics interpreted Finnis as claiming that these norms were somehow derived from the first practical principles. Others read him as claiming that they were underived and,

therefore, self-evident. Neither interpretation was wholly implausible. Clarification of the matter awaited the development of the theory to include an underived first principle of morality.

70 See s. II A for a general explanation of how dialectical arguments may be employed in defense of self-evident propositions.
71 In the next section, I shall discuss the complex question of the relationship between human goods and the persons whom they fulfill.
72 Germain Grisez, Joseph Boyle and John Finnis, 'Practical Principles, Moral Truth, and Ultimate Ends,' *American Journal of Jurisprudence*, 32 (1987), 99, 123.
73 See Joseph M. Boyle, Jr., Germain Grisez and Olaf Tollefsen, *Free Choice: A Self-Referential Argument* (Notre Dame, Ind.: University of Notre Dame Press, 1976), 86–7, citing Gottfried Wilhelm von Leibniz, *Monadology*, § 32 at 235 (Robert Latta translation 1898).
74 Weinreb, *Natural Law and Justice*, 6.
75 On the role of the phenomenalist conception of the self in many arguments against free choice, see Boyle et al., *Free Choice*, 81.
76 Alasdair MacIntyre, 'Determinism,' *Mind*, 66 (1957), 28, 30.
77 See Boyle et al., *Free Choice*, 82.
78 Ibid., 83.
79 On the 'lastingness' of choices, see Finnis, *Fundamentals of Ethics*, 139–44.
80 Weinreb, *Natural Law and Justice*, 6 (emphasis in the original).
81 Hittinger, *A Critique*, 2.
82 MacIntyre, *After Virtue*, 6.
83 Hittinger, *A Critique*, 5.
84 Ibid.
85 Ibid. (emphasis in the original).
86 Ibid.
87 Ibid., 8.
88 Ibid.
89 Henry B. Veatch, *Human Rights: Fact or Fancy?* (Baton Rouge, La.: Lousiana State University Press, 1985), 98.
90 Hittinger, *A Critique*, 198.
91 Ibid., 44–5.
92 Aquinas, *Summa Theologiae*, 1–2, q. 94, a. 2.
93 Germain Grisez, *Contraception and the Natural Law* (Milwaukee, Wis.: Bruce, 1964).
94 Hittinger, *A Critique*, 62.
95 Ibid.
96 Ibid., 63.
97 Ibid.
98 Ibid., 40.
99 Ibid., 28.
100 Ibid., 55.
101 Ibid., 187.
102 Finnis, *Natural Law and Natural Rights*, 371–2.
103 Grisez, *Christian Moral Principles*, 108, reported in Hittinger, *A Critique*, 27.
104 Hittinger, *A Critique*, 29.
105 Ibid. 29–30. It is worth noting that the criticism implicit in the last of these questions will seem especially compelling to anyone who supposes—wrongly—that 'our concern for the goods which fulfill persons' can be judged a 'mere' concern inasmuch as these goods are mere tendencies, inclinations, attractions, or are in some other sense subjective.

106 See Alan Donagan, *The Theory of Morality* (Chicago, Ill.: University of Chicago Press, 1977).
107 Grisez, *Contraception*, 78.
108 Grisez made this point early on as well. See, e.g., ibid.
109 See Grisez et al., 'Practical Principles,' 115, where they formally treat the problem of the relationship between goods and persons, identifying certain respects in which basic goods 'simply are persons—individually and in communion,' and certain other respects in which they are distinguishable from the persons whom they fulfill. For a detailed critique of Donagan's claim that a 'respect persons' approach to ethics is preferable to a 'respect the goods of persons' approach, see Joseph M. Boyle, Jr., 'Aquinas, Kant, and Donagan on Moral Principles,' *The New Scholasticism*, 58 (1984), 391.
110 Hittinger, *A Critique*, 53.
111 Grisez, *Christian Moral Principles*, 576. See also Grisez et al., 'Practical Principles,' 114. ('As intelligible, the basic goods have no proper names attached to them. So they can be understood as goods and provide reasons for acting whether, in a particular case, the agent or another will benefit.')
112 Grisez, *Christian Moral Principles*, 185.
113 Grisez and Finnis are careful not to imply that integral human fulfillment is the fulfillment of communities considered as distinct from the individual persons who comprise them. The 'common good,' under the Grisez–Finnis theory, 'is fundamentally the good of individuals (an aspect of whose good is friendship in community).' Finnis, *Natural Law and Natural Rights*, 168. It is 'the well-being of you and me, considered as individuals with shared opportunities and vulnerabilities, and the concrete conditions under which that well-being of particular individuals may be favoured, advanced, and preserved.' Ibid., 372. Nor does the ideal of integral human fulfillment imply that self-preference in choosing is never consistent with a will to integral human fulfillment. Grisez and Finnis recognize that one's own well-being (and that of those for whom one is in some special way responsible) has a reasonable first claim on one's interest, but they deny that the rational ground of this claim is any judgment that one's own well-being is more valuable simply because it is one's own. See, e.g., ibid., 107.
114 Hittinger, *A Critique*, 51.
115 The 'ideality' of integral human fulfillment does indeed have theological implications. Although we can wish for integral fulfillment, it can only be hoped for in the light of religious faith. If it is to be realized—if its ideality is to be annulled—divine action is required. In Christian terms, grace is needed to perfect nature.
116 Hittinger, *A Critique*, 135 (emphasis added).
117 Ibid.
118 Ibid., 111–12.
119 Finnis, *Natural Law and Natural Rights*, 104, quoting John Rawls, *A Theory of Justice* (Cambridge, Mass.: The Belknap Press of Harvard University Press, 1971), 420.
120 Quoted in Veatch, *Human Rights*, 98.
121 Russell Hittinger, 'The Recovery of Natural Law and the "Common Morality," ' *This World*, 18 (1987), 62, 69.
122 Ibid.
123 Ibid.
124 Grisez et al., 'Practical Principles,' 109.
125 Have I merely drawn a caricature of the neo-scholastic idea of choosing by

reference to an objective hierarchy of values? If so, I would welcome correction. The problem is that neither Hittinger nor the (other?) neo-scholastic critics of the Grisez–Finnis theory seem willing to present a detailed account of how choosing in accordance with a principle of hierarchy is supposed to work across a set of cases. Until they present such an account, one can only speculate.

3

Natural Law and Human Nature

The natural law theory originally proposed by Germain Grisez, and developed and defended over the past twenty-five years by Grisez, John Finnis, Joseph Boyle, William May and Patrick Lee, among others, has been sternly criticized by many philosophers who are sympathetic to the idea of natural law.

Some of these critics suggest that Grisez's view of the relationship between morality and nature disqualifies his theory as a theory of natural law. Russell Hittinger, for example, asserts that the idea of natural law 'obviously requires a commitment to law as in some sense "natural," and nature as in some way normative.'[1] As Hittinger understands Grisez's theory, it suffers from a 'failure to interrelate systematically practical reason with a philosophy of nature.'[2] In other words, it fails to do the very thing that makes a theory of practical reasoning and morality a *natural law* theory.

Lloyd Weinreb advances similar criticism. He maintains that Grisez's approach substitutes a 'deontological' understanding of natural law for the original 'ontological' understanding. According to Weinreb, modern 'deontological' natural law theories such as Grisez's differ from the 'ontological' theories of classical and medieval law theorists insofar as the deontological theories dispense with the idea of a 'normative natural order.'[3] They are theories of 'natural law without nature.'[4] Theories of this sort purport to identify principles of natural law without deriving them from nature. Defenders of such theories, in effect, excuse themselves from providing metaphysical or ontological grounds for the moral propositions they assert. In Weinreb's judgment, they pay a heavy price for refusing to argue from metaphysical or ontological premises: they are forced to rely—as Weinreb supposes Grisez, Finnis, and their collaborators rely—on implausible claims that certain propositions in normative ethics and political theory are self-evidently true.[5]

Yet another critic, Henry Veatch, faults Grisez and his collaborators for erecting a 'wall of separation . . . between practical reason and theoretical reason, between ethics and metaphysics, between nature and morals, between "is" and "ought." '[6] As Veatch interprets their writings, Grisez and Finnis, for example, maintain the 'absolute independence of ethics as over against metaphysics, or of morals with respect to a knowledge of nature,'[7] so that 'principles of morals and ethics are not thought [of] as being in any sense principles of being or nature at all.'[8] Thus Veatch suggests that the theory of morality they propose, whatever its merits, is not a *natural law* theory.

Veatch's suggestion, however, is less extreme than the claim leveled against Grisez and Finnis by Ralph McInerny. According to McInerny, Grisez and Finnis hold a 'Humean' view of practical reasoning 'which regards knowledge of the world to be irrelevant to [practical reasoning].'[9] Obviously, any theory of practical philosophical reasoning that merits identification with the practical philosophy of David Hume cannot plausibly be counted as a natural law theory.

When these critics talk about the need to ground morality in 'nature,' they mean to refer principally to *human* nature and the place of *man* in nature. In their view, a sound natural law ethics derives moral norms from methodologically antecedent knowledge of the nature of man and man's place in nature.

According to this approach, metaphysics—in particular that branch of metaphysics that studies man—precedes ethics. Metaphysical anthropology reveals the facts about human nature; ethics then prescribes or prohibits possible acts (or classes of acts) on the basis of their conformity, or lack of conformity, to these facts.

Grisez and his collaborators reject this approach on a number of grounds. Most importantly, they maintain that it involves 'the naturalistic fallacy' of purporting to infer moral norms from facts about human nature. Logically, a valid conclusion cannot introduce something that is not in the premises. Grisez and his followers insist, therefore, that moral conclusions inasmuch as they state reasons for action can be derived only from premises that include still more fundamental reasons for action. They cannot be derived from premises (e.g., facts about human nature) that do not include reasons from action. According to Grisez and others, natural law theory need not—and a credible natural law theory cannot— rely on this logically 'illicit inference from facts to norms.'[10]

Of course, Grisez's 'neo-scholastic' critics contend that the naturalistic 'fallacy' is no fallacy; for the facts about human nature from which they seek to infer norms of morality are, they say, laden with moral value. Veatch, for example, defends the neo-scholastic approach on the grounds that 'the very "is" of human nature has . . . an "ought" built into it.'[11] Thus, one discovers what one ought to do by understanding the facts about human nature.

My aim in this brief essay is to show: (1) that, contrary to what their critics claim, the natural law theory advanced by Grisez and his collaborators does not entail the proposition that basic human good or moral norms have no connection to, or grounding in, human nature; and (2) that Grisez and his followers are correct in maintaining that our knowledge of basic human goods and moral norms need not, and logically cannot, be deduced, inferred or (in any sense that a logician would recognize) derived from facts about human nature.

II

It would be tedious, but not difficult, to show that neither Grisez nor any of his principal followers has ever denied that basic human goods and moral norms have a grounding in human nature. Nor have they ever alleged that theoretical knowledge (McInerny's 'knowledge of the world') is irrelevant to practical reasoning and morality. Critics who assert the contrary should reread the texts carefully. Indeed, Grisez and his follow-ers affirm that basic human goods and moral norms *are* what they are because human nature *is* what it is. Finnis, for example, in the very section of *Natural Law and Natural Rights* to which Veatch points in making the allegations I have quoted (a section entitled 'The Illicit Inference from Facts to Norms') *endorses* the proposition that 'were man's nature differ-ent, so would be his duties.'[12] More recently, Grisez, Boyle and Finnis have set forth in some detail their account of how theoretical knowledge contributes to our understanding of basic human goods and moral norms.[13]

The real issue, then, is not whether Grisez and his followers deny that morality is grounded in (human) nature; the simple, demonstrable truth is that they do not. The real issue is whether their claim that the most basic practical principles and moral norms are not inferred from prior knowl-edge of human nature somehow entails the proposition that morality is not grounded in nature.

III

If Grisez and his followers are correct to hold that the most basic reasons for action are not derived from facts about human nature, how are these reasons known? They are known in non-inferential acts of understanding in which we grasp possible ends or purposes as worthwhile for their own sakes. The most basics reasons for action are those reasons whose intelli-gibility does not depend on deeper or still more fundamental reasons. As *basic* reasons, they cannot be derived; for there is nothing more fundamen-tal that could serve as a premise for a logical derivation. Therefore, they must be self-evident.

Only intrinsic goods, i.e., things that are intelligibly desirable for their own sakes, can be basic reasons for action. Instrumental goods are reasons for action; they are not, however, basic reasons. They are reasons whose intelligibility depends on deeper or more fundamental reasons (and ultimately basic reasons). Therefore, they are *derived* and are not self-evident.

If Grisez and his followers are correct in supposing that the most basic reasons for action are not inferred from propositions about human nature but are instead self-evident, does that mean that these reasons (and the moral norms whose derivation they make possible) are detached from human nature?

The answer is no. Here is why: only that which is understood to be worthwhile can provide a reason for action. Only that which is humanly fulfilling can be understood to be worthwhile. Intrinsic goods are basic reasons for action precisely because they are (intrinsic) aspects of human well-being and fulfillment. They perfect human beings, i.e., beings with a human nature. As human perfections, 'basic goods' belong to human beings as part of their nature.[14]

Finnis has usefully explicated the relationship between morality and nature by distinguishing an 'epistemological' from an 'ontological' mode of analysis. He began the analysis in the 'epistemological' mode:

> Propositions about primary human goods are not derived from propositions about human nature or from any other propositions of speculative reason; as Aquinas says with maximum clarity, and never wavers from saying, they are *per se nota* and *indemonstrabilia*. [Citations omitted.] For we come to know human nature by knowing its potentialities, and these we know by knowing their actuations, which in turn we know by knowing their objects—and the objects . . . are precisely the primary human goods. (So, if anything, an adequately full knowledge of human nature is derived from our practical and underived (*per se notum*) knowledge of human goods . . .)
>
> But . . . if we shift from the epistemological to the ontological mode, the same methodological principle, in its application to human beings, presupposes and thus entails that the goodness of all human goods (and thus the appropriateness, the *convenientia*, of all responsibilities) is derived from (i.e., depends upon) the nature which, by their goodness, those goods perfect. For those goods—which as ends are the *rationes* of practical norms or 'oughts'—would not perfect that nature were it other than it is.[15]

Neo-scholastic critics of the position Finnis defends have ignored the distinction between ontology and epistemology to which he appeals. They seem to have assumed, gratuitously, that anyone who maintains that our knowledge of human goods is not derived from our prior knowledge of human nature must hold that human goods are not grounded in nature. This assumption, however, is unsound. There is not the slightest inconsistency in holding both that: (1) our knowledge of the intrinsic value of certain ends or purposes is acquired in non-inferential acts of understanding wherein we grasp self-evident truths; and (2) those ends or purposes are intrinsically valuable (and thus can be grasped as self-evidently worthwhile) because they are intrinsically perfective of human beings, i.e., beings with a human nature.

In short: the proposition that our knowledge of basic human goods and moral norms is not derived from prior knowledge of human nature does not entail the proposition that morality has no grounding in human nature. Our knowledge of the most fundamental principles of human well-being and fulfillment may be underived—because these principles are self-evident practical truths—yet remain knowledge of human well-being and fulfillment.

IV

Still, would not our claims to moral knowledge be somehow more secure if they could rest on solid facts about human nature rather than on putatively self-evident propositions?

Perhaps the single most commonly misunderstood feature of Grisez's natural law theory is its appeal to self-evidence. Sometimes Grisez and his collaborators are interpreted as claiming that truths about disputed issues in normative ethics and political theory (such as whether abortion is immoral or whether it ought to be made illegal) are self-evident. No proponent of the theory, to my knowledge, has claimed that the truth about any issue in normative ethics or political theory is self-evident.

Lloyd Weinreb's critique of Grisez's theory miscarries on this very point. It is obvious that truths about issues in normative ethics and political theory are not self-evident. If, as Weinreb supposes, Grisez and Finnis, and the rest were reduced to claiming that their positions on matters of this sort were self-evidently true, then there would be something deeply wrong with their approach. Weinreb, however, is simply mistaken in supposing that Finnis, for example, maintains that his position on abortion is self-evidently true.[16]

According to Grisez, Finnis, and their collaborators, only the most basic reasons for action are self-evident. These reasons provide only the most basic premises for moral arguments. Indeed, moral questions arise because of diversity of basic reasons for action. One may have a basic reason to do X, but at the same time a basic reason not to do X because one also has a basic reason to do or preserve Y, and the doing or preserving of Y is incompatible here and now with X. What is one to do? Which, if either, course of action is not merely rational but fully reasonable? Are both courses of action fully reasonable?

One cannot decide simply by knowing that X and Y are basic reasons for action. One requires some knowledge of *moral norms* that guide one's morally significant choosing, i.e., one's choices between *rationally* appealing but incompatible alternatives. The most basic reasons for action are not themselves moral norms, though it is by reference to their *integral* directiveness that it is possible to identify principles of moral reasoning that distinguish upright from morally wrongful choosing.

Still someone might object: is there not something unsatisfying about appeals to self-evidence even at the level of the most basic premises of moral arguments? After all, people can simply refuse to accept a claim that something is self-evident. That is true. It is also true, however, that people can refuse to accept any claim. Basic reasons for action are simply ends (goods) whose intelligible point can be grasped without the benefit of deduction or inference by anyone who knows what the terms referring to them signify. Such reasons can frequently be defended by indirect (dialectical) arguments that bring other knowledge to bear to highlight the rational unacceptability of denying them.[17] At the same time, because they cannot be argued for directly (for there are no premises from which to derive them)[18] anyone who does affirm them must acknowledge their self-evidence.

It seems to me that appeals to self-evidence, when properly understood, do not fail to provide a solid foundation for moral reasoning. In any event, they provide no less solid a foundation than appeals to the facts of human nature. Someone who fails to see the point in pursuing knowledge just for its own sake is unlikely to be impressed by arguments meant to establish that truth-seeking is natural to human beings. Or, again, someone who finds it baffling that anyone would pursue a friendship just for friendship's sake is unlikely to understand the value of friendship any better by being informed (or even persuaded) that man is by nature a social being.

Moreover, someone who does not grasp the intelligible point of pursuing knowledge or friendships just for their own sake lacks a rational warrant for judging these goods to be reasons for action. To derive reasons for action from more fundamental premises, more fundamental reasons for action must be in those premises. Propositions like 'truth seeking is natural to human beings' or 'man is a social being' do not state reasons for action. Grisez and his followers are correct, then, to conclude that propositions like these logically cannot serve as premises for moral conclusions.

In the end, even Henry Veatch admits as much. 'I concede,' he says in a published debate with Finnis, 'that there can be no *deduction* of ethics from metaphysics, and no *inference* of "propositions about man's duties and obligations" simply from "propositions about his nature." '[19] 'Yet,' Veatch asks, 'is not the soundness of such contentions due to one's taking the terms "deduction" and "inference" in a somewhat straitened and overly technical sense?'

I think the answer to Veatch's inquiry is 'no.' The distinction between what 'is the case' (about human nature or anything else in the natural order) and what 'ought to be' is logically significant.[20] Muddle is the best we can hope for if we ignore this distinction or sweep it under the rug. A pretty good example is Veatch's own claim that 'the very "is" of human nature has an "ought" built into it.' That claim is not flatly wrong; it is just muddled. Knowledge, friendship and the other basic reasons for action are aspects of human well-being and fulfillment. In that sense, human nature has an 'ought' built into it. As Veatch concedes, however, we cannot deduce or infer the 'ought' from the 'is' of human nature. We cannot deduce or infer reasons for action from premises that do not include reasons for action. We cannot deduce or infer *basic* reasons for action from anything. Our knowledge of basic reasons is underived and non-inferential.

In no sense, however, do we simply 'make up' basic reasons for action or manufacture our knowledge of them out of our own subjectivity. Their directiveness and their truth are not mere 'structures of the mind.' According to some of Grisez's neo-scholastic critics, to hold that our knowledge of basic reasons for action is underived is to hold that the truth of practical judgment consists in their 'conformity to practical reason's own inner requirements, i.e., to itself or its directive structure.'[21] But this claim is unwarranted. Although practical judgments are not inferred from prior theoretical knowledge, they do not refer to the 'structure of practical reason' itself; indeed, as Grisez has pointed out, it is scarcely possible to see what such phrases mean.[22] Rather, 'the truth of practical knowledge with respect to its first principles is their adequation to possible human fulfillment considered precisely insofar as that fulfillment can be realized through human action.'[23] To say that possible fulfillment thus considered may be understood (or, when things miscarry, misunderstood) by the inquiring intellect is not to reduce the truth of propositions that refer to such fulfillment to conformity with any 'inner structures' of the mind that grasps those propositions and, thus, knows that truth. To hold that basic reasons for action are underived is not, then to lapse into some form of subjectivism.

At the same time, there are aspects of human nature that are relevant to practical thinking and can indeed be known prior to practical reasoning, for example, ranges of empirical possibility and environmental constraint. Human nature, however, is not a closed nature. It could be known in its fullness only by grasping all the ways that human persons may be ful-filled through their understanding of basic reasons for action and their reasonable and creative choices. Such choices are choices of purpose which will instantiate and realize the human goods that are the basic reasons for action; and it is characteristic of those reasons, those goods, and thus of human nature that many of those possible intelligent purposes remain as yet unenvisaged. A complete theoretical account of *human nature* (unlike accounts of closed natures) would depend, therefore, on data provided by practical inquiry, reflection and judgment. Those who claim that theoretical knowledge of human nature is methodologically prior to basic practical knowledge have things, in this respect, exactly backwards.

NOTES

1 Russell Hittinger, *A Critique of the New Natural Law Theory* (Notre Dame, Ind.: University of Notre Dame Press, 1987), 8.
2 Ibid.
3 Lloyd Weinreb, *Natural Law and Justice* (Cambridge, Mass.: Harvard University Press, 1987), 108–16. Weinreb criticizes Grisez's theory as it appears in John Finnis's *Natural Law and Natural Rights* (Oxford: Clarendon Press, 1980). He cites the theory as an example of contemporary 'deontological theories of natural law.' He judges all such theories to be seriously defective. In their place, he would 'restore [] the original understanding of natural law as a theory about the nature of being, the human condition in particular' (p. 7).
4 The phrase here quoted is the title of ch. 4 of Weinreb's *Natural Law and Justice*. In that chapter, he considers a number of contemporary writers whose theories he classifies as 'deontological natural law theories.' In addition to Finnis, he criticizes Lon Fuller, David Richards and Ronald Dworkin for proposing theories of 'natural law without nature.'
5 For the suggestion that Finnis, for example, maintains that certain conclusions in normative ethics and political theory are self-evidently true, see Weinreb, *Natural Law and Justice*, 112–13. For the specific suggestion that Finnis maintains that his position on the morality of abortion is a self-evident truth, see ibid., 296, n. 32.
6 Henry Veatch, 'Natural Law and the "Is"—"Ought" Question,' *Catholic Lawyer*, 26 (1981), 265.
7 Ibid., 256.
8 Ibid.
9 Ralph McInerny, *Ethica Thomistica* (Washington, DC: The Catholic University of America Press, 1982), 54–5.
10 Finnis, *Natural Law*, 33.
11 Veatch, 'Natural Law,' 258.
12 Finnis, *Natural Law*, 34.
13 Germain Grisez, Joseph Boyle and John Finnis, 'Practical Principles, Moral Truth, and Ultimate Ends,' *American Journal of Jurisprudence*, 32 (1987), 99–151, at 108–109.
14 Cf., ibid., 127.
15 John Finnis, 'Natural Inclinations and Natural Rights: Deriving "Ought" from "Is" According to Aquinas,' in L. J. Elders and K. Hedwig, eds., 'Lex et

Libertas,' *Studi Tomistici*, 30 (Vatican City: Pontificia Accademia di S. Tommaso, 1987), 45–7.

16 On the basis of a misunderstanding of which sorts of propositions Finnis claims to be self-evident, Weinreb charges that Finnis 'has confused self-evidence with personal conviction,' *Natural Law and Justice*, 113. I criticize Weinreb's attribution to Finnis of the view that certain conclusions in normative ethics and political theory are self-evident in 'Recent Criticism of Natural Law Theory,' *University of Chicago Law Review*, 55 (1988) 1386–1389, reprinted herein as Chapter 2.

17 On dialectical arguments in defense of self-evident practical truths see Grisez et al., 'Practical Principles,' 111–12. See also Chapter 2.

18 There are, however, data (experienced inclinations and a knowledge of empirical patters that underlie possibilities of action and accomplishment).

19 Veatch, 'Natural Law,' 254.

20 Ralph McInerny asserts that '[t]he concern not to infer value from fact, Ought from Is, may be a symptom of fastidiousness,' *Ethica Thomistica*, 55. Whether or not one credits Professor McInerny's psychological speculation, it remains logically invalid to move from premises that do not include reasons for action to conclusions that state reasons for action. To conclude to specific moral norms, for example, one's premises must include reasons for actions that are more fundamental than those norms. This is not to say, as McInerny imagines Grisez and Finnis to say, that 'knowledge of the world is irrelevant to [practical reason].' Grisez and Finnis do not argue that such theoretical knowledge is irrelevant to practical inquiry and moral judgment. Their claim is merely that basic practical principles and the specific moral norms derived from them cannot be deduced inferred, or, in any strict sense, derived from purely theoretical premises. They hold, with Aquinas, that practical reasoning, like theoretical reasoning, has its own underived (i.e., *per se nota* and *indemonstrabilia*) first principles (see *Summa Theologica*, Ia Iiae, q. 94, a. 2). These principles are indispensable premises in reasoning that conclude validly to propositions about specific moral norms. Other premises include 'theoretical' propositions about, e.g., the structure of human action as intentional behavior, the causality of means, etc.

21 Brian V. Johnstone, 'The Structures of Practical Reason: Traditional Theories and Contemporary Questions,' *Thomist*, 50 (1986), 417–446, at 432.

22 Germain Grisez, 'The Structures of Practical Reason: Some Comments and Clarifications,' *Thomist*, 52 (1988), 269–291, at 277. See also Grisez, Boyle and Finnis, 'Practical Principles,' 125 and 115–20 (on practical truth).

23 See Grisez, 'The Structures of Practical Reason,' 278, n. 8.

4

Does the 'Incommensurability Thesis' Imperil Common Sense Moral Judgments?

The distinguished legal philosopher, R. George Wright, has recently explored the implications for free speech jurisprudence of the debate among moral philosophers about the 'incommensurability' of values.[1] Wright's analysis suggests that contemporary natural law theorists (and others) who defend the 'incommensurability thesis' hold (or, for the sake of consistency, should hold) that choices between rationally grounded options[2] are necessarily arbitrary. He has argued, for example, that my own defense of the proposition that basic values are incommensurable commits me to the proposition that, under ordinary circumstances, there cannot be a conclusive moral reason for choosing to interrupt 'one's recreational coffee drinking in order to rescue one's friend from a painful accidental death.'[3] In a private communication, Professor Wright has asked how I and other defenders of the incommensurability thesis can maintain that thesis while at the same time holding that someone faced with a choice between, say, risklessly saving a tot's life and spending an extra hour on the golf course should, ordinarily, save the tot's life.[4]

Wright fears that strict adherence to the incommensurability thesis imperils our common sense belief that sometimes people are morally bound to choose one practical option over a competing option despite the fact that the competing option is itself rationally grounded (i.e., grounded in a basic human value).[5] He supposes that we must admit some commensurability of values in order to save the common sense belief. I shall argue that Professor Wright's fear is unwarranted and his supposition mistaken. The incommensurability thesis is perfectly consistent with the non-arbitrariness of morally significant choices.[6] Hence, we may adhere strictly to the incommensurability thesis, as I think we should, without abandoning the common sense belief that many choices between rationally grounded practical possibilities admit of right and wrong answers.

I begin with a few clarifications. Wright marshals the common sense belief that choices between rationally grounded possibilities for action are often non-arbitrary against what he describes as 'the broad assertion that disparate values . . . are [in]commensurable.'[7] In referring summarily to 'disparate values,' however, he neglects to take note of a distinction that is strictly respected by prominent defenders of the incommensurability thesis, namely the distinction between *non-basic* (e.g., instrumental) and *basic* (i.e., intrinsic) values. Intrinsic values, such as human life and health, friendship, knowledge, and skillful work and play, are incommensurable because they provide *ultimate* reasons for choice and action, i.e., reasons whose intelligibility as motives for action are not derivative of other, more fundamental reasons. Basic values, inasmuch as they provide ultimate reasons for action, are irreducible to one another or to some common underlying factor.[8] Any value that is reducible to some more fundamental value is not a *basic* value; any reason for action whose intelligibility is derivative of some more fundamental reason is not an *ultimate* reason for action. By contrast, purely instrumental values, such as money, which provides reasons for action only as means to, or conditions for, the realization (or fuller realization) of more fundamental values, are not ultimate reasons for choice and action. Hence, they are non-basic.

The incommensurability thesis states that *basic* values and their particular instantiations as they figure in options for choice cannot be weighed and measured in accordance with an objective standard of comparison.[9] Defenders of the thesis therefore deny the workability and even the coherence of the consequentialist strategy of deciding between rationally grounded practical possibilities. That strategy directs the chooser to identify and choose the option which promises the net best proportion of good to bad, or benefit to harm, overall and in the long run.[10] Certain non-consequentialists, however, including Professor Wright, worry that by denying the possibility of identifying morally correct choices between rationally grounded options by comparing the weight of the basic values that provide reasons for action on either side of the equation, defenders of the incommensurability thesis undercut the possibility of non-arbitrary solutions in cases of morally significant choice. Russell Hittinger, for example, has described the attack on consequentialism based on the incommensurability thesis as a 'scorched-earth policy.'[11] This description is mistaken, however, if, as I shall demonstrate, the incommensurability thesis does not entail the proposition that choices between rationally grounded possibilities, such as those described in Professor Wright's hypothetical cases, cannot themselves be rationally guided (i.e., guided by objective norms and principles).

Before turning to one of Professor Wright's hypothetical cases, however, I would note that there are certain forms of commensurability which defenders of the incommensurability thesis need not, and, in fact, do not, deny. What is commensurable in the cases I have in mind is something other than basic values or their instantiations. For example, it is obvious that intrinsic human goods are rationally superior to merely instrumental goods; intelligible human goods are rationally superior to merely sensible goods; a fuller realization of the good is manifestly superior to a more meager realization.[12] Moreover, we quite rationally (i.e., in accordance with objective criteria) rank people as chess or tennis players, for example, though if Smith is world champion at chess and Jones at tennis it may well be senseless to ask who is better as a player. Similarly, we sometimes rationally compare things like vacation packages: For example, package Y might be unqualifiedly the best ski holiday (i.e., it is the cheapest, safest and most accessible, while offering the best slopes, the most comfortable accommodation, the most sociable companions). At the same time, package Z might be unqualifiedly the best seaside vacation, being similarly superior to its competitors in every respect considered relevant by the prospective vacationer. Packages Y and Z are comparable precisely insofar as each is 'the best of its type,' though one cannot say that, subjective preferences aside, one or the other is unqualifiedly 'the best vacation package on offer.'

The incommensurability of basic values that provide ultimate reasons for action is important precisely insofar as it bears on the way those values are at stake in options for choice.[13] Thus, it is worth noticing that there is often[14] an incommensurability between options which derives not from the incommensurability of *different* basic values, but from the incommensurability of different possible instantiations of *even a single* basic value, as those instantiations figure in options for choice. This latter sort of incommensurability derives, in turn, from such factors as the diversity of persons in whose lives the values at stake may be instantiated, uncertainty about the outcomes of competing possible choices, differences in attitude towards risk (gravity versus probability schedules), and, perhaps most importantly, the reflexive impact of choices on the character and personality of the chooser.

A final clarificatory point: Basic values and their particular instantiations can sometimes be brought into a certain form of rational commensurability with respect to future choices by a choice or commitment (embodied in a choice) which one reasonably makes here and now. In light of a reasonable personal (e.g., vocational, relational, educational) commitment I have made, it may be perfectly reasonable for me to treat, and, indeed, it may be patently unreasonable for me to fail to treat, certain basic values or certain possible instantiations of a single basic value as superior to others in their directive force (for me). Choosing in harmony with one's past reasonable commitments, and, thus, establishing or maintaining one's personal integrity (in the non-moral as well as the moral sense), constitutes an important moral reason which often guides our choices between rationally grounded options.

With these clarifications in mind, let us now consider Professor Wright's case of a golfer who happens to notice a child drowning in a water hazard near the green at the fourteenth hole. He can, without risk to himself, save the child; the interruption will, however, deprive him of an hour's worth of play and prevent his completing the course. Wright supposes that the facts as he stipulates them create the following dilemma for defenders of the incommensurability thesis. On the one hand, they, like other morally sensitive human beings, want to believe that the golfer has a moral obligation to interrupt his game to save the tot. On the other hand, they believe that the competing values at stake in the choice, namely the goods of 'life' and 'play' are incommensurable. Both 'life' and 'play' are intrinsic values; as such, they provide ultimate reasons for action. A choice for either possibility, therefore, is rationally grounded. Thus, it is impossible to say that it is rationally preferable (i.e., more reasonable) to interrupt the game to save the life of the tot than to allow the tot to perish and avoid interrupting the game. If the goods of 'life' and 'play' really are incommensurable, then, morally speaking, the choice between saving the tot's life and going on with the game is arbitrary. If the choice is not arbitrary—if the golfer has a moral duty to save the tot and forgo finishing the game—it must be because 'life' and 'play' are, at some level, commensurable and the good of 'life' outweighs the good of 'play.'

In fact, I (and, I assume, other defenders of the incommensurability thesis) believe that the golfer has a moral obligation to interrupt his game to save the child. Not only is it more reasonable to save the child, it is (practically) *unreasonable* (i.e., immoral) not to do so. The choice is anything but arbitrary. On the facts as stipulated by Professor Wright, the golfer is under a strict moral obligation to save the child.

I do not believe, however, that the situation is controlled by a moral norm that says: In choosing between options in which competing basic values are involved, identify and choose the option which preserves or advances the weightier value. If, as I think, basic values, qua basic, are irreducible and therefore incommensurable—if, in other words, basic values provide *ultimate* reasons for choice and action—then such a putative moral norm is incoherent. The incommensurability of basic values and their diverse instantiations does not, however, entail the arbitrariness of choice. In fact, the situation *is* controlled by a moral norm, albeit one that does not require the weighing and comparison of values that is ruled out by the incommensurability thesis.

Where one chooses a possibility for a reason, one's choice is not strictly arbitrary. Even under circumstances in which one had a competing reason to choose an incompatible possibility, one's choice remains rationally grounded. To be sure, in a certain case, one may have 'first-order' reasons for incompatible actions (i.e., reasons provided by basic values) neither (or none) of which are defeated by 'second-order' reasons for action.[15] Where one has undefeated first-order reasons for incompatible actions, one's choice, while not strictly arbitrary, is rationally underdetermined; a choice either way, therefore, is not merely rational (i.e., for a reason) but fully reasonable (i.e., fully in accord with reason because not contrary to a conclusive reason, not defeated by any competing reason).[16] In a different case, however, one may have second-order reasons to choose a certain possibility and not choose competing possibilities. In such a case, the first-order reasons grounding the latter possibilities are defeated by second-order reasons to choose the former. The second-order reasons which defeat the latter possibilities provide conclusive reasons to act on the former.

Moral norms are second order reasons for action of a special sort. In situations of morally significant choice, such norms may provide conclusive reasons not to choose certain possibilities, despite the fact that one has, and is aware of, first-order reasons to choose those possibilities. Where a moral norm gives one a conclusive reason not to do something that one nevertheless has a reason to do, that norm defeats (though, by virtue of the incommensurability of the values that provide the first-order reasons for action, it does not destroy[17]) one's reason for doing it. If—in defiance of one's moral duty—one chooses that possibility, one's action is not utterly irrational (insofar as one performs the action for a reason and, if one is successful, realizes whatever benefit for oneself or others grounds the intelligibility of the reason); nevertheless, one's action is practically unreasonable, i.e., immoral.

The incommensurability thesis entails that one cannot have (as consequentialists suppose we sometimes have) conclusive reasons for adopting by choice a proposal to damage or destroy a basic value in any of its instantiations. The good (or quantum of good) available in a certain possibility cannot provide a conclusive reason to damage or destroy the instantiation of another (putatively commensurable and less weighty) basic human good. Indeed, one always has a conclusive reason *not* to adopt by choice any such proposal. If the incommensurability thesis holds, then the entailment of which I speak yields a moral norm strictly forbidding one to *intend* evil, even for the sake of good consequences; and this norm, where it applies, provides a conclusive (second-order) reason which defeats the (first-order) reasons one might very well have for choosing directly to destroy basic human goods.[18]

Basic values are not suprapersonal realities or platonic forms; rather they are *intrinsic* aspects of real and possible persons, their well-being and fulfillment. Were it otherwise, such values simply could not provide ultimate intelligible reasons for action. Thus, although people sometimes have literally no reason not to damage or destroy things that are merely instrumentally valuable, there is always *a* reason not to destroy or damage what one understands to be intrinsically worthwhile. Of course, as I have already suggested, such a reason may compete with genuine reasons one has to go ahead and destroy or damage the basic value in question.[19] However, one's reason not to destroy or damage the value could be defeated by the competing reasons, and the option to destroy or damage the value providing that reason could therefore reasonably be chosen, only if it were possible prior to the choosing to identify a conclusive reason for choosing that option. And such a reason could be available only if the basic values and their instantiations involved in the case were commensurable in such a way as to enable one to identify that option as offering 'the greater good.'

One need not, however, deny the incommensurability thesis in order to identify a (non-consequentialist) moral norm that provides a conclusive reason for the golfer to save the child and forgo completing the course. Under the facts as stipulated by Professor Wright, the 'Pauline Principle,' i.e., the norm against intending evil even for the sake of good, is not among the norms relevant to the golfer's choice.[20] To be sure, the golfer is faced with a morally significant choice (precisely because the incommensurable goods of 'life' and 'play' provide incompatible reasons for action). But the Pauline Principle is only one norm among a set of moral norms that may guide choice in such situations. Another member of that set is the 'Golden Rule'—and it is *this* norm that (most obviously) governs the golfer's choice by defeating his reason not to spend the time required to save the tot, i.e., the possibility of continuing his participation in the good of playing golf.[21]

Of course, the golfer might fail to do what the Golden Rule requires. His love for the game (or his love of winning, or some other emotional motive) might overwhelm his rational grasp of his moral duty of fairness to the child. This failure, however, constitutes ordinary, garden variety immorality rooted in poor character or weakness of the will. If he attempts to rationalize his immoral choice by observing that he *had a reason* (i.e., the intrinsic value of playing golf) to do what he did, we should reply: 'Yes, you had a reason to continue doing what you did; the fact that you had incompatible reasons for action provided by competing basic values created the moral problem in the first place. But you knew (or should have known by applying straightforward Golden Rule analysis) that you had a conclusive reason not to do what you did, and this reason (the second-order reason provided by the Golden Rule) defeated your (first-order) reason to do it. Your immoral choice was not without benefit, for it instantiated the good of play; the instantiation of benefit does not, however, redeem an immoral choice.'

Notice that the moral offense in not interrupting the game in order to save the child is not the offense of intending (or otherwise willing) the child's death. (Nor, of course, would the golfer have been guilty of intending to destroy the good of 'play' had he chosen the morally correct option and interrupted his game to save the child.) The norm violated by the golfer is not the rule against doing evil that good may come of it; rather it is the rule that enjoins us to treat others as we would have them treat us— a rule that applies with full force to accepting or refusing to accept foreseen albeit unintended side effects of actions which one has reasons to perform.

Notice, too, that nothing in the reasoning I have proposed is based on the supposition that 'play' is not a basic good or that 'life' is a greater good than 'play.' Thus, not only is my reasoning non-consequentialist, it is also consistent with a certain common sense belief that is placed in jeopardy by consequentialism and, indeed, by any theory that affirms the commensurability of basic values and asserts that 'life' ranks higher than 'play,' namely the belief that one ordinarily has no moral duty to forgo one's ordinary pursuits, including playing golf, to devote oneself to life saving or to join famine relief projects and other worthy lifesaving endeavors in far off places. Although he may very well have a moral duty to contribute money or goods in kind to the effort, and, perhaps, to pray for its success, a professional golfer who lives in Scotland does not violate the Golden Rule (or any moral norm) when he declines to abandon his career in order to, say, join the relief effort in Bangladesh. Of course, the absence of a moral duty to abandon golf to go to Bangladesh does not entail the presence of a moral duty *not* to give up the good of playing golf in order to help save famine victims in Bangladesh. It may turn out that a choice either way is not only rationally grounded (and, therefore, not strictly arbitrary) but morally permissible (i.e., not excluded by any moral norm).[22]

Common sense moral judgments have nothing to fear from, and may, indeed, presuppose, the incommensurability of basic values and their instantiations that accounts for the multiplicity of moral principles (including, notably, the Golden Rule and the Pauline Principle) that common sense morality recognizes.[23] If basic values were commensurable, as consequentialists suppose they are, then we would need only one moral rule to resolve problems of morally significant choice, one second-order reason for action, namely the consequentialist principle enjoining us to choose the greater good and/or the lesser evil.

NOTES

1 R. George Wright, 'Does Free Speech Jurisprudence Rest on a Mistake?: Implications of the Commensurability Debate,' *Loyola of Los Angeles Law Review*, 23 (1990), 763–790. I am grateful to Professor Wright, both for this article and for the personal communication cited *infra*, n. 4. He has, with characteristic elegance and good humor, articulated a non-trivial concern about the possible

implications of a position that I and other contemporary natural law theorists have vigorously defended. Even if I am correct in suggesting, as I shall, that his concern reflects a misunderstanding of the 'incommensurability thesis' and its implications, I credit him for lucidly setting forth his challenge and thank him for providing an opportunity for me to clear up a misunderstanding that is not his alone: See *infra*, n. 5.

2 A 'rationally grounded option' is an option whose intelligible appeal is provided by the opportunity it presents for someone to instantiate in himself or others some basic value.

3 Wright, 'Does Free Speech Jurisprudence Rest on a Mistake?,' 772–3.

4 Letter from R. George Wright to Robert P. George, dated May 9, 1991, on file with the author.

5 Professor Wright's fear is shared by other commentators on contemporary natural law theory. See Pannier, 'Finnis and the Commensurability of Goods,' *The New Scholasticism*, 61 (1987), 440, 443; Russell Hittinger, *A Critique of the New Natural Law Theory* (Notre Dame, Ind.: University of Notre Dame Press, 1987), 74–9. For a critique of Hittinger's analysis, see Robert P. George, 'Recent Criticism of Natural Law Theory,' *University of Chicago Law Review*, 55 (1988), 1371–1429, reprinted herein as Chapter 2. Also see Finnis, 'Concluding Reflections,' *Cleveland State Law Review*, 38 (1990), 231, 235–241.

6 Paradigmatically, morally significant choice is between rationally grounded possibilities for action, i.e., possibilities shaped by (practical) reason's grasp of basic values for the sake of which one may choose to act.

7 Ibid., 773. I leave it to the reader to decide whether Professor Wright has fairly characterized my defense of the incommensurability thesis as a 'broad assertion'. See Robert P. George, 'Human Flourishing as a Criterion of Morality: A Critique of Perry's Naturalism,' *Tulane Law Review*, 63 (1989), 1455–1474, reprinted herein as Chapter 14. In that essay, I argued that: (1) a value is 'basic' if it provides an ultimate reason for choice and action; (2) an ultimate reason, qua ultimate, is not reducible to other, more fundamental reasons, nor does an ultimate reason depend for its intelligibility as a rational motive for action on some underlying factor that it has in common with other ultimate reasons; and (3) qua irreducible, the basic values that provide ultimate reasons for choice and action are incommensurable. My challenge to Professor Michael Perry (and others who maintain that moral judgments can and should be made on the basis of an objective comparison of values) is to escape the logical paradox of maintaining that irreducible values that provide ultimate reasons for action are nevertheless commensurable. For an argument that desire, feeling or other sub-rational motives for action cannot supply the required principle of commensuration, see George, 'Self-Evident Practical Principles and Rationally Motivated Action: A Reply to Michael Perry,' *Tulane Law Review*, 64 (1990), 887–894.

8 As a leading defender of the incommensurability thesis has observed, '[i]t is crucial to avoid the misleading picture of there being something, enigmatically known as "value," the quantity of which is increased by people having rewarding friendships, enriching occupations, etc.' Joseph Raz, *The Morality of Freedom* (Oxford: Oxford University Press, 1986), 344.

9 The point at issue between critics and defenders of the incommensurability thesis is whether basic values, and their diverse instantiations as they figure in options for choice, are *objectively* commensurable, i.e., commensurable by *reason*. The question is not whether *subjective* commensuration, i.e., commensuration by *feelings*, is possible. Obviously, people can and do (subjectively) *prefer*

one basic value to another, or possible instantiation of a basic value to a competing possible instantiation. The commensurability required, according to Professor Wright and others, to warrant the conclusion that choices between rationally grounded possibilities for action are non-arbitrary, is *objective* commensurability. It is this sort of commensurability that consequentialism presupposes and that defenders of the incommensurability thesis deny. Whatever is to be said for and against the possibility of objective commensurability, I wish to show that the incommensurability thesis does not entail the proposition that choices between rationally grounded options are necessarily arbitrary.

10 For an application and defense of the consequentialist strategy, see McCormick, 'Ambiguity in Moral Choice,' in *Doing Evil to Achieve Good*, in Richard A. McCormick and Paul Ramsey, eds. (Lanham, Md.: University Press of America, 1978). For a careful critique, see John Finnis, *Fundamentals of Ethics* (Washington, DC: Georgetown University Press, 1983), 86–94.

11 Hittinger, *A Critique*, 24.

12 For a fuller account of these commensurabilities and their significance, see Grisez, Boyle and Finnis, 'Practical Principles, Moral Truth, and Ultimate Ends,' *American Journal of Jurisprudence*, 32 (1987), 99, 137–139.

13 In stating that 'saving a life . . . [outweighs] undisturbed coffee drinking,' Professor Wright mistakenly supposes that he is commensurating values. In fact, he is commensurating not values, but options.

14 In a weak sense of 'option,' in which it refers to any available purpose of course of action, there are sometimes 'rationally commensurable options' one of which is utterly dominant in the way I have explained. Rarely does one encounter this sort of commensurability outside purely technical or instrumental contexts, however. Even in the case of competing ski vacation packages, for example, it is unusual to find that one package is superior to all the others in *every* relevant respect.

15 'Second-order' reasons are reasons that guide choices between incompatible possibilities for which one has 'first-order' reasons for action which are provided by basic values. Moral norms, as I shall explain, provide conclusive second-order reasons.

16 For a concise explanation of how choices between rationally grounded possibilities can be rationally underdetermined, see Raz, *The Morality of Freedom*, 388–9.

17 If basic values were somehow commensurable such that it would be possible to identify one among competing options that promised unqualifiedly great good, then one's reason to choose that option would not merely defeat one's reasons to choose competing options, it would destroy them. Where one option promises everything of value available in competing options *plus something more*, there can be no *reason* to choose a competing option. (The only possible motives for choosing a competing option would be subrational, e.g., emotional love of comfort, aversion to hardship or pain, desire to please others.) Hence, some philosophers have concluded that consequentialism requires that two incompatible conditions be met: (1) that a morally significant choice be made ('morally significant choice' being paradigmatically between rationally grounded options); and (2) that the person making the choice be able to identify one option as offering unqualified greater good or lesser evil. Once someone identifies an option as offering, say, unqualifiedly greater good, thus fulfilling condition (2), he is left with no *reason*, no *rational* ground, to choose a competing option, and, hence, no possibility of fulfilling condition (1), i.e., of

making a morally significant choice. See John Finnis, Joseph M. Boyle, Jr. and Germain Grisez, *Nuclear Deterrence, Morality, and Realism* (New York: Oxford University Press, 1987), 254–60. For an attempt to rebut this argument, see McKim and Simpson, 'On the Alleged Incoherence of Consequentialism,' *The New Scholasticism*, 62 (1988), 349. The proponents of the argument reply to McKim and Simpson in 'Incoherence and Consequentialism (or Proportionalism)—A Rejoinder,' *American Catholic Philosophical Quarterly*, 64 (1990), 271.

18 The moral norm against 'doing evil that good might come of it' (sometimes called 'the Pauline Principle') is a second-order reason never to choose directly against (i.e., intend to destroy or damage as an end-in-itself or as a means to some other end) any of the basic values that provide first-order reasons for action. A research scientist could violate this norm by, for example, kidnapping an innocent person and subjecting him to deadly experiments in the sincere hope of finding a cure for AIDS—the curing of AIDS being a genuine reason for action, rooted in the basic values of life and health, and providing a rational motive for the scientist's immoral scheme.

19 In the example I set out in the preceding note, the research scientist has a reason not to destroy the life of an innocent person which is provided by the basic (irreducible, incommensurable) value of that person's life. At the same time, he has competing reasons to destroy that person's life, namely, the lives of those who would benefit from a cure for AIDS.

20 A choice either way is consistent with the Pauline Principle.

21 The same norm applies *a fortiori* to the case of the recreational coffee drinker.

22 Depending on the circumstances—in particular, on any special duties he might have as a father, husband, colleague, valuable participant in worthy local causes, etc.—we might commend (and even recommend) his going to Bangladesh as a supererogatory act.

23 For a more complete list of 'second-order' reasons ('intermediate moral principles') that govern situations of morally significant choice, see John Finnis, *Natural Law and Natural Rights* (Oxford: Clarendon Press, 1980), 100–33. Finnis refers to the moral norms which provide these reasons as 'basic (methodological) requirements of practical reasonableness.'

5

Natural Law and Positive Law

I. NATURAL LAW

As I understand the natural law,[1] it consists of three sets of principles: first, and most fundamentally, a set of principles directing human choice and action toward intelligible purposes, i.e., basic human goods which, as intrinsic aspects of human well-being and fulfillment, constitute reasons for action whose intelligibility as reasons does not depend on any more fundamental reasons (or on sub-rational motives such as the desire for emotional satisfactions) to which they are mere means; second, a set of 'intermediate' moral principles which specify the most basic principle of morality by directing choice and action toward possibilities that may be chosen consistently with a will toward integral human fulfillment and away from possibilities the choosing of which is inconsistent with such a will;[2] and third, fully specific moral norms which require or forbid (sometimes without exceptions) certain specific possible choices.[3]

II. BASIC PRACTICAL PRINCIPLES

The first, and, as I say, most fundamental, principles of natural law are not, strictly speaking, moral norms. They do not resolve questions of which option(s) may uprightly be chosen in situations of morally significant choice. Indeed, the multiplicity of these most basic practical principles *creates* situations of morally significant choice, and makes it necessary for us to identify norms of morality in order to choose uprightly in such situations.

The most basic practical principles refer to ends or purposes which provide non-instrumental reasons for acting. These principles identify intrinsic human goods (such as knowledge, friendship and health) as ends to be pursued, promoted and protected, and their opposites (ignorance, animosity, illness) as evils to be avoided or overcome.

Of course, not all ends to which action may be directed are provided by reasons, much less non-instrumental reasons. All of us sometimes want things we have no reason to want. Such desires, though not rationally grounded, are perfectly capable of motivating us to act. One may, for example, experience thirst and desire a drink of water. It may well be that no intelligible good is to be advanced or protected by one's having a drink. One desires a drink not for the sake of health, or friendship, or any other intelligible good which would provide a *reason* for going to the water fountain. Still, one has a motive, albeit a sub-rational motive, to have a drink. One's acting on this motive is perfectly explicable and may, depending on other factors, be perfectly reasonable.[4]

In addition to the distinction between reasons and (non-rationally grounded) desires (and other sub-rational motives), there is the distinction between instrumental and non-instrumental reasons for action. Instrumental goods provide reasons for acting only insofar as they are means to other ends. Money, for example, is a purely instrumental good. It is of value only insofar as one can buy or do things with it. Intrinsic goods, on the other hand, though they may, to be sure, also have considerable instrumental value, are worthwhile for their own sakes. As ends-in-themselves, intrinsic goods provide reasons for action whose intelligibility as reasons does not depend on more fundamental reasons (or on ends ultimately provided by sub-rational motives) to which they are mere means.

Following Germain Grisez, I (and others) refer to intrinsic goods as 'basic human goods.' We do so to stress the point that such goods are not 'platonic forms' somehow detached from the persons in and by whom they are instantiated. Rather, they are intrinsic aspects of the well-being and fulfillment of flesh and blood human beings in their manifold dimensions (that is to say, as animate beings, as rational beings and as agents through deliberation and choice.) Basic human goods provide reasons for action precisely insofar as they are constitutive aspects of human flourishing.

III. MORAL PRINCIPLES

Taken together, the first principles of practical reason that direct action to the basic human goods outline the (vast) range of possible rationally motivated actions, and point to an ideal of 'integral human fulfillment.' This is the ideal of the complete fulfillment of all human persons (and their communities) in all possible respects. The first principle of morality, which is no mere ideal, directs that our choosing be compatible with a will toward integral fulfillment. The specifications of this principle, in, for example, the Golden Rule of fairness or the Pauline Principle that evil may not be done even that good might come of it, take into account the (necessarily sub-rational) motives people may have for choosing or otherwise willing incompatibly with such a will.

Moral principles—whether the most basic and general principle prior to its specification, or those specifications which are intermediate between the most basic principles and fully specific moral norms, or the fully specific norms themselves—are intelligible as principles of action and relevant to practical thinking only because, at the most basic level of practical reflection, rational human beings are capable of grasping a multiplicity of intelligible ends or purposes that provide reasons for action. Paradigmatically, moral principles govern choice by providing conclusive second-order reasons to choose one rather than another, or some rather than other, possibilities in cases in which one has competing, first-order reasons, i.e., where competing possibilities each offer some true human benefit and, thus, hold some genuine rational appeal.[5] Paradigmatically, moral norms exclude the choosing of those possibilities which, though rationally grounded, fall short of all that reason requires.

This conception of the role of moral norms in practical reasoning is captured in the tradition of natural law theorizing by the notion of *recta ratio*—'right reason.' Right reason is reason unfettered by emotional or other impediments to choosing consistently with what reason fully requires. Often enough, a possibility for choice may be rationally grounded (i.e., for a (first-order) *reason* provided by the possibility of realizing or participating in some true human benefit, some basic human good) yet at the same time be contrary to *right* reason (i.e., contrary to at least one conclusive (second-order) reason provided by a moral norm which excludes the choosing of that possibility).

Of course, most of our choices are not between right and wrong options, but rather between incompatible right options. Where a choice is between or among morally acceptable possibilities, one has a reason to do X and a reason to do Y, the doing of which is incompatible here and now with doing X, yet no conclusive reason provided by a moral norm to do X or not to do X for the sake of doing Y. In situations of this sort, one is considering possibilities made available by the practical intellect's grasp of the most basic principles of practical reason and precepts of natural law. These pertain to the first set of principles of natural law I identified at the beginning of this chapter. Yet practical reason is unable to identify principles in the second and third sets (i.e., second-order principles or norms) to determine one's choice. One's choice, then, though rationally grounded, is in a significant sense rationally underdetermined.[6] Doing X or not doing X in order to do Y are both fully reasonable, are both fully compatible with *recta ratio*.

IV. NATURAL LAW PRACTICAL REASONS, AND MORALITY

As choosing subjects, or 'acting persons,' we make the natural law effective by bringing the principles of natural law into our practical deliberation and judgment in situations of morally significant choice. This task is not merely a job for the natural law theorist or a believer in natural law. It is something that every rational agent does to some extent, and every responsible agent does to a large extent.

Even in the most mundane aspects of our lives, in matters of no great moral moment, we regularly and effortlessly identify and act upon the first-order reasons that constitute the most basic principles of natural law. In fact, countless choices in which these principles centrally figure are so commonplace that ordinary people would be shocked to learn that they were acting on principles at all. They would characterize their choices as merely 'doing what comes naturally,' or even 'doing what I like.' And, in a sense, they would be absolutely right. They are choosing and acting, with minimal reflection or deliberation, for the sake of reasons (and, thus, on principles) that are so patently obvious, that are grasped so effortlessly, that fit into the established patterns of their lives so easily, that they require hardly any thought at all.

Beyond this, everyone who deliberates among competing possibilities each or all of which have at least some rational appeal, and who, upon reflection, identifies a principle of rectitude in choosing which will enable him to judge correctly that one of those options is, uniquely, right (and should therefore be chosen) and others are wrong (and therefore, despite their elements of rational appeal, should not be chosen), makes the second and third sets of principles of natural law effective in his own willing and choosing. In cases of this sort, one is acting not only on the *prima principii*, the most basic precepts of natural law that are, as it were, the foundations of any sort of rational action (whether morally upright or defective), but also on the basis of moral norms that distinguish fully reasonable from practically unreasonable, morally upright from immoral, choosing.

Now, here it is worth pausing to avert a misunderstanding. By saying that the choosing subject 'makes the natural law effective,' I do not mean to imply that the subject creates the natural law or confers upon it its morally binding nature or its force. No one should infer from my willingness to put the choosing subject in an active role with respect to the natural law ('making it effective') that the natural law, as I understand it, is somehow subjective. On the contrary, the reasons constitutive of each of the three sets of principles of natural law are, in a stringent sense, *objective*. They are grasped (only) by *sound* practical judgment and missed (only) when inquiry and judgment miscarry. They correspond to aspects of the genuine fulfillment of human persons, as such, and to the real (and strictly non-optional) requirements of reasonableness in human willing and choosing (i.e., the norms of morality) that obtain for human beings, as such, and which do not depend upon, or vary with, people's beliefs, wishes, desires, or subjective interests or goals. The principles of natural law possess and retain their normative and prescriptive force

independently of anyone's decision to adopt or refuse to adopt them in
making the practical choices to which they apply.[7]

That being said, it remains true that we make the natural law effective
in our lives precisely by grasping and acting on these principles. In doing
so, we exercise the human capacity for free choice. A free choice is a choice
between open practical possibilities (to do X or not do X, perhaps for the
sake of doing Y) such that nothing but the choosing itself settles the
matter.[8] The existence of basic reasons for action (and, thus, of the primary
principles of natural law) are conditions of free choice. If there were no
such reasons, then all of our actions would be determined—determined
either by external causes or by internal (sub-rational) factors such as
feeling, emotion, desire, etc.[9] The denial of free choice, which is central to
the various modern reductionisms in philosophy, psychology and the
social sciences, is, then, closely connected to the denial of the possibility of
rationally motivated action. To deny free choice and the existence of basic
goods, reasons and principles that are its conditions, is to suppose that
people are nothing more than animals with a well-developed capacity
for theoretical and instrumentally practical rationality. If people were
nothing more than that, then natural law could never be effective for them
and would, indeed, hardly be intelligible conceptually.

Because persons can make free choices, they are self-constituting
beings. In freely choosing—that is, in choosing for or against goods that
provide non-instrumental reasons—one integrates the goods (or the damaging and consequent privation of the goods, i.e., the evils) one intends
into one's will. Thus, one effects a sort of synthesis between oneself as an
acting person and the object of one's choices (i.e., the goods and evils one
intends—either as ends-in-themselves or as means to other ends). One's
choices perdure in one's character and personality as a choosing subject
unless or until, for better or worse, one reverses one's previous choice by
choosing incompatibly with it or, at least, resolves to choose differently
should one face the same or relevantly similar choices in the future.[10]

Of course, ethical theory is a complicated business in part because
different types of willing bear on human goods and evils in interestingly
and importantly different ways. Thus it is necessary to distinguish, as the
tradition of natural law theorizing does, as distinct modes of voluntariness, 'intending' a good or evil (as an end or as a means to some other end)
from 'accepting as a side-effect' a good or evil that one foresees as a
consequence of one's action but does not intend. Although one is morally
responsible for the bad side-effects one knowingly brings about, one is not
responsible for them in the same way one is responsible for what one
intends. Often, one will have an obligation in justice or fairness to others
(and thus a conclusive moral reason) not to bring about a certain evil
that one knows or believes would likely result, albeit as an unintended

side-effect, from one's action. Sometimes, though, one will have no obligation to avoid bringing about a certain foreseen bad side-effect of an action
one has a reason (perhaps even a conclusive reason) to perform.

V. NATURAL LAW, POSITIVE LAW AND THE COMMON GOOD

Communities, like individual persons, make choices. Their choices have
to do with the ordering of the common lives of members of communities.
Sometimes, especially in small communities, many of these choices or
decisions are made by consensus, by achieving unanimity about what to
do. It is the rare community, however, that can rely exclusively on unanimity. Most communities must rely on authority to coordinate the
actions of individuals and sub-communities within the larger community
for the sake of the common good. This is obviously true of political
communities. Although there are many different forms of government, all
political communities must create and rely upon authority of some sort.[11]

Political authorities serve the common good in large measure by creat-
ing, implementing and enforcing laws. Where the laws are just (and
expedient), authorities serve their communities well; where they are
unjust (or inexpedient) they serve their communities badly. The moral
purpose of a system of laws is to make it possible for individuals and
sub-communities to realize for themselves important human goods that
would not be realizable (or would not be fully realizable) in the absence of
the laws. Hence, according to Aquinas, 'the end of the law is the common
good.'[12]

It is tempting to think of authority and law as necessary only because of
human selfishness, inconstancy, weakness or intransigence. The truth,
however, is that the law would be necessary to coordinate the behavior of
members of the community for the sake of the common good even in a
society of angels. Of course, in such a society legal sanctions—the threat of
punishment for law-breaking—would be unnecessary; but laws themselves would still be needed. Given that no earthly society is a society of
angels, legal sanctions are—quite reasonably—universal features of legal
systems. They are not, however, essential to the very concept of law.

But, someone might object, certain familiar laws would not be necessary
in a society of angels—laws against murder, rape, thefts, etc. The actions
forbidden by such laws are plainly immoral—contrary to natural law—
and would never be performed by perfectly morally upright beings. True.
And since the moral point of law is to serve the good of people as they
are—with all their (perhaps I should say our) faults—laws against these
evils are necessary and proper. The natural law itself requires that someone (or some group of persons or some institution) exercise authority in

political communities and the authority fulfills his (or their or its) moral functions by translating certain principles of natural law into positive law and reinforcing and backing up these principles with the threat of punishment for law-breaking. Thus, a morally valid authority, in a sense, derives the positive law from the natural law; or, as I have said, translates natural principles of justice and political morality into rules and principles of positive law.

Aquinas, following up a lead from Aristotle, observed that the positive law is derived from the natural law in two different ways. In the case of certain principles, the legislator translates the natural law into the positive law more or less directly. So, for example, a conscientious legislator will prohibit grave injustices such as murder, rape and theft by moving by a process akin to deduction[13] from the moral proposition that, say, the killing of innocent persons is intrinsically unjust to the conclusion that the positive law must prohibit (and punish) such killing.

In a great many cases, however, the movement from the natural law to the positive law in the practical thinking of the conscientious legislator cannot be so direct. For example, it is easy to understand the basic principle of natural law that identifies human health as a good and the preservation and protection of human health as important purposes. A modern legislator will therefore easily see, for example, the need for a scheme of coordination of traffic that protects the safety of drivers and pedestrians. The common good, which it is his responsibility to foster and serve in this respect, requires it. Ordinarily, however, he cannot identify a uniquely correct scheme of traffic regulation which can be translated from the natural law to the positive law. Unlike the case of murder, the natural law does not determine once and for all the perfect scheme of traffic regulation. A number of different schemes—bearing different and often incommensurable costs and benefits, risks and advantages—are consistent with the natural law. So the legislator must exercise a kind of creativity in choosing a scheme. He must move, not by deduction, but rather by an activity of the practical intellect that Aquinas called *determinatio*.[14]

Unfortunately, no single word in English captures the meaning of *determinatio*. 'Determination' captures some of the flavor of it; but so do 'implementation,' 'specification,' and 'concretization.' The key thing to understand is that in making *determinationes*, the legislator enjoys a kind of creative freedom that may be analogous to that of the architect. An architect must design a building that is sound and sensible for the purposes to which it will be put. He cannot, however, identify an ideal form of a building that is uniquely correct. Ordinarily, at least, a range of possible buildings differing in a variety of respects will satisfy the criteria of soundness and usability. Obviously, a building whose 'doors' are not more than 3 ft. high ordinarily fails to meet an important requirement for a usable building. No principle of architecture, however, sets the proper height of a door as such at 6 ft. 2 in. as opposed to 6 ft. 8 in. In designing any particular building, the conscientious architect will strive to make the height of the doors make sense in light of a variety of other factors, some of which are themselves the fruit of something akin to *determinatio* (e.g., the height of the ceilings); but even here he will typically face a variety of acceptable but incompatible design options.

It is meaningful and correct to say that the legislator (including the judge to the extent that the judge in the jurisdiction in question exercises a measure of law-creating power) makes the natural law effective for his community by deriving the positive law from the natural law. The natural law itself requires that such a derivation be accomplished and that someone (or a group or institution) be authorized to accomplish it. Because no human individual (or group or institution) is perfect in moral knowledge or virtue, it is inevitable that even conscientious efforts to translate the natural law into positive law, whether directly or by *determinationes*, will sometimes miscarry. Nonetheless, the natural law itself sets this as the task of the legislator and it is only through his efforts that the natural law can become effective for the common good of his community.

Of course, the body of law created by the legislator is not itself natural law. The natural law is in no sense a human creation. The positive law (of any community), however, *is* a human creation. It is an object—a vast cultural object composed of sometimes very complicated rules and principles, but an object nonetheless. Metaphysically, the positive law belongs to the order Aristotle defines as the order of 'making' rather than of 'doing.' For perfectly good reasons, it is made to be subject to technical application and to be analyzed by a kind of technical reasoning—hence the existence of law schools that teach students not (or not just) moral philosophy, but the distinctive techniques of legal analysis, e.g., how to identify and understand legal sources, how to work with statutes, precedents, and with the (often necessarily) artificial definitions that characterize any complex system of law.

At the same time, the creation of law (and a system of law) has a moral purpose. It is in the order of 'doing,' (the order, not of technique, but rather of free choice, practical reasoning and morality—the order studied in ethics and political philosophy) that we identify the need to create law for the sake of the common good. The lawmaker creates an object—the law—deliberately and reasonably subject to technical analysis—for a purpose that is moral, and not itself merely technical. To fail to create this object (or to create unjust laws) would be inconsistent with the requirements of the natural law, it would be a failure of legislative duty precisely in the moral order.

VI. NATURAL LAW, POSITIVE LAW AND THE JUDICIAL ROLE

The fact that the law is a cultural object that is created for a moral purpose generates a great deal of the confusion one encounters today in debates about the role of moral philosophy in legal reasoning. The vexed question of American constitutional interpretation is the scope and limits of the power of judges to invalidate legislation under certain allegedly vague or abstract constitutional provisions. Some constitutional theorists, such as Professor Ronald Dworkin, who wish to defend an expansive role for the judge, argue that the conscientious judge must bring judgments of moral and political philosophy to bear in deciding hard cases.[15] Others, such as Judge Robert Bork, who fear such a role for the judge, and hold, in any event, that the Constitution of the United States does not give the judge such a role, maintain that moral philosophy has little or no place in judging, at least in the American system.[16]

Some people who are loyal to the tradition of natural law theorizing are tempted to suppose that Professor Dworkin's position, whatever its faults in other respects, is the one more faithful to the tradition. This temptation should, however, be resisted. While the role of the judge as law-creator reasonably varies from jurisdiction to jurisdiction[17] according to each jurisdiction's own authoritative *determinationes*—that is to say, each jurisdiction's own positive law—Judge Bork's idea of a body of law that is properly and fully (or almost fully) analyzable in technical terms is fully compatible with classical understandings of natural law theory.

Natural law theory treats the role of the judge as itself fundamentally a matter for *determinatio*, not for direct translation from the natural law. It does not imagine that the judge enjoys (or should enjoy) as a matter of natural law a plenary authority to substitute his own understanding of the requirements of the natural law for the contrary understanding of the legislator or constitution maker in deciding cases at law. On the contrary, for the sake of the Rule of Law, understood as ordinarily a necessary (albeit not a sufficient) condition for a just system of government, the judge (like any other actor in the system) is morally required (that is, obligated as a matter of natural law) to respect the limits of his own authority as it has been allocated to him by way of an authoritative *determinatio*. If the law of his system constrains his law-creating power in the way that Judge Bork believes American fundamental law does, then, for the sake of the Rule of law, he must respect these constraints, even where his own understanding of natural justice deviates from that of the legislators or constitution makers and ratifiers whose laws he must interpret and apply. None of this means that Judge Bork is more nearly correct than Professor Dworkin on the question of what degree of law-creating power *our* law places in the hands of the judge; it merely means that the question whether Dworkin or Bork is more nearly correct is properly conceived as itself a question of positive law—not natural law.

Bork, who is understood by some of his critics as denying the existence of natural law or any type of objective moral order, has recently clarified his position: 'I am far from denying that there is a natural law, but I do deny both that we have given judges the authority to enforce it and that judges have greater access to that law than do the rest of us.'[18]

If Bork's view is sound (and subject, perhaps, to one or two minor qualifications I am prepared to believe that it is sound), that leaves us with the question whether the natural law itself—quite independently of what the Constitution may say—confers upon the judge a sort of plenary power to enforce it. One of my central aims in this essay has been to argue that the correct answer to this question is 'no.' To the extent that judges are not given power under the Constitution to translate principles of natural justice into positive law, that power is not one they enjoy; nor is it one they may justly exercise. For judges to arrogate such power to themselves in defiance of the Constitution is not merely for them to exceed their authority under the positive law; it is to violate the very natural law in whose name they purport to act.

NOTES

1 For a fuller account of the understanding of natural law set forth in this paragraph, see Joseph M. Boyle, Germain Grisez and John Finnis, 'Practical Principles, Moral Truth and Ultimate Ends,' *American Journal of Jurisprudence*, 32 (1987), 99–151. I defend this understanding against various criticisms in 'Recent Criticism of Natural Law Theory,' *University of Chicago Law Review*, 55 (1988), 1371–1429, reprinted herein as Chapter 2.

2 Examples of moral principles in this category are the 'Golden Rule' of fairness and the 'Pauline Principle' which forbids the doing of evil even as a means of bringing about good consequences.

3 Examples of norms in this category are those forbidding such specific possible choices as willfully refusing to return borrowed property to its owner upon his request (which is a good example of a moral norm which admits of exceptions) and directly killing an innocent person (which is a good example of an exceptionless moral norm). Note that 'direct' killing refers to the intending of death—one's own or someone else's—as an end in itself (as killing for revenge) or as a means to another end (as in terror bombing the civilian population of an unjust aggressor nation). It is sometimes permissible to accept the bringing about of death—one's own or someone else's—as the foreseen and accepted side effect of a choice in which one does not intend death (either as end or means).

4 To act on one's sub-rational motive is not necessarily unreasonable or morally wrong. Moral questions arise only when one has a reason not to do something which one also has a reason, or a non-rationally grounded desire, to do. So, to stay with the example, where one is thirsty and has no reason not to slake one's

thirst, then there is nothing wrong with having a drink. Visiting the water fountain, in these circumstances, is an innocent pleasure.

5 I defend this conception of the role of moral principles in 'Does the "Incommensurability Thesis" Imperil Common Sense Moral Judgments?,' *American Journal of Jurisprudence*, 37 (1992), 185–195. Reprinted herein as Chapter 4.

6 See Joseph Raz, *The Morality of Freedom* (Oxford: Clarendon Press, 1986), 388–9.

7 On the objectivity of the principles of natural law, see John Finnis, *Natural Law and Natural Rights* (Oxford: Clarendon Press, 1980), 69–75; and *Fundamentals of Ethics* (Oxford: Oxford University Press, 1983), 56–79.

8 For a thorough explanation and defense of this conception of free choice, see Joseph M. Boyle, Jr., Germain Grisez and Olaf Tollefsen, *Free Choice: A Self-Referential Argument* (Notre Dame, Ind.: University of Notre Dame Press, 1976).

9 I explain this point at length in 'Free Choice, Practical Reason and Fitness for the Rule of Law,' in *Social Discourse and Moral Judgment*, Daniel N. Robinson, ed. (San Diego, Calif: Academic Press, 1992), 123–32, reprinted herein as Chapter 6.

10 On the lastingness and character-forming consequences of free choices, see John Finnis, *Fundamentals of Ethics*.

11 See Finnis, *Natural Law and Natural Rights*, 231–59.

12 *Summa Theologiae*, 1–2, q. 96, a. 1.

13 *Summa Theologiae*, 1–2, q. 95, a. 2.

14 Ibid. For a sound exposition and valuable development of Aquinas's understanding of *determinatio*, see Finnis, *Natural Law and Natural Rights*, 285–90. Also see Finnis, 'On "The Critical Legal Studies Movement,"' *American Journal of Jurisprudence*, 30 (1985), 21–42.

15 For the most fully developed articulation of Dworkin's position, see his *Law's Empire* (Cambridge, Mass.: Harvard University Press, 1986).

16 See Robert H. Bork, *The Tempting of America: The Political Seduction of the Law* (NY: The Free Press, 1990), esp. 251–9.

17 I am concerned here with the role and duty of judges in basically just legal systems, i.e., systems which do not deserve to be subverted and which judges and others would do wrong to subvert. Different considerations apply in sorting out the obligations of judges in fundamentally unjust legal systems. I do not take up these considerations in this essay.

18 Bork, *The Tempting of America*, 66.

6

Free Choice, Practical Reason and Fitness for the Rule of Law

I. ON THE RULE OF LAW

Occasionally one encounters overblown claims on behalf of the rule of law. For example, thirty years ago, Lon L. Fuller, the theorist who has in our own time best explicated the content of the rule of law,[1] seemed to assert that tyrannical rulers cannot pursue their pernicious ends while at the same time scrupulously observing the requirements of the rule of law. Fuller argued, or, in any event, his critics took him to be arguing, that the rule of law operates as a procedural guarantee against serious substantive injustice.[2]

Fuller's critics responded by pointing out that wicked rulers sometimes have purely self-interested motives for eschewing official lawlessness and binding themselves to act in accordance with legal procedures. They contended that the strict observance of legal forms by such rules cannot guarantee that the laws they enact and enforce will not be substantively unjust.

In a celebrated exchange with Fuller, Herbert Hart maintained that nothing prevents wicked regimes from pursuing manifestly evil ends through procedures that exemplify the qualities of process that Fuller correctly identified as constitutive of the rule of law.[3] Fuller responded by claiming that grossly wicked regimes, such as the Nazi regime, do not observe even formal principles of legality. In practice, regimes of this sort depart freely from the rule of law whenever it suits their purposes. He defied Hart to provide 'significant examples of regimes that have combined a faithful adherence to the [rule of law] with a brutal indifference to justice and human welfare'.[4]

Fuller's critics, however, remained skeptical. Indeed, Joseph Raz went a step beyond Hart in attempting to deflate Fuller's claims for the rule of law. Raz suggested that the rule of law is simply an efficient instrument, not unlike a sharp knife, that may be useful and even necessary for government to pursue morally decent purposes but is equally serviceable in the causes of tyranny and injustice.[5]

At one point, Neil MacCormick shared Raz's understanding of the desiderata of the rule of law as morally neutral (and largely technical) requirements of legal efficiency. 'After all,' MacCormick has remarked, these requirements 'can in principle be as well observed by those whose laws wreak great substantive injustice as by those whose laws are in substance as just as can possibly be'[6]. Recently, however, MacCormick has modified his view. While he continues to insist that strict observance of the rule of law is compatible with grave substantive injustice, he is now inclined to give some credit to Fuller's claim that the elements of the rule of law constitute a kind of 'internal morality' of law.

There is always something to be said for treating people with formal fairness, that is, in a rational and predictable way, setting public standards for citizens' conduct and official's responses thereto, standards with which one can judge compliance or noncompliance, rather than leaving everything to discretionary and potentially arbitrary decision. That indeed is what we mean by the 'Rule of Law.' Where it is observe, people are confronted by a state which treats them as rational agents due some respect as such. It applies fairly whatever standards of conduct and of judgment it applies. This has real value, and independent value, even where the substance of what is done falls short of any relevant ideal of substantive justice.[7]

MacCormick's analysis of the intrinsic, albeit limited, value of the rule of law is, I think, quite sound. I would merely add that an unjust regime's adherence to preannounced and stable general rules, so long as it lasts, will have the additional virtue of limiting the rulers' freedom of maneuver and is therefore likely to reduce, to some extent, the efficiency of their evil-doing. Even those subjected to unjust rule will be made somewhat better off to the extent that their rulers, regardless of their motives, operate according to law. To be sure, the substance of the laws may be spectacularly unjust; nevertheless, a wicked government's decision to act within the procedural constraints of the rule of law affords the general population at least some measure of security.

Plato warned that wherever the rule of law enjoys ideological prestige evil men will find it convenient to adhere to constitutional procedures and other legal forms as means of maintaining or enhancing their power.[8] He had no illusions that a ruler's willingness to operate according to law would guarantee that the particular laws he enacted and enforced would, even in general, be just. Nevertheless, he noticed that, quite apart from the self-interested motives that evil rulers sometimes have for acting according to law, men of goodwill always and everywhere have reason to respect the rule of law: for such respect manifests a degree of procedural fairness that in itself is desirable in human relations and, in particular, in the relations between ruler and ruled. While this reciprocity is often useful in securing other desirable ends—such as enabling people to understand the legal consequences of the actions they contemplate and, thus, to plan and order their lives—it is not *merely* a means to other ends (nor, I would suggest, may it lightly be sacrificed for the sake of other goods).

I think it is fair to conclude, then, that if Fuller claimed too much for the rule of law, his more extreme critics have acknowledged too little. Fuller was wrong to suppose (if he did, in fact, suppose) that the strict observance of the procedural forms of legality would guarantee substantive justice; nevertheless, *pace* Raz, a ruler's willingness to observe these forms is likely to constitute a benefit to the ruled even when it is motivated by something other than a sincere regard for the morally compelling reasons that those in possession of political authority have for respecting the rule of law.

Sober accounts of the rule of law acknowledge both the contribution of formal legality to the morally upright ordering of human affairs and the limits to that contribution. Even the most illuminating of these accounts, however, typically say little about a certain very important philosophical question: What is it about (most) people that makes them fit for the rule of law?

The correct answer, I think, is suggested by MacCormick's claim that rulers ought to govern by law because people are 'due some respect as rational agents.' There is, however, more to be said; for today when one speaks of human rationality (in virtually any context) one will be understood to be referring to what Aristotle labeled 'theoretical' rationality. *Merely* theoretically rational agents, however, could not be ruled by law and would, in any event, no more deserve to be ruled by law than computers deserve such rule. Even theoretically rational agents who: (1) experienced felt desires; and (2) were capable of bringing intellectual operations to bear in order to satisfy their desires—if this were all to be said of their capacities for 'practical' reasoning—would hardly be due the respect implied by the rule of law. Such agents would certainly not be capable of exercising moral judgment and making moral choices.

The rationality for which people are 'due some respect' in the form of the rule of law is not primarily the rationality that enables people to solve mathematical problems, or understand the human neural system, or develop cures for diseases, or inquire into the origins of the universe or even the existence and attributes of God. It is, rather, the rationality that enables them to judge that mathematical problems are to be solved, that the neural system is to be understood, that diseases are to be cured and that God (if He exists) is to be known and loved.[9] It is, moreover, the capacity to distinguish fully reasonable possibilities for choice and action from possibilities that, while rationally grounded, fall short of all that reason demands. In sum, fitness for the rule of law depends on our capacities as *practically* intelligent beings, that is, our capacities to grasp and act on reasons and to distinguish defeated from undefeated, and conclusive from nonconclusive, reasons for action. These capacities are, in turn, connected with our capacity for free choice, that is, our capacity to deliberate and choose (often, but not always, for conclusive reasons) between and among possibilities that provide reasons for action.

In what follows I shall explicate the phenomenon of free choice and discuss, in general terms, the relationship between free choice, practical reasoning and morality. I shall also say why I think that beings who can make free choices and be practically reasonable are not only fit for the rule of law, but in most circumstances, deserve to be governed in accordance with it.

II. FREE CHOICE AND PRACTICAL REASON

People make choices; and some of the choices people make are quite unlike the 'choices' made by non-rational animals. A mule may hesitate when faced with the possibilities of drinking from a pail of water or eating from a bale of hay. In the end, it will do one or the other first. Now, let us suppose that on this occasion the mule drinks the water before eating the hay. In a loose sense, the animal can be said to have 'chosen' to drink before eating. Nothing *external* to the mule determined that it would drink first; what settled the matter in the end was something *internal* to the mule, namely, the mule's own desires or preferences. The animal hesitated between the pail and the bale because it was experiencing a conflict of felt desires: it felt a desire for the water and, at the same time, a desire for the hay. Eventually, the desire for the water prevailed and the mule drank.

Like mules, people can be motivated by hunger, thirst and other felt desires. They can experience conflicts of felt desires and make 'choices' in the loose sense in which mules and other animals can be said to make choices. Unlike mules and other animals, however, people can 'choose' in a stricter and philosophically more interesting sense. The choices that people can make that are quite unlike the 'choices' made by other animals are what philosophers mean by 'free choices.'

A free choice is a choice between two or more open practical possibilities which no factor by the choosing itself settles which possibility is chosen.[10] Inasmuch as the mule's choice to drink before eating was *determined* (albeit by its own desires) it was not a *free* choice. Insofar as similar choices made by human beings are similarly determined they are not free choices. Free choices are choices that are not determined by desire. Free choices are not determined by anything. They are, in short, not determined.

Choice in any sense is possible only where someone has motives for incompatible actions. *Free* choice is only possible where these motives are reasons for action or, at least, where reasons for action are among these motives. There can be no free choice where the *only* possible motives for action are *sub-rational*, for example, feelings, desires, preferences, habits, emotional inertia.

Because mules can be motivated by possibilities that appeal to feelings, desires, preferences, habits, inertia, etc., they sometimes *hesitate* between incompatible possibilities and 'choose' in the looser sense of the term. Because mules cannot, we must suppose, appreciate the *rational* appeal of some possibilities for choice, they cannot *deliberate* between incompatible possibilities that provide reasons for action and make free choices between or among them. People and other rational beings, precisely insofar as they can understand certain possibilities as providing reasons for action, *can* deliberate between incompatible possibilities and make free choices.

It is important to notice that reasons for action, though they are conditions of free choice, are not causes (in any modern sense of 'cause') of the actions they are capable of motivating.[11] One can choose not to perform a certain act that one has a reason (and, thus, a rational motive) to perform and one can choose to perform a certain act that one has a reason (and, thus, a rational motive) not to perform. In the simplest case, one may have a reason to perform an act yet have a strong aversion to performing it (and, thus, an emotional motive for not performing it). One's failure to perform it may be due to weakness of the will.[12]

In a more interesting case, one may have a reason to perform a certain act and, at the same time, a reason not to perform it. One may freely choose to act on the latter reason. In a case of this sort where one has a conflict of reasons and no conclusive reason to act on one reason rather than the other, the choice between the two is rationally underdetermined. Nevertheless, a choice either way remains rationally grounded.[13] If one performs the act, one does so for a reason; if one refrains from performing the act, one also does so for a reason.

Let us consider an example. Suppose that Ferdinand is a bright young college senior who is trying to decide on a career. He has talent and interest in psychology and could, no doubt, contribute to the advancement of knowledge in that field. Thus, he has a reason to enroll in a doctoral program in psychology at, say, Georgetown. At the same time, however, he has talent and interest in medicine. Thus, he has a reason to forgo graduate work in psychology and go to medical school. A choice either way would be 'for a reason' and, thus, rationally based; yet Ferdinand has no conclusive reason for making it one way rather than the other. A choice in favor of either possibility would be consistent with those principles of reasonableness in practical affairs that we usually refer to as moral norms. Hence, no such norm provides a reason for action that defeats one or the other of the conflicting reasons and dictates a choice one way rather than the other.

There are cases of conflicting reasons, however, in which moral norms do provide conclusive reasons to do something that one has a reason not to do or not to do something that one has a reason to do. Nevertheless, one may freely choose to defy a conclusive reason. In such cases, one's action, while not utterly irrational, is not fully reasonable. An act in defiance of a conclusive reason remains rationally grounded insofar as one performs it for a reason. Yet inasmuch as one's reason for performing it has been defeated, one's nevertheless choosing to act in this way is practically unreasonable.

Let us suppose that Ferdinand has opted for medical school. In the course of his medical studies, it becomes clear to him that it would be possible to learn a great deal about the etiology of a certain deadly cancer by performing damaging and ultimately fatal experiments on a living human subject. Naturally, Ferdinand desires to acquire this knowledge— both for its own sake and in the hope of finding a cure for the cancer. Now, it occurs to him that he could probably get away with performing the necessary experiments on an advanced Alzheimer's patient who has no family and resides in a hospice that Ferdinand regularly visits as part of his practical training. So, Ferdinand faces a choice between performing the experiments and declining to do so. Like his earlier choice between going to graduate school in psychology or going to medical school, this choice is between rationally grounded possibilities. That is to say, Ferdinand has reasons for a choice either way. Here however, he has a conclusive reason for making the choice one way rather than the other, namely, the moral norm that forbids the taking of innocent human life.

Moral norms are norms for free choice; they are principles of practical reasonableness that guide choices between incompatible possibilities in which one has a reason, or reasons, for action. As action-guiding principles, moral norms are, moreover, themselves reasons for action. They are not the most basic reasons for action, however; for the most basic reasons are principles that guide action by directing choice toward rational possibilities and away from what is utterly irrational. And certain possibilities, while holding some rational appeal (and therefore available for choice in the strong sense of the term), are, nevertheless, not fully reasonable (i.e., the reasons for choosing them are defeating). Moral norms guide action by directing choice toward *fully reasonable* possibilities and away from possibilities that, while not utterly irrational, are practically unreasonable.

Moral norms (such as the norm that forbids the direct killing of innocent human beings) are conclusive reasons for action that exclude certain possibilities despite the fact that one has (non-moral) reasons to choose these possibilities. Where a moral norm excludes a possibility, one's reason for choosing that possibility (assuming that one had a reason and not merely an emotional motive for it) has been defeated. Defeated reasons are reasons on which it is unreasonable to act. Nevertheless, such reasons retain some rational appeal. In declining to act on them, one forgoes some real benefit. By declining to act on a defeated reason, Ferdinand, for example, forgoes genuine goods, namely, knowledge of the etiology of the cancer in question together with the possibility of developing a cure.

Let us suppose, however, that Ferdinand chooses, reluctantly, to perform the experiments on the unsuspecting Alzheimer's victim. Perhaps he has been reading the works of Jeremy Bentham or one of his contemporary followers and has decided that the evil of performing the experiments would be outweighed by all of the good that the knowledge they would yield would make possible. In accounting for his choice, we might take note of the irrationality of supposing that the goods and evils at stake here can be commensurated in a way that would enable someone to identify a choice one way or the other as promising the net best proportion of good to evil.[14] We would not conclude, however, that his choice was utterly irrational. His reasons for making it, namely, the knowledge to be gained and the possibility of a cure, while defeated here by the absolute norm against directly killing the innocent, remain reasons. In view of the conclusive reason for action provided by the norm, however, his choice would fall short of what reason requires: it would thus be unreasonable, irresponsible, immoral.

III. ON THE INTRANSITIVE SIGNIFICANCE OF FREE CHOICE

There are two additional points about the significance of free choice that are, I think, relevant to the question of how people, as moral beings, are fit for the rule of law. Free choices are events or states of affairs in the world; they are not *merely* events or states of affairs, however, like the events and states of affairs that they bring about. In addition to their transitive significance as events that shape the world external to the chooser they have a profound intransitive significance.

First, free choices reflexively shape the personality and character of the chooser. In freely choosing we integrate ourselves around the principles of our choices. Thus, we constitute (or reconstitute) ourselves as particular sorts of persons. We construct (or reconstruct) our moral selves. Typically, this self-constitution or moral self-construction is not the precise reason for our choosing; nevertheless, it is an unavoidable side effect of that choosing. And it is the capacity for moral self-construction (and destruction) that makes us moral beings.

The second point I wish to make about the intransitive significance of free choice is that precisely insofar as our choices are self-constituting they persist beyond the behavior that executes them. Indeed, they persist in the personality and character of the chooser until, for better or worse, he repents of his prior choice and either makes a new choice that is incompatible with that prior choice or genuinely resolves not to repeat the choice he has now repudiated.[15]

The possibility of repentance of an immoral choice manifests a lack of complete integration in the human personality. Someone who has by his immoral choices constituted a wicked character can, with difficulty, reconstitute himself. Fiction and even biography are replete with examples. So long as this lack of complete integration continues, the constitution of a wicked character does not preclude the possibility of repentance and reconstitution around upright principles of action. Nor, of course, does the constitution of a good character eliminate the possibility of evil choices and the reconstitution of one's character around immoral principles. Biography and even fiction provide examples here, too.

IV. FREEDOM, REASON AND FITNESS FOR THE RULE OF LAW

The fact that people can grasp and act on reasons, thus constituting themselves by their own free choices, does not mean that they may not legitimately be governed. The human capacities for practical deliberation and judgment and morally significant choice do not somehow make people fit for anarchy. The possibility of morally upright choice entails the possibility of immoral choice; and with respect to a great many possibilities for choice the common good of everyone in society is served by legal restrictions on the freedom of individuals to do whatever they please.

Moreover, insofar as law provides concrete norms for coordinating various types of human activity in complex societies, it is plain that legal rules would have a place even in a society of perfectly virtuous individuals.[16] Laws provide beings capable of grasping and acting on reasons with (additional) reasons for action. Where the laws are just, they provide conclusive reasons for action. The reasons for action provided by just laws are conclusive even in cases of norms (e.g., coordination norms) that come into force by virtue of the sheer legislative acts of duly qualified political authorities.[17]

Most people are capable of grasping and acting on reasons, including the reasons for action provided by laws. To subject people fit for the rule of law to rule by, say, whim or terror is an affront to their dignity. People really are 'due some respect as rational agents.' And such respect entails, at a minimum, the observance by political authorities of the desiderata of the rule of law.

It is true, of course, that even the most scrupulous adherence to the rule of law does not exhaust the debt owed by rulers to the ruled. As Fuller's critics insisted, the formal requirements of legality may be observed even where the substance of the law is gravely unjust. So respect for the rule of law, while (generally) required as a matter of political morality, is not all that political morality requires. Beings that are fit for the rule of law deserve, moreover, to be ruled by laws that are just.

NOTES

1 Fuller explicated the content of the rule of law in terms of eight constitutive elements or 'desiderata' of legality: (1) the prospectivity (i.e., non-retroactivity) of legal rules; (2) the absence of impediments of compliance with the rules by those subject to them; (3) the promulgation of the rules; (4) their clarity; (5) their coherence with one another; (6) their constancy through time (enabling people to be guided by the rules); (7) their generality; and (8) the congruence between official action and declared rule. He observed that these desiderata are matters of degree; thus, legal systems exemplify the rule of law *to the extent that* the legal rules are prospective, susceptible of being complied with, promulgated, clear, etc. What was, perhaps, most controversial about Fuller's account of the rule of law was his claim that these 'demands of legality' constitute an 'internal morality of law.' See Lon Fuller, *The Morality of Law* (New Haven, Conn.: Yale University Press, 1969), ch. 2.
2 Ibid., ch. 4.
3 See H. L. A. Hart, *'Fuller's The Morality of Law'*, Harvard Law Review, 78 (1965), 1281–96.
4 Fuller, *The Morality of Law*, 154.
5 Joseph Raz, 'The Rule of Law and Its Virtue', Law Quarterly Review, 93 (1977), 208.
6 Neil MacCormick, 'Natural Law and the Separation of Law and Morals' in Robert P. George (ed.), *Natural Law Theory: Contemporary Essays* (Oxford: Clarendon Press, 1992) p. 122.
7 *Id* at 123.
8 Plato, Statesman, 291a–303d.
9 On the distinction between 'theoretical' and 'practical' rationality as herein understood, see John Finnis, *Fundamentals of Ethics* (Washington, DC: Georgetown University Press, 1983); Also, see generally, John Finnis et al., 'Practical Principles, Moral Truth, and Ultimate Ends,' *The American Journal of Jurisprudence*, 32 (1987), 99–151.
10 For a full defense of the possibility of free choice as here defined see Joseph M. Boyle, Jr., Germain Grisez and Olaf Tollefsen, *Free Choice: A Self-Referential Argument* (Notre Dame, Ind.: University of Notre Dame Press, 1976).
11 On the distinction between reasons and causes see Daniel N. Robinson, *Philosophy of Psychology* (New York: Columbia University Press, 1985), especially 50–7.

12 See David Wiggins, 'Weakness of Will, Commensurability, and the Objects of Deliberation and Devise', in Amelie Oksenberg Rosty (ed.) Essays on *Aristotle's Ethics* (Berkeley: University of California Press, 1980).

13 For a useful explanation of how choices between rationally grounded possibilities can be rationally underdetermined, see Joseph Raz, *The Morality of Freedom* (Oxford: Clarendon Press, 1986).

14 For powerful arguments against consequentialism based (in part) on problems of incommensurability, see Germain Grisez, 'Against Consequentialism,' *American Journal of Jurisprudence*, 23 (1978); Finnis, *Fundamentals of Ethics*, chs. 4–5; Raz, *The Morality of Freedom*, ch. 13; and Philippa Foot, 'Utilitarianism and the Virtues,' *Mind*, 94 (1985). For additional arguments that complement the argument based on incommensurability, see Alan Donagan, *The Theory of Morality* (Chicago, Ill.: University of Chicago Press, 1977), esp. 149–57, 172–209; Bartholomew Kiely, 'The Impracticality of Proportionalism,' *Gregorianum*, 66 (1985), 655–686; and D. H. Hodgson, *The Consequences of Utilitarianism* (Oxford: Clarendon Press, 1967). For an ingenious, albeit ultimately self-defeating, attempt to rescue consequentialism from its critics, see Derek Parfit, *Reasons and Persons* (Oxford: Clarendon Press, 1984), wherein the author proposes the category of 'self-effacing theory,' that is a consequentialist theory that requires, for the sake of optimizing consequences, its own abandonment 'by some process of [deliberate] self-deception that, to succeed, must also be forgotten' (p. 42).

15 The resolution required to effect a reconstitution of one's character based upon repentance of one's earlier choice cannot be merely the resolution to avoid the circumstances in which one would feel it necessary to make the choice one now regrets. It can be nothing short of the resolution to choose differently even in those circumstances.

16 On the role of law in providing solutions to coordination problems, see generally Edna Ullmann-Margalit, *The Emergence of Norms* (Oxford: Oxford University Press, 1977).

17 For a useful review of the contemporary debate over the question of a prima facie (defeasible) moral obligation to obey the law, and for a defense of the position herein adopted, see John Finnis, 'Law as Co-ordination,' *Ratio Juris*, 2 (1989), 97–104. For a vigorous argument on behalf of the counterposition, see Joseph Raz, 'The Obligation to Obey: Revision and Tradition,' *Notre Dame Journal of Law, Ethics, and Public Policy*, 1 (1984), 139–155.

Part Two

MORAL AND POLITICAL QUESTIONS

7

Religious Liberty and Political Morality

Practical reasoning not only applies but also identifies reasons for choice and action. These reasons include moral reasons. A full theory of practical reasoning includes a theory of morality. A theory of morality—a critical reflective account—seeks to identify the moral norms available to guide choice and action by distinguishing fully reasonable from practically unreasonable—albeit not simply irrational—choices.

Moral norms are themselves reasons for choice and action, albeit reasons of a particular sort. They guide choice and action in situations in which one has a reason (or, at least, an emotional motive) to do X, but at the same time a reason not to do X because, for example, one also has a reason to do or preserve Y, and the doing or preserving or Y is incompatible here and now with doing X. A moral norm forbids doing X when it provides a conclusive reason not to do X. Such a reason defeats, though it does not destroy,[2] whatever reason one has to do X. By the same token, if a moral norm requires one to do X, then it provides a conclusive reason for doing X. Such a reason defeats, but, again, does not destroy, one's reason to do or preserve Y. If, however, no moral norm dictates a choice one way or the other, then the choice is between morally acceptable, albeit incompatible, options. One may, for example, have an undefeated reason to do X and at the same time an undefeated reason to do Y. A choice for either of these possibilities is thus rationally grounded. Nevertheless, inasmuch as one lacks a conclusive reason for choosing one over the other (though one may have a conclusive reason to choose one or the other over some third alternative, e.g., the possibility of doing nothing), the choice between them is rationally underdetermined.[3]

Not all reasons for action are moral norms.[4] All moral norms are, however, reasons for action. Where a moral norm dictates a certain course of action, it is a conclusive reason for that action; it defeats any reasons one may have for doing what it forbids or not doing what it requires. Only by acting in accord with the moral norm does one act in a fully reasonable, i.e., morally responsible, manner.

Consider a case in which one has a reason for doing X, but one's reason is not itself a moral norm. If one has a non-moral reason to do X and is not forbidden by a moral norm from doing it, then one has an undefeated, albeit non-conclusive, reason to do X. One can reasonably opt to do X or not do it. If, in the circumstances, however, a moral norm forbids one's doing X, then that norm provides a conclusive reason not to do it that defeats one's reason to do it. Of course, in the opposite situation, where a moral norm requires one's doing X, then one has a conclusive reason to do it. Any reason one may have for not doing it is defeated by the moral norm requiring one to do it. The key point is that a choice is fully reasonable (as opposed to merely rationally grounded) when it is not only for a reason, but is also in conformity with all (i.e., when it is not forbidden by any) moral norms. Even actions that are motivated by one's regard for an end whose *intelligible* (and not merely emotional) appeal qualifies it as a *reason* (and not merely a sub-rational motive) for action can be practically unreasonable. It cannot be reasonable to do what one has a conclusive reason not to do. An action motivated by one's regard for a reason is nevertheless unreasonable precisely insofar as one is under a moral obligation not to do it.

In the case of immoral choices (at least insofar as they are not merely the products of conscientious but mistaken moral judgments), reason is fettered by emotion. Commonly, though not always, the emotion that motivates an immoral choice is allied with a (defeated and therefore morally inadequate) reason for that choice. In such circumstances, reason is typically instrumentalized and harnessed by emotion not merely in the cause of satisfying desires, but, also, for the purpose of producing rationalizations for immoral actions. My point can be illustrated by a hypothetical case. The acquisition of scientific knowledge is undeniably a reason for action. Knowledge of this sort is typically both intrinsically and instrumentally worthwhile; it is both an end-in-itself and a means to other valuable ends. Now, consider the case of a gifted research scientist who wishes to understand the etiology of AIDS. He desires to acquire this knowledge both for its own sake and in the hope of finding a cure. His preliminary research suggests a strategy for further research that, though promising, requires the performance of deadly experiments on a living human being. Lacking a volunteer, he considers the possibility of secretly performing the experiments on an unsuspecting patient who is in an advanced stage of AIDS. Of course, the proposal that he is considering violates various moral norms; but his desire to have the knowledge is strong. So he begins to rationalize his plan: 'The life I will be destroying is, after all, a poor and unhappy one; and the experiments do promise to advance science significantly and may even lead to a cure that will save thousands of lives. Surely the great good to be achieved outweighs the little bit of evil I will have to do to achieve it.'

Such a rationalization is possible because the advancement of science and the saving of lives really are reasons for action. They are reasons for the scientist to carry out his plan. They are not, however, the only relevant reasons in these circumstances. The scientist also has reasons to abandon his scheme. The life that the scientist would destroy is a reason for action too, as is his own character which will be corrupted (or further corrupted) by his freely adopting a proposal to commit murder. Faced with reasons to perform the experiments and reasons not to perform them, what should he do?

If there were no (moral) norms to provide reasons to prefer one course of action to the other, the choice between them would be rationally underdetermined. It would be a choice between morally acceptable options. Here, however, that is not the case. The moral norms enjoining us to treat every human being fairly and every human life as an end rather than as a mere means clearly exclude the option of carrying out the experiments. These norms provide conclusive reasons not to carry them out, despite the great goods that really may be achieved by doing so. Of course, the scientist may decide to carry them out anyway. He may fetter his own reason and subordinate it to his emotional desire to realize those goods: To act on one's emotional desire to realize goods that can only be realized here and now by doing what one has conclusive reasons not to do is, it is fair to say, the textbook case of practical unreasonableness.

II. REASONS FOR POLITICAL ACTION AND NORMS OF POLITICAL MORALITY

A theory of political morality seeks to identify reasons for political choice and action. Among these reasons are norms of political morality that distinguish morally acceptable political choices and public policies from immoral choices and policies. Political action, for purposes of normative political theory, is action undertaken for the sake of the common good of such a society.

Are the basic reasons for political action some subset of the universe of basic reasons for action? Or are all the basic reasons for action reasons for political as well as for other sorts of action? To answer these questions it is necessary to clarify the notion of a basic reason for action.

A basic reason for action is a reason whose intelligibility does not depend on further or deeper reasons for action. Those ends or purposes that are intrinsically worthwhile provide basic reasons for action. While such ends or purposes may also be instrumentally desirable, i.e., desirable as means to other ends, they are distinguishable from purely instrumental goods inasmuch as they can be intelligently sought as ends-in-themselves. Instrumental goods do indeed provide reasons for action; they are reasons whose intelligibility depends, however, on further or deeper reasons.

Thus, they are not basic reasons. The intelligibility of instrumental goods depends upon the intrinsic goods whose realization by choice and action they make possible. If there were no intrinsic goods, no basic reasons for action, practical reason would be what Hume, for example, thought it to be, namely, purely instrumental; and rationally motivated action would be impossible.[5] Intrinsically choiceworthy ends or purposes provide us with the basic reasons for action that make rationally motivated action possible.[6]

Qua basic reasons for action, the value of intrinsic goods cannot and need not be inferred from more fundamental reasons for action. Nor, as Germain Grisez has rightly insisted, can basic reasons for action be deduced from purely theoretical premises (i.e., premises that do not include reasons for action). As first principles of practical thinking, basic reasons for action are, as Aquinas held, self-evident (*per se nota*) and indemonstrable (*indemonstrabilia*).[7] As fundamental aspects of human well-being and fulfillment, they belong to human beings as parts of their nature; they are not, however, derived (in any sense that the logician would recognize) from methodologically antecedent knowledge of human nature drawn from anthropology or any other theoretical discipline. Rather, they are grasped in acts of non-inferential understanding by the mind working inductively on the data of inclination and experience.[8]

What are the basic reasons for action? John Finnis has usefully classified them as follows: life (in a broad sense that includes health and general vitality); knowledge; play; aesthetic experience; sociability (i.e., friendship broadly conceived); practical reasonableness; and religion.[9] Practically reasonable action in respect of the plurality of basic reasons for action is guided and structured by moral norms that are, as it were, methodological requirements of the good of practical reasonableness. That good, then, has a peculiar strategic or architectonic role in the moral life. To live in accordance with its requirements is to realize a fundamental aspect of the human good precisely by making one's self-constituting choices in pursuit of other goods intelligently and uprightly.

Let us now return to the question of whether the basic reasons for political action are some subset of the universe of basic reasons for action. According to one view, some intrinsic human goods are aspects of the common good while others are private goods and therefore not legitimate reasons for political action (or, at least, certain forms of political action). The extreme version of this view identifies some good, say, peace or justice, as the sole legitimate reason for political action. According to a familiar contemporary liberal position, for example, justice is the sole legitimate reason for any political action that limits legal liberty; legal prohibitions enacted for the sake of goods other than justice are themselves unjust.[10]

At one point Germain Grisez and Joseph M. Boyle, Jr. defended a political theory that bore some affinities to the liberal position. In *Life and Death with Liberty and Justice*, a book published in 1979, they argued that laws prohibiting voluntary euthanasia, while justifiable, could not legitimately be based on a putative public interest in preserving the lives of those who might wish to do away with themselves. Bodily life, they maintained, is a purely 'private' good in the respects relevant to the question of whether people ought to be legally free to destroy their own lives. As such, it is not in itself a legitimate ground for limiting legal liberty.

Grisez and Boyle argued that '[t]he very notion of a *common* good or of a *public* interest suggests that there is a contrasting category of good which are *individual* or *private*.'[11] Their criterion for distinguishing the two categories was the effectiveness of political society in pursing the goods in question: 'the common good includes goods which the political society as such can *effectively* pursue.'[12] Other goods, they maintained, provide reasons for action, but not for political action.

According to Grisez and Boyle, the primary purpose of public authority is to establish and maintain a just social order. To this end, those exercising public authority must forbid certain sorts of acts and require others. The requirements of justice frequently provide conclusive reasons for laws that restrict liberty. Thus, public authorities are ordinarily required, for the sake of the common good, to prohibit murder, rape and theft, for example, and to require the payment of taxes. At the same time, the requirements of justice often provide public authorities with conclusive reasons not to enact laws that limit people's liberty. And, as Grisez and Boyle viewed the matter, those requirements provide conclusive reasons not to forbid acts (including immoral acts) that do not unjustly harm others: '[f]or the sake of justice and human dignity the liberty to act immorally must be respected and protected by law.'[13]

Where, as in the case of legal prohibitions on self-administered suicide, for example, a law is motivated not by a concern to protect people from wrongs committed against them by others, but rather by a commitment to the 'private' good of preserving bodily life, Grisez and Boyle argued that the law is unjust. 'Although the law should not facilitate such acts, it should take care to avoid interfering with competent adults who freely choose to kill themselves.'[14]

According to Grisez and Boyle, 'liberty must be respected by political society, almost as an absolute, limited only by the demands of justice.'[15] As we have seen, they did not hold liberty to be inviolable. Nor did they treat liberty as a basic good. They argued, rather, that liberty must be limited for the sake of justice; but, at the same time, liberty may not legitimately be limited except for the sake of justice. To limit liberty for the sake of other goods violates the good of justice. Justice is the sole reason for political action that directly limits individual freedom.

Grisez and Boyle did not take the extreme libertarian view that justice is the sole reason for any form of political action. They held that other goods could rightly be understood as reasons for political action in a restricted sense. The good of knowledge, for example, could serve as a legitimate reason for a system of public education; similarly the goods of beauty and play could serve as valid reasons for public museums, parks and recreation facilities; and indeed the goods of life and health could be sound reasons for public hospitals and publicly funded medical research. The restriction on treating these goods as reasons for political action, however, was that they could not serve as legitimate reasons for direct prohibitions of types of action deemed to be unwise, imprudent or even immoral. Thus, the goods of knowledge, beauty, play, life and health, together with the goods of personal integrity and authenticity (or what Finnis calls 'practical reasonableness'), were, according to Grisez and Boyle, 'private,' goods in a way that the good of justice was not. Qua 'private,' these goods could not serve as valid reasons for public authorities to prohibit wrongful acts.

As I see it, there are two problems with Grisez and Boyle's position. First, to the extent that their argument relied on the claim that governments cannot promote or protect goods other than justice effectively except insofar as government action to promote or protect these goods is ultimately motivated by a concern for justice, it seems implausible. The fact is that governmental action—even coercive governmental action—can be effective in discouraging people from doing wicked things even when their immoral actions harm only themselves or those who collaborate with them. Laws designed to uphold public morality, for example, not only contribute to the moral education of the public, they may help to establish or maintain a milieu which encourages virtue and discourages at least the grosser forms of vice. But if political action to protect public morals with respect to putatively 'victimless' immoralities such as pornography, prostitution, drug abuse and suicide can have beneficial effects, then the goods of life, health, friendship and practical reasonableness really are aspects of the common good and reasons for political action, even by the standard of effectiveness articulated by Grisez and Boyle.

My second criticism to the position once defended by Grisez and Boyle is that I see no warrant for the claim that direct limitations on liberty imposed otherwise than for the sake of justice are themselves unjust. I grant that in particular circumstances prudential considerations may very well tip the balance against the enactment or enforcement of laws to uphold public morality, for example. A legislator may reasonably judge that under the conditions prevailing in his society a particular morals law may be too costly, or doomed to failure, or even likely to do more harm than good. Even where morals laws are, for prudential reasons, however, inadvisable, they are not necessarily unjust.

One of the ways that a law can be unjust is by depriving people of goods that are rightfully theirs. And it is certainly true that laws can unjustly deprive people of liberties to which they are entitled. People are morally entitled to decide for themselves without arbitrary governmental restrictions whether or whom to marry, for example, or what profession to pursue, where to live and how to spend their leisure time. For the government to deprive people of these or other honorable liberties is unjust. There is no warrant, however, for believing that people are entitled to the liberty to corrupt, pervert or destroy themselves simply because the law cannot effectively prevent them from doing so. Whether or not they are effective, morals laws that do not imperil honorable liberties do not unjustly deprive people of goods to which they are entitled.

Another way in which laws can be unjust is by arbitrarily favoring the interests and well-being of some citizens over others. Are morals laws unjust in this way? Not if they are based on sound moral judgments and not on mere prejudices. To encourage virtue and discourage vice is not to favor the interests or welfare of the virtuous over the vicious. Laws that forbid the sale or possession of pornography, for example, do not favor the interests of people who happen to dislike pornography over those who happen to like it. If pornography is wicked, and thus destructive of one's character, then no one has a true interest in using it—not even pornography-lovers. On the contrary, everyone has an interest in not using it. In light of this common interest, reasonable efforts to curtail the availability of pornography are 'for the common good.' They are in the interest of everyone—especially those who are most vulnerable to the temptation to use pornography (and therefore benefit most from the maintenance of a social milieu free of pornography's corrupting influences). To be sure, such efforts, to the extent they are successful, frustrate the *desires* of those who wish to use pornography; these efforts do not, however, fail to regard their interests and well-being as just as important as the interests and well-being of everybody else.[16]

Are there, then, no inherently private reasons for action? Are all the basic reasons for action aspects of the common good of civil society?

III. RELIGIOUS LIBERTY AND POLITICAL MORALITY

There is surely one item on Finnis's list of basic goods that will strike many Americans, even many devoutly religious Americans, as inherently private. Religion, they will say, is manifestly not a reason for political action. Getting right with God, if there is a God, is a matter for individuals and the churches and other communities of faith they freely choose to join. Religion therefore is in no way an aspect of the common good of civil society. Political action for the sake of religion is contrary to sound political morality.

Misguided constitutional interpreters will allege that the principle that government has no business concerning itself with the good of religion, if religion is a good, is laid down in the Constitution of the United States. The most that can be said for this claim is that it has impressed a fair number of modern Supreme Court justices. Under the most plausible interpretation of the Establishment Clause of the First Amendment, the federal government is forbidden to establish a national church or interfere with established churches in the states.[17] At most, the Establishment Clause requires what commentators sometimes call 'non-preferentialism,' i.e., the principle that government must be even-handed in its treatment of competing religious groups. Despite its popularity in elite circles, there is surprisingly little textual or historical warrant for the so-called 'strict-separationist' view that the Establishment Clause forbids the states or even the federal government from promoting religion generally or preferring religion to irreligion.[18]

Constitutional interpretation aside, what is the truth as a matter of political morality? Is religion a purely private good? Is it in no sense an aspect of the common good of civil society? The correct answer, I think, is that the good of religion is a reason for political action and an aspect of the common good of civil society. To see why, however, it will be necessary first to get clear on the sense in which religion is a basic reason for action, and second to analyze more closely the concept of the common good. After that, I shall say a word about how the status of religion, as a basic reason for political action, grounds and harmonizes two norms of political morality identified in *Dignitatis Humanae*, Vatican II's *Declaration on Religious Liberty*; one requiring governments to respect the immunity of persons from coercion in matters of religious belief and practice, and the other enjoining governments 'to take account of the religious life of the people and show it favor, since the function of government is to make provision for the common welfare.'[19]

Whether or not unaided reason can conclude on the basis of a valid argument that God exists—indeed, even if it turns out that God does not exist—there is an important sense in which religion is a basic human good. Agnostics and even atheists can easily grasp the intelligible point of considering whether or not there is some ultimate, more-than-human source of meaning and value, of inquiring as best one can into the truth of the matter, and of ordering one's life on the basis of a reasonable judgment. As Finnis explains, 'if there is a transcendent origin of the universal order-of-things and of human freedom and reason, then one's life and actions are in fundamental disorder if they are not brought, as best one can, into some order of harmony with whatever can be known or surmised about that transcendent other and its lasting order.'[20] Religion is a basic reason for action, then, inasmuch as one has reason, even without appeal to ulterior reasons, to ascertain the truth about ultimate or divine realities and, if possible, to establish 'peace with God, or the gods, or some non-theistic but more-than-human source of meaning and value.'[21]

Let us turn now to the concept of the common good. According to Finnis, the central sense of the common good is as 'a set of conditions which enables the members of a community to attain for themselves reasonable objectives, or to realize reasonably for themselves the value(s), for the sake of which they have reason to collaborate with each other (positively and/or negatively) in a community.'[22] As he observes, however, this sense of common good is related to two other senses: (1) there is a common good inasmuch as the basic goods are goods for every member of the community and, indeed, for all human beings; and (2) each of the basic goods can be participated in by innumerable persons in innumerable ways.

As a common good in both of these senses, religion, like all the other basic goods, is an aspect of the common good in Finnis's central sense. People have reason to cooperate with each other in their efforts to understand religious truth and order their lives in accordance with it. Obviously, religion is the central common good of religious communities. While religious communities enable their members to realize other goods, e.g., friendship, knowledge, aesthetic appreciation and play, these communities are organized precisely for the sake of religion. Of course, these points establish nothing more than that religion is a reason for common or cooperative action. Even if religion cannot be considered 'private' in the extreme sense that would make nonsense of common worship and organized (or even disorganized) churches and religious orders, it may nevertheless be 'private' precisely in the sense that it is not a reason for political action.

Do people ever have reason to make political judgments and support or enact public policies based on their grasp of the value of religion? Does concern for the good of religion give people reason to collaborate (positively and/or negatively) in the political community?

In positive collaboration, the collaborators work together on a common project. In negative collaboration, they collaborate precisely by taking care not to interfere with one another. I submit that the good of religion gives people reason to collaborate both positively and negatively in the political community. A concern for religion, that is to say, gives people reason to support and enact certain public policies that they would have less or no reason to support or enact were it not for the value of religion.

It is the value of religion, for example, that grounds the right to religious liberty and the corresponding duty of government not only to refrain from coercing people on the basis of theological objections to their religious beliefs and practices but also to protect individuals and religious communities from others who would coerce them on the basis of such objections. The point comes more sharply into focus when we consider that even where a proposal for governmental suppression of a religious practice is not grounded (at least not exclusively) in a theological objection to the practice—I have in mind here everything from a proposal to suppress the use of drugs even as part of a bona fide religious ritual to a proposal to suppress bona fide rituals involving human sacrifice—the good of religion provides a reason for government not to suppress the practice. I hasten to add that the reason may well be defeated. Clearly there are conclusive reasons to prevent human sacrifice, for example, and perhaps even to prohibit the smoking of peyote even at the cost of impeding people's sincere religious practice. Where there are not conclusive reasons to suppress a practice, however, the good of religion provides a compelling reason to grant exceptions to general laws whose application forbids that practice in cases where the practice is important to the religious lives of some citizens.[23]

Political morality requires respect for religious liberty for reasons set forth eloquently in the first part of *Dignitatis Humanae*. The appropriation of religious truth and the general religious well-being of men and women is impeded rather than advanced by attempts to coerce religious belief and practice. Coercion is self-defeating, and usually counterproductive, even when it is exercised on behalf of the Church in which the fullness of religious truth subsists:[24] 'For, of its very nature, the exercise of religion consists before all else in those internal, voluntary, and free acts whereby man sets the course of his life directly toward God. No merely human power can either command or prohibit acts of this kind'.[25]

It is precisely at this point, however, that the Declaration reminds its readers that religion is not a purely private matter, that religion indeed provides a reason for collaboration: 'However, the social nature of man itself requires that he should give external expression to his internal acts of religion; that he should participate with others in matters religious; that he should profess his religion in the community.'[26] And only an instant later the Declaration unambiguously affirms the status of religion as a reason for positive collaboration in the political community:

There is a further consideration. The religious acts whereby men, in private and in public and out of a sense of personal conviction direct their lives to God transcend by their very nature the order of terrestrial and temporal affairs. Government, therefore, ought indeed to take into account of the religious life of the people and show it favor, since the function of government is to make provision for the common welfare.[27]

Just as the common good of religion provides a reason for negative collaboration in the political community in the form of governmental respect for (and protection of) religious liberty, it provides a reason for positive governmental action to encourage religious reflection, faith and practice. Of course, norms of political morality, especially the norm requiring respect and protection for religious liberty, limit the means by which government may legitimately act for the sake of the range of ends that constitute the basic reasons for political action.

Because prudential concerns of various sorts and other countervailing reasons will often militate against particular policies for promoting religion, the norm of political morality enjoining government to 'show favor' to the religious life of the people is not an especially stringent one. By contrast, the norm requiring government to respect and protect religious freedom is quite stringent. Nevertheless, where there are undefeated reasons for government to support and encourage religion, such support and encouragement is for the common good.

There are many ways in which government can serve the common good by acting for the sake of religion. An obvious way is by collaborating (both positively and negatively) with religious schools. At the same time, government sponsored schools can help children to develop rich spiritual lives by, for example, cooperating with parents and religious leaders to provide opportunities for children to practice their religions and receive religious instruction as parts of the regular school week.

Outside the area of education, government can encourage and support religious broadcasting, especially the sort of broadcasting that fosters inter-faith understanding. It can, as our government does, grant tax exemptions to religious organizations and permit contributors to those organizations to deduct their contributions. Moreover, government can involve responsible religious leaders and their organizations in public policy deliberations and employ them in social services roles without requiring them to compromise their moral and religious scruples. And for the sake of people's spiritual lives, among other goods, it can carefully refrain from taking over social welfare functions that are better served in particular communities by religious institutions, inter-denominational and non-denominational charities, families and other non-governmental providers.

Government can and should concern itself (acting again both positively and negatively) with the health and well-being of various communities of faith, just as it should concern itself with the well-being of families and other subsidiary communities, especially when these communities are threatened, as many religious people believe they are today, by powerful secularizing forces that would employ the principal institutions of cultural transmission to spread a pseudo-gospel of materialism and self-indulgence.

NOTES

1 Readers who are familiar with the natural law theory of practical reasoning and morality that I have set forth and defended in earlier chapters may move forward to section II of this chapter.

2 If it *destroyed* one's reason to do X, then a decision to do X despite the moral norm against doing it would be not merely unreasonable but irrational and, therefore, in a certain sense, unintelligible.

3 For a careful explanation of how choices between rationally grounded possibilities can be rationally underdetermined see Joseph Raz, *The Morality of Freedom* (Oxford: Clarendon Press, 1986), 388–9.

4 Even non-moral reasons for action are subject, however, to moral norms.

5 In Hume's famous statement, 'reason is, and ought only to be, the slave of the passions, and can never pretend to any office, other than to serve and obey them.' *A Treatise of Human Nature*, kb. 2, pt. 3, s. III. Hume's thinking here is fully in line with his great predecessor, Thomas Hobbes, who said that 'the Thoughts, are to the Desires as Scouts and Spies to range abroad, and find the way to things desired.' *Leviathan*, pt. 1, ch. 8.

6 I have explicated and defended the claim that the practical intellect can grasp such ends or purposes in 'Recent Criticism of Natural Law Theory,' *University of Chicago Law Review*, 55 (1988), 1371–1429, reprinted herein as Chapter 2.

7 See *Summa Theologiae*, 1–2, q. 94, a. 2.

8 As the fruit of intellectual acts made possible by reflection on data, basic reasons for action are not mere intuitions or innate ideas. Nor does the truth of our knowledge of basic reasons for action consist in their 'conformity to practical reason's own inner requirements, i.e., to itself or its directive structure.' (Brian V. Johnstone among others, has mistakenly attributed this latter position to Germain Grisez. See Johnstone, 'The Structures of Practical Reason: Traditional Theories and Contemporary Questions,' *Thomist*, 50 (1986), 417–466. For Grisez's reply rejecting this view and criticizing Johnstone's claim that it is implied by Grisez's theory of practical reasoning see 'The Structures of Practical Reason: Some Comments and Clarifications,' *Thomist*, 52 (1988), 269–291.) Our knowledge of basic reasons for action has its truth, rather, in the adequation of those reasons to possible fulfillment that can be realized through human action. See my 'Natural Law and Human Nature,' in Robert P. George, ed., *Natural Law Theory* (Oxford: Clarendon Press, 1991), reprinted herein as Chapter 3. Of course, our knowledge of the possibilities of such fulfillment will depend, in any particular circumstances, on a measure of theoretical knowledge including a knowledge of empirical possibilities and environmental con-

straints. To hold that the basic reasons for action, as self-evident first principles of practical reasoning, are not inferred from prior theoretical principles is by no means to imply, then, that there is a 'wall of separation' between practical and theoretical reasoning, *pace* Henry Veatch, 'Natural Law and the Is–Ought Question,' *Catholic Lawyer*, 26 (1981), 251–265, or that knowledge of the world is irrelevant to practical thinking, *pace* Ralph McInerny, *Ethica Thomistica* (Washington, DC: The Catholic University of America Press, 1982), 54–5.

9 John Finnis, *Natural Law and Natural Rights* (Oxford: Clarendon Press, 1980), 86–90.

10 In Ronald Dworkin's equality-based liberal conception of justice, for example, 'government must be neutral on what might be called the question of the good life.' See *A Matter of Principle* (Cambridge, Mass.: Harvard University Press, 1985), 191. I have criticized Dworkin's liberalism in 'Individual Rights, Collective Interests, Public Law, and American Politics,' *Law and Philosophy*, 8 (1989), 245–261, and in *Making Men Moral: Civil Liberties and Public Morality* (Princeton, NJ: Princeton University Press, 1993).

11 Germain Grisez and Joseph M. Boyle, Jr., *Life and Death With Liberty and Justice* (Notre Dame, Ind.: University of Notre Dame Press, 1979), 36 (emphasis on the original). The authors no longer hold strictly to the theory of political morality that they defended in this book. See Germain Grisez, Joseph Boyle and John Finnis, 'Practical Principles, Moral Truth, and Ultimate Ends,' *The American Journal of Jurisprudence*, 32 (1987), 99–151, 150. Their revised position is closer to the view that has been defended in various places by John Finnis and myself, though differences probably remain.

12 Grisez and Boyle, *Life and Death*, 37 (emphasis on the original).

13 Ibid., 58.

14 Ibid., 450.

15 Ibid., 456.

16 For a compelling argument that desire-satisfaction is not intrinsically valuable and therefore ought not to be confused with human goods that provide reasons for action, see Raz, *The Morality of Freedom*, 140–5.

17 Established churches were still in existence in some states more than forty years after the ratification of the First Amendment. For an account of these establishments see generally Gerard V. Bradley, *Church–State Relationships in America* (NY: Greenwood Press, 1987). For the argument that a central purpose of the Establishment Clause was the protection of state establishments, see William C. Porth and Robert P. George, 'Trimming the Ivy: A Bicentennial Re-Examination of the Establishment Clause,' *West Virginia Law Review*, 90 (1987), 109–170.

18 For a devastating critique of 'strict separationism' see Bradley, *Church–State Relationships*, especially chs. 1 and 7.

19 *Dignitatis Humanae*, 3.

20 Finnis, *Natural Law*, 155.

21 Grisez, Boyle and Finnis, 'Practical Principles,' 108.

22 Finnis, *Natural Law*, 155.

23 I offer no opinion here as to whether judicially enforceable constitutional provisions ought to require such exceptions. Nor do I take a position on whether the 'free exercise' clause of the First Amendment of the Constitution of the United States requires such exceptions absent a 'compelling state interest' in enforcing general laws that happen to conflict with conscientious religious belief or practice. As to the latter question, the Supreme Court of the

United States has held that such exceptions are not required. See *Employment Division, Department of Human Resources of Oregon, et al.* v. *Smith et al.*, Slip Opinion No. 88–1213. Decided April 17, 1990.

24 *Dignitatis Humanae*, 1 makes it plain that the *Declaration on Religious Liberty* in no way alters Catholic teaching that the 'one true religion subsists in the catholic and apostolic Church, to which the Lord Jesus committed the duty of spreading it abroad among all men.'

25 *Dignitatis Humanae*, 3.

26 Ibid.

27 Ibid.

8

Marriage and the Liberal Imagination[1]

In an article marked by the intelligence and fair-mindedness for which his work is widely—and rightly—admired, Stephen Macedo has argued against the view that sodomy, including homosexual sodomy, is intrinsically non-marital[2] and immoral. His goal is to show that natural law theorists have no sound argument for drawing moral distinctions[3]—which would, in turn, provide a basis for legal distinctions (particularly in the area of marriage)—between the sodomitical acts of 'devoted, loving, committed homosexual partners'[4] and the acts of genital union of men and women in marriage. We propose in this response to defend our view against Macedo's criticisms.

We heartily commend Macedo's efforts to understand and accurately represent the view of contemporary natural law theorists. Nevertheless, we are not entirely happy with his formulations of the natural law position regarding sexual morality. Neither Germain Grisez, nor John Finnis, nor either of us perceives the central moral wrongness of sodomitical and other non-marital sex acts as consisting in their being 'distractions from' genuine human goods. A more adequate, though unavoidably more complex, formulation of our position is the following:

(1) Marriage, considered not as a mere legal convention, but, rather, as a two-in-one-flesh communion of persons that is consummated and actualized by sexual acts of the reproductive type,[5] is an intrinsic (or, in our parlance, 'basic') human good; as such, marriage provides a non-instrumental reason for spouses,[6] whether or not they are capable of conceiving children in their acts of genital union, to perform such acts.

(2) In choosing to perform non-marital orgasmic acts, including sodomitical acts—irrespective of whether the persons performing such acts are of the same or opposite sexes (and even if those persons are validly married to each other)—persons necessarily treat their bodies and those of their sexual partners (if any) as means or instruments in ways that damage their personal (and interpersonal)[7] integrity;[8] thus, regard for the basic human good of integrity provides a conclusive moral reason not to engage in sodomitical and other non-marital sex acts.[9]

Macedo attacks the claims we have formulated in (1) above by offering to show that whatever values can possibly be realized in the acts of genital union of sterile spouses can equally be realized by those spouses—or similarly committed couples, whether of the same sex or opposite sexes—in oral or anal sex acts. His challenge to proponents of the natural law position is to identify a valid reason for sterile married couples to engage in acts of genital union that is not, at the same time, a valid reason for such couples (or others, married to each other or not, fertile or infertile, 'gay' or 'straight') to engage in oral or anal sex if they prefer or desire it.

In effect, Macedo denies that what we refer to as the 'reproductive-type acts' of spouses can have the special value and moral significance we ascribe to them. He attempts to show that we hold a 'double standard' in maintaining that: (a) sodomitical acts cannot be marital; and (b) penile–vaginal acts, even of spouses who know (or at least believe) themselves to be temporarily or permanently sterile, can be marital.[10]

Macedo also rejects the claims we have formulated in (2) above about the damage to personal (and interpersonal) integrity, and hence, the intrinsic immorality, of choosing to perform non-marital orgasmic acts. He affirms, and claims that many people will find it 'deeply unreasonable'[11] of us to deny, that pleasure (including sexual pleasure) is a good in itself and, as such, provides a basic reason for acting. Relatedly, he argues that there is something implausible about our claim that it is necessarily wrong for persons sometimes to use their bodies as mere instruments in the pursuit of pleasure and other extrinsic goals. He attempts to show, by way of a *reductio ad absurdum*, that the principle that we believe excludes sodomitical and other non-marital sex acts as immoral would, on our argument, also exclude as immoral such obviously innocent pleasures as chewing sugarless gum, 'which gives pleasure but has no nutritional value.'[12]

In Part I of this chapter, we rebut Macedo's charge of maintaining a double standard in holding that acts of genital union of sterile spouses can be marital and, as such, intrinsically good, while sodomitical acts are intrinsically non-marital. In Part II, we reply to his critique of our claim that non-marital sex acts damage integrity and are thus morally bad, and we suggest that, in rejecting central tenets of our view, he undermines his own apparent moral objections to promiscuity and to the sexual liberationist ideology that licenses it. And in Part III, we reply to some claims he makes regarding the political relevance of our view of marriage and sexual morality.

I. THE ABSENCE OF A DOUBLE STANDARD

Macedo asks: 'What is the point of sex in an infertile marriage?'[13] We answer that the point of sex in such a marriage is exactly the same as the point of sex in a fertile marriage, namely, the intrinsic good of marriage itself, which is consummated and actualized in marital acts.

But isn't procreation the point of sex in fertile marriages, at least according to the natural law tradition? It is true that St Augustine, among others, seems to have treated marriage as a purely instrumental good whose primary value has to do with procreation and the nurturing of new human beings.[14] Others, however, including Grisez, Finnis and ourselves, reject the instrumentalizing of marriage and marital intercourse to any extrinsic end, including the great good of having and rearing children.[15] In our view, children conceived in marital intercourse participate[16] in the good of their parents' marriage and are themselves non-instrumental aspects of its perfection; thus, spouses rightly hope for and welcome children, not as 'products' they 'make,' but, rather, as gifts, which, if all goes well, supervene on their acts of marital union.[17] The intrinsic intelligible point of the sexual intercourse of spouses, however, is, in our view, marriage itself, not procreation considered as an end to which their sexual union is the means.

Macedo's argument against our position presupposes that the point and value of sex can only be instrumental. Notice the difference between the answer we just gave and the answer Macedo himself gives to the question: 'What is the point of sex in an infertile marriage?'

Not procreation: the partners (let us assume) know that they are infertile. If they have sex, it is for pleasure and to express their love, or friendship, or some other shared good. It will be for precisely the same reasons that committed, loving gay couples have sex.[18]

He then asks, posing the question as a challenge to those who deny that sodomitical acts can be marital, 'Why are these good reasons for sterile or elderly married couples but not for gay and lesbian couples?'[19]

It is our position, however, that the reasons Macedo identifies are not adequate reasons for spouses—fertile or infertile—to engage in sexual relations. Nor is procreation an adequate reason for fertile spouses to have sex. We reject the proposition that sex can legitimately be instrumentalized, that is, treated as a mere means to any extrinsic end, including procreation.[20] Any such instrumentalization, we believe, damages the basic human good of integrity.[21] Again, the intrinsic point of sex in any marriage, fertile or not, is, in our view, the basic good of marriage itself, considered as a two-in-one-flesh communion of persons that is consummated and actualized by acts of the reproductive type. Such acts alone among sexual acts can be truly unitive, and thus marital; and marital acts, thus understood, have their intelligibility and value intrinsically, and not merely by virtue of their capacity to facilitate the realization of other goods.

Macedo's argument presupposes the truth of the very proposition we deny, whether we are arguing with people to our 'left,' such as Macedo and other liberals, or with strict Augustinians to our 'right': namely, that the value—the point—of marriage and marital intercourse can only be instrumental. Thus, we believe, Macedo's challenge begs the central question in dispute between those, like Macedo himself, who believe that justice requires the legal recognition of same-sex 'marriages,' and those of us who deny that such 'marriages' are morally possible. For however much we and other natural law theorists share the view that marital intercourse should be not only chaste, but also pleasurable and expressive of tender feelings—indeed, however much we believe that procreation, rightly desired,[22] is a great good and a perfection of marriage—we hold that marriage and marital intercourse are intrinsically good; and, again, we deny that sexual intercourse may legitimately be instrumentalized to any extrinsic end.

If our view is correct, then there is no real problem of 'homosexuality and the conservative mind,' at least insofar as natural law theorists of our stripe qualify as 'conservatives.' There is, rather, a problem of marriage and the liberal imagination. Criticisms of our view along the lines of those advanced by Macedo seem compelling to liberals because they cannot imagine that the point and value of sexual relations, inside or outside of marriage, can be anything other than instrumental. They presuppose that the sexual relationship of partners in marriage, if it has any point and value at all, must be instrumental either to pleasure, the expression of feelings, and the like on the one hand, or to procreation on the other.

This problem of imagination is analogous to the problem some people have—though Professor Macedo himself is most decidedly not among them—in affirming the intrinsic value of 'pure' scientific study and humanistic learning. Some people simply fail to 'see the point' of an education that is not, in some sense, instrumentalized to the extrinsic goals it helps enable students to achieve, such as marketable skills and enhanced social status. They cannot imagine why someone would pursue intellectual knowledge just for its own sake. (A doctoral student working on, say, *The Canterbury Tales* is bound at some point to be asked by an apparently baffled friend or relative: What is the point of studying Chaucer so that you can teach his writings to other people, who will be studying them in order to teach them to other people, and so forth?) In fact, skeptics about the intrinsic value of intellectual knowledge suppose that rational people who claim to be engaging in such an enterprise must, in reality, have at the back of their minds some extrinsic goal that renders intelligible their choice to spend time, money and effort on intellectual pursuits.

Of course, values such as knowledge and (if we are correct) marriage, in addition to their intrinsic worth, typically have significant instrumental value. Consequently, people who fail to grasp the intrinsic value of such basic human goods ordinarily do not judge them to be valueless. People who are skeptical of the intrinsic value of marriage need not, and typically do not, find the idea of marriage pointless and baffling. They cannot imagine, however, why spouses would perform marital acts, not (or not merely) as a means to, or of, procreation, pleasure, expressing feeling and the like, but above all, and decisively, for the sake of marriage itself, understood as actualized in such acts.

Intrinsic value cannot, strictly speaking, be demonstrated. Qua basic, the value of intrinsic goods cannot be derived through a middle term. Hence, if the intrinsic value of marriage, knowledge or any other basic human good is to be affirmed, it must be grasped in non-inferential acts of understanding.[23] Such acts require imaginative reflection on data provided by inclination and experience, as well as knowledge of empirical patterns, which underlie possibilities of action and achievement. The practical insight that marriage, for example, has its own intelligible point, and that marriage as a one-flesh communion of persons is consummated and actualized in the reproductive-type acts of spouses, cannot be attained by someone who has no idea of what these terms mean; nor can it be attained, except with strenuous efforts of imagination, by people who, due to personal or cultural circumstances, have little acquaintance with actual marriages thus understood. For this reason, we believe that whatever undermines the sound understanding and practice of marriage in a culture—including ideologies that are hostile to that understanding and practice—makes it difficult for people to grasp the intrinsic value of marriage and marital intercourse.

Although much in our culture has tended in recent years to undermine the institution of marriage and the moral understandings upon which it rests, longstanding features of our legal and religious traditions testify to the intrinsic value of marriage as a two-in-one-flesh communion. Consummation has traditionally (though, perhaps, not universally) been recognized by civil as well as religious authorities as an essential element of marriage.[24] 'Physical defects and incapacities which render a party unable to consummate the marriage, existing at the time of the marriage, and which are incurable are, under most statutes, grounds for annulment. . . .'[25] This requirement for the validity of a marriage, where in force, has never been treated as satisfied by an act of sodomy, no matter how pleasurable. Nothing less (or more) than an act of genital union consummates a marriage;[26] and such an act consummates even if it is not particularly pleasurable. Unless otherwise impeded, couples who know they are sterile can lawfully marry so long as they are capable of

consummating their marriage by performing such an act.[27] By the same
token, a marriage cannot be annulled for want of consummation on the
ground that one of the spouses turned out to be sterile. A marriage can,
however, be annulled on the ground that impotence (or some other condition) prevents the partners from consummating it.[28]

We believe that the law, in its rules regarding consummation, embodies
an important insight into the nature of marriage as a bodily—no less than
spiritual and emotional—union that is actualized in reproductive-type
acts. Liberals, however, may well consider the law simply to be misguided
on this point. Marriage, they may argue, is a one-flesh union only in a
metaphorical sense. It is, in reality, they may say, an emotional union that
is served in various ways by the mutually satisfying orgasmic acts of
spouses. Consummation, they may contend, ought not to be a requirement for the validity of marriage, or, if it is to be a requirement, it should
be considered to have been satisfied by a wider range of possible sexual
behaviors.

In the end, we think, one either understands that spousal genital intercourse has a special significance as instantiating a basic, non-instrumental
value, or something blocks that understanding and one does not perceive
correctly. For the most part, our liberal friends, such as Stephen Macedo,
honestly[29] do not see any special point or value in such intercourse.[30] For
them, spouses have no reason, apart from purely subjective preference,
ever to choose genital intercourse over oral or anal intercourse. And
because oral and anal intercourse are available to same-sex couples, such
couples have as much interest in marriage and as much right to marry as
couples of opposite sexes.

By contrast, many other people perceive quite easily the special value
and significance of the genital intercourse of spouses, and see that this
value and significance obtains even for spouses who are incapable of
having children, or any more children. They are therefore confident that
sodomitical acts cannot be marital (though they divide over the question
whether contracepted intercourse retains its marital quality).[31] Thus, as a
matter of common sense, they deny that marriage, as a moral reality, is
possible for couples of the same sex.

The central issue can be brought into focus by considering the case of an
elderly married couple who simply no longer experience pleasure in their
acts of genital intercourse. They are, however, still physiologically capable
of performing such acts and can do so without emotional repugnance. Is
there any point to their continuing to perform them? Can it be reasonable
for them to do so, at least occasionally, as a way of actualizing and
experiencing their marriage as a one-flesh union? We say yes. We suspect
that Macedo and most other liberals would say no. Our answer is valid if
marriage, and the genital acts that actualize it, are intrinsically good and,

thus, have an intelligible point even apart from their capacity to produce pleasure.

What we have said so far is sufficient to establish that there is no logical inconsistency in our approving of the marital acts of spouses, fertile or otherwise, while disapproving of their—or anyone else's—sodomitical or other non-marital sex acts. We maintain no 'double standard.' Still, a logically flawless position may nevertheless be false. The proposition that alligators are good opera singers suffers from no logical faults; it just happens to be false (or, at best, a metaphor). Someone who believed that proposition to be true in a literal sense would simply be wrong. By the same token, it is possible that we are simply wrong in believing that marriage, as a one-flesh communion of persons, is possible. Perhaps marriage, thus conceived, is an illusion or, at best, a mere metaphor to describe a relationship marked by more or less intense psychological closeness combined with sexual intimacy and certain sorts of commitments and obligations.

Do spousal acts of genital union have the intrinsic value we ascribe to them? If not, then such acts have no more value than other orgasm-inducing acts that spouses might perform on each other's bodies, should they mutually prefer to do so, and which may be performed by couples of the same sex as well as by those of opposite sexes. If marital acts, as we describe them, have no intrinsic value—if, that is to say, marriage as a one-flesh union is impossible for anyone—then the situation of sterile heterosexual couples is indistinguishable from that of similarly committed homosexual couples. Either couples of both sorts should refrain from sex altogether, or couples of either sort may more or less freely engage in any mutually agreeable sex acts of their choosing.

Macedo declares that 'the "one-flesh communion" of sterile couples would appear ... to be more a matter of appearance than reality.'[32] Because procreation is unattainable for sterile spouses, they cannot really be united biologically; 'their bodies,' he asserts, 'like those of homosexuals, can form no "single reproductive principle," no "real unity."'[33]

We disagree. When animals (including humans) mate, they are united biologically whether or not conception is possible. In mating, the male and female pair is, indeed, a 'single reproductive principle.' Reproduction is one act; yet the act is performed by the mated pair as an organic unit. So, as Grisez remarks:

Though a male and a female are complete individuals with respect to other functions—for example, nutrition, sensation, and locomotion—with respect to reproduction they are only potential parts of a mated pair, which is the complete organism capable of reproducing sexually. Even if the mated pair is sterile, intercourse, provided it is the reproductive behavior characteristic of the species, makes the copulating male and female one organism.[34]

Of course, non-human animals cannot mate for reasons and by choice, the way humans can.[35] And, as we see things, their mating cannot have the intrinsic value and moral significance of human mating. (Even animals that mate for life do not marry, at least under our conception of marriage.) Marriage is a 'reflexive' good; it includes the free choices of the parties' consent. And, as Grisez points out, marriage 'fulfills both biological and moral capacities by making two bodily and free persons into one . . . without in the least compromising their individuality.'[36]

Macedo's claims would be plausible, we think, only on an understanding of reproductive organs and their functioning that we find highly implausible. According to this understanding, which is implicit in his frequent references to sexual organs as 'equipment,' these organs cease being reproductive organs during times at which they are not effectively performing, or, in any event, are not capable of effectively performing, reproductive functions. At these times, a penis or a vagina is no more a reproductive organ than a finger, tongue, mouth or rectum. So, under this understanding, animals (including humans) performing during infertile periods the precise behaviors that constitute mating during fertile periods are not, in fact, mating.

In contrast, Finnis has argued that the inseminatory union of male with female genital organs, though it only occasionally results in procreation, is 'the behavior that unites biologically because it is the behavior which, as behavior, is suitable for generation.'[37] Macedo, in response, offers an analogy (borrowed from Andrew Koppelman): 'pointing a gun at someone and pulling the trigger is in general behavior suitable for murder, but not when the gun is unloaded.'[38]

This analogy would hold if, and only if, it were true that human (and other animal) acts of inseminatory union are in general behavior suitable for reproduction, but not when the non-behavioral conditions of reproduction do not obtain. But this proposition is not true. Animal (including human) intercourse, unlike pulling the trigger of an unloaded gun, is part of a complex biological function, namely, reproduction. Such intercourse constitutes reproductive functioning, even if the process of which it is a part is, due to non-behavioral factors, incomplete. This is why we easily recognize the mating of animals we know to be sterile as mating, and not as failed attempts to mate.[39]

The unloaded gun analogy breaks down further when we consider the specifically human acts we refer to as marital acts. The sexual organs of human beings are not instruments, or 'equipment,' which have their value and intelligibility as means of accomplishing ends extrinsic to them. Rather, sex organs are parts of the personal reality of the human being. Thus, when spouses unite genitally—when they mate—their biological unity is truly interpersonal. If, as we believe, this unity has intrinsic, and not merely instrumental, value, it provides the spouses with a non-instrumental reason for performing marital acts. Thus, the intelligibility of these acts in no way depends on the possibility of procreation.

Guns, unlike sexual organs, are not parts of the personal reality of human beings. The value of guns is purely instrumental. Their intelligibility depends entirely upon their utility in accomplishing the ends of those who own and use them (for example, the hit man, the soldier, the hunter, the gun collector). An unloaded gun is simply useless to, say, a hit man. It is pointless for him to take aim at an unsuspecting victim and pull the trigger. It simply does no good, even in the hit man's rather perverse sense of 'good.' As action, it is unintelligible. But if, as we believe, the genital union of spouses makes them truly one-flesh, then the marital acts of spouses, fertile or not, are perfectly intelligible. They are not pointless. On the contrary, qua unitive, they are intrinsically good.

The mating of spouses, then, is something altogether different from shooting a gun. Mating is mating, not because it is in fact reproductive (human mating usually is not reproductive), but precisely because it is, in Grisez's words, 'the reproductive behavior characteristic of the species,'[40] or, in Finnis's words, 'the behavior which, as behavior, is suitable for generation.'[41] Mating is fundamentally unlike shooting in that it is an irreducibly unitive activity; and its unitive significance obtains for the mated pair irrespective of the procreative potential of their particular acts of genital intercourse. And, inasmuch as the interpersonal unity achieved in the mating—the reproductive-type acts—of spouses is intrinsically good, spouses have a reason to mate quite irrespective of whether their mating will, or even can, be productive.

II. THE MORAL HARM OF NON-MARITAL SEX ACTS

We have argued that sodomy is intrinsically non-marital. Is it immoral? In our view, all non-marital sex suffers from at least one grave moral defect: Sex that is not for the intrinsic good of marriage itself—sex, that is to say, which is wholly instrumentalized to pleasure or some other goal—damages personal (and interpersonal) integrity by reducing persons' bodies to the status of means to extrinsic ends.

The body, as part of the personal reality of the human being, may not be treated as a mere instrument without damaging the integrity of the acting person as a dynamic unity of body, mind and spirit. To treat one's own body, or the body of another, as a pleasure-inducing machine, for example, or as a mere instrument of procreation, is to alienate one part of the self, namely, one's consciously experiencing (and desiring) self, from another, namely, one's bodily self. But these parts are, in truth, metaphysically inseparable parts of the person as whole. Their existential separation in acts that instrumentalize the body for the sake of extrinsic goals, such as producing experiences desired purely for the satisfaction of the conscious self, dis-integrates the acting person as such.

So, in our view, while sexual intercourse is valuable and morally good when it actualizes (and, thus, allows spouses to experience) the one-flesh communion of their marriage, sex that is wholly instrumentalized is intrinsically morally bad, even when the ultimate goals to which orgasmic activity is chosen as a means (for example, sharing a pleasurable experience, getting a good night's sleep, expressing tender feelings, generating feelings of closeness) are in themselves innocent and even desirable. This, we believe, is the idea Finnis had in mind when he provoked Macedo's vigorous objections by saying:

In reality, whatever the generous hopes and dreams and thoughts of giving with which some same-sex partners may surround their sexual acts, those acts cannot express or do more than is expressed or done if two strangers engage in such activity to give each other pleasure, or a prostitute pleasures a client to give him pleasure in return for money, or (say) a man masturbates to give himself pleasure and a fantasy of more human relationships after a grueling day on the assembly line.[42]

However harsh this judgment sounds, it is certainly true if, as we believe, the sexual acts of same-sex partners, unlike the reproductive-type acts of spouses (but like the sodomitical acts even of spouses), cannot be truly unitive and, thus, marital. Hence, the sexual acts of same-sex partners (and the non-marital acts of partners of opposite sexes—even if married to each other) cannot realize a truly common good, but can, at best, do no more than, as Finnis says, 'provide each partner with an individual gratification.'[43] And thus:

for want of a common good that could be actualized and experienced by and in this bodily union, that conduct involves the partners in treating their bodies as instruments to be used in the service of their consciously experiencing selves; their choice to engage in such conduct thus dis-integrates each of them precisely as acting persons.[44]

It is precisely in response to Finnis's claim that instrumentalized sex damages integrity that Macedo declares that 'many will find deeply unreasonable . . . the judgment that pleasure is not in and of itself a good.'[45] Drawing an analogy between sex and eating, he asks: 'Is eating for the sake of mere pleasure unnatural or irrational? Is it permissible to chew sugarless gum, which gives pleasure but has no nutritional value, . . . or is doing so the gastronomic equivalent of masturbation (assuming that we are not doing it to exercise the jaw or clean the teeth)?'[46]

However others may judge the matter, we certainly deny that pleasure is an intrinsic good. Pleasure can motivate people, but it does not provide a basic reason for acting. Pleasure motivates by appealing not to the practical intellect of the deliberating and choosing subject, but rather to some sentient part of the self. Thus, pleasure must be distinguished from basic human goods, such as knowledge and, as we argue, marriage, which provide rational (as well as emotional) motivation.[47]

Now, this is by no means to suggest that pleasure is bad. Rather, its value depends on the moral quality of the acts in which pleasure is sought and experienced. In morally good acts, pleasure is rightly sought as an experiential aspect of the perfection of persons' participation in the basic goods that provide reasons for their acts. Integrated with the good of marriage, for example, pleasure is rightly sought and welcomed as part of the perfection of marital intercourse (just as, in our view, procreation may be rightly desired). However, to simply instrumentalize intercourse to pleasure (or procreation) is to vitiate its marital quality and damage the integrity of the genital acts even of spouses.

The body is not rightly treated as a machine for having experiences; it is, rather, a part of the personal reality of the human being whose every act (including spiritual acts) is also a bodily act, and whose body, as an intrinsic (and not merely instrumental) part of the person, participates in his or her fulfillment. Among the fulfillments of persons is their integrity as unified actors. This integrity is no mere means of accomplishing ends extrinsic to itself; it is, rather, an end in itself, and, as such, provides a non-instrumental reason for action (and restraint). To be rationally concerned about, and to act to maintain, their personal integrity, people need no reason other than the basic good of personal integrity itself.

Thus, we believe that it is contrary to reason—bad and immoral—to sacrifice one's psychosomatic integrity, or to instrumentalize a part of oneself, for the sake of some desired experience, whether it is getting drunk, enjoying a psychedelic drug trip or having an orgasm. But what about eating just for the pleasure of it? What about chewing sugarless gum?

Grisez has observed that people regularly perform bodily acts without reducing their bodies to the status of mere means to extrinsic ends. In eating, for example, as in speaking, watching a film, playing a musical instrument or engaging in marital intercourse, 'the body functions as part of oneself, serving the whole and sharing in the resulting benefits.'[48] In masturbation and other non-marital sex acts, by contrast, 'one does not choose to act for a goal which fulfills oneself as a unified, bodily person. The only immediate goal is satisfaction for the conscious self; and so the body, not being part of the whole for whose sake the act is done, serves only as an extrinsic instrument.'[49]

As Macedo himself notes, the analogy between sex and eating becomes interesting only in a case in which one, say, eats purely for pleasure.[50] Ordinarily, if usually unreflectively, the pleasure of eating is integrated into people's larger worthwhile projects. In eating, people typically do not treat their bodies as mere machines for inducing pleasurable experiences for the satisfaction of their conscious selves. That is to say, people typically do not choose satisfaction of some want or desire merely as sentient beings, rather than as integrated persons. Thus, the fact that people may seek and obtain pleasure in eating does not render the act disintegrative.

The same is true of chewing gum. People ordinarily, if usually unreflectively, chew gum as part of larger projects, just as rocking in a chair, twirling a pencil or going for a walk are characteristically parts of larger projects (such as our project of trying to think through the argument we are presenting in these pages). People typically do not chew gum to 'pleasure themselves' in a manner akin to masturbation. The nature of the pleasure available in chewing gum or in eating offers people little in the way of sub-rational motivation to treat their bodies as mere instruments of their consciously experiencing selves, and, thus, to compromise their psychosomatic integrity. In this respect, the pleasure of chewing gum or eating is like the pleasure of rocking in a chair or taking a walk, and unlike the pleasure of having an orgasm or, we suppose, using hallucinogenic drugs.

Chewing gum, rocking in a chair and taking a walk are examples of 'innocent pleasures.' For most people these activities present no hazard to any aspect of the person's well-being. (Chewing or smoking tobacco, by contrast, presents a different sort of case, not because these activities are disintegrative, but rather because they may imperil physical health.) The important point is that in the activity of chewing gum, no existential separation of the bodily self and the consciously experiencing self is typically effected. In that activity, the body is not typically commandeered into the service of a project that is fully and accurately described (and, thus, morally specified) as producing pleasure, whether as an end in itself or as means to other ends.

The above argument shows, we think, that masturbation and other non-marital sex acts are not morally similar to eating or even to chewing sugarless gum. It does not, however, show that eating or chewing sugarless gum could never share the moral defect we claim is common to all such acts—hence, our use of the term 'typically' as a hedge. In the extreme case, someone could, we suppose, produce an ingestible product—a genetically re-engineered broccoli, perhaps—that could induce orgasms or pleasurable experiences of that order. Less dramatically, a person could, we imagine, pursue pleasure in eating or chewing gum in a way divorced from larger projects such that his activity could only accurately be described as 'pleasuring himself' in a way analogous to the masturbator or psychedelic drug-tripper. It is difficult to imagine what—short of hallucinogenic mushrooms or orgasm-inducing broccoli—would tempt a person to take such a turn, but anything, we suppose, is possible. In that case, we would say that eating and gum chewing damage personal integrity insofar as those acts effect an existential alienation of the body from the conscious self by simply using the body as an experience-inducing machine. Thus, such behavior should, for moral reasons, be avoided.

Our view about the disintegrative quality of non-marital sex tends to strike liberals as exceedingly odd. Something like our view, however, must be affirmed by anyone who supposes, as Macedo seems to, that there can be something morally wrong, and not merely imprudent, about some forms of consensual sex. 'Sexual liberationists' can afford casually to dismiss the idea that sex can damage integrity. They have no interest in developing a principled moral critique of consensual adultery, promiscuity, prostitution ('sex work'), bestiality and the like. Liberals who reject liberationism, however, had better take care before dismissing our view.

Our goal has been to identify a principle that makes sex something other than an instrumentalization of the body and disintegration of the bodily self. Macedo himself, it is clear, has some sympathy with this goal. 'Liberationists,' however, will rightly challenge him to produce a principled moral critique of promiscuity that really distinguishes non-promiscuous homosexual relations from the promiscuous lifestyles they prefer, which, they will say, 'intrinsically realize' goods such as play, bonhomie, friendliness to strangers and, to be sure, 'pleasure.' We do not believe that Macedo will be able to meet this challenge.

III. THE POLITICAL RELEVANCE OF OUR VIEW

Now, suppose that our view of marriage and sexual morality (or something quite like our view) is morally correct. Macedo argues that it is, nevertheless, politically irrelevant. Noting that Grisez and Finnis, like the two of us, believe that contracepted sex, no less than sodomitical acts, is non-marital and morally bad, he says:

To the extent that the state has an interest in discouraging homosexuality on . . . natural law grounds, it has an equal interest in acting against all extramarital and contracepted sex. To the extent that the state exhibits no interest in discouraging the use of contraceptives, it has evidently rejected new natural law reasoning and must find some other grounds to justify discouraging homosexuality.[51]

Acknowledging that our view does not 'single out homosexuality as singularly perverse and "unnatural,"'[52] he argues that its very 'fair-mindedness and broad sweep' in rejecting all non-marital sex acts, even those engaged in by spouses, 'may also make [it] politically irrelevant. . . . This natural law philosophy cannot be of help to any but those few Americans who accept its extremely broad strictures.'[53]

It is true that most Americans do not agree with us about the immorality of contraception, at least in the case of contraception within marriage; it is also true, however, that most Americans do not agree with Macedo about the moral possibility of same-sex 'marriage.' We suspect that most Americans—or, at the very least, a minority substantial enough to be politically salient—hold a basic view of sexual morality that resembles ours in understanding marriage to be a one-flesh communion and, precisely as such, the principle of rectitude in sexual behavior. If many, or even most, of these Americans differ with us on contraception (or divorce, though divorce raises issues that are much more complicated), their difference does not go to the root. They simply disagree with our claim that contraception vitiates the marital quality of spousal genital acts.[54] Although their view is opposed to ours in this respect, and though, we suppose, it rests on a certain ('physicalist') misunderstanding of what constitutes a reproductive-type act, it is defended by responsible people who affirm the fundaments of our understanding of marriage and sexual morality.[55] It is on these fundaments that we, and they, hold that sodomitical acts cannot consummate and actualize marriage.

Moreover, even those who share our views about contraception need not hold, as Macedo thinks we must, that the state has an 'equal interest in acting against all extramarital and contracepted sex.'[56] A huge variety of prudential considerations enter into the questions of whether and how the state should act against any immoral conduct, especially conduct that typically involves little or no injustice.[57] Such considerations might militate strongly in favor of a legal immunity for married couples to use contraceptives. On this basis, someone opposed to contraception on moral grounds might nevertheless support the decision of the Supreme Court in *Griswold* v. *Connecticut*.[58] Indeed, given the stated ground of that decision, one might even affirm the Court's reasoning, namely, the 'perfectionist'[59] argument that the centrality of confidentiality and spatial privacy to marital friendship require legal immunity for married couples from investigation and prosecution for using contraception without regard to the question of whether contracepting is morally good or bad.[60] People can, in other words, consistently hold that contraception is bad for marriage but that laws against contraception are worse. At the same time, they can hold (though they need not) that the state should ban the distribution of contraceptives to unmarried people and strongly discourage, if not forbid, extra-marital sex. Certainly, at a minimum, they can hold that the state ought not to institutionalize (or otherwise support or promote) same-sex or other intrinsically non-marital sexual relationships or recognize 'marriages' between people of the same sex or others who cannot consummate marriage as a one-flesh communion.[61]

NOTES

1 The author would like to thank his co-author Gerard V. Bradley, for permission to reprint this essay.

2 We hold that marriage, as a one-flesh communion of persons, is intrinsically, and not merely instrumentally, good. In marital acts—that is, sexual intercourse that consummates and actualizes marriage by uniting the spouses in a reproductive-type act, thus making them, in no merely figurative sense, two-in-one-flesh—spouses participate in this intrinsic goodness. Because the biological reality of human beings is 'part of, not merely an instrument of,' their personal reality,' the biological union of spouses in marital acts constitutes a truly interpersonal communion. John Finnis, 'Law, Morality, and "Sexual Orientation,"' *Notre Dame Law Review*, 69 (1994), 1049, 1066. Sodomitical acts, by contrast, lack this unitive capacity, and thus cannot actualize marriage. Such acts are, therefore, non-marital even when performed by persons who are married to each other. It is precisely in this sense that sodomy is intrinsically non-marital.

3 Stephen Macedo, 'Homosexuality and the Conservative Mind,' *Georgetown Law Journal*, 84 (1995), 261, 264.

4 Ibid. at 279.

5 The concept of a reproductive-type act is biological-functional. It refers to the species-specific pattern of behavior suited to the reproductive function. Although that function is completed only if certain non-behavioral conditions also obtain, the pattern of behavior remains the same even if those conditions do not obtain. The reproductive-type acts of humans and other mammals are acts of inseminatory union of male with female genital organs. The freely chosen reproductive-type acts of spouses are marital in that they actualize and enable the spouses to experience their interpersonal communion, of which such acts are the biological matrix. It is important to see that, though all marital acts are reproductive in type, not all reproductive-type acts are marital. Acts of fornication and adultery can be reproductive in type, though they are intrinsically non-marital. And even the reproductive-type acts of spouses lose their marital quality when they are wholly instrumentalized to ends extrinsic to marriage. The marital quality of spousal intercourse is not vitiated, however, by the fact that reproduction is impossible for all married couples most of the time—due to the periodic infertility of the female spouse, even during her fertile years, and eventually the permanent loss of fertility with age—and for some married couples all of the time—due to some defect in the functioning of reproductive organs.

6 'Marriage,' 'reproductive-type acts,' and 'spouses' are thus so interdefined that (as would have gone without saying down to yesterday) marriage is inherently

heterosexual and a man's spouse is necessarily a woman (and vice versa)—and the terms are used in this way throughout our response. This terminology begs no questions, because we confront and respond openly, and with reasons, to all the relevant questions in appropriate terminology.

7 We believe that acts that damage personal integrity also damage interpersonal integrity in two ways: first, they unavoidably damage the ability of persons performing them to relate properly to others as bodily persons; second, in acts in which two or more persons cooperate in immorality, they also damage the integrity of their specific relationship, which, like every friendship, is perfected precisely by cooperation in good and upright activities.

8 Although we do not make the argument here, we follow Grisez in holding that non-marital sex acts also damage the capacity of persons for bodily self-giving in marriage. Also, note that we use the term 'integrity' for what Grisez refers to as 'self-integration.'

9 Paul Gilbert has observed that 'few philosophers have . . . developed an ethic of sexuality as something other than an appetite requiring regulation.' Paul Gilbert, 'Sexual Morality,' in *The Oxford Companion to Philosophy*, Ted Honderich, ed. (NY: Oxford University Press, 1995). As this formulation of our position makes clear, those of us associated with what Macedo calls 'the new natural law theory' are among the few.

10 See Macedo, 'Homosexuality,' 278–81. It is important to notice that nothing in our claim that sodomitical acts are intrinsically non-marital, or in Macedo's strategy for rebutting our claim, turns on whether the acts in question are performed by persons of the same sex or of opposite sexes. We do not hold—indeed, we deny—that oral or anal sex acts can consummate and actualize heterosexual, but not homosexual, marriages. Macedo does not argue that such acts can consummate and actualize homosexual, but not heterosexual, marriages. We maintain that only the reproductive-type acts of spouses can be marital. Macedo denies that acts of penile–vaginal intercourse between spouses that cannot be reproductive—or, at least, acts that are known (or thought) by them to be incapable of being reproductive—can have value and significance that is lacking in other orgasmic sexual acts that they (or persons in similar relationships of commitment) might perform for the sake of pleasure, feelings of closeness or some other end or combination of ends. See ibid.

11 Ibid., 282.

12 Ibid.

13 Ibid., 278.

14 See, e.g., St Augustine, *De bono coniugali* (9.9).

15 See, e.g., Germain Grisez, 'The Christian Family as Fulfillment of Sacramental Marriage,' Paper Delivered to the Society of Christian Ethics Annual Conference (Sept. 9, 1995) (unpublished manuscript, on file with *The Georgetown Law Journal*).

16 On the idea of basic goods as 'participated in' by persons, see John Finnis, *Natural Law and Natural Rights* (NY: Oxford University Press, 1980), 64. On the participation of children in their parents' marriage, see Grisez, 'Christian Family,' 1–8. What Grisez says in these pages pertains to marriage as a natural (and basic) human good, and not exclusively to sacramental marriage as fulfilled by the Christian family. His theological treatment of marriage as a sacrament follows. Ibid., 8–10.

17 This understanding of children as gifts to be accepted and valued for their own sake—rather than as objects that may be willed and brought into being for

one's own purposes—obviously coheres well with certain theistic metaphysical views, including Jewish and Christian views. It can, however, also be accommodated by Buddhist and certain other nontheistic views. We believe that some understanding along these lines of the moral relationship of parents to the children they may conceive is essential to the rational affirmation of the dignity of children as persons: i.e., as ends in themselves, and not mere means of satisfying desires of their parents; as subjects of justice (including fundamental and inviolable human rights), rather than objects of will. Alternative understandings, we believe, run into severe difficulties in explaining why children may not properly be understood—and rightly treated—as the property of their parents.

    Liberals are often puzzled by the tendency of natural law theorists—'new' as well as old—to object on moral grounds to the production of human beings by *in vitro* fertilization. After all, the natural law tradition strongly affirms the goodness of transmitting life to new persons. Why, then, should couples who are incapable of begetting children in acts of marital intercourse not resort to *in vitro* processes in order to become parents? The short answer is that the manufacturing of children is inconsistent with respect for their basic equality and human dignity. For a careful articulation and defense of this position, see 'In Vitro Fertilization and Public Policy, Evidence Submitted to the Government Committee of Inquiry into Human Fertilization and Embryology by the Catholic Bishops Joint Committee on Bio-Ethical Issues, on Behalf of the Catholic Bishops of Great Britain,' (May 1983).

18 Macedo, 'Homosexuality,' 278.

19 Ibid.

20 Suppose that King Henry VIII engages in sexual intercourse with a wife—one whom he has for all other intents and purposes cast aside—precisely and solely for the sake of producing an heir. (He would, let us further suppose, just as soon produce that heir by *in vitro* means, were they available to him.) Do Henry and his wife perform a marital act? Not in our view. Although their act of sexual intercourse occurs in the context of marriage, and is, indeed, reproductive in type (and perhaps even in result), its marital quality is vitiated precisely by its instrumentalization to what is for him an extrinsic end (i.e., producing an heir).

    The situation is different, of course, if Henry loves his wife and hopes for an heir. In this case, their marital intercourse is valued for its own sake and as a way of attaining another good. Moreover, in hoping that their marital act will be fruitful, Henry and his wife are not seeking a child as a product. See *infra*, n. 21.

21 This is not to suggest that other goals may not rightly be sought and realized in and through marital intercourse. Marriage, like other basic human goods, has important instrumental as well as intrinsic value. Goals compatible with marital love—playfulness, cheer ups, distractions from grief, etc.—may properly be integrated with the intrinsic good of marital union without reducing that basic good to the status of a mere means.

22 That is, desired under a description that does not reduce the child to the status of a product to be brought into existence at its parents' will and for their ends, but rather treats him or her as a person—possessing full human dignity—which the spouses are eager to welcome (and take responsibility for) as a perfective participant in the community established by their marriage (i.e., their family). (It is in this sense that we speak of children as 'gifts' that

'supervene' on marital acts.) This is not to suggest that there is anything wrong with spouses engaging in marital intercourse because they 'want' a child. It is merely to indicate the description under which the 'wanting' of the child is consistent with his or her dignity as a person, and to highlight our view that the marital significance of properly motivated spousal intercourse obtains whether or not conception is hoped for, results, or is even possible. Perhaps we should also record here our view that the intrinsic worth and dignity of a child is in no way diminished by any moral defect in the act that brings that child into existence.

23 Finnis, *Natural Law*, 34.

24 Ga. CODE ANN. § 19–2–1 (1991), states the prerequisites to a valid marriage as '(1) Parties able to contract; (2) An actual contract; and (3) Consummation according to law.' On the legal duty of husband and wife to consummate marriage by penile–vaginal intercourse in English law, see Tony Honore, *Sex Law* (London: Duckworth, 1978), 16–18. Homer H. Clark, Jr. claims that the 'conventional view' in the United States is that a 'ceremonial' (i.e., non-common law) marriage 'is valid notwithstanding that it is not consummated.' Homer H. Clark, Jr., *The Law of Domestic Relations in the United States* (St Paul, Minn.: West Publishing Co., 2nd ed. 1988), 39. However that may be, Clark concedes that the rule continues to be otherwise in various jurisdictions in which 'an unconsummated ceremonial marriage is "little more than an engagement to marry," ' ibid. (quoting *Akrep* v. *Akrep*, 63 A.2d 253 (NJ, 1949)). Clark nowhere suggests that 'consummation' refers to anything other than the (initial) coition of spouses, defined as 'physical union of male and female genitalia . . . leading to the ejaculation of semen from the penis into the female reproductive tract,' *Webster's New Collegiate Dictionary* (Springfield, Mass.: G. and C. Merriam Co., 1977). Clark himself professes to find the requirement of physical consummation, in effect, to be an 'impenetrable mystery.' See Clark, *Domestic Relations*, 39, n. 66. From the viewpoint of liberal morality, the requirement is indeed mysterious. But the liberal understanding of marriage and sexual morality, as we have labored to show, is hardly the sole possibility. Nor is it the understanding embedded in the English or American law of marriage. An alternative moral understanding along the lines of the one we defend makes perfect sense of the consummation requirement as well as certain other features of marriage law as it has traditionally stood (e.g., monogamy).

25 4 Am. Jur. 2D Annulment of Marriage § 30 (1962) (footnote omitted); see also Honore, *Sex Law*, 21.

26 See 4 Am. Jur. 2D Annulment of Marriage § 32 (1962) ('Capacity for imperfect or unnatural copulation is not enough; sexual intercourse in the proper meaning of the term is ordinarily [sic] and complete intercourse.'); see also Honore, *Sex Law*, 18.

27 See 4 Am. Jur. 2D Annulment of Marriage § 30 (1962) ('Barrenness or inability to beget or bear children, if associated with complete power of copulation, is . . . not a ground for annulling a marriage.'); see also Honore, *Sex Law*, 18. Honore supposes that 'from this it follows, if the law is to be consistent, that a marriage can be consummated even if husband or wife use contraceptives,' ibid. As a logical or philosophical matter, however, this does not in fact follow. There is no inconsistency in holding both: (a) that sterile acts of genital union of spouses can be marital; and (b) that the choice to contracept vitiates the marital quality of spousal intercourse. See *infra*, n. 30. In any event, as Honore points out, English law since 1948 as a matter of fact treats contracepted

intercourse—so long as it is 'ordinary and complete' penile–vaginal intercourse—as sufficient to consummate marriage. Honore, *Sex Law*, 18. English
law here has been made consistent with the teaching of the Church of England,
which reversed its position on the immorality of contraception earlier in this
century.

28 'The legal definition of impotency within the meaning of annulment statutes
implies some malformation or organic defect existing at the time of marriage,
by reason of which there cannot be natural and perfect coition—vera copula—
between the parties,' 4 Am. Jur. 2D Annulment of Marriage § 32 (1962) (footnote omitted). 'Vera copula' plainly refers to what we have called acts of the
reproductive type, whether or not they are, or can be, reproductive in fact. See
JG v. *HG*, 33 Md. 401 (1870) ('The rudimentary condition of [the appellee's]
sexual organs, and their imperfect development, not only rendered conception
impossible, but there was on her part an incapacity for vera copula. That is to
say, she was not capable of the act of generation in its natural and ordinary
meaning, but only of incipient and imperfect coition.'); see also Honore, *Sex
Law*, 17–18.

29 This is not to say that the culture in which such failures of understanding
can honestly occur can come into being without culpable and bad faith
rationalizations of morally corrupt dispositions and choices. In this respect, as
in most others, there is nothing special about sexual immorality or its cultural
impact.

30 The failure of imagination, which, we believe, obscures for many people the
intrinsic value of marriage and marital acts, is rooted in certain moral and
metaphysical beliefs they have come to hold about the human person and
human good(s) more generally. People who reject traditional standards of
sexual morality tend to understand human beings dualistically, that is, as non-
bodily persons who inhabit non-personal bodies. This dualism subserves a
psychologistic conception of value that effaces the distinction (which is strictly
maintained in the natural law tradition) between human goods on the one
hand, and good human feelings on the other. On this distinction and its
importance for practical philosophy, see generally John Finnis, *Fundamentals of
Ethics* (Washington, DC: Georgetown University Press, 1983); 'Human
Flourishing as a Criterion of Morality: A Critique of Perry's Naturalism,'
Tulane Law Review, 63 (1989), 1455–1474, reprinted herein as Chapter 14. On
person–body dualism and some of its implications for normative ethics, see
David Braine, *The Human Person: Animal and Spirit* (Notre Dame, Ind.: Univer-
sity of Notre Dame Press, 1992); John Finnis et al., *Nuclear Deterrence, Morality,
and Realism* (NY: Oxford University Press, 1987), 304–9; Robert P. George, 'Life
as an Evil; Death as a Good: A Critique of Callahan's Inversion,' in *Set No
Limits: A Rebuttal to Daniel Callahan's Proposal to Limit Health Care to the Elderly*,
Robert L. Barry and Gerard V. Bradley, eds. (Urbana, Ill.: University of Illinois
Press, 1991), 15 [hereinafter George, 'Life as an Evil']; Patrick Lee, 'Human
Beings Are Animals,' in *Natural Law and Moral Inquiry: Ethics, Metaphysics, and
Politics in the Work of Germain Grisez*, Robert P. George, ed. (Washington, DC:
Georgetown University Press, 1998).

31 Those who argue that contraception vitiates the marital quality of spousal
genital acts have the stronger case. Nobody, we believe, performs a reproductive-type act when he or she deliberately thwarts that act's reproductive potential. Many thoughtful scholars have, however, taken an opposing view,
arguing that particular contracepted acts within marriage remain marital so

long as the marriage as a whole is open to children. See generally John T. Noonan, Jr., *Contraception: A History of Its Treatment by the Catholic Theologians and Canonists* (Cambridge, Mass.: Belknap Press of Harvard University Press, 1965); James T. Burtchaell, *The Giving and Taking of Life* (Notre Dame, Ind.: University of Notre Dame Press, 1989); David Novak, 'Religious Communities, Secular Society, and Sexuality: One Jewish View, Paper Presented at Brown University' (Apr. 1995) (unpublished manuscript, on file with author).

32 Macedo, 'Homosexuality,' 279.

33 Ibid., 278. Macedo goes so far as to argue that even fertile couples who conceive a child in sexual intercourse do not really unite biologically, because, in his view, 'penises and vaginas do not unite biologically, sperm and eggs do.' Ibid. at 280. Sperm and eggs, however, are parts of the biological reality of persons, just as penises and vaginas are. Neither sperm nor eggs, neither penises nor vaginas, are properly conceived as non-personal 'equipment' that is 'used' by persons, considered as standing over and apart from these and other aspects of their biological (i.e., bodily) reality. So, in our view, persons—males and females—who unite genitally in marital acts really do unite biologically (and, because—as Finnis has observed (see Finnis, *supra*, n. 1)—the biological reality of human beings is part of their personal reality, they unite interpersonally), whether or not, as a result, egg and sperm unite in the conception of a child. In denying that human males and females really unite biologically when they mate—whether or not their mating is, or is even intended to be, procreative—Macedo slips into person–body dualism, as he does elsewhere, in claiming, for example, that 'if the presence of nonworking equipment [in the case of sterile couples] of the "right" sort is a crucial distinguishing feature of permissible sexual relationships, artifice might supply [by way of a partial sex change operation, for example] what nature has not.' Macedo, *supra* n. 2, at 280. For what we believe is a decisive argument against the most plausible forms of person–body dualism, see Lee, 'Human Beings as Animals.' For arguments that complement and reinforce the one Lee advances, see Braine, *The Human Person*, 29, at 19–68; Finnis et al., *Nuclear Deterrence*, 304–9; George, 'Life as an Evil,' 23–7.

34 Grisez, 'The Christian Family,' 6.

35 However, even sterile (non-human) animals do mate, and nobody has any difficulty recognizing that as a reproductive-type performance on their part.

36 Grisez, 'The Christian Family,' 6.

37 Finnis, 'Law, Morality, and "Sexual Orientation,"' 1066, n. 46.

38 Macedo, 'Homosexuality,' 280.

39 By contrast, where a male mounts a female but, for whatever reason, does not manage to achieve vaginal penetration, what we have is precisely a failed attempt to mate.

40 Grisez, 'The Christian Family,' 6.

41 Finnis, 'Law, Morality, and "Sexual Orientation,"' 1066, n. 46.

42 Ibid., 1067.

43 Ibid. What Finnis says, and we say, is necessarily true of the sexual acts of same-sex partners is, as we have tried to make clear, no less true of the sodomitical and other non-marital sexual acts of partners of opposite sexes, including partners in marriage.

44 Ibid., 1066–67 (footnote omitted). Macedo asks rhetorically: 'Is it plausible that there are no distinctions to be drawn here? My guess is that most committed loving couples—whether gay or straight—are sensitive to the difference be-

tween loving sexual acts expressing a shared intimacy and mere mutual masturbation.' Macedo, 'Homosexuality,' 282. Our claim, however, and Finnis's
as we read him, is not that no distinctions of any sort can be drawn, but
rather that non-marital sex acts of all types share a decisive moral flaw:
they instrumentalize the body in a way that damages the integrity of those who
choose such acts. Unlike masturbatory acts, acts of fornication, adultery and
sodomy can seem to unite persons. It is therefore entirely understandable that
people who perform such acts prefer them to mere masturbation and, generally, prefer to perform them with people for whom they have affection. At
some level, such people are, we believe, interested in the one-flesh union of
persons we understand as marriage. If, however, acts of fornication, adultery
and sodomy cannot, in reality, unite persons in this way, then, as Finnis says,
'those acts cannot do more than is expressed or done if . . . a man masturbates
to give himself pleasure and a fantasy of more human relationships . . .' (Of
course, there are important respects in which distinctions among non-marital
sex acts certainly can be drawn. Even if, as we believe, no non-marital sex act
can be morally good, some—for example, those involving injustice and other
evils beyond that of the wrongful instrumentalizing of one's body and that of
one's partner—are worse than others.)
45 Macedo, 'Homosexuality,' 282.
46 Ibid.
47 Although we disagree with ethical noncognitivists who (following David
Hume) deny the possibility of ultimately rationally motivated action, we share
with them the view that pleasure and other sub-rational motivating factors
ought not to be confused with basic reasons for action. Of course, speaking
loosely, one can refer to any cause or motive as a 'reason.' In moral analysis,
however, it is critical to distinguish those ends (if any) that provide rational
motivation from those that provide merely emotional motivation. The former
are reasons, strictly speaking; the latter are not. See Robert P. George, 'A
Defense of the New Natural Law Theory,' *American Journal of Jurisprudence*,
41 (1996), reprinted herein as Chapter 1. For a useful exposition and skillful
defense of ethical noncognitivism, see Jeffrey Goldsworthy, 'Fact and Value in
the New Natural Law Theory,' *American Journal of Jurisprudence*, 41 (1996).
48 Germain Grisez, *The Way of the Lord Jesus: Living a Christian Life* (Chicago:
Franciscan Herald Press, 1983), 650.
49 Ibid.
50 Macedo, 'Homosexuality,' 282.
51 Ibid., 276.
52 Ibid., 277.
53 Ibid.
54 See *supra*, n. 30.
55 We have in mind here, particularly, the scholars whose work we cite in *supra*,
n. 30.
56 See the discussion of *Griswold* v. *Connecticut*, 381 U.S. 479 (1965), in Gerard V.
Bradley, 'Life's Dominion: A Review Essay,' *Notre Dame Law Review*, 69 (1993),
329, 350–353.
57 For a classic expression of this idea in the natural law tradition, see St Thomas
Aquinas, *Summa Theologiae*, 1–2, q. 96, a. 2. See also Robert P. George, *Making
Men Moral: Civil Liberties and Public Morality* (Princeton, NJ: Princeton University Press, 1993) at viii–x (discussing prudence); 31–3 (discussing Aquinas); 42–
7 (discussing value and limits of 'perfectionist' law and policy).

58 381 U.S. 479 (1965) (recognizing that right of privacy in marriage allows use of contraception). Finnis, for example, rejects contraception on moral grounds yet supports this decision. See Finnis, 'Law, Morality, and "Sexual Orientation,"' 1076.
59 On 'perfectionism' and perfectionist reasons for limiting governmental means of enforcing morality, see George, *Making Men Moral*, 129–30, 161–88 (discussing Joseph Raz's 'perfectionist' liberalism).
60 As far as we can tell, neither Justice Douglas nor any other Justice in *Griswold* stated or clearly implied a view about the morality of contraception. We suppose (on other grounds) that most, if not all, the Justices believed that contraception in marriage is morally acceptable. A Justice who took the opposite view could, however, have concurred in the decision.
61 Society, in our view, has a compelling interest in marriage (rightly understood) and stable family life. This does not mean that there are no moral limits to the means that governments may employ to protect the institution of marriage. It does mean, however, that governments may, and should, decline to treat all sexual relationships as legally equal or confer the status of marriage on intrinsically non-marital relationships. What Joseph Raz—who does not agree with our moral analysis of homosexual sexual activity—says of monogamy applies to the constitutive aspects of marriage more generally: 'Monogamy, assuming that it is the only valuable form of marriage, cannot be practiced by an individual. It requires a culture which recognizes it, and which supports it through the public's attitude and through its formal institutions.' Joseph Raz, *The Morality of Freedom* (NY: Oxford University Press, 1986), 162.

9

What Sex Can Be: Self-Alienation, Illusion or One-Flesh Union[1]

The law of marriage has long embodied the understanding that marriage, as a moral reality, is an inherently heterosexual institution. Nowhere is this more evident than in the legal rules regarding the consummation of marriage by, and only by, sexual acts which are reproductive in type. These rules, and the understanding of marriage from which they flow, have lately been called into question by people who propose the revision of marriage law on the ground that acts traditionally condemned as sodomitical may, in some cases, be the moral equivalent of reproductive-type acts. In particular, advocates of 'same-sex marriage' claim that sound moral analysis demonstrates that homosexual sex can unify the whole lives of people as committed partners in just the way that the reproductive-type acts of spouses actualize and enable them to experience their true marital union. In this article we argue that sexual acts are morally right only within marriage. Understanding this will enable one to see why non-marital sexual acts, including homosexual acts, are intrinsically incapable of actualizing true marital union, and why the law ought not to treat such acts as equivalent in human significance to marital acts. Indeed, we shall argue that non-marital sexual acts are always and in principle contrary to an intrinsic personal good, and as such harm the character of those freely choosing to engage in them.

It is often assumed in treatments of sexual ethics that the central argument from natural law theory against non-marital sexual acts is simply that such acts are unnatural, that is, contrary to the direction inscribed in the reproductive or procreative power. This argument, often described as 'the perverted faculty argument,' is easily disposed of.[2] It is then assumed that only prejudice motivates the conviction that homosexual acts, for example, are morally wrong.[3]

Some contemporary natural law theorists, however, have articulated much more powerful arguments in sexual ethics. In this article we present a natural law argument for the proposition that sexual acts are morally right only within marriage, an argument first developed in detail by Germain Grisez,[4] and subsequently presented by others influenced by his thought.[5]

The argument we propose centers on the choice to engage in a non-marital sexual act, and the relationship between this choice and what is genuinely fulfilling for the persons involved in that act. We argue that in order for a choice to engage in sex to be respectful of the basic, intrinsic goods of persons, this choice must: (1) respect the integration of the person as bodily with the person as intentional agent; and (2) constitute a choice to participate in the real and basic good of marital union, rather than to induce in oneself and one's partner(s) a merely illusory experience of interpersonal unity. We shall argue that chaste marital intercourse[6] is really and literally love-making, that it really consummates or renews the marriage, that is, the two-in-one-flesh unity of a man and a woman. And we shall argue that if sexual acts do not consummate or renew marriage, they involve either self-alienation (and so violate the first requirement) or constitute the pursuit of a merely illusory experience (and so violate the second requirement). So, if our view is right, sex offers a unique and profound human possibility, a possibility denied, incidentally, by liberationists who claim to have a more enlightened and appreciative view of sex. At the same time, the abuse of sex is a degradation of persons, justifying the cautious attitude toward sex adopted by some of history's most profound thinkers.

Under what conditions is a sexual act morally right? There are, basically, three positions contending for dominance in the contemporary debate. First, some hold the 'liberationist' position that as long as no other, more general moral norms are violated, such as those prohibiting lying, deception, exploitation and so on, sexual acts are morally good (or, at least, innocent), since they are pleasurable. Second, others adopt the 'liberal' view that sexual acts between people are morally right as long as they in some way express genuine love or affection; the relationship such acts symbolize or express, on this view, need not be marital. Third, the position we shall argue for is the 'traditional' view that to be morally right sexual acts must embody or actualize marital union. In section one we criticize the liberationist position. In section two we explain how in marriage sexual acts initiate or renew marital communion. In section three we criticize the liberal position. In section four we reply to objections. And in section five we argue that only the traditional position can give a plausible account of why incest, pedophilia, bestiality, sex with multiple partners and so on, are morally wrong.

I. SEX AND PLEASURE

On the first view, while some sexual acts may have a tremendous emotional (or other) significance or depth, there is no valid reason why all sexual acts must have such significance. In fact, on this view, as long as concerns about health, honesty and liberty are met, there is nothing wrong with even the most promiscuous forms of sexual behavior. Frederick Elliston presents an argument for this position: 'For at least some of the people some of the time sex is fun. Whatever else may be true of it, at the barest level sex remains an intensely pleasing physical activity. . . . Granted the two earlier provisos [no coercion, no deception], sex is good for this reason, if for no other.[7] Later he sums up this view: 'Insofar as promiscuity maximizes the pleasures that can be derived from sex, it is good; and insofar as the prohibition against promiscuity is a limitation on the pleasures to be derived from sex, it is unwarranted—in a word, "bad." '[8] He adds that one can, arguing in the spirit of John Stuart Mill, maintain that 'the freedom to be promiscuous can contribute to the full growth of the human personality.'[9]

Among the implications of this view, it would seem to follow that there is nothing wrong, at least in principle, with prostitution. For if it is pleasant for one party, why may it not be legitimately profitable for the other party? Proponents of the morality of prostitution grant that there is often coercion, exploitation and other bad effects associated with prostitution. But, they argue, these are not necessary or inevitable features of commercial sex. On this basis, Lars Ericsson concludes that prostitution should be viewed as morally upright: 'If two adults voluntarily consent to an economic arrangement concerning sexual activity and this activity takes place in private, it seems plainly absurd to maintain that there is something intrinsically wrong with it.'[10]

However, we argue that it is wrong to treat one's body, or another's, as a mere extrinsic instrument, and that this is done in sexual acts chosen for the sole immediate purpose of pleasure (even when there is an ulterior end, such as commercial gain or relaxation). Sexual acts done for the sole immediate purpose of pleasure, and not intended as embodying or expressing personal communion, constitute mere masturbation, either solitary or mutual. And we shall argue that masturbation is objectively morally wrong.

It is often said that there are two types of pleasure: first, a specific type of sensation, such as the taste of an apple, or the euphoric sensation produced by a drug; second, an aspect of an activity, desired for its own sake, of which one is conscious, such as the pleasure in playing tennis (not a specific sensation, but the enjoyment or satisfaction of the game as a whole). Clearly, in this second sense of 'pleasure' it is impossible literally to choose the activity for the sake of the pleasure. 'To play tennis for the sake of the pleasure it produces,' (in this sense) is actually just to play tennis for its own sake.[11] However, there is also a third type of pleasure. While playing tennis, one has the experience or consciousness of playing tennis, and one enjoys this experience. That experience can, of course, be artificially produced. One can have the experience of playing tennis without actually doing so. Of course, not all experiences are artificially produced. Still, the experience of an activity is (or can be) distinct from the activity itself, and so it is possible to pursue the activity for the sake of the experience. So, 'pleasure' may refer either to: (1) a sensation; (2) an aspect of an activity (of which one is conscious); or (3) the experience of an activity, whether one is actually engaging in the activity or not.

As a result, the phrase, 'pursue an activity for the sake of the pleasure,' is ambiguous. It could mean three different things, corresponding to the three different senses of 'pleasure.' If the pleasure sought is actually an aspect of an activity that is genuinely fulfilling, then, obviously, the choice need not be morally wrong.[12] However, if the pleasure sought is a particular sensation or an experience distinct from the fulfilling activity, then the pleasure sought may not be connected to an activity that actualizes a human good. If the pleasure is chosen as separate from a real human good, and it is chosen instead of pursuing a real good, then the choice is morally wrong. Our choices ought to be in accord with a respect and love for real human goods, precisely because such goods are intrinsic aspects of the well-being and fulfillment of human persons—ourselves and others. So, just as we should not be deterred by contrary emotions from choosing a genuine good, so we should not be deterred from choosing a real good by a mere desire for pleasure.[13] However, a choice to pursue pleasure apart from a real good may also involve a denigration of one's bodily self. If one chooses to actualize one's bodily, sexual power as an extrinsic means to producing an effect in one's consciousness, then one separates in one's choice oneself as bodily from oneself as intentional agent. The content of such a choice includes the dis-integration attendant a reduction of one's bodily self to the level of an extrinsic instrument.

How does such a choice include dis-integration? It is not that a perfection is pursued in which the body does not in some sense share. For, since we are bodily beings, there are no such perfections. Nor is it the same as, say, a student-athlete who merely has trouble harmonizing his athletic pursuits with his studies. A simple lack of integration is not necessarily morally problematic. Nor is it that in such acts the body is ignored, for there is, of course, intense attention toward the body. Rather, the problem is that in such a choice one treats the body as a mere extrinsic means: one regards the body as something outside or apart from the subject, and so as a mere object. A certain contempt for the body inheres in such choices.[14]

An analogy will clarify the point. Suppose a husband begins to regard his wife as a mere servant, or as a mere means toward his own ends. To regard her in this way in itself diminishes the personal harmony between them. He has ceased to regard her as an end in herself, as a subject, and regards her as merely a means, merely an object. His relation to her, then, lacks what it should have. This is true even before he performs any external act to manifest this defect in his relation to her. Something similar happens with the masturbator and his body, only here the disharmony involves different aspects of the same person, rather than two distinct persons. The masturbator treats his body as a mere means in relation to a feeling, a feeling regarded not in its reality (as a bodily act), but simply in its aspect as feeling. And so the body is regarded as a mere extrinsic means in relation to the goal of a certain type of feeling. The body is regarded as something outside the self, not as an aspect of the subject, and so as a mere object. Therefore, the choice to masturbate is a choice whose object includes a disharmony between the conscious aspect of the self and the bodily aspect of the self.

Not every use of another person or of parts of one's body is wrong. Treating one's body, or another's, as an extrinsic instrument (extrinsic to the person as intentional agent) is wrong, however, precisely because it separates in one's intention the person as bodily from the person as intentional agent. And in that way it includes personal dis-integration in the object of choice.

What is it for A to use B? A uses B when A has a purpose to attain and A moves B to produce or help produce this purpose. The relation between user and used is not symmetrical. If the purpose for which A works is equally a purpose of B, then A is not using B to attain that purpose, rather, the relation is one of cooperation for a common good. On the other hand, if B does want to help A, it does not follow necessarily that he is not being used at all by A. If the purpose is A's primarily, even if (as a result of their interaction) B is willing to help A attain his purpose, then A is using B.

But A may use B either as an extrinsic instrument or as an intrinsic instrument. One uses an instrument as intrinsic to oneself when, for example, one uses one's hand to write, one's legs to walk, and so on. Indeed, parts of one's body are called organs, a word derived from the Greek word for instruments. How do extrinsic instruments, such as hammers, lawn mowers and so on, differ? And, more to the point, what is it in A's attitude that is inconsistent with his regarding B as intrinsic to himself? Part of the difference consists in the nature of B. A hammer is an extrinsic instrument partly because it is not internally oriented toward the purpose of pounding nails. Therefore—and this is the decisive point— when Jones uses the hammer to pound nails, the subject of the action is Jones, not Jones plus the hammer as aspects of a larger whole. A hand is an intrinsic instrument because it is internally oriented to the whole, rather than its own activities being oriented to a further, alien purpose. Therefore, the hand shares in the activities of the whole, of which it is a part. Where the instrument is intrinsic, there is a unitary activity in which this part shares; where the instrument is extrinsic (or is treated as extrinsic), there are several activities, and the activities of the extrinsic objects (which have their own quite distinct teleology) are extrinsically oriented to a purpose external to them.

How does this apply to the body (other persons' bodies and one's own) in sexual acts? The body, or rather, parts of the body, can be used in two ways. Where the body is treated as extrinsic to the person, the body is used for purposes external to the 'person,' and so is a stranger to the purpose(s) for which it is (now) conscripted. Where the body is rightly treated as intrinsic to the person, there is a unitary activity, and various bodily actions share in this activity, not being oriented to extrinsic purposes. This applies to sexual acts. If in the sexual act a man and woman act for the sake of bodily marital unity, their action qua intentional agents and their action qua bodies are one and the same; for their intention is precisely this bodily union, as an intrinsic aspect and the biological matrix of their total marital communion. However, this is not the case in masturbatory acts. Or rather, in a masturbatory act, with respect to its intentionality, the bodily act and the intentional act are not the same.[15] This is true in masturbation involving two or more people as well as in solitary masturbation. With two parties: John uses Susan's body to obtain sexual gratification. In that case her personal presence is irrelevant; that it is Susan, and not some other woman, is irrelevant—is not essential—to the intentional action he is performing, which is obtaining gratification or pleasure. But similarly in solitary masturbation: here, of course, it does matter whose body it is, but it does not matter what sort of stimulation produces the pleasures the masturbator desires. Whether the cause of the pleasurable sensation be a caress, a poke or an electrical stimulus in the brain, is irrelevant. Thus, what happens in his body is irrelevant, so long as it produces the end desired, a certain sort of experience. (This, of course, is in striking contrast to chaste marital intercourse.) So in masturbatory acts the body is treated as an extrinsic instrument. In one's intentional act there is a separation—a dis-integration—of the self as bodily and the (same) self as personal.

The integration of the various aspects of the self in action or in self-awareness is a basic human good, an intrinsic aspect of fulfillment, the lack of which is a privation. The integration consists, partly, in an awareness and appreciation (which may, of course, be quite informal) of the ontological unity of the different aspects of the self. Also, the inner harmony certainly includes a love of self and a certain degree of self-esteem.

Privations in these areas are privations in self-integration.[16] A choice to use one's body as an extrinsic instrument includes in its object self-alienation. So, the use of one's own body, or of another person's body, as an instrument extrinsic to the self or selves as personal agents, unavoidably violates the basic human good of self-integration.

Thus, masturbation, whether solitary or with two or more participants, is morally wrong. To be morally right a sexual act must involve more than a fair and non-violent pursuit of pleasure.[17]

II. SEX AND MARRIAGE

What we have said so far might seem consistent with the position that sex is morally right as long as the persons involved love each other, or at least have a certain affection for each other,[18] and their sexual acts express that love or affection. On this view, no moral norm requires that one be married to someone to have sex with him or her. It is enough if two people (of opposite sexes or the same sex) have a friendly relationship. To see why this view is mistaken, we must first see (in a general way) what marriage is and what values are realized by chaste sexual intercourse within marriage.

There are three main views of marriage. First, some thinkers have held that marriage is an institution which is defined by its instrumental relation to procreation.[19] On this view, marriage is essentially a contractual union, and its extrinsic purpose is the conceiving and rearing of children. Proponents of this view usually hold that marriage should also, ideally, involve a friendship between the husband and wife. Marital union involves an agreement concerning acts of sexual intercourse, and sexual intercourse within marriage is conceived not only as serving procreation, but also, secondarily, as symbolizing the marital friendship. Still, the relationship between husband and wife is conceived as in itself non-bodily, and sexual intercourse is viewed as extrinsic (an extrinsic means) to the marital friendship.

A second view, certainly more popular these days, is that marriage is essentially a friendship, procreation is an extrinsic addition and sexual acts are extrinsic symbols or expressions of love or of the couple's personal communion. On this view there is no intrinsic or essential relationship between marriage and procreation. A couple may wish to have children, and having children may even be viewed as contributing to their marital relationship. But procreation is not viewed as intrinsically linked with marriage. As a consequence, on this view there is no reason why 'marriage' should refer only to man–woman relationships, or, to express the same point in a different way, why (if this view is consistently worked out, which is not always the case) there is any morally significant difference between homosexual and heterosexual relationships.

The third view of marriage is the one we propose. On this view, marriage is the community formed by a man and a woman who publicly consent to share their whole lives, in a type of relationship oriented toward the begetting, nurturing and educating of children together. This openness to procreation, as the community's natural fulfillment, distinguishes this community from other types. It makes sexual intercourse within marriage appropriate because, in such a community, sexual intercourse can immediately actualize (initiate or renew) the good of marriage.

On this third view, marriage is good in itself, and not merely an instrumental good in relation to procreation. At the same time, marriage is naturally fulfilled or unfolds in bearing and bringing up children; children are not related to marriage merely as an extrinsic addition or afterthought. Thus, if a married couple do not have children for some reason, their marriage is fully a marriage and remains good in itself (which is difficult to maintain on the first view), but also lacks its complete natural fulfillment (which is denied on the second view).[20]

In this type of community, sexual intercourse is not merely an extrinsic symbol or a pursuit of pleasure. In sexual intercourse between a man and a woman (whether married or not), a real organic union is established. This is a literal, biological point. Human beings are organisms, albeit of a particular type.[21] An organic action is one in which several bodily parts—tissues, cells, molecules, atoms and so on—participate. Digestion, for example, involves several smaller, chemical actions of individual cells. But the several components of digestion form a unitary, single action. The subject of this action is the organism. So the organism is a composite, made up of billions of parts. Its unity is manifested and understood in its actions. Now, for most actions, such as sensation, digestion, walking and so on, individual male or female organisms are complete units. The male or female animal organism uses various materials as energy or instruments to perform its actions, but there is no internal orientation of its bodily parts to any larger whole of which it is a part, with respect to those actions. (This is precisely why we recognize individual male and female organisms as distinct, complete organisms, in most contexts.) However, with respect to one function the male and the female are not complete, and that function, of course, is reproduction. In reproductive activity the bodily parts of the male and the bodily parts of the female participate in a single action, coitus, which is oriented to reproduction (though not every act of coitus is reproductive), so that the subject of the action is the male and the female as a unit.[22] Coitus is a unitary action in which the male and the female become literally one organism.[23] In marital intercourse, this bodily unity is an aspect—indeed, the biological matrix—of the couple's more comprehensive, marital communion.

Now, when a couple chooses to form the kind of community distinguished by its openness and orientation to procreation, then the organic unity effected in sexual intercourse has a continuity with their community. In sexual intercourse they unite (become one) precisely in that respect in which their community is distinct and naturally fulfilled. So this bodily unity is not extrinsic to their emotional and spiritual unity. The bodily, emotional, and spiritual are the different levels of a unitary, multileveled personal communion. Therefore, in such a community sexual intercourse actualizes the multileveled personal communion. The sexual intercourse of spouses is not an extrinsic symbol of their love, or a mere means in relation to procreation. Rather, their sexual intercourse embodies, or actualizes, their marital communion. In that way the chaste sexual intercourse of husband and wife instantiates a basic human good: the good of marital union.

In sexual intercourse, the husband and the wife become one organism, but they do so precisely as man and woman, precisely as potential father and mother. Thus, in this act they share their procreative power (even if some condition distinct from their sexual act makes procreation impossible).[24] The full exercise or fulfillment of this potential would include conception, gestation, bearing and raising the child, that is, bringing the child, the concrete prolongation and fruit of their love, to maturity physically, emotionally, intellectually and morally. Thus in their sexuality, in the procreative potential which they share with each other, there is a dynamism toward fatherhood and motherhood, and so, a dynamism which extends the present unity of the spouses indefinitely into the future. This reality is the basis for the profound significance that most people sense or feel is attached to sexual intercourse.

We do not, of course, deny that there are relationships in the first two senses—contractual unions in the first case, and friendships in the second case. In some societies men have viewed their wives only as mothers of their children, and have sought romantic relationships elsewhere (as on the first view). Also, many couples today regularly perform sexual acts together, but view their relationships as having nothing inherently to do with procreation (as on the second view). Both of these types of relationships have at times been called 'marriage.' But our position is that these are specifically distinct from the intrinsic good of marriage.

In the first two types of relationship, sexual acts are extrinsic to the personal communion of the two, or more, persons engaging in the sexual act. Only in the third type, only in marriage as a one-flesh union of spouses, is the sexual intercourse part of, or constitutive of, the personal bodily communion itself.

III. SEX, LOVE AND AFFECTION

So far we have argued that engaging in sex merely for pleasure is wrong in that it separates in one's intention the person as bodily (both oneself and the other) from the person as intentional agent, treating the body as a sub-personal, extrinsic instrument. So, unless the sexual act embodies or actualizes a real union of persons, it will involve the instrumentalization of both the other person(s) and oneself. We now argue that only in marriage can sexual acts constitute a real union of persons. There are four common types of non-marital sexual acts: masturbation (solitary or mutual), sodomy, fornication and adultery. We do not formally discuss adultery here: if masturbation and fornication are wrong, then adultery, which involves additional moral defects, is certainly wrong. We considered the morality of masturbation above. In this section we discuss sodomy and fornication.

A. Sodomy

By 'sodomy' here is meant: (1) anal or oral intercourse between persons of the same sex; or (2) anal or oral intercourse between persons of opposite sexes (even if married), if it is intended to bring about complete sexual satisfaction apart from penile–vaginal intercourse. If a couple use their sexual organs for the sake of experiencing pleasure or even for the sake of an experience of unity, but do not become one organism, then their act does not actually effect unity. If Susan, for example, masturbates John to orgasm or applies oral stimulation to him to bring him to orgasm, no real unity has been effected. That is, although bodily parts are conjoined, and so there is juxtaposition and contact, the participants do not unite biologically; they do not become the subject of a single act, and so do not literally become 'one flesh.' They may be doing this in order simply to obtain or share pleasure. In that case the act is really an instance of mutual masturbation, and is as self-alienating as any other instance of masturbation. However, they might intend their act as in some way an expression of their love for each other. They might argue that this act is no different from the penile–vaginal intercourse they performed two nights before, except that this one involves a merely technical or physical variation—a rearrangement of 'plumbing.'

However, in sodomitical acts, whether between persons of the same sex or opposite sexes, between unmarried or married persons, the participants do not unite biologically. Moreover, an experience of pleasure, just as such, is not *shared*. Although each person may experience pleasure, they experience pleasure each as an individual, not as a unit. For a truly common good, there must be more than experience; the experiences must be subordinated to a truly common act that is genuinely fulfilling (and as such provides a more than merely instrumental reason for action). If, on the contrary, the activities are subordinated to the pleasurable experiences, if the physical stimulation administered to one another is merely a means to attain what are (and can only be) individual, private gratifications, then unity is not achieved.

We could express this point in a different way. It is clear that in some sexual acts couples are engaging in the activity simply as a means of having (and giving each other) a pleasurable experience. In that case, we have argued, they are instrumentalizing their bodies in order to obtain an effect in their consciousnesses. Moreover, such acts do not really foster bodily communion between the participants, and may actually drive them apart, since the gratifications are private experiences, not shared activities. Now, what feature must a sexual act have so that one is not merely using another's body (and one's own)? The answer is that it must be an act in which a real good is realized or participated in. If this is so, then it is an act in which the two share and therefore become one in jointly performing this act. In that case, their pleasurable experiences will be aspects of a real good, rather than their acts being subordinated to the pleasurable experiences. Now, in the case of chaste marital intercourse, spouses participate in the real good of marital bodily union. In marital intercourse the man and the woman become organically one in an act of copulation, and this physical union initiates or renews their total marital communion: that is, distinct from the pleasurable experiences, there is an identifiable, real act and basic human good in which they share, namely, the act of initiating or renewing their marital union in their becoming organically one.

Confusion may arise on this point. It might seem that we are begging the question. For we are saying, first, that there must be some real act, definable independently of its pleasure, in which the couple share—a common good—in order for their act to be unifying. And yet we then say that with married people the act which they share is their becoming truly one, that is, one organism. Aren't we saying that the common act that makes them one is their becoming one? And if their common act can be their becoming one, why can't homosexuals (or, for that matter, heterosexuals) do this in sodomitical acts?

The answer is that there are three types of unity referred to here: unity of persons, unity of action (which promotes or actualizes the unity of persons), and the organic unity of male and female in coitus. It is true in general, for any two (or more) people, that actions which they perform make them one only if there is a real, common good of their actions (unity of action). The common good could be health (sharing a meal), aesthetic experience (going to a play or movie), play (bridge, checkers) and so on. In each case there is a unity of action, that is, an action sharing in a real, common good, performed jointly. Moreover, this unity of action promotes or actualizes interpersonal unity, or unity of persons. In the case of the sexual act of a married couple, their act of physically or organically becoming one (organic unity) is the common good, the shared pursuit of which (unity of action) also brings about or enhances their interpersonal unity (unity of persons). But if the participants in a sexual act do not become physically or organically one, then, whatever goods they may be seeking as ulterior ends, their immediate goal is mere pleasure or illusory experience. So there is in such an experience no *common* good, the common pursuit of which makes them one. There is no real unity of action to effect or enhance their interpersonal unity. So in that case, although they may intend or wish otherwise, their act is in reality a using of their own and each others' bodies as a means of obtaining a pleasurable experience, which might include the illusory experience of a union which they are not by this action promoting or effecting in any way.

B. Fornication

There must, then, be an organic unity so that there is a common good in the sexual act. But, as we showed above, in section one, this organic union is an instance of a real human good only if it is an aspect of a real union of the persons. If they are united as one organism but are not united in other aspects of their lives or selves, then they are treating their bodies as extrinsic instruments.[25] But suppose a heterosexual couple has a friendship, and is even planning marriage in the future. They have intercourse, and intend their act not just as an experience of pleasure, but (perhaps confusedly) as an embodiment of their personal, but not-yet-marital, communion. In this case they really do become one flesh in the sexual act, and so their act seems to be a sharing in a common good. They become one flesh, and they intend this union to be an actualization and experience of their (less-than-marital) personal communion. What about this type of act, which has traditionally been designated as 'fornication'? Discussing precisely this issue, Germain Grisez replied:

However, the part of the good of marital communion which fornicators choose, bodily union, is not an intelligible good apart from the whole. Although bodily union provides an experience of intimacy, by itself it realizes only the natural capacity of a male individual and a female individual to mate. Sexual mating contributes to an intelligible good, which fulfills persons, only insofar as it is one element of the complete communion by which a man and a woman become, as it were, one person.[26]

In other words, an interpersonal communion is actualized only by an act that is proper to it.

The interrelationship of family members, for example, is actualized and experienced in the family meal. Friends actualize and experience their relationship in conversation. Sexual activity does not actualize an ordinary friendship. But reproductive-type acts, acts in which spouses become one flesh and share their procreative potentiality, actualize and enable them to experience this specific type of personal communion. Only if they are married, only if they consent to marriage, does their becoming one organism actualize (initiate or renew) a basic human good—the good of *marriage*. Thus, only if they have a truly marital relationship can their sexual act embody their personal communion.

In sum, in chaste marital intercourse the couple act in a fully integrated way. Each bodily person relates to the other precisely as a bodily person, because they become one physically and personally. In non-marital sexual acts, however, either the participants unite in a bodily way but not as actualizing a personal communion (fornication), or they do not really unite at all, but use their bodies for an illusory experience of bodily unity or for private gratification (masturbation, sodomy).

IV. OBJECTIONS

There are three important objections to our position, and it will clarify matters to consider them.

A. Objection 1

First, it has been objected that this argument would entail that the sexual acts of sterile married couples are also immoral, and everyone recognizes that is not the case. Paul Weithman has called this 'the sterility objection' (an objection he does not himself advance).[27] Stephen Macedo argues as follows:

If there is no possibility of procreation, then sterile couples are, like homosexuals, incapable of sex acts 'open to procreation.' What is the point of sex in an infertile marriage? Not procreation; the partners (let us assume) know that they are infertile. If they have sex, it is for pleasure and to express their love, or friendship, or some other shared good. It will be for precisely the same reasons that committed, loving gay couples have sex. Why are these good reasons for sterile or elderly married couples but not for gay and lesbian couples?[28]

Macedo argues further that the only reason why homosexual couples cannot perform sexual acts suited to procreation is that they lack 'the physical equipment (the "biological complementarity") such that anyone could have children by doing what they do in bed.'[29] In other words, sterile married couples merely lack some physical condition that would enable them to procreate. But exactly the same situation obtains in the case of homosexual couples. Clearly, the objection concludes, sexual acts between sterile married couples can be morally right; therefore, there is no reason why sexual acts between homosexual couples cannot also be morally right.

Regardless of whether one agrees that the difference is morally significant, the two types of acts do have a clear difference. As Macedo admits, no one could have children by performing sodomitical acts. Yet this is not true of the type of act performed by sterile married couples when they engage in penile–vaginal intercourse. People who are not temporarily or permanently infertile could procreate by performing exactly the same type of act which the infertile married couple perform and by which they consummate or actualize their marital communion. The difference between sterile and fertile married couples is not a difference in what they do. Rather, it is a difference in a distinct condition which affects what may result from what they do. However, the difference between any heterosexual couple engaging in penile–vaginal intercourse and a homosexual couple is much more than that. The lack of complementarity in homosexual couples is a condition which renders it impossible for them to perform the kind of act which makes them organically one.

If a married couple become sterile, this does not change what they have been doing in bed: they still perform the same kind of act they have been doing perhaps for years. Similarly, a fertile married couple may have sexual intercourse several times during a week. If conception results, they may not know which act of sexual intercourse caused it. Still, all of their acts are the kind of acts which could result in procreation. Their sexual acts later in life, for example, after the female spouse has become infertile, are still the kind of acts which could result in procreation—the difference is not a difference in what they do—the kind of act—but in a condition extrinsic to what they do.

This is a clear difference. Is it morally significant? Indeed it is. The heterosexual couple who engage in a reproductive-type act truly become one body, one organism. If they have given marital consent, then this act initiates or renews their marital communion. The good of marriage is a multileveled union. The sexual intercourse of a married couple is an aspect (and, as we have said, the biological matrix) of this multileveled union and so, given marital consent, it initiates or renews that union. If an otherwise eligible heterosexual couple have consented to join their lives in a total personal communion, a communion that is naturally fulfilled in bearing and raising children (whether or not the non-behavioral conditions of procreation obtain for them), then this act initiates or renews that union: it embodies the kind of communion they have, that is, a procreative one. The homosexual couple, on the other hand, lacks not just a condition enabling their act to be procreative, but a precondition of the formation by them of the kind of personal union which is initiated or renewed by marital acts.[30]

Some analogies may clarify the point we are making. Suppose Smith has a temporary digestive disorder so that, although he can eat, he frequently vomits, and thus many of his meals are not digested. As a consequence, when Smith sits down to eat a meal he cannot be sure whether this particular one will result in increased nourishment. Still, he continues to eat, and his meals as a set are ordered to his nourishment. When Smith eats he is exercising his digestive system: what he does is the same for every meal, though many individual instances do not result in nourishment. He is engaging in nourishing activity, even if this particular act does not nourish, because he is performing the behavior that is in his power, which is capable in some instances of nourishing. One could say that he is performing a nourishing-type act.

This means that Smith would be performing a nourishing-type act even if—perhaps because full digestion led to time-consuming elimination—he hoped that this particular act did not result in nourishment. Moreover, his eating would still be a nourishing-type act if his disorder got worse, his stomach was closed, and he obtained his nourishment intravenously. In that case, he might eat in order to exercise that part of his digestive system still functioning, or to share a meal with a friend.[31]

Likewise with reproductive-type acts. Reproduction, or procreation, is not an action directly under our control. Its conditions are non-behavioral as well as behavioral. What is performed is an act which in some instances may result in procreation. Moreover—and here reproduction is distinct from other acts—by performing that act the male and the female become one organism, two-in-one-flesh. When that one-flesh unity is an aspect of a total marital communion, it is a rational and sufficient motive and justification for that act. But humans (and other mammals) become one flesh (one organism) only if they perform the type of act which in some instances procreates, only if they perform a reproductive-type act.

B. Objection 2

We have argued that if a sexual act does not embody a personal communion, then it instrumentalizes the body in pursuit of pleasure or of an illusory experience of personal communion, and that in order to embody a personal communion there must be a commitment to a stable personal relationship suited to acts of this sort (in other words, marriage), and it must be an act in which the two initiate or renew their procreative communion by achieving a real physical or biological union. There are two ways of directly challenging this argument. One way denies our claim that non-marital acts cannot achieve a real union. The other grants that in non-marital sexual acts the participants instrumentalize the body, but denies that instrumentalizing the body is in itself wrong.

So a second objection is to argue that non-marital acts do sometimes realize a basic, common good, that they do, sometimes, somehow embody or express a personal communion. There are three variations on this. The first is to say that such acts symbolize the personal union of the participants, and that in this way such acts contribute to or strengthen the participants' personal relationship. One might argue that sexual acts foster personal communion because they are a sign or expression of love. But if that is so, then why can't sexual acts involving multiple partners, or between partners of the same sex, symbolize love or affection? And why must a couple (or group) have a community suited for procreation (i.e., be married) in order validly to express their love sexually?

It is true that chaste sexual acts are signs or symbols of personal union. However, sexual acts are in their immediate reality much more than symbols. The question is whether the reality that is more than symbolic will involve depersonalization. When one waves at someone, or smiles at someone, or shakes her hand, the gesture is of itself rather trivial, but partly through convention and partly through natural association, it signifies a cordial act of will or emotion. The same is true of a hug or a non-passionate kiss. But insofar as these acts are symbols, the thought is moved away from the sign to the will or emotion which it signifies. However, in a sexual act there is a desire directed toward the body and the desire of the other.[32] The participants' attention is riveted on the action itself. And the desire and attention is not just toward the physical presence of the other (as in a hug). So the action is not primarily a sign for some other reality. Indeed, sexual acts are symbolically powerful precisely because of what sexual intercourse between a man and woman is in reality.

It is true, however, that someone may have sex with another in order to signify something as an ulterior end. For example, an otherwise unwilling teen girl may consent to have sex with her boyfriend in order to show him how much she cares. Still, the immediate reality of the sexual act is not a mere sign. And so if there is not a real union of which the sexual act is a part—in other words if it is not a marital act—then the bodily presence of the other, and the personal presence of the other in his or her body, is used for the sake of the experience of the sexual act, even if that experience has as an ulterior end some signification. In other words, if doing X in itself involves instrumentalizing the body, it does not cease to do so if one does X for the sake of an ulterior end, in this case, signification.

A second variation on this objection (viz., the denial that sodomitical acts instrumentalize the self as bodily) is to claim that sex is simply a type of gift. In sex the participants give each other pleasure, and this giving strengthens or expresses a personal communion. It is an exchange of gifts, and the gift is pleasure.

The difficulty here is that this position presupposes a hedonistic theory of value. Pleasure is not by itself an intrinsic good, but is really good only as an aspect of a genuinely fulfilling activity. So pleasure by itself does not constitute a fitting gift. If pleasure, apart from participation in a real good, is not fulfilling, then giving this experience, or enabling someone else to have this experience, is not a true gift.

A third variation on this argument is to say that there is, in some way, a real bodily unity in sexual acts not suited to procreation, that is, in sodomitical acts. Thus, Michael Perry poses the following question:

The nonprocreative sexual conduct of a man and a woman in a lifelong, monogamous relationship of faithful love can be morally licit if it 'actualizes' and 'allows them to experience' their friendship as a sexual-spiritual union of profound depth and richness. Why, then, can't the sexual conduct of a man and a man or of a woman and a woman also be morally licit—why cannot it also be worthy of those who would be truly, fully human—if it actualizes and allows them to experience their friendship as a lifelong, monogamous, faithful, loving sexual-spiritual union of profound depth and richness?[33]

The answer to this is that not just any act will allow a couple to experience their unity. What is it about a sexual act that enables it to embody a personal communion? The fact that it gives intense pleasure is certainly not what enables it to do so, for many acts do that, without having that kind of implication.

No act—sexual or otherwise—can be just an experience of and actualization of a friendship. Friendship is a unity constituted by common pursuit of genuine goods such as health, knowledge, play[34] and so on. Thus, friendship is actualized and experienced only in the common pursuit or realization of other genuine goods.[35] In truly marital acts the genuine, common good is the bodily, organic unity of spouses, as a noninstrumental aspect and biological basis of the overall (multileveled) reality of their marriage. But no actual organic unity is present in sodomitical acts, and there is not any other human good instantiated by such acts. So, sodomitical acts do not (in any substantial and morally significant sense) unify the two (or more) persons who perform them on each others' bodies.

C. Objection 3

A final objection to our overall argument is to admit that in sodomitical acts the body is instrumentalized, but to deny that instrumentalizing the body is of itself morally wrong. Michael Perry expresses this objection as follows:

Why is conduct morally bad simply because it involves one in treating one's body 'as an instrument to be used in the service of one's consciously experiencing self'? [quoting from John Finnis's article] Assume that from time to time I choose to eat a food that is utterly without nutritional value (and so does me no physical good) but that it is otherwise harmless and satisfies my appetite for a particular taste or sensation. Assume, too, that I do not thereby fail to eat, or make it more likely that someday I will fail to eat, the nutritional foods I need. Have I thereby done something that 'dis-integrates me precisely as an acting person'?[36]

Stephen Macedo also considers analogies with eating, and argues that the sort of pursuit of pleasure which clearly does no damage to persons' self-integration in regard to our eating and drinking must similarly be judged harmless when it comes to sexual acts:

Or as Sabl suggested to me, suppose a person lost his capacity to digest but not the capacity to eat, so that nutrition had to be delivered intravenously. Would it then be immoral to eat for the sake of mere pleasure, or perhaps for the sake of pleasure as well as the camaraderie of dining companions?[37]

This appeal to an analogy with eating could be construed in two different ways. On the one hand, one could use the analogy to support a claim that instrumentalizing the body is not of itself wrong. In other words, one would say that eating just for pleasure does instrumentalize the body, but eating just for pleasure is clearly not wrong, and so instrumentalizing the body is not always wrong (this is Perry's argument). On the other hand, one could argue that, although instrumentalizing the body is wrong, still, eating just for pleasure is clearly not wrong, so one can perform an activity—including sex—just for pleasure without instrumentalizing the body. We reply that 'eating just for pleasure' is not necessarily wrong, but that is because it does not involve treating the body as an extrinsic instrument.

First of all, to regard one's body as an extrinsic instrument is immoral because it involves a contempt for the body; it involves treating the body as if it were outside oneself, a sub-personal object. To treat one's body as a mere object is a violation of the basic good of self-integration. Since we are our bodies (and not merely inhabit them), it is treating a person (ourselves) as a sub-personal object. With respect to eating, 'to eat simply for the sake of pleasure' is not the same in its moral significance as having sex simply for the sake of the pleasure when it does not embody a marital communion. Often, one might choose to eat simply because one is hungry, and one might then take no thought of any intrinsic good, such as health. Still, what one chooses is an intelligible activity that is, at least to some degree, really fulfilling. (Even if for some reason one can't digest one's food, the eating exercises part of one's digestive capacity and one chooses a nourishing-type act, of which the pleasure is an aspect.) Similarly, such acts as twiddling one's thumbs, tapping one's foot, or chewing sugarless gum, are rightly enjoyed simply as physical activities, exercises of one's physical capacities; but that, of course, is not the central reality in a sexual act. One chooses the activity of eating, and the pleasure is a felt aspect of that activity. Such a choice is not necessarily wrong, though it could be wrong for reasons other than its relation to pleasure. Also, it would not be wrong, as we said above, for someone who for some reason could not obtain nourishment from his food at all, to eat for the sake of exercising that part of his digestive system which still functions, for the camaraderie fostered by that common activity, and for the pleasure in the activity. Of course, it is wrong to allow one's mere desire for the pleasure of eating to cause one to eat excessively. To do so is to commit the immoral act of gluttony. However, the wrongness of gluttony does not seem to consist, primarily, at any rate, in self-alienation.

Masturbatory or sodomitical sex is quite different. Here the physical activities (stroking, rubbing) are chosen as merely extrinsic means of producing an effect (gratification) in consciousness, the only thing chosen for its own sake. Although someone who cannot obtain nourishment from his food can still perform that behavior which is suited to nourish (of which one is aware, at some level), the analogous point is not true of masturbatory or sodomitical sex acts. Such acts are not suited to reproduction: they are not, in our parlance, 'reproductive-type acts.'

V. NON-MARITAL SEXUAL ACTS, MULTIPLE PARTNERS, INCEST, BESTIALITY . . .

Most people recognize that incest, bestiality and pedophilia, as well as promiscuity, prostitution and group sex, are morally wrong. Nevertheless, it is not clear how such activities could be immoral if the explanation of the meaning and nature of sexual acts proposed by those opposing our view were correct. If sex is rightly understood and practiced as merely a sign of affection, then why would it not be an appropriate sign to express to one's child, by an adult to his or her friend of minor age, or even to one's pet? If sex is a sign of affection, why would it be improper to use it to express one's gratitude to one's parents or one's teachers? No one sees anything wrong with sharing beautiful music with such people, or sharing a meal with several people at one sitting. Some parents at times give their children massages, to relax them or to help them sleep if they are extremely tense. But what is it about sex that makes it improper in such circumstances?

There must be some feature of sex which distinguishes it from activities which are appropriately shared with children, one's parents, in groups and so on. But what is that feature? Being an intense and pleasurable sign of affection—the only trait distinctive of sex according to many who oppose our view—provides not the slightest reason to refrain from sexual acts in those contexts. Our view, on the contrary, provides an intelligible answer: sexual acts are such that either they embody a marital communion—a communion that is possible only in reproductive-type acts between a man and a woman, in a marital relationship—or they involve instrumentalizing the body for the sake of an illusory experience or fantasy of marital union, an illusion or fantasy that is especially inappropriate with children, one's parents and so on.

Replying to Hadley Arkes's suggestion that permitting homosexual acts would logically compromise the principle forbidding incest, Stephen Macedo fails to perceive the force of this argument. Macedo writes: 'Incest, of course, would lead to a horrible and revolting form of vulnerability for children.'[38] But if sex is essentially what Macedo claims it to be—simply an intense sign of affection—it is hard to see why extending it to children would in any way exploit their vulnerability, or why it would be 'horrible and revolting.' Only if sex necessarily involves more than expressing an extrinsic sign of affection, only if there is some reality made present or simulated, a reality that is unfitting with a child or with one's parent, or with strangers, or in groups, can there be anything truly unfitting about incest.

In sum, in choosing to engage in sexual activity one adopts an attitude toward the relationship between the body and consciousness in both oneself and others with whom one has sex, and one relates to the basic good of personal communion. To engage in sex merely for pleasure separates in one's intention the person as bodily from the person as intentional agent, treating the body (both one's own and others') as a sub-personal object. Moreover, sexual acts aimed at expressing affection or love but outside marriage are choices of an illusory experience. Only if there is a common good realized in and by the sexual act—making the couple one in the cooperative participation in the common good of marriage—do the participants treat each other and themselves as unified bodily persons (and, thus, with respect) and embody a real, basic good. For only then is their pleasure or experience an aspect of participation in a real good, rather than individual, private gratifications or illusory experiences. In marriage, the couple become two-in-one-flesh, and this bodily union is an aspect of their total marital communion, actualizing (initiating or renewing) their marriage. Only if two persons truly unite biologically, and only if this biological union is an aspect of a total personal communion, does their sexual act embody a genuine, common good—marriage. And the sexual act can be an aspect of a total personal communion—that is, actualize or make present their personal communion—only if the personal communion is of the sort that is naturally prolonged and fulfilled in procreation, and the sexual act is a reproductive-type act making them truly two-in-one-flesh. Thus, only in marriage can sexual acts realize a common good rather than induce self-alienation or produce a merely illusory experience of personal unity.

NOTES

1 The author would like to thank his co-author Patrick Lee, the co-author of this essay, for permission to reprint this essay.
2 It is not clear, for example, that acting against the orientation of a biological power is necessarily wrong, nor is it clear that sodomitical and other non-marital acts are really *contrary* to that direction. It is worth noting that among the recent natural law theorists who decline to use the perverted faculty argument one would have to include Pope John Paul II. Cf. *Familiaris Consortio*, Pt. III. The Pope specifically rejects this sort of argument in *Veritatis Splendor*, #48.
3 See, e.g., Andrew Sullivan, *Virtually Normal: An Argument about Homosexuality* (NY: Alfred Knopf, 1995), 19–55.
4 Germain G. Grisez, *The Way of the Lord Jesus, Vol. 2: Living a Christian Life* (Quincy, Ill.: Franciscan Press, 1993), 633–56.
5 John Finnis, 'Law, Morality, and "Sexual Orientation,"' *Notre Dame Law Review*, 69 (1994), 1049; Robert P. George and Gerard V. Bradley, 'Marriage and the Liberal Imagination,' *Georgetown Law Review* 84 (1995), 301–320.
6 By 'chaste' marital intercourse is meant marital intercourse that is done with mutual respect and the right intentions.
7 Frederick Elliston, 'In Defense of Promiscuity,' in *Philosophical Perspectives on Sex and Love*, Robert M. Stewart, ed. (NY: Oxford University Press, 1995), 152.
8 Ibid.
9 Ibid. Mill himself, it should be noted, did not advocate promiscuity.
10 Lars O. Ericsson, 'Charges Against Prostitution: An Attempt at Philosophical Assessment,' *Ethics*, 90 (1980), 338–339.
11 One could not enjoy *it* unless it was desired for its own sake or was a means to something else. On the position that there are two senses of 'pleasure,' cf. William Alston, 'Pleasure,' in *Encyclopedia of Philosophy*; J. L. Cowan, *Pleasure and Pain: A Study in Philosophical Psychology* (NY: Macmillan, 1968); Dan Brock, 'The Use of Drugs for Pleasure; Some Philosophical Issues,' in *Feeling Good and Doing Better; Ethics and Nontherapeutic Drug Use*, Thomas Murray, Willard Gaylin and Ruth Macklin, eds. (Clifton, NJ: Humana, 1984), 83–106.
12 The choice could be wrong for reasons not connected with its relation to pleasure. It could involve injustice, neglecting other duties, and so on.
13 Sometimes simulating an activity is not a pursuit of sheer pleasure or an experience bereft of real fulfillment, but a form of play: for example, simulating the flying of an airplane, or the coaching of a football team, as in computer games. Why couldn't having sex with Susan be justified as 'playing house,' that is playing husband and wife? Note, first, that if this were so it would justify adultery as well as premarital sexual relations. Note also that no one thinks it wrong for John and Susan to pretend to be husband and wife in a play

or movie, provided they do not engage in acts intended to be sexually arousing. The difference is that when people engage in sex their sexual desire and
their physical activity are aimed at something quite real, the sexual arousal and
bodily contact or union with the other, making sexual acts quite different from
saying lines in a play or movie or other types of simulation. It is clear, then, that
the fundamental act in sex is not play (although there may, of course, be some
playfulness during their sexual act).

14 It is in this way, for example, that one might take heroin. A drug addict takes
heroin simply for the feeling; how he gets that feeling, what reality that feeling
is attached to (in this case, a change in the chemicals in his brain) is completely
irrelevant. Thus, he is using his body to get that feeling. His end is the conscious feeling, as a content. His means is a chemical change produced in his
body. But he treats his body as a mere extrinsic means, as a mere object, not as
an intrinsic aspect of the subject, which in reality it is. Such a choice inherently
involves contempt for the body.

15 So, the point is not that the act violates the nature of the teleology of the bodily
part, as if the act were a violation of a bodily part. That would be the same as
the argument that certain acts are wrong solely because they are unnatural.
Rather, the point is that the body is not treated as an aspect of the subject of the
action, and so is treated as an extrinsic tool.

16 One may be deprived of self-integration through no fault of one's own, just as
one can be deprived of physical health (which consists to a great extent in
physical integration) through no fault of one's own.

17 We think it is important to note the logical link between solitary masturbation
and other non-marital sexual acts. Many philosophers and theologians hold
that solitary masturbation is not in itself morally wrong, but hold that prostitution and promiscuity are wrong. We, however, doubt the coherence of such
a position. If doing something by oneself is morally acceptable, then, unless
some incidental injustice is committed when it is done with another, it is hard
to see why doing the same thing with someone else's assistance should be
wrong.

18 And consider that people can develop a certain affection for each other quickly,
indeed, moments after meeting each other for the first time.

19 In *De bono coniugali* St Augustine held explicitly that marriage is an instrumental good. He added, however, that ideally there should be a friendship between
husband and wife, and that this friendship is intrinsically good.

20 For this reason the couple may wish to adopt a child or join together in some
other parental-like activity.

21 See Patrick Lee, 'Human Beings are Animals,' *International Philosophical Quarterly*, 37 (1997), 291–304; David Braine, *The Human Person: Animal and Spirit*
(Notre Dame, Ind.: University of Notre Dame Press, 1992), 69–130, 228–90.

22 It is important to note that the teleology of sexual acts belongs to them as
groups primarily. That is, one cannot say that each and every sperm is designed to join with an ovum, so that if this particular one does not it has failed.
If so, it would be hard to explain teleologically why there are millions of
sperms ejaculated in intercourse. Rather, the design of the bodies is that *some
sperm or other at some time or other* join with an ovum. The same is true with
individual instances of sexual intercourse. That is, the functional orientation
belongs to acts of sexual intercourse as a group, primarily, and only indirectly
to the individual acts. The individual act of intercourse is not *directly* oriented
to reproduction; one could say that it is indirectly oriented to reproduction, as

a member of a set, some of which, if all goes well (and the agents respect the basic good of life in its transmission), will be reproductive.

23 Of course, not every instance of two entities sharing in an action are instances of two entities becoming one organism. In this case, however, the potentiality for a specific type of act, reproduction, can be actualized only in cooperation with the opposite sex of the species. The reproductive bodily parts are internally oriented toward actuation together with the bodily parts of the opposite sex. Thus, the same feature which shows that the various bodily parts of a single horse or human constitute a single organism, is found in the bodily parts of the male and the female engaging in a reproductive-type act. So they are literally, not merely metaphorically, one organism. Also strictly speaking, men and woman engaging in sexual acts do not choose to reproduce, though they can choose to perform reproductive-type acts, with reproduction as their goal.

24 See below.

25 See above.

26 Germain Grisez, *The Way of the Lord Jesus, Vol. 2: Living a Christian Life* (Quincy, Ill.: Franciscan Press, 1993), 651.

27 Paul Weithman, 'Natural Law, Morality and Sexual Complementarity,' in *Laws and Nature*, Martha Nussbaum, ed. (NY: Oxford University Press, 1996).

28 Stephen Macedo, 'Homosexuality and the Conservative Mind,' *Georgetown Law Journal*, 84 (1995), 261–300, at 278. George and Bradley, in reply, observe that pleasure and expressions of feeling are *not*, in truth, the justifying point of sexual relations between spouses; the justifying point is, rather, the intrinsic good of marriage itself considered as a one-flesh communion of persons consummated and actualized by acts which, qua reproductive in type, unite the spouses biologically and interpersonally. See 'Marriage and the Liberal Imagination,' op. cit.

29 Macedo, 'Homosexuality and the Conservative Mind,' 278–9.

30 Notice that there are two distinct points regarding homosexual acts: (1) homosexuals partners cannot form the kind of personal communion with each other which is embodied by reproductive-type acts; (2) nor can they perform with each other a reproductive-type act, that is their sexual acts do not unite them biologically.

31 Also, see below.

32 See above.

33 Michael J. Perry, 'The Morality of Homosexual Conduct: A Response to John Finnis,' *Notre Dame Journal of Law, Ethics and Public Policy*, 9 (1994), 56.

34 As an intrinsic good, to be sure, play provides a basic reason for action. However, the good of play should not be equated with doing whatever one pleases. That would collapse play as a *reason* into a non-rational motive. Play, precisely as a rational motive, gives one reason to pursue more or less complex, frequently rule-based, activities (such as chess or football). It does not provide a reason to do whatever one wants to precisely because one believes that pleasure is to be obtained.

35 Nothing in our analysis implies that friendship is merely instrumental to other goods. On the contrary, friendship is intrinsically valuable. See John Finnis, *Natural Law and Natural Rights* (Oxford: Clarendon Press, 1980), 88.

36 Ibid.

37 Macedo, 'Homosexuality and the Conservative Mind,' 282, n. 85.

38 Ibid., 288.

10

Making Children Moral: Pornography, Parents and the Public Interest[1]

On two occasions in October of 1965, Sam Ginsberg, proprietor of Sam's Stationery and Luncheonette in Bellmore, New York, sold magazines containing photographs of nude women to a sixteen-year-old boy. Ginsberg was tried in state court and convicted of violating Section 484–h of the New York Penal Law, which prohibited the sale of pornographic materials to minors (defined by the statute as persons under seventeen years of age). His conviction was upheld by the relevant department of the Appellate Term of the New York Supreme Court, after which he was denied leave to appeal to the New York Court of Appeals. The Supreme Court of the United States heard the case on appeal and in April of 1968 affirmed Ginsberg's conviction in an opinion by Justice William Brennan.[2] Justice John Marshall Harlan concurred in the judgment and joined the opinion of the Court. Justice Potter Stewart concurred in the result. Justice William O. Douglas, joined by Justice Hugo Black, dissented. Justice Abe Fortas also dissented.

Ginsberg argued that the New York law violated the First Amendment's guarantee of freedom of expression. He did not challenge the authority of the state to ban obscene publications. (The Supreme Court has always held that obscenity—like defamation and certain other types of harmful and valueless expression—is outside the First Amendment's protections of freedom of speech and the press.) Rather, he claimed that the New York law was unconstitutional on its face because it banned the sale (to minors) of non-obscene publications.

Justice Brennan conceded that the pornographic magazines Ginsberg sold were not legally obscene for adults.[3] Thus, according to the prevailing doctrine, New York could not forbid Ginsberg or others from stocking them and selling them to adults. The Court ruled, however, that New York was constitutionally permitted to adopt 'variable concepts of obscenity,' according to which the magazines sold by Ginsberg were, nevertheless, legally obscene for minors.[4] The Justices rejected Ginsberg's argument that 'the scope of the constitutional freedom of expression secured to a citizen to read or see material concerned with sex cannot be made to depend upon whether the citizen is an adult or a minor.'[5]

Brennan identified two interests which, he said, justified the state, acting pursuant to its police powers to protect public health, safety and morals, in placing limitations on the availability of material to minors that it could not constitutionally prohibit to adults.[6] First, he said, is the state's interest in assisting parents in fulfilling their child-rearing responsibilities. Quoting from *Prince* v. *Massachusetts*, Brennan wrote that '[i]t is cardinal with us that the custody, care and nurture of the child reside first in the parents, whose primary function and freedom include preparation for obligations the state can neither supply nor hinder.'[7] But, he continued, '[t]he legislature could properly conclude that parents and others, teachers, for example, who have this primary responsibility for children's well-being are entitled to the support of laws designed to aid discharge of that responsibility.'[8]

The second interest justifying special limitations on children's access to pornographic material, according to Brennan, is the state's 'independent interest in the well-being of its youth.'[9] In defense of this interest, he quoted with approval the concurring opinion of Judge Fuld of the New York Court of Appeals in *People* v. *Kahan*:

While the supervision of children's reading may best be left to their parents, the knowledge that parental control or guidance cannot always be provided and society's transcendent interest in protecting the welfare of children justify reasonable regulation of the sale of material to them. It is, therefore, altogether fitting and proper for a state to include in a statute designed to regulate the sale of pornography to children special standards, broader than those embodied in legislation aimed at controlling dissemination of such materials to adults.[10]

Then, quoting again from *Prince* v. *Massachusetts*, Brennan observed that the Supreme Court had itself recognized the state's independent interest in children's welfare and the need for them to be ' "safeguarded from abuses" which might prevent their "growth into free and independent well-developed men and citizens." '[11] The sole question before the Court, he concluded, was 'whether the New York Legislature might rationally conclude, as it has, that exposure to the materials proscribed by section 484–h constitutes such an "abuse." '[12] His conclusion, and that of a majority of the Justices, was that the New York Legislature might rationally conclude that exposing minors to pornographic materials, even of a sort not considered to be obscene for adults, constitutes an abuse which, as he put it, might impair 'the ethical and moral development of youth.'[13]

There are a great many people today who would disagree with Justice Brennan's conclusion. I, however, think it was right. In fact, Brennan quite correctly identified both the harm of exposing young people (but, I shall argue, not just young people) to pornography and the interests justifying governmental efforts to protect them (and, I think, the rest of us) from that harm.

It is often supposed—particularly by judges who would invalidate anti-pornography laws—that the 'harm' of pornography is offense to the sensibilities of those—like themselves, the judges are often quick to add—who find it distasteful.[14] Pornography, they say, may shock and offend many people; but putting up with being shocked and offended is the price we must pay for the great blessing of freedom of expression. Those who are shocked and offended can simply avert their eyes. Justice Douglas, in his dissent in *Ginsberg*, informed his readers that he personally finds the pornographic material that comes to the Court for review 'exceedingly dull and boring.'[15] Still, he allowed that some people 'can and do become very excited and alarmed and think that something should be done to stop the flow [of pornography].'[16] And, indeed, those who wish to do something about it—Douglas made particular mention of parents and religious organizations—can act in their private capacities, albeit in ways Douglas did not specify, to combat it; they may not, however, implicate the state as a censor. 'As I read the First Amendment,' Douglas declared, 'it was designed to keep the state and the hands of all state officials off the printing presses of America and off the distribution systems for all printed literature.'[17]

I think that this is a very dubious account of what the First Amendment was 'designed' to do. If we are really going to let our constitutional jurisprudence be governed by what the provisions of the Constitution, including the First Amendment, 'were designed to do,' then very little that is pornographic will be given any protection at all—which would be fine with me.[18] The point I wish to make here, though, is that the harm of pornography about which legislators have traditionally (and, in my view, rightly) been concerned, as Brennan seemed to understand perfectly well, but Douglas grasped (or, perhaps, credited) not at all, is not its capacity to shock and offend, but, rather, its tendency to corrupt and deprave. (Indeed, its capacity to shock and offend is, I think, more or less derivative of the judgment that it tends to corrupt and deprave.) Here, I think, the dissenting members of the President's Commission on Obscenity and Pornography which issued its Report in 1970 were right on the mark: 'The government interest in regulating pornography has always related primarily to the prevention of moral corruption and not to . . . the protection of persons from being shocked and/or offended.'[19]

But, it will be objected, in this day and age, when we (whoever 'we' are) are enlightened about sex and have rightly relegated Comstockery to the ash heap of history, who could credit the idea that pornography is a source of moral corruption? Sure, there are still folk—parents and religious organizations—who get themselves worked up ('excited and alarmed,' in Douglas's dismissive characterization) about the prevalence of pornography in our culture and call for its censorship, but, is it not the case, as Justice Douglas was pleased to observe in *Ginsberg*, that '[c]ensors are, of course, propelled by their own neuroses?'[20] Well, if so, permit me to put some of my neuroses on display.

Professor Harry Clor, in his new book, *Public Morality and Liberal Society*, reports on a content analysis he conducted of 'a typical general circulation magazine called Swank.'[21] Clor describes Swank as 'somewhat less crudely salacious than Hustler magazine and somewhat more so than Playboy or Penthouse.'[22] Perusing Swank, he says, 'is, in some sense, like entering a world unto itself; one gets an introduction to the world of pornography.'

First of all, we encounter a number of what the trade calls 'spreader' or 'beaver' pictorials: close-up shots of nude women with their legs spread wide apart and sexual organs prominently displayed. A series of page-size photographs portrays a man and a woman, both completely naked, simulating intercourse; in some scenes oral sex is simulated by both partners. One set of pictures depicts group sex.[23]

Now, it seems to me that images such as those offered to readers of Swank tend to corrupt and deprave by doing precisely what they are designed to do, namely, arousing sexual desire that is utterly unintegrated with the procreative and unitive goods which give the sexual congress of men and women, as husbands and wives, its value, meaning and significance. Such images tend to induce (and/or reinforce) in persons (particularly, I think, in men, who, in any event, tend to be more attracted to and tempted by pornography than women tend to be) a certain disposition—a more-than-merely-temporary state of the imagination and emotions—which makes it difficult for people to understand, intend and experience sexual relations as other than a kind of self-gratification involving, as part of its end, the 'using' and, in some sense, 'possessing' of another.

Even, to take the best possible case for pornography, when spouses employ pornographic materials as means of stimulating their sexual desire for each other or 'spicing up' their sex lives, as morally liberated sex experts frequently advise couples to do, they accomplish their goal by means that unavoidably de-personalize themselves and their relationship. What pornography arouses in, say, Mr Smith is the desire for a woman (perhaps a desire for a certain sort of woman—a woman with large breasts, for example), not a desire for the bodily actualization and expression of his unique relationship of marital union with Mrs Smith as such. Mrs Smith may be willing to go along with this, since Mr Smith might be otherwise uninterested in her, but she ought not to be. Mrs Smith is, after all, a unique person who is uniquely related to Smith as his wife; it is dehumanizing for her to be taken by him (and dehumanizing for him to take her) as 'a mere convenient, available instance of [a] "desirable woman" whose presence in the man's aroused imagination impels him towards her until the moment when his biological tension is released, the appealing figure fades in his imagination, and his failure to integrate his insistent words and actions to a common life of friendship becomes obvious even to him.'[24] This dehumanization—this reduction of persons to the status of things—in and by pornography is highlighted by Harry Clor in his characterization of the contents of Swank, which, you will recall, is by no means the most salacious of the pornographic magazines available for sale in a typical newsstand:

First, this is an area of wholly loveless, affectionless sex. The sexuality it portrays and invites is thoroughly depersonalized; the passion it appeals to is the desire for the possession of someone's body without any interest in the personality to which, in ordinary life, a body belongs. Second, there is an invasion of privacy; physical intimacies and reactions normally protected from public observation are placed conspicuously on display. This 'invasion,' this aggressive intrusion upon the intimately private, is by no means incidental to Swank's pornographic intent and effect; it is an integral element in the experience that Swank is designed to give us, and it is one of the features that make the magazine recognizable as pornography. Third, the magazine presents a pervasive 'objectification' of the erotic experience and the female in particular. The erotic activity is reduced, in graphic detail, to its physical components, and the participants are viewed as instruments for the production of pleasurable sensations.[25]

If Clor's characterization is accurate, however, why would anybody be interested in pornography? Why does it have any appeal to people? Why is there a market for it—indeed, according to a recent cover story on the pornography industry in U.S. News and World Report, a massive international market.[26] The answers, I think, have to do with the complexities of human sexual psychology. As John Finnis has observed:

. . . sexuality is a powerful force which only with some difficulty, and always precariously, can be integrated with other aspects of human personality and well-being—so that it enhances rather than destroys friendship and the care of children, for example. . . . [Moreover,] human sexual psychology has a bias towards regarding other persons as bodily objects of desire and potential sexual release and gratification, and as mere items in an erotically flavored classification (e.g., 'women'), rather than as full persons with personal and individual sensitivities, restraints, and life plans.[27]

Pornography, precisely by arousing sexual desires unintegrated with the human goods to which sexuality is morally ordered, induces in its consumers states of emotion, imagination and sentiment which dispose them to understand and regard themselves and their bodies, and others and their bodies, as, in essence, instruments of sexual gratification—sex objects. Pornography corrupts by appealing to and heightening the tendency towards selfishness which, even in the most virtuous among us, represents a danger to our integrity and to the precious relationships (husband–wife, parent–child, friendships) which depend, in part, on the proper integration of our sexuality into our lives.

Anyone who has the temerity to question the tenets of liberal sexual ideology exposes himself to the risk of being misunderstood and misrepresented. So, as a matter of caution, let me here make explicit what I am *not* saying (and do not believe). I am not saying (nor do I believe) that sex is bad, or, in itself, sinful, or only for procreation (though I think its procreative significance is always a part of what makes sex humanly valuable, even when it is not, and perhaps isn't even intended to be, procreative); nor am I saying that we should be ashamed of our bodies, or of our sexuality, or that we should dress the nude figures painted by Michaelangelo on the ceiling of the Sistine Chapel, or cover up the table legs, or excise the *Song of Songs* from the Bible. In fact, I think that sex, when it is humanly valuable, is intrinsically, and not merely instrumentally valuable.[28] And I think that part of why we should be concerned about sexual immorality generally, and the tendency of pornography to corrupt and deprave in particular, is that it damages people's capacities properly to channel sexual desire so that they can realize in their marriages the intrinsic value of sexual union. This capacity is, I think, utterly dependent on the understandings and self-understandings practically and effectively available to us only to the extent of our self-integration, self-possession and self-control in matters pertaining to our sexuality.[29]

Of course, the judgment that pornography is bad in the ways I claim it is depends on the validity of my more general claims about sexuality and sexual morality.[30] And to many people today my understanding of sexuality and sexual morality is an antiquated and unliberated one. It is denounced by David Richards, for example, who celebrates pornography 'as the unique medium of a vision of sexuality, a "pornotopia," a view of sensual delight in the erotic celebration of the body, a concept of easy freedom without consequences, a fantasy of timelessly repetitive indulgence.'[31] Well, this like other aspects of sexual liberationism, is a fantasy all right. In matters of sexuality, there simply is no 'easy freedom without consequences,' nor should we want there to be. The dignity, beauty and value of our sexuality depend on the fact that it does have consequences, even when the coming to be of new human persons happens not to be among those consequences.

In fact, 'sexual liberationism' is a sort of self-contradiction. Freedom lies not in sexual self-indulgence or self-gratification, but rather in sexual self-integration, self-possession and self-control. Justice Brennan was on to this, I think, in *Ginsberg* when, quoting Judge Fuld, he concluded that the

New York Legislature could quite reasonably conclude that exposing young people to pornography was an 'abuse' that threatened their growth into 'free and independent well-developed men and citizens.' The freedom pornography imperils is freedom from a sexuality which is unintegrated, selfish, impulsive, depersonalized, disordered, out of control.

But vulnerability to the risk of anarchic sexuality is by no means confined to the young. Nor is the harm of such sexuality limited to individuals as opposed to communities. Nor can the young, or anyone else, be protected from the threats posed by pornography to their interests by efforts to keep pornography out of their hands unless those efforts are part of a larger project to restrict its availability. Again, those who dissented from the 1970 Report of the President's Commission on Obscenity and Pornography rightly observed that 'pornography has an eroding effect on society, on public morality, on respect for human worth, on attitudes toward family love, on culture.'[32] Even in defending an alleged 'right to pornography,' Ronald Dworkin conceded this most crucial of all points in the debate about pornography and censorship: Legal recognition of such a right, he observed:

would sharply limit the ability of individuals consciously and reflectively to influence the conditions of their own and their children's development. It would limit their ability to bring about the cultural structure they think best, a structure in which sexual experience generally has dignity and beauty, without which their own and their families' sexual experience are likely to have these qualities in less degree.[33]

So, I think, the very considerations which justify the paternalistic concern to limit the rights of minors to obtain pornographic materials—even the 'soft-core' stuff whose sale to a minor landed Ginsberg in the dock—justify, and indeed demand, a broader concern to protect from the corroding and corrupting effects of pornography the social milieu in which people lead their lives and rear their children. The very interests identified by Justice Brennan as justifying the prohibition of sales of pornography to minors equally, I think, justify a more sweeping prohibition of pornography—a broader definition of 'obscenity' if we are to stick with the idea, which the Court seemed eager to stick with in *Ginsberg*, that whatever lewd material the state is justified in banning gets classified as 'obscene.'

I should say a word here about the feminist argument for repressing pornography. As the reader will have surmised by now, I am a moral traditionalist, as opposed to a feminist. If I understand feminist opponents of pornography, such as Susan Brownmiller and Catharine MacKinnon, they are eager to distance themselves from the 'moralistic' arguments made by people like me. I am less interested, I think, in distancing myself from arguments made by people like them—arguments equally moralistic, and none the worse for that. I think that pornography is degrading and dehumanizing for everyone, but I have no doubt that women and girls get the worst of it in a society in which pornography flourishes. Even when pornography depicts women in dominant and powerful, as opposed to subordinate and humiliating, roles (which, according to Clor and others is not that often), the understandings and self-understandings, the dispositions and feelings, the sentiments and sensibilities it promotes conduce to a 'cultural structure,' as Dworkin says, where sexuality lacks 'dignity and beauty.'[34] In the context of such a cultural structure in the real world of male and female sexual psychology and relationships, women and girls are bound to suffer even more than men and boys. Women, for example, are more likely to be abandoned and left unsupported by their sexual partners. They are overwhelmingly more likely to be 'traded in' for younger and sleeker models, even by 'respectable' husbands. It would be very surprising if they were not more likely to suffer domination, exploitation and abuse.

Now, legal prohibition of anything works well only when supported by a widespread recognition of the evil of the thing prohibited. This is not only because effective enforcement requires public support for the law; it is also because law is only effective where most people recognize moral reasons (and thus have motives other than respect for law as such or fear of punishment) for refraining from the activity prohibited by the law. There is a core of truth in the idea that laws work best when they are needed least. Or, to state things the other way around, laws are likely to be least effective when they are needed most. So, it seems, the damage to the moral ecology (Dworkin's 'cultural structure') of modern societies already done by the traffic in pornography (and other desiderata of the sexual revolution) limits the social pay-off of strengthening the legal attack on the pornography industry. Still, I believe that it is worth doing.

At the same time, public and private institutions, including schools, libraries, museums and the like, should do their part by observing the maxim: first do no harm. Such institutions should not abet the pornography trade by catering in any way to the desire for pornography. Anyone who makes the stuff available—from street vendors to libraries—does an injustice to decent people, particularly decent men, by putting what will in many cases be a powerful temptation in their way, and to everybody, and particularly to women (and children), since everybody has a stake in the moral ecology of the community that pornography degrades. Where these injustices are perpetrated by public institutions whose very reason for existence is to serve the public good, it is a special outrage and scandal.

Now, even if I am right in thinking that pornography damages the moral environment (and, thus, the public interest) of communities in which it flourishes, and that those communities are therefore entitled to enact and enforce laws restricting and even prohibiting it, difficult questions remain. Even non-pornographic artistic and literary evocations of sexual love—the *Song of Songs*, for example—can be used as stimuli or occasions for the indulgence of unintegrated sexual desire of the sort deliberately aroused by pornography. And there are certainly borderline cases in which it is difficult to distinguish the pornographic from the non-pornographic. What is to be done?

Here, I think, there is no hope of identifying strict rules. A certain sort of practical or prudential judgment is required, and democratic deliberation must take place in every community. Although I know that it is supposed to be especially unenlightened to consider concerns about the pornographic use of non-pornographic materials to be in any way legitimate, these concerns do strike me as worth taking seriously, particularly when it comes to young people. So I think that public (and private) institutions ought to do what they can, in Brennan's words, to 'support' parents in 'the discharge of their responsibilities.' So, warnings, ratings systems, restricted access, requirements that children be accompanied by adults, all have their place where the access of minors to sexually oriented material is concerned. Free speech considerations are relevant here, but should not be treated as trumps. Instituting such policies should not, however, be permitted to become a pretext for expanding the offering of pornographic materials in the public media. This, according to George Will, was an effect of the movie rating system; he fears, as I do, that it could be a consequence of the television rating system and the v-chip.

Nudity in anything like a sexual context should, I think, be kept off television precisely because easy access by young people makes the already difficult task of parents even more difficult. I don't know enough about the technology of the Internet to have any very firm idea of whether or how the presentation of questionable material there could be controlled, but certainly any conceivable ways of supporting parents ought to be explored and considered. I recognize that where legitimate material with sexual content is concerned, there is a trade-off. Protecting the young means making access to some such material more difficult for adults. Balances can be struck in different ways, and I see no reason in principle why different communities (and, indeed, different institutions) ought not to be able to strike them differently. My real point is that absolutism (or, dare I call it, 'fundamentalism') ought to be eschewed by everybody: Parents have no absolute right to raise their children in an antiseptic environment entirely free from materials which, though legitimate, can constitute for young people what, in the old language, was called 'an occasion of sin.' At the same time, adults have no absolute right to easy access even to non-pornographic materials where the interests of young people may be adversely affected.

When it comes to the borderline cases of legitimacy, it seems to me that here, too, prudential judgment, exercised in light of local and contingent circumstances, is required. I am not sufficiently impressed by John Stuart Mill's argument in *On Liberty* to agree with his judgment that in civilized societies we can always count on 'the salutary permanent effects of freedom.'[35] Rather, different circumstances and conditions call for different policies. Different societies differ even as to the degree of personal autonomy that is consistent with the maintenance of a minimally decent moral environment. And while it is true that in some societies a puritanical spirit threatens genuine progress in the arts and literature, in others, licentiousness, abetted, as always, by a false vision of freedom, imperils the interest of all in a morally decent cultural milieu. In any society, careful deliberation by citizens committed to the common good, informed both by sound moral judgment and prudent practical understanding, needs to be brought to bear in the effort to, at the same time, preserve honorable liberties and protect public morality.

NOTES

1 Adapted from an address delivered at the Conference on Free Speech and Community sponsored by the Arizona Humanities Council and the Arizona State University College of Law, Feb. 7, 1997.
2 *Ginsberg* v. *New York*, 390 U.S. 629 (1968).
3 Ibid., 634.
4 Ibid., 635–7.
5 Ibid., 636.
6 Ibid., 638–43.
7 Ibid., 639 (quoting *Prince* v. *Massachusetts*, 321 U.S. 158, 166 (1944) (upholding in the face of constitutional challenge the conviction of the guardian of a minor child for permitting the child to sell religious tracts on the streets of Boston, in violation of Massachusetts' child labor laws)).
8 Ibid., 639.
9 Ibid., 640.
10 15 N.Y. 2d 311, 312 (1965).
11 *Ginsberg*, 390 U.S. at 640–641 (quoting *Prince*, 321 U.S. at 165).
12 Ibid., 641.
13 Ibid., 640–1.
14 A typical example: On January 22, 1997, a federal district court in New York City invalidated the Military Honor and Decency Act of 1996, which prohibited the sale of pornographic magazines and videotapes on military bases. The judge, Shira A. Scheindlin, ruled that the ban violated constitutionally

protected free speech rights. 'While the majority of Americans may wish to ban pornography,' she wrote, 'in the final analysis, society is better served by protecting our cherished right to free speech, even at the cost of tolerating speech that is outrageous, offensive, and demeaning.' *General Media Communications, Inc.* v. *Perry*, 952 F. Su 1072, 1074 (SDNY 1997). Predictably, she went on to assure her readers that she shared the view that 'the result of permitting such speech is often unfortunate and unpleasant.' Ibid. It is plain, I think, that Judge Scheindlin supposes that the motivating purpose of the Military Honor and Decency Act was, above all, to prevent offense. But this supposition is gratuitous and almost certainly incorrect. The purpose, rather, was to uphold public morality on military bases by protecting people (and the moral environment in which they live) from the morally corrosive effects of pornography. (One may, of course, deny that pornography has 'morally corrosive' effects, but that denial does not entitle one to suppose that the people responsible for laws against pornography share one's own view of the matter and must therefore be motivated, in reality, not by a concern to protect public morality, but rather by a desire to prevent offense.) Scheindlin's supposition is connected to other highly questionable aspects of her reasoning. For example, why should her views, or those of other judges, about what is, after all, the factual question of whether society is 'better served' by permitting pornography than prohibiting it prevail over the contrary opinions of the American people or their elected representatives? It simply begs the question to say that her views should prevail because she is a judge and is therefore responsible for enforcing constitutional guarantees.

15 *Ginsberg*, 390 U.S. at 655 (Douglas, J., dissenting).
16 Ibid.
17 Ibid.
18 On what the First Amendment was designed to do—and how far prevailing free speech doctrine diverges from that design—see Walter Berns, *The First Amendment and the Future of American Democracy* (Chicago, Ill.: Gateway Editions, 1985).
19 Morton A. Hill and Winfrey C. Link, Separate Statements By Commission Members, in 'The Report of the Commission on Obscenity and Pornography,' 456, 457 (1970) [hereinafter Commission Report].
20 *Ginsberg*, 390 U.S. at 655 (Douglas, J., dissenting).
21 Harry M. Clor, *Public Morality and Liberal Society: Essays on Decency, Law and Pornography* (Notre Dame, Ind.: University of Notre Dame Press, 1996), 190.
22 Ibid.
23 Ibid.
24 John Finnis, *Pornography* (unpublished manuscript, on file with author, 1973), 19.
25 Clor, *Public Morality*, 190–1.
26 Eric Schlosser, 'The Business of Pornography,' *US News and World Report* (Feb. 10, 1997), 4.
27 John Finnis, *Natural Law and Natural Rights* (NY: Oxford University Press, 1980), 217.
28 The sexual intercourse of spouses is the biological matrix of the multilevel (bodily, emotional, dispositional, spiritual) relationship and good of their marriage. The climactic one-flesh union of husband and wife in marital intercourse not only expresses, but enables them to consummate, actualize and experience the uniquely sexually unitive form of friendship that marriage is. Sex is not a

'necessary evil' that good people need to engage in and tolerate in order to continue the human race; rather, it is a central and more-than-merely-instrumental aspect of the great and intrinsic good of marriage. This view of sexual morality differs from both the strict Augustinian view that understands sex as instrumental to procreation and the dominant liberal view that understands sex as instrumental to procreation (if that is the wish of the persons involved), or to pleasure, or as a means of promoting emotional closeness or expressing affectionate feelings. See, generally, Robert P. George and Gerard V. Bradley, 'Marriage and the Liberal Imagination,' *Georgetown Law Review*, 84 (1995), reprinted herein as Chapter 8.

29 John Finnis provides a valuable explication and defense of Aquinas's account of this dependency in *Aquinas*, Ch. 7, s. 2 (Oxford: Clarendon Press, 1998).

30 For the defense of these claims, see George and Bradley, 'Marriage'; see also John Finnis, 'Law, Morality, and "Sexual Orientation,"' *Notre Dame Law Review*, 69 (1994), 1049; John Finnis, 'The Good of Marriage,' *The American Journal of Jurisprudence* (1997).

31 D. A. J. Richards, *The Moral Criticism of Law* (Encino, Calif.: Dickenson Publishing Co., 1977), 71 (footnote omitted).

32 Commission Report, 458.

33 Ronald Dworkin, 'Do We Have a Right to Pornography?,' in *A Matter of Principle* (Cambridge, Mass.: Harvard University Press, 1985), 335, 349.

34 Ibid.

35 John Stuart Mill, *On Liberty* (Longmans, Green, Reader and Dyer, 1873).

11

Public Reason and Political Conflict: Abortion and Homosexuality

Is it possible for people who sharply disagree about important questions of morality, including those pertaining to abortion and homosexuality, to constitute a stable political society whose basic constitutional principles can be affirmed as just by all reasonable parties? This question is not about the possibility of political compromise; rather, it concerns the possibility of a certain type of moral agreement. This type of moral agreement is not agreement about whether abortion or homosexual conduct, for example, are right or wrong. Instead, it is agreement about basic principles of justice for a society composed of people who disagree about such issues.

One possibility is for people who disagree about the morality of particular acts or practices to agree upon fair procedures for the political resolution of moral disagreements. For example, people who disagree about the morality of abortion might, as a constitutional matter, agree upon democratic procedures for setting public policy on abortion. However, people of strong and settled conviction on either side of the debate over abortion cannot reasonably be satisfied of the justice of the fundamental law of their country simply because the procedures used to arrive at a resolution were democratic. From the pro-life point of view, any regime of law (including one whose pedigree is impeccably democratic) that deprives unborn human beings of their right to legal protection against homicide is gravely unjust.[1] Similarly, from the pro-choice viewpoint, restrictions on a woman's right to abortion are seriously unjust even if they were put in place by democratic procedures. From either perspective, the question of abortion is viewed as a matter of fundamental justice whose proper resolution is essential to the full moral legitimacy of the constitutional order. In this respect, the social conflict over abortion closely resembles the conflict over slavery. Of course, pro-life and pro-choice advocates may, for their own partisan reasons, or as part of a modus vivendi, agree to a constitutional requirement that public policy on abortion be settled by democratic procedures. But agreement of this sort is not agreement on basic principles of justice.

A number of leading liberal political theorists have proposed a different, and more radical, possibility. They contend that people who disagree about abortion, homosexuality and other matters of allegedly 'private' or 'personal' morality can and should agree as a matter of fundamental justice to a constitutional principle that forbids government from substantially restricting or burdening people's liberty, or denying them equality of treatment, on the basis of controversial moral judgments about such matters.[2] This principle is one version of what is sometimes referred to as 'anti-perfectionism.' Its proponents seek to provide the ground of a moral right, for example, to legal abortion and the legal recognition of same-sex unions, a ground which can rationally be affirmed as a principle of political justice even by people who believe that abortion and homosexual conduct are seriously immoral.

Why should people agree to the anti-perfectionist principle? After all, the question of whether abortion and homosexuality are purely 'private' or 'personal' matters—matters that implicate no significant public interests—is as much in dispute as the question of whether these acts are immoral. From the pro-life point of view, abortion is no more 'private' than infanticide and other forms of homicide. From the perspective of those who object to the public recognition or promotion of same-sex sexual relationships, the issue is no more a matter of merely 'personal' morality than was (and is) the issue of polygamy. Understandably, critics of anti-perfectionism suspect that it represents a kind of philosophical sleight of hand designed to induce dissenters from substantive liberal moral beliefs to accede to liberal hegemony in matters of public policy pertaining to issues such as abortion and homosexuality.[3]

Are anti-perfectionism's critics correct? Or can a sound argument in defense of anti-perfectionism be developed? In this chapter, I shall consider the recent effort of John Rawls and some of his followers to defend anti-perfectionist liberalism in the form of a doctrine of 'political justice.' Their criteria of legitimate political advocacy and action in societies marked by group conflict over issues such as abortion and homosexuality centers around the idea of 'public reason.' I shall try to show that their arguments fail to provide compelling grounds for embracing anti-perfectionism, and I shall illustrate this point by criticizing: (1) the sketch of a defense of a right to abortion proposed by Rawls in *Political Liberalism* and developed in greater detail by Judith Jarvis Thomson; and (2) Stephen Macedo's Rawlsian argument for the legal recognition of same-sex 'marriages.' I will then provide suggestions as to how people with such disagreements can discuss and debate their beliefs in a peaceful and civil manner.

I. POLITICAL LIBERALISM AND THE RATIONALIST BELIEVERS

A. The Rawlsian Conception

In his profoundly influential book, *A Theory of Justice*, Rawls defended a strict anti-perfectionism.[4] This defense was embedded in a general theory of justice ('justice as fairness') that Rawls now says relied on a premise which the theory itself rules out, namely, the idea that 'in the well-ordered society of justice as fairness, citizens hold the same comprehensive doctrine, and this includes aspects of Kant's comprehensive liberalism, to which the principles of justice as fairness might belong.'[5] The problem with this idea is that neither liberalism, considered as a 'comprehensive doctrine,' nor any other comprehensive view is held by citizens generally in pluralistic societies such as ours. Nor is it reasonable under the circumstances of political freedom that characterize modern constitutional democratic regimes to expect that 'comprehensive liberalism,' or any competing comprehensive view, ever would be adopted by citizens generally. Rawls refers to this state of affairs as 'the fact of reasonable pluralism,' and it is the starting point of his revised argument for an anti-perfectionist resolution of the problem of moral disagreement.[6]

Rawls labels his revised proposal 'political liberalism.' His idea (or ideal) is that, for constitutional democratic societies such as ours:

citizens are to conduct their public political discussions of constitutional essentials and matters of basic justice within the framework of what each sincerely regards as a reasonable political conception of justice, a conception that expresses political values that others as free and equal also might reasonably be expected reasonably to endorse.[7]

In this framework, 'deeply opposed though reasonable comprehensive doctrines may live together and all affirm the political conception of a constitutional regime.'[8] Debates over constitutional essentials and matters of basic justice are, for moral reasons (and not as a mere modus vivendi), to be conducted in terms of a 'strictly political conception of justice,'[9] such as 'justice as fairness'[10] as revised by Rawls in *Political Liberalism*. These debates are not to be conducted in terms of moral doctrines of justice, whether secular (e.g., Kantian or Millian liberalism) or religious (e.g., Catholic or Jewish), which are 'general in scope'[11] and in dispute among reasonable citizens. In sharing a common 'political' conception of justice, the partisans of competing reasonable comprehensive doctrines participate in an 'overlapping consensus' on basic principles of justice,[12] thus making social stability (despite the fact of pervasive moral disagreement about personal and social life) not only possible, but also possible 'for the right reasons.'[13]

The alternative to a common commitment to a 'political' conception of justice is for citizens in pluralistic societies to debate issues of constitutional essentials and matters of basic justice by appealing to general moral doctrines of justice connected to their various reasonable comprehensive views. In that case, liberalism—representing one comprehensive view with its own reasonable, but controversial, moral and metaphysical doctrines—would compete for ascendancy in the public square with a range of alternative religious and secular comprehensive views, some reasonable, some not,[14] but all characterized by controversial moral and metaphysical doctrines of their own. Rawls argues against this alternative, not on pragmatic grounds (such as fear that the conflict of comprehensive views at this level could lead to civil strife), but on moral grounds.[15] A strictly 'political' conception of justice is, he maintains, the fairest and most reasonable way of settling constitutional essentials and matters of basic justice. 'Political,' as opposed to 'comprehensive' or 'metaphysical,' liberalism consists precisely in the adoption of such a conception.

What this means concretely is that, whenever constitutional essentials and matters of basic justice are at stake, political actors—including citizens as voters and public political advocates—are forbidden to act on the basis of principles drawn from their comprehensive doctrines, except to the extent that 'public reasons, given by a reasonable political conception, are presented sufficient to support whatever the comprehensive doctrines are introduced to support.'[16] In this way, political liberalism constrains—sometimes quite radically—appeals to, and actions based upon, comprehensive doctrines including comprehensive liberalism. It does so on grounds entirely separate from the putative falsity, unsoundness or unreasonableness of those doctrines or the specific principles drawn from them. Appeals to comprehensive doctrines are never legitimate in legislative assemblies or in the public acts and pronouncements of executive officers.[17] Nor, above all, may judges in a constitutional democracy with judicial review justify their decisions by appealing to principles drawn from comprehensive doctrines.[18]

Undoubtedly having in mind criticisms of *A Theory of Justice* advanced by Alasdair MacIntyre, Michael Sandel, Charles Taylor and others,[19] Rawls insists that 'political liberalism is not a form of Enlightenment liberalism, that is, a comprehensive liberal and often secular doctrine founded on reason and viewed as suitable for the modern age now that the religious authority of Christian ages is said to be no longer dominant.'[20] It is, rather:

a political conception of political justice for a constitutional democratic regime that a plurality of reasonable doctrines, both religious and nonreligious, liberal and nonliberal, may freely endorse, and so freely live by and come to understand its virtues. Emphatically, it does not aim to replace comprehensive doctrines, religious or nonreligious, but intends to be equally distinct from both and, it hopes, acceptable to both.[21]

'Political liberalism' claims to be 'impartial' between the viewpoints represented by the range of competing reasonable comprehensive doctrines, be they liberal or non-liberal, secular or religious.[22] Indeed, according to Rawls, 'political liberalism does not attack or criticize any reasonable view.'[23] He says that 'rather than confronting religious and nonliberal doctrines with a comprehensive liberal philosophical doctrine, the thought is to formulate a liberal political conception that those nonliberal doctrines might be able to endorse.'[24]

If Rawls is correct, not only people who subscribe to one or another comprehensive form of liberalism, but also traditional Catholics, evangelical Protestants, and orthodox Jews—assuming their viewpoints are reasonable (something Rawls seems to suggest he is willing to assume)— ought to be able reasonably to embrace a purely 'political' liberalism while in no way compromising their fundamental moral and religious beliefs and commitments. Precisely to the extent that they are reasonable, various comprehensive views, including religious ones, can be part of the overlapping consensus of political liberalism which ensures social stability.[25]

Although he observes that a de facto modus vivendi might, in particular circumstances, develop into an overlapping consensus,[26] Rawls emphatically denies that the overlapping consensus constitutes, or necessarily results from, a mere modus vivendi.[27] The key is that the overlapping consensus is characterized by a certain type of reasonable moral agreement about what, at a basic level defined by principles and ideals, constitute fair terms of social cooperation among people who, being reasonable, view each other as free and equal citizens. Thus, 'political liberalism,' though representing a 'freestanding' conception of justice,[28] is a moral conception, containing 'its own intrinsic normative and moral ideal.'[29]

Terms of cooperation offered by citizens to their fellow citizens are fair, according to Rawls, only to the extent that 'citizens offering them . . . reasonably think that those citizens to whom such terms are offered might also reasonably accept them.'[30] Rawls refers to this requirement as 'the criterion of reciprocity.'[31] It is the core of what Rawls calls 'the liberal principle of legitimacy,' namely, that 'our exercise of political power is fully proper only when it is exercised in accordance with a constitution the essentials of which all citizens as free and equal may reasonably be expected to endorse in the light of principles and ideals acceptable to their common human reason.'[32] Only when political power is thus exercised do political actors (including voters) act consistently with the ideal of 'public reason.' [33]

B. The 'Rationalist Believers'

A central point and effect of the liberal principle of legitimacy and the ideal of public reason is to exclude as illegitimate, in the framing of a constitution and in legislative and judicial deliberations touching upon constitutional essentials or basic matters of justice,[34] certain principles and other propositions even though they are, or may well be, true. It is easy enough to see how such an exclusion might, in certain circumstances, be reasonable, prudent, and thus warranted as part of a modus vivendi.[35] It is far from obvious, however, that people are obligated morally, in circumstances in which they are not obliged as a matter of political prudence, to refrain from acting on principles that they reasonably believe to be true and that are not ruled out as reasons for political action by their reasonable comprehensive doctrines of justice and political morality.

Of course, a particular comprehensive view might identify reasons, even reasons of principle and not mere prudence, for declining to enforce by law or otherwise to take political action based on certain types of moral obligations. Certain comprehensive liberalisms, such as the liberalisms of John Stuart Mill[36] and Joseph Raz,[37] purport to identify such principles. It is, of course, crucial to Rawls's project to avoid an appeal to any such comprehensive liberalism. His claim is that the rational moral force of the liberal principle of legitimacy and of the ideal of public reason depends in no way on the truth of comprehensive liberalism in any form.

When citizens disagree with one another about certain basic moral, political and religious questions, what does it mean for them to propose terms of social cooperation that they reasonably think their fellow citizens can reasonably accept? If the criterion of reciprocity and the principle of legitimacy are interpreted narrowly, it simply requires that those citizens proposing terms of social cooperation must reasonably think that they are giving their fellow citizens who disagree with them about particular fundamental matters sound reasons, accessible to them as rational persons, for changing their minds. Under such a narrow interpretation, the scope of public reason would be correspondingly wide. Although it would exclude appeals to sheer authority, or 'secret knowledge,' or to putative truths revealed only to an elect few and not accessible to reasonable persons as such, it would not rule out in advance of argument on the merits any principle or proposition, however controversial, which is (or can be) defended by rational argument.[38]

Of course, this interpretation (and the very wide view of public reason it would authorize) is not one Rawls can accept, for it does not limit the field of acceptable doctrines of political morality to political liberalism. It will not serve to exclude ideals and principles drawn from comprehensive forms of liberalism, for example. More to the point, it will not rule out certain notable non-liberal comprehensive views which similarly appeal to our 'common human reason.' The broad tradition of natural law thinking, for example, proposes what amounts to its own principle of public reason when it asserts that questions of fundamental law and basic matters of justice ought to be decided in accordance with natural law, natural right, natural rights and/or natural justice.[39] If Rawls is to sustain his bold claim that 'only a political conception of justice that all citizens might reasonably be expected to endorse can serve as a basis of public reason and justification,'[40] he must defend a broad version of the legitimacy principle, one that restricts the scope of public reason sufficiently to exclude not only comprehensive doctrines that appeal to secret knowledge or private revelation, but also comprehensive doctrines that appeal to publicly accessible reasons. Relatedly, he must show that the putatively strictly 'political' conception of justice can guarantee the liberal conclusions he favors on questions that from the liberal point of view touch upon constitutional essentials and matters of basic justice, without smuggling into the justification for these conclusions disputed principles or propositions drawn from a comprehensive liberalism.

In *Political Liberalism*, Rawls considers the case of 'rationalist believers who contend that [their] beliefs are open to and can be fully established by reason.'[41] Oddly, he says that this contention is 'uncommon,'[42] when it is, in fact, the claim of what Sir Isaiah Berlin, whose own sympathies were plainly liberal, has called 'a central strand in the whole tradition of western thought.'[43] In any event, Rawls's remarkably brief argument against the so-called rationalist believers is based entirely on the claim that they unreasonably deny 'the fact of reasonable pluralism.'[44] If I understand accurately what Rawls means by 'rationalist believers,' then I am something of one myself. I certainly do not deny that people in our culture, including reasonable people, disagree about fundamental moral questions, such as the morality of abortion and homosexual acts. Nor need people like me deny that some measure of moral disagreement is in some sense inevitable under circumstances of political and religious freedom. In precisely what sense, then, do we, according to Rawls, deny the fact of reasonable pluralism?

To be faithful to his own methodological scruples, Rawls must avoid denying the truth of the reasonable, albeit controversial, moral, metaphysical and religious claims that he wishes to exclude as reasons for political action under the principle of legitimacy. He must, therefore, adduce grounds other than their falsity for their exclusion. If he is reduced to arguing on the merits for the falsity of these claims, the case for 'political liberalism' has been fatally compromised. Rawls's strategy is not to deny the truth of the claims of rationalist believers, but merely to deny that their claims 'can be publicly and fully established by reason.'[45] This denial can be sustained, however, only by addressing the merits of the actual arguments that the rationalist believers publicly advance in support of their beliefs—arguments which the liberal principle of legitimacy and the Rawlsian ideal of public reason are meant to rule out in advance, irrespective of their soundness, on grounds independent of the truth or falsity of the principles the arguments are meant to vindicate.

Rawls's insistence that he is not denying the truth of rationalist believers' beliefs, but only their assertion that these beliefs can be publicly and fully established by reason, is therefore unavailing. Rationalist believers do not claim on the basis of secret knowledge or special revelation that their beliefs are publicly justifiable by rational argument; on the contrary, they defend their views precisely by offering public justification, that is, rational arguments in support of the principles and propositions on the basis of which they propose political action.[46] These arguments are either sound or unsound. If sound, there is no reason to exclude the principles and propositions they vindicate as 'illegitimate' reasons for political action. If unsound, they should be rejected—on rationalist believers' own terms—precisely for that reason.

Consider the matter from the viewpoint of people to whom the arguments of rationalist believers are addressed. Those who, upon reflection, are persuaded by arguments that appeal to their 'common human reason' obviously have no grounds for excluding as in principle 'illegitimate' or 'contrary to public reason' these principles and propositions as reasons for political action. People who are not persuaded will consider that the arguments advanced for these principles and policies are unsound or, in any event, insufficient to warrant belief in, and action based on, the principles and propositions in support of which they are advanced. They will, of course, consider those who are persuaded to be in error (and vice versa), but they have no grounds for supposing them to be acting in violation of a principle of legitimacy by preparing to exercise public power, or to support the exercise of such power, for 'non-public' reasons.

Do rationalist believers deny the possibility of reasonable disagreement? Rawls says that, 'it is unrealistic—or worse, it arouses mutual suspicion and hostility—to suppose that all our differences are rooted in ignorance and perversity, or else in the rivalries for power, status, or economic gain.'[47] True, but rationalist believers recognize that many differences, including certain political differences, arise from considerations that are underdetermined by reason such as matters of taste or sentiment, or from reasonably guided, albeit still rationally underdetermined, prior commitments and the distinctive perspectives and responsibilities flowing from them, or from the diversity of reasonable beliefs about the likely consequences of alternative possible courses of action. There may be in such cases a variety of unreasonable opinions; but there need not be a uniquely reasonable or correct one.

In other matters, however, including fundamental political matters such as questions of human rights, there are uniquely morally correct beliefs that are, in principle, available to every rational person, or so rationalist believers hold. Differences with regard to such matters may be 'reasonable,' in the sense that reasonable persons can err about such matters (which may be complicated and difficult), and, indeed, can sometimes err without subjective moral fault. Still, some error of reason must be responsible for anyone's failure to arrive at a correct opinion with regard to such matters. Errors may be rooted in inattention to or ignorance of certain facts or values, sub-rational influences that block insight but may be subjectively non-culpable, logical failure or other mistakes in judgment that can be induced or at least facilitated by particular cultures.[48]

Is this view unreasonable? Rawls speaks of competing comprehensive views that are 'perfectly reasonable'[49] and of persons subscribing to different views who are nonetheless 'fully reasonable.'[50] Unless he is to violate his own methodological scruples by appealing to some form of moral relativism, Rawls cannot declare the view of rationalist believers to be unreasonable because they hold that conflicting views on moral questions, including some questions of human rights, on which 'reasonable people disagree' cannot be equally reasonable. There is nothing unreasonable in holding that the view of those in error is less than fully or perfectly reasonable, and that they, to the extent that their view deviates from the correct one, are (perhaps non-culpably) being less reasonable than their opponents who have managed to get to the truth of the matter at issue.

Indeed, it is difficult to see how Rawls himself could defend a contrary position. After all, there are reasonable people who reject 'political liberalism.' Rawls must suppose that they are in error. Persons who consider other people to be in error can, of course, do so compatibly with a recognition of their own fallibility. Nevertheless, to the extent that their view deviates from the correct one—perhaps because they misunderstand or fail to appreciate the force of one or more of Rawls's central arguments— Rawls must suppose that they are being less reasonable than those who grasp his arguments, appreciate their force, and therefore affirm the superiority of 'political liberalism' to its alternatives.

Must rationalist believers reject Rawls's account of the sources of reasonable disagreement in connection with what he calls 'the burdens of judgment?'[51] That account is not without its ambiguities. If, however, it is read in such a way as to avoid its collapse into relativism, then Rawls's idea of 'fully reasonable,' or even 'perfectly reasonable,' though erroneous, views refers to false beliefs that are formed by people without subjective fault. This is what people generally have in mind when, although themselves persuaded of the truth of a certain view, they nevertheless allow that the relevant subject matter is one about which 'reasonable people can disagree.' The possibility of reasonable disagreement in this sense is, however, no reason to exclude public argument as to the truth of the matters in question. John Finnis's remark on this point strikes me as entirely apt: 'Public reasoning should be directed to overcoming the relevant mistakes, not pre-emptively surrendering to them.'[52]

In *A Theory of Justice*, Rawls defended his substantive principles of justice by way of a 'political constructivism' that asked what principles reasonable parties in an original position, behind a 'thick' veil of ignorance, and thus possessed of merely a 'thin' theory of the good, would choose for a society in which they would eventually occupy a place.[53] In *Political Liberalism*, he indicates that the principle of legitimacy and the limits or guidelines of public reason 'have the same basis as the substantive principles of justice.'[54] This is shaky, for neither Rawls nor his followers have ever provided any reason to believe that perfectionist principles that would not be chosen under conditions of artificial ignorance by the unnaturally risk-averse parties in the original position are unjust, or are not valid principles of justice. The key point is this: From the proposition that principles that would be chosen by such parties under such conditions are just (and are principles of justice), it simply does not follow that perfectionist principles that might very well be chosen by reasonable and reasonably well-informed persons outside the Rawlsian original position are unjust (or are not principles of justice).

II. ABORTION AND PUBLIC REASON

Although his desire to defend 'political liberalism' requires Rawls to resist the very wide view of public reason that could be endorsed by natural law theorists or other so-called rationalist believers, he is nevertheless eager to show that the scope of his doctrine of public reason is not excessively narrow.[55] For example, his 'political liberalism' allows people to resort to beliefs drawn from their comprehensive doctrines in a variety of areas that do not touch upon 'constitutional essentials' and matters of 'basic justice.'[56] Even in areas that do touch upon such matters, Rawls's theory allows appeals to comprehensive doctrines subject to the proviso that citizens making such appeals 'in due course' show that their position can be justified in terms of public reason.[57]

In *Political Liberalism*, Rawls offers the following explanation of the demands of public reason:

What public reason asks is that citizens be able to explain their vote to one another in terms of a reasonable balance of public political values, it being understood by everyone that of course the plurality of reasonable comprehensive doctrines held by citizens is thought by them to provide further and often transcendent backing for those values. In each case, which doctrine is affirmed is a matter of conscience for the individual citizen. It is true that the balance of political values a citizens holds must be reasonable, and one that can be seen to be reasonable by other citizens; but not all reasonable balances are the same. The only comprehensive doctrines that run afoul of public reason are those that cannot support a reasonable balance of political values.[58]

Precisely at this point, Rawls inserts a footnote, which, 'as an illustration,' takes up what he describes as 'the troubled question of abortion.'[59] After stipulating 'that we are dealing with the normal case of mature adult women,' he asks the reader to 'consider the question in terms of these three important political values: the due respect for human life, the ordered reproduction of political society over time, including the family in some form, and finally the equality of women as equal citizens.'[60] After acknowledging, parenthetically, that these are not the only important political values, he declares that 'any reasonable balance of these three values will give a woman a duly qualified right to decide whether or not to end her pregnancy during the first trimester.'[61]

How, one may ask, could this bold conclusion be justified without appeal to moral or metaphysical views widely in dispute about the status of embryonic and fetal human beings, or the justice or injustice of choices either to bring about their deaths or to perform acts with the foreseeable side effect of bringing about their deaths? Here is Rawls's entire justification: 'At this early stage of pregnancy the political value of the equality of women is overriding, and this right is required to give it substance and force.'[62]

Why does the value of women's equality override the value of fetal life? Rawls does not say. The absence of argument for this claim is especially remarkable in view of the fact that opponents of abortion contend that the right to life (which, in their view, the unborn share with all other human beings) is fundamental and inviolable and, as such, cannot be 'balanced' against other considerations. Rawls goes on to comment that he does not think that the introduction of other political values into the calculation would alter his conclusion, and, indeed, that a reasonable balance of political values might allow a right to abortion even beyond the first trimester, 'at least in certain circumstances.'[63] He explicitly declines to argue the point further, however, stating that his purpose in raising the question of a right to abortion at all is simply 'to illustrate the point of the text by saying that any comprehensive doctrine that leads to a balance of political values excluding that duly qualified right in the first trimester is to that extent unreasonable.'[64]

Needless to say, Rawls's footnote has elicited vigorous criticism.[65] As an argument for a right to abortion, it does worse than beg centrally important questions—it ignores them altogether. Moreover, it seems plainly, if silently, to import into the analysis of the question a range of undefended beliefs of precisely the sort that 'political liberalism' is supposed to exclude. This smuggling in of controversial moral and metaphysical beliefs is especially egregious in view of the fact that abortion is often put forward as a question that simply cannot be resolved, one way or the other, without introducing such beliefs into the deliberations.[66] As such, it presents a particular challenge to Rawls's central argument that constitutional essentials and matters of basic justice ought to be resolved by appeal to a purely 'political' conception of justice, rather than to general doctrines of justice as parts of reasonable comprehensive views.

In a footnote to the introduction of the new paperback edition of *Political Liberalism*,[67] Rawls acknowledges the force of some of these criticisms and offers a brief reply:

Some have quite naturally read the [original] footnote . . . as an argument for the right to abortion in the first trimester. I do not intend it to be one. (It does express my opinion, but an opinion is not an argument.) I was in error in leaving it in doubt that the aim of the footnote was only to illustrate and confirm the following statement in the text to which the footnote is attached: 'The only comprehensive doctrines that run afoul of public reason are those that cannot support a reasonable balance [or ordering] of political values [on the issue].' To try to explain what I meant, I used three political values (of course, there are more) for the troubled issue of the right to abortion, to which it might seem improbable that political values could apply at all. I believe a more detailed interpretation of those values may, when properly developed at public reason, yield a reasonable argument. I don't say the most reasonable or decisive argument; I don't know what that would be, or even if it exists.[68]

At this point, Rawls cites with approval, noting only that he would add several (unspecified) 'addenda' to it, Judith Jarvis Thomson's argument for a right to abortion in her then recent article 'Abortion: Whose Right?'.[69] Here is Thomson's summation of her argument:

First, restrictive regulation [of abortion] severely constrains women's liberty. Second, severe constraints on liberty may not be imposed in the name of considerations that the constrained are not unreasonable in rejecting. And third, the many women who reject the claim that the fetus has a right to life from the moment of conception are not unreasonable in doing so.[70]

The affinities of Thomson's approach with Rawlsian political liberalism are obvious. The central pro-life claims are: (1) human beings in the embryonic and fetal stages, like innocent human beings at all other stages of life, have a right not to be directly (or otherwise unjustly) killed; and (2) like all other human beings, they are entitled to the (equal) protection of the laws against homicide.[71] Thomson defends the right to abortion, not by claiming that the central pro-life claims are false, but by arguing that their truth or falsity is irrelevant to the political resolution of the question of abortion.[72] What matters is that people are 'not unreasonable' in judging the central pro-life claims to be false. Therefore, even those who judge them to be true should refrain from taking political action that would restrict women's freedom based on their judgment. They should join those who consider the central pro-life claims to be false in a sort of Rawlsian overlapping consensus that recognizes a woman's right to abortion.

Here, I submit, we have fully on display all the equivocations, ambiguities and weaknesses of the Rawlsian criterion of reciprocity, liberal principle of legitimacy and doctrine of public reason. Immediately after offering the summary of her argument I quoted a moment ago, Thomson, evidently struggling to be generous, says that, 'there is of course room for those who accept Catholic doctrine on abortion to declare it in the public forum';[73] but, she adds, 'those who accept the doctrine ought not say that reason requires us to accept it, for that assertion is false.'[74] What is Thomson claiming here? Is it that the central pro-life claims should be rejected because they are untrue or, even if true, somehow unreasonable? To establish that, she would have to engage pro-life arguments on the merits and refute them. She makes no serious effort to do so. To have done so would, in any event, have shifted the ground of the argument for a right to abortion from the sphere of Rawlsian 'public reason' to an unrestricted debate of a sort that would engage, in violation of Rawlsian scruples, principles connected with competing comprehensive doctrines.[75]

What Thomson seems to mean is that not all 'reasonable people' accept pro-life claims, or that the rejection of pro-life claims does not mark a person as 'unreasonable.' There are, as I suggested earlier, important ways in which assertions like these are true. Contrary to what Thomson supposes, however, nothing follows from the ways in which they are true for the questions whether women have a right to abortion or the unborn have a right not to be aborted. If, in truth, the latter right obtains, and thus the pro-life position is more reasonable than its alternative, then the fact that reasonable people, perhaps without culpability, hold the contrary view in no way vitiates the human right of the unborn not to be killed, or confers upon women a moral right to the more or less unrestricted legal freedom to bring about their deaths. What matters, from the moral point of view, is that basic human rights be identified where they obtain and, to the extent possible, protected.

In the end, Thomson's argument that people are 'not unreasonable' in rejecting the pro-life position boils down to an assertion that the argument over the moral status of the human conceptus and early embryo ends in a sort of stalemate: 'While I know of no conclusive reason for denying that fertilized eggs have a right to life, I also know of no conclusive reason for asserting that they do have a right to life.'[76] Yet one is entitled to this conclusion about the moral status of newly conceived human beings (Thomson's 'fertilized eggs') only if one can make an argument sufficient to support it. Such an argument also would have to rebut the arguments put forward to show that the unborn have a right to life even in the earliest stages of their existence. Apart from a few references to *Evangelium Vitae*, Thomson cites no such arguments at all. There is all the difference in the world between rebutting these arguments and ruling them out in advance on the ground that they implicate deep moral and metaphysical questions in dispute among reasonable people subscribing to competing comprehensive doctrines.

What are the arguments to be rebutted if Thomson is to show that there is nothing unreasonable in rejecting the central pro-life claims? Perhaps these arguments are so tendentious, obscure or otherwise lacking in rational force that she is justified in ruling them out in advance as legitimate grounds for political action on pro-life principles. In considering the claim that 'a human being's life begins at conception,' Thomson observes parenthetically, and without further comment or citation, that 'we are invited to accept that premise on the ground that the conceptus—a fertilized human egg—contains a biological code that will govern its entire future physical development, and therefore is already a human being.'[77] Her suggestion, it seems, is not that the ground adduced for accepting the premise is false, but rather that it is inadequate. It is worth pausing here to consider the implications of the genetic coding and completeness of the human conceptus and early embryo. A human being is conceived when a human sperm containing twenty-three chromosomes fuses with a human egg also containing twenty-three chromosomes (albeit of a different kind) producing a single cell human zygote containing, in the normal case, forty-six chromosomes that are mixed differently from the forty-six chromosomes as found in the mother or father.[78] Unlike the gametes (that is, the sperm and egg), the zygote is genetically unique and distinct from its parents. Biologically, it is a separate organism. It produces, as the gametes do not, specifically human enzymes and proteins. It possesses, as they do not, the active capacity or potency to develop itself into a human embryo, fetus, infant, child, adolescent and adult.

Assuming that it is not conceived in vitro, the zygote is, of course, in a state of dependence on its mother. But independence should not be confused with distinctness. From the beginning, the newly conceived human being directs its own integral organic functioning. It takes in nourishment and converts it to energy. Given an hospitable environment, it will 'develop continuously without any biological interruptions, or gaps, throughout the embryonic, fetal, neo-natal, childhood and adulthood stages—until the death of the organism.'[79] Thus, according to Dianne Nutwell Irving:

> The biological facts demonstrate that at syngamy we have a truly human nature. It is not that he or she will become a human being—he or she already is a human being. . . . [A] human zygote or embryo is not a possible human being; nor is he or she potentially a human being; he or she is a human being.[80]

Jed Rubenfeld, in his influential article, '*On the Legal Status of the Proposition that "Life Begins at Conception"*',[81] asserts the contrary. He claims that arguments that life begins at conception are 'virtually unintelligible.'[82] If this were true, then Thomson would seem to be justified in effectively ruling such arguments out in advance as reasons for legal restrictions on abortion. The trouble with Rubenfeld's assertion is that he engages no serious scholarly argument in favor of the proposition he claims to be not merely false or inadequate but 'virtually unintelligible.' Although he cites serious scholarly work in his analyses of claims that 'life begins' at various biological marker events in prenatal development such as the point in brain development at which interneural connections within the cerebral cortex make possible higher mental functioning,[83] he fails to engage a single serious scholarly defense of the proposition whose legal status the title of his article promises to explore. The sole citation he gives for 'these arguments' before declaring them to be 'virtually unintelligible' is a 'well-known antiabortion pamphlet written by Dr John Willke of the National Right to Life Committee.'[84] To make matters worse, it is unclear whether Rubenfeld has even read this source, since he refers to it only parenthetically as having been discussed by Frances Olsen (a pro-choice scholar) in a 1989 *Harvard Law Review* article.[85]

Had Rubenfeld examined the scholarly literature, he could not have imagined, as Thomson did, that the ground of the belief that the lives of new human individuals begin at conception is the bare proposition that 'fertilization may be said to represent the moment of genetic completion.'[86] This is what Thomson seems to have in mind in referring to the 'biological code that will govern its entire future physical development.'

In response to the argument that life begins at conception, as he imagines it, Rubenfeld says that 'every cell in our bodies is genetically complete,'[87] yet nobody supposes that every human cell is a distinct human being with a right to life. This misses the point of the argument that there comes into being at conception, not a mere clump of human cells, but a distinct, unified self-integrating organism, which develops itself, truly himself or herself, in accord with its own genetic blueprint. The significance of genetic completeness for the status of newly conceived human beings is that no outside genetic material is required to enable the zygote to mature into an embryo, the embryo into a fetus, the fetus into an infant, the infant into a child, the child into an adolescent, the adolescent into an adult. What the zygote needs to function as a distinct self-integrating human organism, a human being, it already possesses.

At no point in embryogenesis does the distinct organism that came into being when it was conceived undergo substantial change or a change of natures. It is human and will remain human. This was the point of Justice Byron White's remark in his dissenting opinion in *Thornburgh* v. *American College of Obstetricians & Gynecologists*[88] that 'there is no nonarbitrary line separating a fetus from a child.'[89] Rubenfeld quotes White's observation and then purports to demolish what he takes to be 'the argument based on the gradualness of gestation,' by pointing out that, 'no nonarbitrary line separates the hues of green and red. Shall we conclude that green is red? That night is day?'[90]

The point of the argument is not that development is 'gradual,' but rather that it is continuous and is the development of a single lasting being. The human zygote that actively develops itself is, as I have pointed out, a genetically complete organism directing its own integral organic functioning. As it matures, in utero and ex utero, it does not 'become' a human being, for it is, as Dianne Irving observes, a human being already, albeit an immature human being, the way a newborn infant is an immature human being who will undergo quite dramatic growth and development over time.

These considerations undermine the familiar argument, recited by Rubenfeld, that 'an unfertilized ovum also has the potential to develop into a whole human being, but that does not make it a person.'[91] The ovum is not a whole human being. It is, rather, a part of another human being (the woman whose ovum it is) with merely the potential to give rise to, in interaction with a part of yet another human being (a man's sperm cell), a new and whole human being. Unlike the zygote, it lacks both genetic distinctness and completeness, as well as the active capacity to develop itself into an adult member of the human species. It is living human cellular material, but, left to itself, however hospitable its environment, it will never become a human being. It will 'die' as a human ovum, just as

countless skin cells 'die' daily as nothing more than skin cells. If successfully fertilized by a human sperm, which, like the ovum (but dramatically
unlike the zygote), lacks the active potential to develop into an adult
member of the human species, then substantial change—a change of
natures—will occur. There will no longer be merely an egg, which was
part of the mother, sharing her genetic composition, and a sperm, which
was part of the father, sharing his genetic composition; there will be a
genetically complete, distinct, unified, self-integrating human organism
whose nature differs from that of the gametes—not mere human material,
but a human being.

These considerations also make clear that Michael Lockwood, who
takes a line on these issues similar to Rubenfeld's, is quite incorrect to say
that 'we were never week-old embryos, any more than we were sperm or
ova.'[92] It truly makes no sense to say that 'I' was once a sperm (or an
unfertilized egg) that matured into an adult. Conception was the occasion
of substantial change (that is, change from one complete individual entity
to another) that brought into being a distinct self-integrating organism
with a specifically human nature. By contrast, it makes every bit as much
sense to say that I was once a week-old embryo as to say that I was once
a week-old infant or a ten-year-old child. It was the new organism created
at conception that, without itself undergoing any change of substance,
matured into a week-old embryo, a fetus, an infant, a child, an adolescent
and, finally, an adult.

Rubenfeld has another argument: Cloning processes give to non-
zygotic cells the potential for development into distinct, self-integrating
human beings; thus to recognize the zygote as a human being is to recognize all human cells as human beings, which is absurd.[93] It is true that a
distinct, self-integrating human organism which came into being by a
process of cloning would be, like a human organism that comes into being
as a monozygotic twin, a human being. That being, no less than human
beings conceived by the union of sperm and egg, would possess a human
nature and the active potential to mature as a human being. However,
even assuming the possibility of cloning human beings from non-zygotic
human cells, the non-zygotic cell must be activated by a process which
effects substantial change and not mere development or maturation. Left
to itself, apart from an activation process capable of effecting a change of
substance or natures, the cell will mature and die as a human cell, not as
a human being.[94] When speaking of the conceptus, Thomson refers to the
biological code that will govern 'its entire future physical development';[95]
her syntax points to the relevant entity and reveals the truth that each
of us is the human being—that is, the distinct, self-integrating human
organism—we were as an adolescent, a child, an infant, a fetus, an embryo
and a zygote. Each of us is the 'it' who has now experienced the physical

development that was in *its* future when, at conception, *it* was coded for that development.

I have set forth in some detail the argument that the life of a human being begins at conception, and considered some (though by no means all) of the counterarguments, not to show that the unborn have a right to life (though I believe that they do) or that there is no general right to abortion (though I believe there is not), but to show that the case for the right to life cannot be easily rebutted, nor can the case for a right to abortion—even a 'duly qualified' right to abortion 'in the first trimester'—be established without engaging the deep moral and metaphysical questions on the basis of which people divide over the question of abortion. If I am correct, Rawlsian 'political liberalism' does not offer a way of resolving the social and political conflict surrounding the issue on the basis of principles of justice which can be identified and applied independently of any particular view on these questions. Neither the considerations suggested by Rawls himself nor those advanced by Thomson give those on the pro-life side anything approaching a sufficient reason to surrender in their political struggle for legal protection of the unborn against abortion. They, like their opponents on the pro-choice side, may have good reasons to seek political compromises with their opponents on legislative proposals for the restriction or regulation of abortion, or even to seek a modus vivendi at the constitutional level on the best terms they can obtain. But nothing in the idea of 'public reason' gives them grounds to suppose that justice itself requires them to shift from being 'politically pro-life' to being merely 'personally opposed to abortion, but politically pro-choice.'

III. HOMOSEXUAL ACTS, MARRIAGE AND PUBLIC REASON

If abortion is the most explosive issue in our 'culture war,' questions pertaining to the legal treatment of homosexual acts and relationships are emerging as the second most incendiary. Assuming that public policy issues regarding sex and marriage go to matters of constitutional essentials and basic justice, Rawlsian political liberalism offers itself as the morally best, or most reasonable, way to resolve political issues concerning homosexual acts and other questions of public policy pertaining to sex and marriage. This way avoids, indeed rules out, appeal to underlying moral and metaphysical questions in dispute among people who give their allegiance to competing comprehensive views. If Rawls is right, reasonable people who reject comprehensive liberalism in favor of views which include more conservative positions on homosexual acts and other questions of sexual morality ought reasonably to be able to join comprehensive liberals in an overlapping consensus on the proper political resolution of these questions.

Disagreements over public policies regarding homosexual conduct and relationships certainly reflect different, incompatible understandings of sexual morality connected to different 'comprehensive views.' Underlying and informing these different understandings are, once again, profound differences about the nature of human persons and values. Is pleasure intrinsically good and, as such, a non-instrumental reason for action? Or can pleasure, in itself, provide nothing more than sub-rational motivation? Is the body an aspect of the personal reality of the human being whose body it is? Or is the body a sub-personal part of the human being whose personal reality is the conscious and desiring self which uses the body as an instrument? Is the idea of a true bodily union of persons in marital acts an illusion? Or are marital acts realizations of precisely such a union? Do non-marital sexual acts instrumentalize the bodies of those performing them in such a way as to damage their personal integrity? Or are mutually agreeable sexual acts of whatever type morally innocent and even valuable means of sharing pleasure and intimacy and expressing feelings of tenderness and affection?

People's judgments and understandings regarding these and related issues, judgments and understandings that are rarely formal and are usually merely implicit, determine their places on the spectrum ranging from various forms of sexual liberationism to strict forms of conservative sexual morality.[96] Some proponents of moderate liberalism on questions of sexual morality oppose promiscuity and adultery but maintain that the judgment of traditional natural law theorists and others that fornication and sodomy are intrinsically non-marital and immoral is misguided.[97] They believe that non-adulterous and non-promiscuous sexual acts and relationships between loving and devoted partners, whether of opposite sexes or the same sex, can be morally good even outside of marriage. Moreover, they argue that the state should, to be fair to people who are homosexually oriented, make marriage licenses, or at least benefits equivalent to those conferred by legal marriage, available to otherwise eligible same-sex couples.

Together with a co-author, Gerard V. Bradley, I recently debated issues of marriage and sexual morality, including the question of homosexual acts and relationships, with Stephen Macedo in the pages of the Georgetown Law Journal.[98] Professor Macedo argues that government has an obligation in justice to its homosexually oriented citizens to issue marriage licenses on a nondiscriminatory basis to same-sex couples.[99] If I understand Macedo's argument correctly, he defends a conception of marriage as essentially an emotional and, possibly, spiritual union of two loving and devoted persons who may be of opposite sexes or the same sex. The intimacy and overall value of their union is, or may be, enhanced by the partners' cooperation in the performance of mutually agreeable sexual acts.[100] Professor Bradley and I defend an alternative conception of marriage—one which we believe to be reflected in traditional American and British marriage law, especially in the law governing consummation of marriage. We argue that marriage is a one-flesh (i.e., bodily, as well as emotional, dispositional and spiritual) union of a male and a female spouse consummated and actualized by sexual acts that are reproductive in type. Such acts consummate and, we maintain, actualize the intrinsic good of marriage whether or not reproduction is desired by the spouses in any particular marital act, or is even possible for them in a particular act or at all.[101]

Macedo is no sexual liberationist. He evidently opposes promiscuity and believes that even consensual sex acts can, in some cases, violate personal integrity or some other moral value.[102] Nor does he maintain that marriage is a mere social or legal convention that lacks a nature of its own and can therefore legitimately be manipulated to serve the subjective ends of individuals or the state, whatever they happen to be. He shares with people such as Bradley and me the view that not all forms of consensual sexual association ought to be recognized as marriages by the state.[103] He disagrees with us, however, on questions of the nature of marriage and the role and value of sex within it.[104]

Bradley and I summarize our argument as follows:

(1)   Marriage, considered not as a mere legal convention, but, rather, as a two-in-one-flesh communion of persons that is consummated and actualized by sexual acts of the reproductive type, is an intrinsic . . . human good; as such, marriage provides a non-instrumental reason for spouses, whether or not they are capable of conceiving children in their acts of genital union, to perform such acts.

(2)   In choosing to perform non-marital orgasmic acts, including sodomitical acts—irrespective of whether the persons performing such acts are of the same or opposite sexes (and even if those persons are validly married to each other)—persons necessarily treat their bodies and those of their sexual partners (if any) as means or instruments in ways that damage their personal (and interpersonal) integrity; thus, regard for the basic human good of integrity provides a conclusive moral reason not to engage in sodomitical and other non-marital sex acts.[105]

Macedo denies these claims. He argues that the organic bodily union of persons we believe to be possible in marital intercourse, whether or not procreation is possible, is illusory.[106] Thus the reproductive-type acts of spouses cannot possibly have the unitive value and significance we ascribe to them. Marital intercourse cannot be what we claim it is, namely, the biological matrix of the multilevel reality of marriage. The most sex can do for people, beyond making it possible for them to become parents, is to enable them to share pleasure, thus enhancing and enabling them to express in a special way the caring, affectionate and intimate emotional bond between them.[107]

Macedo also argues that, by confining humanly valuable and morally upright sex to marital intercourse, natural law theorists such as Bradley and I unreasonably exclude sex acts which, though non-marital (at least in our sense), are nevertheless humanly valuable in their capacity to express and enhance the emotional bonds between lovers.[108] Moreover, he maintains that we are wrong to deny, as we do, that pleasure is an intrinsic good, or that the instrumentalizing of the body to the end of gaining or sharing pleasurable sensations is intrinsically bad.[109] Thus he denies that non-marital sex inevitably damages personal or interpersonal integrity. Bradley and I respond to Macedo's critique of our views by arguing that his understanding of sex and marriage implicates him in a philosophically untenable person-body dualism.[110] This is most apparent in his denial that human males and females unite biologically when they mate, and in his related understanding of sexual organs as 'equipment' that serves the goods of pleasure and procreation but cannot make possible a truly personal union of spouses as the biological matrix of the multilevel (bodily, emotional, dispositional, spiritual) reality of their marriage. Implicit in these denials, we believe, is the idea that the body is a sub-personal aspect of the human being that serves the conscious and desiring aspect—the true 'self'—which inhabits and uses the body. Were Macedo to acknowledge what we believe to be the case, namely 'that the biological reality of human beings is "part of, not merely an instrument of, their personal reality," '[111] then it is difficult to see how he could resist our claim that 'the biological union of spouses in marital acts constitutes a truly interpersonal communion,'[112] whose value is intrinsic, and not merely instrumental to pleasure or the sharing of pleasure, the expression of tender and affectionate feelings, or any other extrinsic goal.

My point in recalling the debate between Macedo and Bradley and myself is not to try to settle the issues but merely to illustrate that the arguments advanced on both sides plainly implicate a body of assumptions reflective of our respective commitments to very different 'comprehensive views.' As a result, I suspect, people whose comprehensive view is essentially liberal will find Macedo's argument much more persuasive than ours; those with non-liberal comprehensive views—including traditional Christians, Jews, and other believers—are likely to find our argument more compelling. Still, neither side makes any appeal to principles or propositions that are not publicly available to rational persons. Neither side invokes any form of secret knowledge or revelation. Each side offers people on the other side reasons, which such people may or may not find persuasive, for changing their minds.

My concern for now is not with the truth or falsity of the claims made on either side, or the validity of the arguments advanced on either side to support its claims, but with the relevance of the truth or falsity of these claims to the resolution of questions of public policy pertaining to sex and marriage and particularly to questions of homosexual acts and relationships. My claim is that political liberalism does not provide a workable alternative to the conflict of comprehensive views on such questions. On the contrary, law and policy in this area should be shaped in accordance with the truth and will inevitably be shaped by people's ideas about the truth of the moral and metaphysical claims at stake in the debate among advocates of competing comprehensive views.

The case for resolving policy questions in this area on the basis of 'political liberalism' is articulated by Macedo himself. Although he contends that the view of marriage and sexual morality that Bradley and I put forward as a ground for public policymaking ought to be rejected as unreasonably narrowing the range of morally valuable sexual conduct and relationships, he argues, in the alternative, that our view constitutes an illegitimate ground for public policy even if it is true and the competing moral view he defends is false.[113] The upshot of his position for questions of public policy pertaining to homosexual acts and relationships is that justice requires the state to grant marriage licenses to same-sex partners and to recognize their relationship as marital even if, in truth, their sex acts cannot be marital (or morally upright) and their relationship cannot, morally speaking, be a marriage. That is the proposition I am interested in here.

Noting that 'it may be, indeed, that Bradley and George and I disagree . . . deeply in our understandings of what it is to have reasons for action, about the nature of goods, and perhaps even about the relationship between mind and body,' Macedo argues that, 'if our disagreements indeed lie in these difficult philosophical quarrels, about which reasonable people have long disagreed, then our differences lie precisely in the territory that John Rawls rightly . . . marks off as inappropriate to the fashioning of our basic rights and liberties.'[114] He continues:

It is inappropriate to carve up basic rights and principles of justice on the basis of reasons and arguments whose force depends on accepting particular religious convictions. So too it is inappropriate to deny people fundamental aspects of equality based on reasons and arguments whose force can only be appreciated by those who accept difficult to assess claims about the nature and incommensurability of basic goods, the relationship between intrinsic and instrumental value, and the dispute over whether pleasure is a reason for action.[115]

Macedo's Rawlsian argument is certainly appealing on its face. The deep moral and metaphysical questions to which he refers are indeed difficult ones about which reasonable people have long disagreed. Claims on either side of these questions are, as he says, difficult to assess. How could it be right, then, to 'deny people fundamental aspects of equality' on the basis of such claims? I certainly do not think it is ever right to deny people fundamental aspects of equality. The question is whether we can identify fundamental aspects of equality pertaining to marriage while prescinding from questions of the nature and value of marriage which, inevitably, implicate deeper moral and metaphysical questions of the sort that Rawls and Macedo wish to rule out of bounds as grounds for public policymaking. Macedo implicitly supposes that we can; I think we cannot.

Macedo's claim about 'denying fundamental aspects of equality' can be sustained only if we presuppose the truth of his own comprehensive liberalism. If the nature and value of marriage are, in truth, what Macedo's comprehensive view supposes them to be, then it is indeed a violation of equality to deny marriage licenses and the full legal benefits of marriage to same-sex partners. This violation occurs, however, only because homosexual partners can in fact realize in their sexual acts and relationships the same constitutive value or values (pleasure, intimacy, the expression of tender feelings) that can be realized by heterosexual spouses. No principle of equality is violated, however, if, in truth, homosexual sexual acts and relationships cannot realize the constitutive value or values of marriage—if marriage truly is, as Bradley and I contend, a bodily communion of persons consummated and actualized by sexual acts which are reproductive in type.

On Macedo's view and on mine, marriage is an important value which society and government have an obligation to help make available to people and which the government should not deny to people who are capable of fulfilling its requirements. What follows from this, in my view, is society's obligation to 'get it right,' that is, to embody in its law and policy a morally sound conception of marriage. This obligation seems to me especially stringent in view of the fact that whatever understanding of marriage is embodied in law and public policy will profoundly shape the public's understanding of the nature and value of marriage, and, thus, affect people's capacities to live out true marriages and participate in their value. This is an area in which moral neutrality strikes me as not only undesirable, but unattainable. The conflict of comprehensive views is unavoidable.

IV. CIVILITY, RECIPROCITY AND THE CONFLICT OF 'COMPREHENSIVE VIEWS'

The morally charged political disputes of our day, particularly the dispute over abortion, are often compared with the conflict over slavery in the

United States in the middle of the nineteenth century. By that point in time, some supporters of slavery were no longer content to defend the 'peculiar institution' as a 'necessary evil,' the toleration of which was required where abolition would allegedly produce disastrous, and therefore morally unacceptable, social and economic consequences. Instead, they contended that slavery was morally good and right, and that the position of their abolitionist opponents constituted, not a noble—albeit practically unattainable—moral ideal, but a form of moral and religious fanaticism that threatened the rights of slaveholders.[116] The conflict of comprehensive views over slavery ultimately defied political compromise and proved to be incompatible with peace and social stability. The matter was finally resolved, but only after a civil war and at a price of nearly three-quarters of a million lives.

Anyone who reflects on the carnage of the American Civil War will applaud Rawls and others for their efforts to come to terms with 'the fact of moral pluralism.' For those of us who judge, however, that 'political liberalism' cannot provide a rational alternative to the conflict of comprehensive views, at least when it comes to morally charged issues such as abortion and homosexuality, the question arises whether it is possible to identify rational standards or ideals of political discourse and action to regulate the conflict. How should people treat those of their fellow citizens with whom they sharply disagree about profoundly important questions of morality, justice and human rights? What, if anything, do citizens who find themselves in such disagreement owe to each other as a matter of justice in the sphere of political advocacy?

The question of one's obligations toward fellow citizens with whom one disagrees is itself a moral question, indeed, a moral question which implicates, or may implicate, constitutional essentials and matters of basic justice such as questions of freedom of speech and the press, and the right to vote. Deliberation about one's obligations to those who advocate policies which one believes to be seriously unjust will be informed by one's general or 'comprehensive' views about justice. There is, I believe, no reason to suppose that people can or should attempt to prescind from their 'comprehensive views' in determining their obligations to those with whom they find themselves in morally charged political conflict.

However, a certain substantial 'overlapping consensus' in fact exists between a great many thoughtful people on both sides of contemporary debates over issues such as abortion and homosexuality regarding people's obligations to their political opponents. Most fundamentally, perhaps, there is a significant level of moral as well as pragmatic agreement about the need to respect basic freedoms of speech, press, and religion, and the right to vote. Of course, there is a measure of disagreement at the margins about the scope of some of these rights. Differences break out, for example, over the free speech rights of advertisers of abortion services, on the one hand, and of protesters and sidewalk counselors at abortion clinics, on the other.[117] Nevertheless, most pro-life and pro-choice advocates respect the rights of their opponents to express and publicize their views and arguments.

Furthermore, it seems at least possible for citizens who differ fundamentally over certain basic moral questions to share a 'deliberative' conception of democracy that includes the mutually recognized obligations of citizens to treat those with whom they disagree with civility and respect. In a valuable book on the subject of moral conflict in the context of democratic politics, Amy Gutmann and Dennis Thompson have remarked that the 'core idea' of 'deliberative democracy' is that 'when citizens or their representatives disagree morally, they should continue to reason together to reach mutually acceptable decisions.'[118] Gutmann and Thompson do not suppose that these efforts will always be successful, or that, somehow, by reasoning together, differences of 'comprehensive views' can be made to melt away. Nor do they imagine that regulative principles of debate and discussion—such as the principles of 'reciprocity,' 'publicity' and 'accountability' which figure centrally in what they call 'the constitution' of deliberative democracy—will dictate substantive policies, liberal or otherwise, on issues such as abortion.[119] Their claim, rather, is that 'reciprocity,' which they consider to be deliberative democracy's 'first principle,'[120] demands that people recognize that others who come down on what they judge to be the wrong side of a disputed moral question may nevertheless be reasonable and honest people who deserve, therefore, to be reasoned with and treated with respect. Yet reasoning with people and treating them with respect does not entail tolerating what one judges to be grave injustices so as not to offend those who judge otherwise. Nor does it mean that one ought not to oppose injustices resolutely and forcefully in one's advocacy and action. Nor does it mean that one may not protest against injustices or even practice civil disobedience to prevent them.[121] It does mean, however, that one has certain obligations to one's opponents, obligations that are not mere matters of politeness.

Deliberative democracy is more than a matter of competing to assemble majorities for positions that one believes to be in one's interest or even morally right. In a deliberative democracy, citizens understand and accept the duty to justify their positions to their fellow citizens who disagree with them. In this respect, it includes something like an ideal of 'public reason,' but not one so narrow as to exclude, as Rawls's ideal of public reason purports to do, reasonable alternatives to liberal positions on such issues as abortion and homosexuality. In other words, it does not 'load the dice' in favor of substantive liberal policies.

A sound principle of public reason for a deliberative democracy would indeed require citizens and policymakers to justify their political advocacy and action by appeal to principles of justice and other moral principles accessible to their fellow citizens by virtue of their 'common human reason.' It would, however, exclude no reasonable view in advance of its dialectical consideration 'on the merits' in public debate. Nor would it exclude religious views as such. What it would exclude, rather, as grounds of public policymaking generally, are appeals to sheer authority (religious or otherwise) or to 'secret knowledge,' or the putative truths revealed only to an elite (or the elect) and not available, in principle, to rational persons as such.[122] A sound principle of public reason would, in short, be very wide. Its goal would be the 'perfectionist' one of settling law and public policy in accordance with what is true as a matter of justice, human rights and political morality generally.

I have indicated elsewhere my own broad agreement with the conception of deliberative democracy advanced by Gutmann and Thompson, albeit indicating certain areas in which I would be inclined to amend, and, more importantly, extend their conception of 'reciprocity.'[123] Inasmuch as Gutmann and Thompson plainly are committed to a broadly liberal comprehensive view, and I am not, this agreement of moral principle about regulative ideals which should govern morally charged political conflict reflects an 'overlapping consensus' that goes beyond the mutual recognition of basic political rights. A consensus of this sort holds out the promise that reasonable people of goodwill who have arrived at sharply different conclusions about basic questions of morality, justice and human rights may nevertheless recognize moral reasons to conduct their political disputes with civility and enjoy the common goods of peace and social stability that are the fruit of such civility.

NOTES

1 See Pope John Paul II, *The Gospel of Life* (NY: Random House, 1995), 78 (arguing that moral value of democracy 'is not automatic, but depends on conformity to the moral law to which it, like every other form of human behavior, must be subject'). On the interpretation of the Pope's teaching, see Robert P. George, 'The Tyrant State,' *First Things*, 67 (1996), 39.

2 See, e.g., Bruce A. Ackerman, *Social Justice in the Liberal State* (New Haven, Conn.: Yale University Press, 1980), 349–78; Ronald Dworkin, *A Matter of Principle* (Cambridge, Mass.: Harvard University Press, 1985), 191; Robert Nozick, *Anarchy, State, and Utopia* (NY: Basic Books, 1974), 33; John Rawls, *A Theory of Justice* (Cambridge, Mass.: Belknap Press of the Harvard University Press, 1971), 327.

3 See John Finnis, 'Legal Enforcement of "Duties to Oneself": Kant v. Neo-Kantians,' *Columbia Law Review*, 87 (1987), 433; Alasdair McIntyre, 'The

Privatization of Good,' *Review of Politics*, 52 (1990), 344. See, generally, Robert P. George, *Making Men Moral: Civil Liberties and Public Morality* (Princeton, NJ: Princeton University Press, 1993), 83–109, 129–60. Of course, not all defenders of liberalism or specific liberal positions embrace anti-perfectionism. Joseph Raz, for example, is among anti-perfectionism's most powerful critics. See Joseph Raz, *The Morality of Freedom* (Oxford: Clarendon Press, 1986); Joseph Raz, 'Facing Diversity: The Case of Epistemic Abstinence,' *Philosophy and Public Affairs*, 19 (1990), 3; see also William A. Galston, *Liberal Purposes: Goods, Virtues, and Diversity in the Liberal State* (Cambridge: Cambridge University Press, 1991), 79–162, criticizing premise that liberalism should or can be 'neutral.'

4 See Rawls, *Theory of Justice*, 327–30.

5 John Rawls, *Political Liberalism* (NY: Columbia University Press, 2nd ed., 1996), xlii. For a powerful critique of this work (including a valuable summary of criticisms and defenses of Rawls advanced by others), see Heidi M. Hurd, 'The Levitation of Liberalism,' *Yale Law Journal*, 105 (1995), 795 (book review). My own critique of Rawls in the pages that follow is concerned with different problems than those identified by Professor Hurd. In particular, I aim to show that Rawls fails to justify his claim that certain principles, despite the fact that they are (or may be) true principles of justice (or political morality more generally), are not legitimate grounds of political advocacy and action in pluralistic societies such as ours because they are drawn from 'general' or 'comprehensive' doctrines which are in dispute among reasonable people. I challenge Rawls's 'political liberalism' insofar as it treats such principles, at least when it comes to debates about 'constitutional essentials and matters of basic justice,' as being outside the bounds of 'public reason.'

Readers familiar with discussions of Rawls's thought will notice that my concerns are, at most, only indirectly related to 'communitarian' criticisms of Rawls which claim that his liberal individualism reflects an inadequate regard for community values and the value of community. My goal is to cast doubt upon the philosophical tenability of Rawls's anti-perfectionism. Thus, my critique has points in common with critiques of Rawls by Miriam Galston, 'Rawlsian Dualism and the Autonomy of Political Thought,' *Columbia Law Review*, 94 (1994), 1842; Lawrence E. Mitchell, 'Trust and the Overlapping Consensus,' *Columbia Law Review*, 94 (1994), 1918; Michael P. Zuckert, 'The New Rawls and Constitutional Theory: Does It Really Taste That Much Better?,' *Constitutional Commentary*, 11 (1994), 227; and Michael J. Sandel, 'Political Liberalism,' *Harvard Law Review*, 101 (1994), 1765 (book review).

6 See Rawls, *Political Liberalism*.

7 Ibid., 1 (citation omitted).

8 Ibid., xx.

9 Ibid., xvii.

10 Ibid.

11 Ibid.

12 Rawls explains that 'in an ideal overlapping consensus, each citizen affirms both a comprehensive doctrine and the focal political conception, somehow related.' Ibid., xxi.

13 Ibid., xlii, 390, 392.

14 Rawls says that political liberalism 'supposes that a reasonable comprehensive doctrine does not reject the essentials of a democratic regime.' Ibid., xviii.

15 See, ibid., 173–212.

16 Ibid., li. Rawls refers to this as 'the wide view' of public reason. Ibid., lii. He introduces it in the Introduction to the paperback edition of *Political Liberalism* as a revision of the somewhat more restrictive view (though referred to as 'the inclusive view' inasmuch as it was less restrictive than 'the exclusive view' of public reason to which he was originally inclined) set forth later in the text. See, ibid., at 247–52.

17 See, ibid., 215–16.

18 See, ibid., 216.

19 See, generally, Alasdair MacIntyre, *After Virtue: A Study in Moral Theory* (Notre Dame, Ind.: Notre Dame University Press, 2nd ed., 1984), 246–52; Michael J. Sandel, *Liberalism and the Limits of Justice* (NY: Cambridge University Press, 1982), 28–46; Charles Taylor, *Sources of the Self: The Making of the Modern Identity* (Cambridge, Mass.: Harvard University Press, 1989), 88–9.

20 Rawls, *Political Liberalism*, xl.

21 Ibid.

22 See, ibid., xxi.

23 Ibid. By way of criticism, it is worth remarking here that 'political liberalism' imposes a heavy burden on comprehensive doctrines by delegitimizing the expression of certain views in the field of political advocacy and relegating their significance to the purely private realm.

24 Ibid., xlvii.

25 See, ibid., xlii.

26 See, ibid., 158–68.

27 See, ibid., 146–8.

28 A 'freestanding' conception is one that is not presented as in any sense derived from or a part of a comprehensive doctrine. See, ibid., 10.

29 Ibid., xliv.

30 Ibid. As discussed below, this conception of the fairness of terms of cooperation, interpreted narrowly, is neither controversial nor original. Rawls, however, interprets it broadly so as to delegitimize any independent appeal, in the political arena, to a 'comprehensive view' of justice and the common good. It is difficult to see how someone could reasonably embrace this position and thereby rule out public advocacy based on the most deeply held attachments of one's fellow citizens. It is far from obvious that reason obliges anyone to sacrifice such attachments or to stay silent about them, and it is strikingly unreasonable to think that people would willingly forbear such witness. Moreover, it is curious that Rawls's principle seems to be anything but even-handed in effect (as between the policy preferences of, say, secular liberals and traditional religious believers), and there can be no doubt that some persons embrace it with a content-partial desire to foreclose specific advocacy from specific quarters. Cf. Paul F. Campos, 'Secular Fundamentalism,' *Columbia Law Review*, 94 (1994), 1814, 1825. ('Political Liberalism is ultimately a paean to a secular creed that has within it the potential to become every bit as monistic, compulsory, and intolerant of any significant deviation from social verities as the traditional modes of belief it derided and displaced.'); Gary C. Leedes, 'Rawls's Excessively Secular Political Conception,' *University of Richmond Law Review*, 27 (1993) 1083, 1086 (arguing that Rawls's principle is used to exclude religious viewpoints).

31 Rawls, *Political Liberalism*, xliv.

32 Ibid., 137. According to Rawls, 'political rights and duties are moral rights and duties, for they are part of a political conception that is a normative

(moral) conception with its own intrinsic ideal, though not itself a comprehensive doctrine.' Ibid., xliv.

33 See, ibid., 137. ('Only a political conception of justice that all citizens might be reasonably expected to endorse can serve as a basis of public reason and justification.')

34 See, ibid.

35 Depending on circumstances, one might, therefore, affirm what Judith Shklar called 'the liberalism of fear.' See Judith N. Shklar, *Ordinary Vices* (Cambridge, Mass.: Belknap Press of Harvard University Press, 1984), 192–226. John Rawls has noted that Shklar's idea that the 'liberalism of fear,' or the form of liberalism represented by thinkers such as Montaigne and Montesquieu, finds its historical origins in a pragmatic response to the cruelties of the Reformation and its aftermath. See Rawls, *Political Liberalism*, xxvi and n. 10.

36 See John Stuart Mill, *On Liberty* (Longmans, Green, Reader and Dyer, 1873), 44–57 (stating that principle of liberty forbids others from interfering with individual's purely 'self-regarding' conduct, even on ostensibly moral grounds).

37 See Joseph Raz, 'Liberty and Trust,' in *Natural Law, Liberalism, and Morality*, Robert P. George, ed. (Oxford: Clarendon Press, 1996), 122–6.

38 See *infra*, Part IV.

39 In Aquinas's natural law theory, something is good, right or just 'by nature' insofar as it is reasonable. See Thomas Aquinas, *Summa Theologiae*, 1–2, q. 71, a. 2, translated in John Finnis, *Natural Law and Natural Rights* (Oxford: Clarendon Press, 1980), 36. ('The good of the human being is being in accord with reason, and human evil is being outside the order of reasonableness.') Finnis has explained that 'for Aquinas, the way to discover what is morally right (virtue) and wrong (vice) is to ask, not what is in accordance with human nature, but what is reasonable.' Finnis, *Natural Law*, 36; see also John Finnis, *Aquinas: Moral, Legal, and Political Theory* (forthcoming, 1998).

40 Rawls, *Political Liberalism*, 137 (emphasis added).

41 Ibid., 152–3.

42 Ibid., 153.

43 Isaiah Berlin, *The Crooked Timber of Humanity: Chapters in the History of Ideas* (London: John Murray, 1990), 24.

44 Rawls, *Political Liberalism*, at 153.

45 Ibid.

46 See, e.g., Hadley Arkes, *First Things: An Inquiry into the First Principles of Morals and Justice* (Princeton, NJ: Princeton University Press, 1986); Finnis, *Natural Law*; John Finnis et al., *Nuclear Deterrence, Morality, and Realism* (Oxford: Clarendon Press, 1987); Germain G. Grisez, *Abortion: The Myths, the Realities, and the Arguments* (NY: Corpus Books, 1970); Robert P. George and Gerard V. Bradley, 'Marriage and the Liberal Imagination,' *Georgetown Law Journal*, 84 (1995), 301, reprinted herein as Chapter 8.

47 Rawls, *Political Liberalism*, 58.

48 See Robert P. George, 'Law, Democracy, and Moral Disagreement,' *Harvard Law Review*, 110 (1997), 1388, reprinted herein as Chapter 18.

49 Rawls, *Political Liberalism*, 24, n. 27.

50 Ibid., 58.

51 See, ibid., 54–7.

52 John Finnis, 'Rawls and Political Liberalism' (Feb. 24, 1996), 8 (unpublished manuscript, on file with author).

53 See Rawls, *Theory of Justice*, 118–42.
54 Rawls, *Political Liberalism*, 225.
55 See, ibid., lii.
56 Ibid., 214–15.
57 See, ibid., lii.
58 Ibid., 243.
59 Ibid., 243, n. 32.
60 Ibid.
61 Ibid.
62 Ibid.
63 Ibid.
64 Ibid.
65 See Thomas McCarthy, 'Kantian Constructivism and Reconstructivism: Rawls and Habermas in Dialogue,' *Ethics*, 105 (1994) 44, 53, n. 16; see also Michael J. Sandel, 'Judgmental Toleration,' in George, *Natural Law*, 107, 109–10; Sandel, 'Political Liberalism,' 1777–8, 1790.
66 See, e.g., Kent Greenawalt, *Religious Convictions and Political Choice* (NY: Oxford University Press, 1988).
67 Rawls, *Political Liberalism*, lv–lvi, n. 31.
68 Ibid.
69 The article to which Rawls plainly is referring is Judith Jarvis Thomson, 'Abortion,' *Boston Review*, (Summer, 1995), 11.
70 Ibid., 15.
71 See, e.g., Patrick Lee, *Abortion and Unborn Human Life* (Washington, DC: Catholic University of America Press, 1996); Robert E. Joyce, 'Personhood and the Conception Event,' *New Scholasticism*, 52 (1978), 97; Francis C. Wade, 'Potentiality in the Abortion Discussion,' *Review of Metaphysics*, 29 (1975), 239; Helen Watt, 'Potential and the Early Human,' *Journal of Medical Ethics*, 22 (1996), 222.
72 See Thomson, 'Abortion,' 14–15.
73 Ibid., 15. Thomson does not object 'to constraining access to abortion on the ground that the fetus has a right to life [because] this is Catholic, and hence religious doctrine.' The 'Catholic doctrine' on the subject condemns abortion as homicidal and unjust as a matter of publicly accessible scientific fact and rational (natural law) morality.
74 Ibid.
75 Moreover, it would undercut the support Thomson's argument supplies to what many find to be the politically attractive (though obviously questionable) idea that people can accept pro-life claims as a basis for being 'personally opposed to abortion,' yet affirm at the same time support for a legal right to abortion on the ground that the truth of pro-life claims is not relevant to (or, at least, is not determinative of) the question whether women are morally entitled to the legal freedom to abort.
76 Thomson, 'Abortion,' 13.
77 Ibid., 11.
78 I will deal with issues raised by the possibility of human cloning later in this section.
79 Dianne Nutwell Irving, 'Scientific and Philosophical Expertise: An Evaluation of the Arguments on "Personhood," ' *Linacre Quarterly* (Feb. 1993), 18, 23.
80 Ibid., 24.

81 Jed Rubenfeld, 'On the Legal Status of the Proposition that "Life Begins at Conception,"' *Stanford Law Review*, 43 (1991), 599.
82 Ibid., 625.
83 See, ibid., 617–26.
84 Ibid., 625, n. 115.
85 See, ibid. (citing Frances Olsen, 'Unraveling Compromise,' *Harvard Law Review*, 103 (1989), 105, 127–28).
86 Ibid., 625.
87 Ibid.
88 476 U.S. 747 (1986) (White, J., dissenting).
89 Ibid., 792 (White, J., dissenting).
90 Rubenfeld, 'On the Legal Status,' 625.
91 Ibid.
92 Michael Lockwood, 'When Does Human Life Begin?,' in *Moral Dilemmas in Modern Medicine*, Michael Lockwood, ed. (NY: Oxford University Press, 1985), 9, 29.
93 See Rubenfeld, 'On the Legal Status,' 625–6.
94 For a valuable examination of the issues Rubenfeld raises, see Michael B. Burke, 'Sortal Essentialism and the Potentiality Principle,' *Review of Metaphysics*, 49 (1996), 491, 500–14, which analyzes the beginning of persons through the lens of Aristotelian essentialism. When 'Dolly,' the sheep brought into being by cloning, was announced in February of 1997, it was evident that the time Dolly began was when the nucleus from a somatic cell of Sheep A was fused (electrically) with the denucleated ovum of Sheep B.
95 See Thomson, 'Abortion,' 11 (emphasis added).
96 For a defense of sexual liberationism, see David A. J. Richards, *Sex, Drugs, Death, and the Law* (Totowa, NJ: Rowman and Littlefield, 1982), 29–63; see also Frederick Elliston, 'In Defense of Promiscuity,' in *Philosophical Perspectives on Sex and Love*, Robert M. Stewart, ed. (NY: Oxford University Press, 1995). For a classic statement of conservative sexual morality in its strictest form, see St Augustine, *De Bono Coniugali*, in *St Augustine, Treatises on Marriage and Other Subjects*, 21–2 (Roy J. Deferrari ed. and Charles T. Wilcox et al. trans., 1955).
97 See Stephen Macedo, 'Homosexuality and the Conservative Mind,' *Georgetown Law Journal*, 84 (1995), 261; see also Andrew Sullivan, *Virtually Normal: An Argument About Homosexuality* (NY: Knopf, 1995); Paul Weithman, 'Natural Law, Morality and Sexual Complementarity,' in *Laws and Nature*, Martha Nussbaum, ed. (1996).
98 See Macedo, 'Homosexuality'; George and Bradley, 'Homosexuality,' 46.
99 See Macedo, 'Homosexuality,' 287.
100 See, ibid., 285–300.
101 See George and Bradley, 'Homosexuality,' 303–13.
102 See Macedo, 'Homosexuality,' 286–7.
103 See, ibid., 287–9.
104 See, ibid., 289–93.
105 George and Bradley, 'Homosexuality,' 301–2 (citations omitted).
106 See Macedo, 'Homosexuality,' 278–81.
107 See, ibid., 281–5.
108 See, ibid.
109 See, ibid.
110 See George and Bradley, 'Homosexuality,' 311, n. 32.

111 Ibid., 301, n. 1 (quoting John Finnis, 'Law, Morality, and "Sexual Orientation,"' *Notre Dame Law Review*, 69 (1994), 1049, 1066).
112 George and Bradley, 'Homosexuality,' at 301, n. 1. We argue that 'when
animals (including humans) mate, they are united biologically whether or not
conception is possible. In mating, the male and female pair is, indeed, a
"single reproductive principle." Reproduction is one act; yet the act is performed by the mated pair as an organic unit,' ibid., 311. As we go on to
observe, citing work by Germain Grisez, though individual males and females are complete organisms with respect to other functions (including, for
example, nutrition and sensation), they are, for reproductive purposes, only
potential halves of a mated pair. It is the mated pair that is the complete
organism that carries out the reproductive function. The mated pair may, of
course, happen to be sterile, but their intercourse, insofar as it is the reproductive behavior characteristic of the species, unites the copulating male and
female as a single organism. See, ibid., 311–13 (citing non-theological sections
of Germain Grisez, 'The Christian Family as Fulfillment of Sacramental Marriage, Paper Delivered to the Society of Christian Ethics Annual Conference'
(Sept. 9, 1995) (unpublished manuscript, on file with author)).
113 See Stephen Macedo, 'Reply to Critics,' *Georgetown Law Journal*, 84 (1995), 329,
334–354.
114 Ibid.
115 Ibid., 335
116 For an illuminating account of the arguments over slavery in this period, see
generally William Lee Miller, *Arguing About Slavery* (NY: Knopf, 1996), 36,
which observes that 'the use of the word "fanatic" to describe the [anti-
slavery] petitioners became so constant as to verge on the automatic.'
117 See, e.g., *Schenck* v. *Pro-Choice Network*, 65 U.S.L.W. 4109 (U.S. Feb. 19, 1997);
Madsen v. *Women's Health Ctr., Inc.*, 512 U.S. 753 (1994).
118 Amy Gutmann and Dennis Thompson, *Democracy and Disagreement* (Cambridge, Mass.: Belknap Press of the Harvard University Press, 1996), 1.
119 On the content and significance of these regulative principles and other principles comprising the constitution of deliberative democracy, see, ibid.
120 Ibid., 2.
121 For a succinct and, in my view, sound treatment of the morality of civil
disobedience, see Finnis et al., *Nuclear Deterrence*, 354–7. On the vexed question of when violence may be used to combat injustices, see, ibid., at 308–18.
122 My idea of a sound conception of public reason is similar to the one defended
by Michael Sandel, who rejects Rawls's restrictions on public reason in favor
of 'a more expansive conception, a public reason of moral and religious
engagement.' Michael Sandel, in 'Symposium, Political Liberalism: Religion
and Public Reason,' *Religion and Values in Public Life*, 3 (1995), 1, 3. Also
noteworthy are Sandel's comments regarding religious contributions to
moral reasoning about abortion. See, ibid., 9; see also Sandel, 'Political Liberalism,' 1789–94.
123 See George, 'Law, Democracy, and Moral Disagreement,' 48.

12

Natural Law and International Order

Among the achievements of recent analytical jurisprudence is its virtual elimination of false oppositions between 'natural law theory' and 'legal positivism.' Theorists of natural law such as John Finnis[1] and legal positivists such as Neil MacCormick[2] have developed refined understandings of relationships between law and morality in the light of which it no longer makes sense to suppose that a commitment to legal positivism logically excludes belief in natural law. Legal positivists, whatever their metaethical and normative commitments, recognize that nothing in the idea of legal positivism as such necessarily commits them to moral skepticism or cultural relativism; natural law theorists, acknowledging important respects in which law and morality are, indeed, 'conceptually distinct,' recognize concepts of law which, for valid theoretical purposes, systematically prescind from questions of the justice or injustice of laws or legal systems.[3]

The concern of the legal positivist is fundamentally with the accurate and theoretically interesting *description* of laws, legal institutions and legal systems. His endeavor is to describe the social practices that constitute the phenomenon of law at various times and in various places. Thus, H. L. A. Hart begins *The Concept of Law* by advising the reader to regard his book 'as an essay in descriptive sociology.'[4] By contrast, the concern of the natural law theorist is fundamentally with *justification*, that is to say, moral evaluation or prescription. Insofar as laws, legal institutions and legal systems are concerned, he is interested in their moral goodness or badness, their justice or injustice. Thus, John Finnis begins *Natural Law and Natural Rights* by declaring that:

there are human goods that can be secured only through the institutions of human law, and requirements of practical reasonableness that only those institutions can satisfy. It is the object of this book to identify those goods, and those requirements of practical reasonableness, and thus to show how and on what conditions such institutions are *justified* and the ways in which they can be (and often are) defective.[5]

In this chapter, I consider understandings of international order as they are, or could be, advanced by theorists operating within the tradition of natural law theorizing. I have, in other chapters and works, argued in support of the new classical natural law theory deployed by Finnis, though originally developed by Germain Grisez in collaboration with Finnis and Joseph M. Boyle, Jr.; but I will make no effort in this chapter to defend that theory or the tradition of which it is a part. My goal, rather, is to provide a sound exposition of the natural law tradition, and of the new classical theory (which draws on the work of Aquinas and other theorists in the tradition, yet criticizes them in certain respects and enters into the broader debate about ethical theory), and to relate some of what the tradition and the theory have to say about international society.

Along the way, I will refer to pronouncements on natural law and international order in papal encyclicals and other official documents of the Roman Catholic Church. I cite these pronouncements, not because the Church or her officials have any special authority that it is appropriate to invoke in philosophical discussion or debate, but rather because the Church is, I believe, the principal institutional bearer of the tradition of natural law theorizing in the modern world. And, of course, the Church is herself an international institution and a longstanding actor in international affairs.

I. NATURAL LAW THEORY[6]

The natural moral law, if there is such a thing, is a body of practical principles comprising at least two types or sets of non-instrumental reasons for action: first, reasons provided by 'basic human goods' which make available to human agents rationally grounded options for choice ('practical possibilities'); and second, reasons provided by moral norms that exclude some of these practical possibilities as in one way or another unreasonable.[7] Moral norms, where they are in force, provide conclusive 'second-order' reasons not to choose certain practical possibilities despite one's 'first-order' reasons (or other motives) to choose them.[8] Natural law theories are accounts of basic human goods, moral norms, and the reasons for action they provide.

Plainly, natural law theorists are cognitivists or 'objectivists' about morality. They are not accurately classified as either 'teleologists' or 'deontologists,' however. Unlike deontologists, they give basic human goods a crucial structural role in their accounts of practical reasoning and moral judgment; at the same time, they reject the consequentialist methods of moral judgment favored by contemporary teleologists.

Any comprehensive theory of human good(s) will say something about the common good, just as any comprehensive theory of morality will say something about political morality. It is hardly surprising, then, that natural law theorists have something to say about law (including international law), economics (including international economics) and politics (including international politics). It is generally unhelpful, however, to attempt to classify natural law theories or theorists as 'liberal' or 'conservative,' 'capitalist' or 'socialist,' 'individualist' or 'communitarian,' and so forth. The natural law tradition itself tends to be rather undogmatic about the proper solution to many of the political, social and economic issues that divide people into such camps. For example, while modern popes have, in the name of natural law, defended certain 'capitalist' principles, such as the market economy and the private ownership of property, they have at the same time allowed that a significant measure of economic regulation and governmental intervention in the economy can be permissible and may even be required as a matter of justice.[9] Furthermore, the popes have made no effort conclusively to settle questions of the proper scope of economic regulation and governmental intervention; nor have they provided precise guidelines as to when public ownership of this or that type of property is in order. Rather, they treat questions of this sort as prudential ones on which people may (within limits established by the requirements of justice and other moral principles) legitimately differ, and whose proper solution will, in any event, vary with the circumstances of any particular society at a given time. Sometimes a plurality of morally acceptable policy options will be available to political authorities in a community; other times, a uniquely morally correct option can be identified, but not without the degree of detailed knowledge of the facts on the ground that is likely to be possessed only by those actually on the scene.

The natural law tradition's well-known commitment to the idea of moral absolutes, forcefully reiterated by Pope John Paul II in his encyclical letter *Veritatis Splendor*, should not obscure the degree to which the tradition recognizes that many important issues of social and economic policy do not admit of a single uniquely correct solution that should, as a matter of natural moral law, govern in all places and at all times. In politics, as in personal affairs, the natural law may exclude only some (or, indeed, none) of the interesting options, leaving the matter to be settled by prudential judgment or, indeed, sheer preference. In one set of circumstances (in a great economic depression, for example) prudence might dictate a strongly interventionist economic policy, while in other circumstances (such as during periods of full employment or economic expansion) a policy of nonintervention or governmental withdrawal from certain sectors of the economy might be indicated. Relativities of this sort in fact abound when one considers the implications of natural law theorizing for international society.

II. THE NEW CLASSICAL THEORY

Before turning to the question of international order, however, let me fill out my sketch of natural law theorizing by describing in a little more detail the foundations of the new classical theory.

According to this theory, the first principles of natural law are not themselves moral principles. They are principles that extend to and govern all intelligent practical deliberation, regardless of whether it issues in morally upright choice, by directing action toward possibilities that offer some intelligible benefit (and not *merely* emotional satisfaction). Such principles refer to non-instrumental (and, in that sense, 'basic' or 'ultimate') reasons for action. Reasons of this sort are provided by ends that can be intelligently identified and pursued, not merely as means to other ends, but as ends-in-themselves (even when pursuit of some such end, in the particular circumstances in which one finds oneself, or by the only means available to one here and now, would be morally wrong).[10] Many philosophers refer to such ends as 'intrinsic goods'; Grisez, Boyle and Finnis call them 'basic human goods.'

Qua basic, such goods, and the fundamental practical principles which direct choice and action toward them, cannot be deduced from still more fundamental practical principles or from truths (such as putative facts about human nature) that are not themselves practical principles or derived from premises that include practical principles.[11] They are, rather, underived and, strictly speaking, 'self-evident.'[12] They come to be known in non-inferential acts of understanding wherein one grasps, in reflecting on the data of one's experience, the intelligible point of possible action (whether or not it is morally upright) directed toward the realization of (or participation in) the good in question by oneself or others (whether or not one happens to be interested in pursuing that good oneself here and how).

Following Aquinas,[13] proponents of the new classical theory identify a plurality of basic human goods, including life and health, knowledge and aesthetic appreciation, excellence in work and play, and various forms of harmony within each person and among persons (and their communities) and between persons (and their communities) and any wider reaches of reality.[14] These basic goods can be realized and participated in by an unlimited number of persons, in an unlimited number of ways, on an unlimited number of occasions. This multiplicity of basic goods, and of their possible instantiations in alternative interesting possible lines of action, entails great complexity in intelligent motivation. The incommensurability (that is, the rational irreducibility) of motives, at least one of which bears on an anticipated benefit whose unique goodness can come to be only through following practical reason's direction (which is often a nonexclusive direction) toward it, requires free choice—that is, a making up of one's indeterminate self to act on this motive rather than that one.

The plurality of basic human goods has a number of implications for how the new classical theory understands rational choice. Paradigmatically, one may have, and be aware of, a non-instrumental reason to do X, yet at the same time, have, and be aware of, a non-instrumental reason not to do X, or to do Y, the doing of which is incompatible with doing X. (In the limiting case, one makes a free choice between options, one of which is rationally grounded and the other of which is supplied by a purely emotional motive, like anger or repugnance.) Whichever option one chooses, one chooses for a non-instrumental reason; in that sense, the choosing of either option is *rational*.

Where it is the case that, of each of some set of incompatible options one has a reason to choose it, yet one has no *conclusive* reason to choose one option rather than the other(s), one chooses between options each of which presents an undefeated reason for acting. Where one has, and is aware of, undefeated competing reasons for acting, one's choice, though rationally grounded, is rationally underdetermined.[15] In such cases, reason does not narrow one's options to a single possibility. More than one practical possibility is not only rationally grounded, but fully reasonable. Sometimes, however, a moral norm (the Golden Rule of fairness) provides a *conclusive* reason not to choose one (or some) option(s), despite one's reason to choose it (or them). In such cases, at least one of one's first-order reasons (that is, reasons provided by basic human goods) is defeated by a second-order reason (that is, a reason provided by a moral norm) that provides a conclusive reason (and, thus, a moral obligation) to choose the undefeated option.

Still, one's first-order reason, though defeated, is not destroyed or eliminated; the morally excluded option retains intelligible appeal. For one to choose that option, while practically unreasonable (inasmuch as one's reason for choosing it has been defeated by a conclusive reason not choose it), is not utterly irrational; this is because one's action in choosing it, however immoral, is for the sake of some true good, and will, to the extent one succeeds, instantiate some intelligible benefit for oneself or someone else. If, *per impossibile*, a moral norm were to eliminate one's basic reason to choose a certain option, then one's choosing that option would not merely be unreasonable, but irrational, and, as such, intelligible, if at all, only as action motivated purely by feeling or some other sub-rational factor.

According to the new classical theory, the basic human goods that motivate and guide rational human choice are not 'Platonic forms' somehow detached from human persons; rather, they are constitutive aspects of the well-being and fulfillment of flesh-and-blood individuals in their manifold dimensions, that is to say, as animate, as rational and as agents through deliberation and choice. Basic human goods provide reasons for action precisely, and only, insofar as they are constitutive aspects of human well-being or flourishing.

Taken together, the first principles of practical reason that direct action toward these goods and reasons outline the (vast) range of possible rationally motivated actions, and point to an ideal of 'integral human fulfillment,' that is to say, the compete fulfillment of all human persons (and their communities) in all possible respects. Of course, no choice or series of choices can actually bring about integral human fulfillment; it is an ideal rather than an operational objective. Nevertheless, it is morally significant inasmuch as the first principle of morality (which, contrary to the representations of some expositors and critics of the new classical theory,[16] is no mere ideal) directs that choice and action for the sake of basic human goods be compatible with a will toward this ideal.

Given its abstractness and generality, the first principle of morality must be specified if it is to be useful in actually guiding people's choosing. Its specifications take account of the (necessarily sub-rational) motives people may have for choosing and otherwise willing incompatibly with a will toward integral human fulfillment; to act on such motives (that is, in defiance of moral norms) is to permit one's reason to be fettered by emotion and, typically, harnessed to it for the purpose of producing rationalizations for immoral conduct. The specifications of the first principle of morality guide action by excluding options that seem reasonable only if one's reason has been thus fettered.

These specifications are not, however, the most specific moral norms. They state propositions such as 'do unto others as you would have them do unto you,' and 'evil may not be done that good may come of it,' rather than more specific norms (of which they are, to be sure, principles) such as 'thou shalt not steal,' and 'thou shalt not kill the innocent and just.' They are, as it were, midway in generality between the first principle and fully specific norms. Finnis refers to these moral principles as 'requirements of practical reasonableness'; Grisez and Boyle (and Finnis in his collaborative writings with them) refer to them as 'modes of responsibility.' They provide conclusive second-order reasons not to choose certain practical possibilities, despite one's first-order reasons (and one's more or less powerful emotional motives) to choose them.

Moral principles, according to the new classical theory, are norms for free choice. In freely choosing, that is to say, in choosing for (or against) reasons provided by basic human goods, one integrates the goods (or the damaging and consequent privations of the goods, that is, the evils) one intends—whether as ends or as means to other ends—into one's will, thus effecting a sort of synthesis between oneself as an acting person and the objects of one's choices, that is to say, the goods and evils one intends. (This is in no way to deny that free choice is exercised and self-constitution effected also by the accepting of side effects.) Hence, one's free choices are self-constituting: they persist as virtues or vices in one's character and personality as a choosing subject unless or until, for better or worse, one reverses one's previous choice by choosing incompatibly with it, or, at least, resolves to choose differently should one face the same or relevantly similar options in the future.[17]

Noting the different ways that different types of willing bear on human goods and evils, proponents of the new classical theory distinguish as distinct modes of voluntariness 'intending' a good or evil (as end or means) from 'permitting' or 'accepting' (as a side effect) a good or evil that one foresees as a consequence of one's action but does not intend (that is, which serves as neither an instrumental or non-instrumental reason for one's choice and action). Although one is morally responsible for the bad side effects one knowingly brings about, one is not responsible for them in precisely the same way one is responsible for the evils one intends. And sometimes no moral norm excludes one's bringing about as a side effect of an action one has a reason (perhaps even a conclusive reason) to perform, some evil that one could not legitimately intend. On the other hand, often one will have an obligation in justice or fairness to others (and thus a conclusive reason supplied by a moral norm) not to bring about a certain evil that one knows or believes would probably result, though as an unintended side effect, from one's action.

III. 'COMMON GOOD' AND 'COMPLETE COMMUNITY'

Aristotle treated the *polis* as the paradigm of a complete community, that is one capable of securing the overall well-being and fulfillment of its members. Later theorists working in the tradition he established retained the term 'politics' for the affairs of a complete community, but treated the territorial state as the truly 'complete community' and the politics of such states as 'politics' in its focal sense. Similarly, they treated the territorial state as the paradigm of a legal system and the law of such states as 'law' in its focal sense. Yet again, they treated the common good of the territorial state as the paradigmatic case and focal sense of 'the common good.' Of course, the tradition of natural law theory recognizes that any group or association can have a 'politics,' a 'law' and a 'common good.' To the extent, however, that a community is 'incomplete,' that is to say, less than fully self-sufficient, it has a politics, law and common good in a derivative or, in any event, non-focal sense.

What does it mean, though, to speak of a 'common good' in any sense? Finnis's primary definition has gained wide acceptance among natural law theorists: 'a set of conditions which enables the members of a community to attain for themselves reasonable objectives, or to realize reasonably for themselves the value(s), for the sake of which they have reason to collaborate with each other (positively or negatively) in a community.'[18] In light of this definition, we may ask: Is there a common good of the 'international community'? Indeed, is there an international 'community' at all?

A central feature of medieval and modern natural law theory is belief in a universal human nature. In the absence of such a belief, the tradition could not speak meaningfully of a *common* good of members of different tribes, clans, nations or races, or, indeed, of an international *community* at all. Even with such a belief in place, however, the mainstream of the tradition has tended to treat the international community, and its politics, law and common good, as nonparadigmatic. Increasingly, however, natural law theorists are coming to view the territorial or national state as crucially 'incomplete,' that is to say, incapable of doing all that can and must be done to secure conditions for the all-round flourishing of its citizens. Finnis states the implications of this change in view for the natural law theory of the international order:

If it now appears that the good of individuals can only be fully secured and realized in the context of international community, we must conclude that the claim of the national state to be a complete community is unwarranted and the postulate of the national legal order, that it is supreme and comprehensive and an exclusive source of legal obligation, is increasingly what lawyers call a 'legal fiction.'[19]

In other words, the national state can no longer (if it ever could) secure the conditions of its citizens' overall well-being (that is, their common good) without more or less systematically coordinating its activities with other nation states and, indeed, without the active assistance of supranational institutions,[20] at least some of which must possess powers to enforce multilateral agreements and international law. Hence, it has become necessary to develop institutions that will enable the international community to function as a complete community and, therefore, as a community whose politics, law and common good are paradigmatic and focal.

One need not accept any of the distinctive claims of the natural law tradition in order to recognize the urgent need for international cooperation, and, indeed, for the (further) development of international institutions, to deal with modern social, economic and political problems. The distinctively modern problems of nuclear and other weapons of mass destruction, not to mention global environmental problems such as ozone depletion, oceanic pollution and mass deforestation, simply do not admit of effective solutions without substantial international cooperation. Moreover, international action is necessary to combat mass starvation and other evils, whether they are the intended or unintended consequences of human action or the result of earthquakes, hurricanes or other natural catastrophes, as well as to promote the economic development of poor nations and to protect human rights.

Does this mean that natural law theory, as applied to the problems of today, envisages the institution of a world government? The answer is, I think, 'yes'; however, it is subject to certain clarifications and, perhaps, qualifications. Ideally, a central political authority would attend to the common good of mankind in, for example, avoiding (or at least limiting) war, protecting the physical environment, preventing starvation and other forms of misery, promoting economic development, and protecting human rights. Such authority would be justified, as is political authority generally, by its capacity efficiently to generate and implement fair and otherwise reasonable solutions to the community's 'coordination problems.'[21] At the same time, it must be observed that concentrating power, and particularly the force of arms, in a central government that is not subject to effective countervailing power is obviously risky. To be sure, some risks are entailed by the creation of any central authority; and risks of this sort are often worth bearing. At the same time, ways must be found to lessen the risks, by, for example, constitutional schemes that divide, check and limit governmental powers. Moreover, the risks of permitting individuals and communities subject to a world government to retain armaments must be weighed prudentially against the risks of disarming them. The concerns that prompted late-eighteenth-century Americans to entrench in their federal constitution a right of the people to keep and bear arms may not be anachronistic.[22] Perhaps those in power in a world government should not be left entirely secure against the possibility of armed resistance, should their rule degenerate into tyranny.

IV. *'DETERMINATIO'* IN INTERNATIONAL SOCIETY

According to natural law theory, just and good positive law, including constitutional law, is always in some sense derived from the natural law. As Aquinas observed, however, this derivation is accomplished in at least two quite different ways. In the case of certain principles, the legislator translates the natural law into positive law more or less directly. So, for example, a conscientious legislator will deal with grave injustices, such as murder, rape and theft, by moving according to an intellectual process akin to deduction[23] from the moral proposition that, say, the killing of innocent persons is unjust to the legal prohibition of such killing. In a great many cases, however, the movement from natural to positive law in the practical thinking of the conscientious legislator cannot be so direct.

It is easy, for example, to understand the basic practical principle that identifies health as a basic human good and the preservation of human health as an important goal. A modern legislator will therefore easily see, for example, the need for a scheme of coordination of vehicular traffic to protect the health and safety of drivers and pedestrians. The common good, which it is his responsibility to foster and serve in this respect, clearly requires such a scheme. Ordinarily, however, he will not be able to deduce from the natural law a uniquely correct scheme of traffic regulation. The natural law does not determine once and for all the perfect scheme of traffic regulation or establish one or another set of tradeoffs (so much convenience or efficiency for so much safety, for example) as uniquely or definitively right. A number of different schemes—attended by different and often incommensurable costs and benefits, risks and advantages—may be consistent with the requirements of natural law. So the legislator must exercise a certain creative freedom in authoritatively choosing from among competing reasonable schemes. He must move, not by deduction or any intellectual process akin to it, but rather by an activity of the practical intellect which Aquinas called *determinatio*.[24]

Unfortunately, no single word in English adequately captures the meaning of *determinatio*. 'Determination' has some of the flavor of it; but so do 'implementation,' 'specification' and 'concretization.' The key thing to understand is that in making *determinationes*, the legislator enjoys a creative freedom that Aquinas analogizes to the freedom exercised by an architect. An architect must design a building that is sound and sensible for the purposes to which it will be put. Ordinarily, however, he cannot identify a form of the building that would be uniquely suitable. A range of possible designs will likely satisfy the relevant criteria. Obviously, a design with 'doors' no more than three feet high is unlikely to meet an important requirement for a functional building. No principle of architecture, however, sets the proper height of a door at six feet two inches as opposed to six feet eight inches. In designing a particular building, the architect will strive to make the height of the doors make sense in light of a variety of factors, some of which are themselves the fruit of *determinationes* (the height of the ceilings, for example); but even here he will typically face a variety of acceptable but incompatible design options.

Contemporary legal theory has brought to light the importance of authoritative legal enactments as norms for regulating and coordinating human action for the common good.[25] More often than not, such enactments are not direct 'deductions' from the natural law; rather, they are *determinationes*. Whether they are products of legislation or multilateral agreements, the norms of international law that have been, or could be, put into force to regulate and coordinate the activities of states, corporations and other actors in international affairs for the sake of the common good would, in the majority of cases, be *determinationes*. For example, in the case of a particular international environmental problem, the natural law may well require that some action be taken, but not prescribe any particular scheme among the range of possible reasonable schemes for dealing with the problem. Nor, perhaps, will the natural law dictate a uniquely correct solution if, in the case, a choice must be made between tolerating a certain amount of environmental pollution and sacrificing a certain measure of economic development. Where tradeoffs of this sort must be made, natural justice requires only that choices be made by fair procedures which take fully into account the rights and interests of all parties who will be affected.

Indeed, key questions about the proper constitution of the international order are themselves matters for *determinatio*. They do not admit of uniquely correct answers. Rather, choices must be made from among a range of reasonable constitutional schemes. Natural law requires that one of these schemes be selected for the sake of the human goods to be fostered and protected by international authority; however, there is no scheme of international authority that is uniquely required as a matter of natural law.

Is natural law theory completely relativistic, then, on the question of the proper constituting of the international order and on other questions pertaining to the common good of international society? No. The principles of natural law rule out certain possibilities, usually on the ground that they are unjust. For example, a constitutional scheme based on racist suppositions would be excluded as a matter of natural law. So, too, would any scheme that unfairly distributed the burdens and benefits of international cooperation in dealing, to stay with the example, with ecological problems. The relativism of the natural law theory of international order is limited. It follows from the belief that the principles of natural law, which exclude certain possibilities as unjust or otherwise immoral, will not necessarily narrow the possibilities for a just and upright ordering of international society, or a fair and effective solution to global environmental problems, to a single uniquely correct option.

I repeat, however, that a substantively acceptable scheme for constituting a society, or the international society, or for solving other problems pertaining to the common good of national or international societies, might nevertheless be judged according to natural law theory to be morally unacceptable on the ground that the procedures used to select that scheme from among the range of possible reasonable schemes were themselves unjust. For example, wealthy and powerful nations might arbitrarily or otherwise unjustly exclude poor and weak nations from participating effectively in decisions affecting the organization of international society. Or the interests and preferences of developing nations might be left out of account in making tradeoffs between, say, environmental protection and economic development.

V. 'SUBSIDIARITY' AND INTERNATIONAL ORDER

I have suggested that contemporary natural law theory envisages a world government that would function as the central authority in a 'complete community.' Does this mean that natural law theory is 'statist'? I think not. I have already noted that risks, as well as benefits, would attend the creation of any world government, and have spoken of the recognition by natural law theory of the need to lessen these risks, where possible, by checking and limiting the powers of that government. In addition to prudential considerations, however, natural law theory proposes principled grounds for decentralizing power wherever practicable.

Recall Finnis's definition of the common good as 'a set of conditions which enables the members of a community to attain *for themselves* reasonable objectives, or to realize reasonably *for themselves* the value(s) for the sake of which they have reason to collaborate . . . in a community' (emphasis supplied). Under the natural law account of human good(s), it is important not only that basic human goods be realized, but that people, and peoples, realize these goods *for themselves*, that is, as the fruits of their own deliberation, judgment, choice and action. On the basis of this consideration, the tradition of natural law theorizing has identified and endorsed the principle of 'subsidiarity.'[26] The meaning and implications of subsidiarity were nicely stated by Pope Pius XI in his 1931 encyclical letter *Quadragesimo Anno*:

just as it is wrong to withdraw from the individual and commit to a group what private initiative and effort can accomplish, so too it is an injustice . . . for a larger and higher association to arrogate to itself functions which can be performed efficiently by smaller and lower associations. This is a fundamental principle. . . . Of its very nature the true aim of all social activity should be to help members of a social body, and never to destroy or absorb them.[27]

As applied to the question of international order and a possible world government, the principle of subsidiarity would restrict the authority of any world government to those problems which cannot be successfully dealt with by national governments, just as it restricts the authority of national governments to those problems which cannot be successfully dealt with by regional governments, of regional governments to those problems which cannot be dealt with successfully by local governments, of local governments to those problems which cannot be dealt with successfully by neighborhood groups and other private associations, and of such groups and associations to problems which cannot be dealt with successfully by families.

Toward the end of his 1963 encyclical letter *Pacem in Terris*, Pope John XXIII reflected on the implications of the principle of subsidiarity for the precise question of constituting international society. He unambiguously affirmed the idea of an international or 'world-wide' public authority which would serve 'the universal common good'[28] by coming to grips with problems that 'the public authorities of individual states are not in a position to tackle . . . with any hope of a positive solution.'[29] This universal public authority would, he said, 'have as its fundamental objective the recognition, respect, safeguarding and promotion of the rights of the human person.'[30] But, he insisted:

the world-wide public authority is not intended to limit the sphere of action of the public authority of the individual state, much less to take its place. On the contrary, its purpose is to create, on a world basis, an environment in which the public authorities of each state, its citizens and intermediate associations, can carry out their tasks, fulfill their duties and exercise their rights with greater security.[31]

In the understanding of Pope John, and the tradition in which he speaks, world government is, in principle, limited government. Although such government is envisaged as the central authority of a complete community, it is not meant to displace regional, national or local authorities. Indeed, a world government may legitimately exercise power only where regional, national or local authorities are not competent to solve the problems at hand.

Of course, the application of the principle of subsidiarity is more a matter of art than of science; and, in the modern world, the principle must be applied under constantly shifting conditions. In many cases, problems that are appropriately dealt with at one level in the conditions prevailing today may more appropriately be dealt with at another level (higher *or lower*) in the conditions prevailing tomorrow. And often enough it will prove impracticable to shift authority to deal with a certain problem from one level of government to another, or from governmental to private hands, or vice versa, at every point at which it would be ideal to do so.

Natural law theorists are confident that the principle of subsidiarity can guide the practical thinking of conscientious statesmen, but they do not pretend that it can be applied mechanically or with anything approaching mathematical precision.

VI. A CONTRACTUAL ASSOCIATION OF NATIONS?

If the tradition of natural law theorizing envisages world government as limited in the scope of its just authority by the principle of subsidiarity, and if it maintains that such government must refrain from displacing national governments (and, indeed, sub-national governments) or interfering with the exercise of their authority in matters within their competence, does the tradition conceive of international society as a contractual association of nations?

Certainly no nation is under an obligation of natural justice to submit to the jurisdiction of a world government that is in itself unjust, or which was brought into being by procedures which excluded that or any other nation from fair participation in the *determinationes* embodied in its design. The substantive or procedural injustice of an international authority can provide an undefeated reason (and, indeed, under some circumstances, a conclusive reason) for a nation to refuse to submit to the jurisdiction of that authority. The fact that the international common good demands the institution of (limited) world government does not impose on any nation the obligation to accept the first offer of world government that comes along.

At the same time, the tradition of natural law theorizing does not suppose that a nation may justly fail to submit to the jurisdiction of a just world government which has been, or is being, created in accordance with basically just procedures. The tradition does not view international cooperation to secure the worldwide common good as somehow optional for states or peoples. The reality of international problems demanding international responses imposes on every nation, as a matter of natural justice, a duty to cooperate with other nations to secure the international common good. Thus, submission to the jurisdiction of a just world government is not morally optional in the way that participating in a contract is ordinarily morally optional. The common goods to be achieved (and common evils to be avoided) by the institution of a central international authority provide *conclusive* reasons for nations to submit to the jurisdiction of a just world government. For any nation to resist the jurisdiction of such a government is contrary to the international common good, and, as such, constitutes the sort of practical unreasonableness in political affairs that the natural law tradition treats as a paradigmatic case of injustice.[32]

None of this should be taken to imply, however, that there would be no place for bilateral or multilateral treaties and other contracts between nations in a properly constituted international order. Nor should it be taken to mean that the contractual *form* is inappropriate for the establishment of a world government or other international political institutions.

VII. CULTURAL DIVERSITY

For the natural law tradition, the obligation of international authority to respect cultural autonomy, and therefore to permit cultural diversity, is rooted in the principle of subsidiarity and in the diversity of basic human goods and of the reasonable ways that individuals and communities instantiate these goods in their lives. Contemporary natural law theory recognizes that dramatically different cultures can provide people with the resources they need to live fulfilling and morally upright lives. This recognition is perfectly compatible with the natural law tradition's historic rejection of cultural relativism. To say that some cultures are morally bad (or, more precisely, that certain practices deeply rooted in, or central to, some cultures are morally bad) is not to say that there is only one culture that is morally good.

In speaking of the obligation of international institutions to assist the economic and social development of impoverished nations, Pope Paul VI in his 1967 encyclical letter *Populorum Progressio* was careful to highlight both the principle of subsidiarity and belief in legitimate cultural autonomy and diversity:

We hope . . . that multilateral and international bodies . . . will discover ways that will allow peoples which are still under-developed to break through the barriers which seem to enclose them and to discover *for themselves, in full fidelity to their own proper genius*, the means for their social and human progress.[33]

According to Pope Paul VI and the natural law tradition, international cooperation, and even the institution of international authority, for the sake of the universal common good, entails neither statism nor cultural uniformity. Indeed, it is important to protect the human values to be realized by people, and peoples, precisely in their acting 'for themselves' and 'in fidelity to their own proper genius.'

Natural law theory rejects the idea that we must choose between cultural chauvinism and cultural relativism. Far from supposing that the natural moral law imposes a single cultural norm to which all peoples should aspire, contemporary natural law theorists maintain that respect for the integrity of diverse legitimate cultures is itself a requirement of natural justice. They hold that international law and government must, to the extent possible, not only permit diverse national and subnational communities to control their own affairs, but also respect (and, if necessary, help to protect) the right of such communities to preserve, by legitimate means, their distinctive languages, customs, traditions and ways of life.

This in no way implies that international authority acts illegitimately in forbidding and repressing violations of human rights, even when they are sanctioned by cultural norms. The question here, of course, is what constitutes a violation of human rights. Natural law theorists are by no means in agreement among themselves on this question; and everyone recognizes certain 'hard cases.' Natural law theorists generally do agree, however, in recognizing a wide-ranging legitimate cultural diversity, and in holding that the repression of cultural practices by public authority is justified only for the sake of preventing fundamental injustices or other grave evils.

NOTES

1 See John Finnis, *Natural Law and Natural Rights* (Oxford: Oxford University Press, 1980), esp. chs. 1 and 12, and Finnis, 'The Truth in Legal Positivism,' in Robert P. George, ed., *The Autonomy of Law: Essays on Legal Positivism* (Oxford: Oxford University Press, 1996).
2 See Neil MacCormick, 'Natural Law and the Separation of Law and Morals,' in Robert P. George, ed., *Natural Law Theory: Contemporary Essays* (Oxford: Oxford University Press, 1992).
3 Hence, natural law theorists need not object to 'positivism' in either of the two major senses discussed by Terry Nardin in chapter 1 of *The Constitution of International Society: Diverse Ethical Perspectives* (Princeton: Princeton University Press, 1998). At the same time, it is worth noting that natural law theorists lay particular emphasis on the proposition—denied today by few legal positivists—that the description of social phenomena cannot be utterly value-free. As Finnis has observed, 'there is no escaping the theoretical requirement that a judgment of *significance* and *importance* must be made if [descriptive] theory is to be more than a vast rubbish heap of miscellaneous facts described in a multitude of incommensurable terminologies.' Finnis, *Natural Law*, 17.
4 H. L. A. Hart, *The Concept of Law* (Oxford: Oxford University Press, 1961), vi.
5 Finnis, *Natural Law*, 3 (emphasis supplied).
6 Readers who are familiar with the natural law theory I have set forth and defended in earlier chapters may move forward to section III of the present chapter.
7 As I explain below, it is possible to distinguish moral principles of varying levels of generality. Taking these varying levels into account, one can speak of natural law as consisting of more than two sets of principles.
8 For a fuller explanation, see Robert P. George, 'Does the Incommensurability Thesis Imperil Common Sense Moral Judgments?,' *American Journal of Jurisprudence*, 37 (1992), 185–195, reprinted here as Chapter 4.

9 For example, Pope Paul VI, in harmony with the tradition of papal social teaching inaugurated in the late nineteenth century by Pope Leo XIII in *Rerum Novarum*, taught that 'without abolishing the competitive market, it should be kept within limits which make it just and moral, and therefore human.' *Populorum Progressio*, para. 61.

10 I explain the idea and significance of ultimate reasons for action in 'Recent Criticism of Natural Law Theory,' *University of Chicago Law Review*, 55 (1988), 1390–1394, reprinted here as Chapter 2.

11 In this respect, the new classical theory differs markedly from familiar neo-scholastic accounts of natural law, such as the one propounded by Thomas Higgins, *Man as Man: The Science and Art of Ethics* (Milwaukee, Wis.: Bruce Publishers, 1958).

12 For a careful explanation of the much misunderstood claim that the most basic practical principles are self-evident, see Joseph Boyle, 'Natural Law and the Ethics of Traditions,' in George, ed., *Natural Law Theory*, 23–7.

13 *Summa Theologiae*, 1–2, q. 94, a. 2., on which see Germain Grisez's path-breaking article, 'The First Principle of Practical Reason: A Commentary on the *Summa Theologiae*, I–II, q. 94, a. 2,' *Natural Law Forum*, 10 (1965), 168, n. 201.

14 See John Finnis, Joseph M. Boyle, Jr. and Germain Grisez, *Nuclear Deterrence, Morality and Realism* (Oxford: Oxford University Press, 1987), 279–80; also Germain Grisez, Joseph Boyle and John Finnis, 'Practical Principles, Moral Truth, and Ultimate Ends,' *American Journal of Jurisprudence*, 32 (1987), 107–108.

15 See Joseph Raz, *The Morality of Freedom* (Oxford: Oxford University Press, 1986), 339.

16 See, e.g., Russell Hittinger's exposition and critique in *A Critique of the New Natural Law Theory* (Notre Dame, Ind.: University of Notre Dame Press, 1987), 50–1.

17 On the lastingness and character-forming consequences of free choices, see John Finnis, *Fundamentals of Ethics* (Washington, DC: Georgetown University Press, 1983), 139–44.

18 Finnis, *Natural Law*, 155.

19 Finnis, *Natural Law*, 15.

20 See Second Vatican Council, *Gauduem et Spes*, para. 84.

21 On the justification of political authority in the natural law tradition, see Finnis, *Natural Law*, ch. 10.

22 The Second Amendment to the Constitution of the United States: 'A well regulated Militia, being necessary to the security of a free State, the right of the people to keep and bear arms, shall not be infringed.'

23 See St Thomas Aquinas, *Summa Theologiae*, 1–2, q. 95, a. 2.

24 *Summa Theologiae*, 1–2, q. 95, a. 2. In describing *determinatio* as 'an activity of the practical intellect,' as I do here (and have done elsewhere), I do not mean to deny that *determinatio* crucially involves choosing. My point is to affirm that the choosing is guided by 'an intellectual process which is not deductive and does involve free choice (human will) and yet is intelligent and directed by reason.' John Finnis, 'On "On the Critical Legal Studies Movement,"' *American Journal of Jurisprudence*, 30 (1985), 23.

25 See Edna Ullmann-Margalit, *The Emergence of Norms* (Oxford: Oxford University Press, 1980).

26 From the Latin *subsidium*, 'to help.'

27 *Quadragesimo Anno*, para. 79. According to John Finnis, 'an attempt, for the

sake of the common good, to absorb the individual altogether into common enterprises would be disastrous for the common good, however much the common enterprises might prosper.' Finnis, *Natural Law*, 168.

28 *Pacem in Terris*, para. 139.
29 *Pacem in Terris*, para. 140.
30 *Pacem in Terris*, para. 139.
31 *Pacem in Terris*, para. 141.
32 My focus on the question of world government here is not meant to obscure the natural law tradition's recognition of mutual obligations among nation states even prior to the creation of central authority. This recognition is certainly evident in the idea of the *ius gentium*, as it figures in the thought of classical and Christian theorists of natural law. These thinkers stressed the obligation of states to cooperate to solve common problems and provide assistance to one another.
33 *Populorum Progressio*, para. 64, emphasis supplied. The phrase 'for themselves' reflects Pope Paul VI's commitment to the principle of subsidiarity; the phrase 'according to their own proper genius' reflects his belief in legitimate cultural diversity, not only as a matter of past practice, but as something that rightly continues as peoples progress.

Part Three
DIALECTICAL ENGAGEMENT

13

Moral Particularism, Thomism and Traditions

Replying to critics in the postscript to the second edition of *After Virtue*, Alasdair MacIntyre took note of the apparently paradoxical—even Quixotic—quality of his own project:

An historicist defense of Aristotle is bound to strike some sceptical critics as paradoxical as well as a Quixotic enterprise. For Aristotle himself, as I pointed out in my discussion of his own account of the virtues, was not any kind of historicist . . . To show that there is not paradox here is therefore one more necessary task; but it to can only be accomplished on the larger scale that the successor volume to *After Virtue* will afford me.[1]

That successor volume appeared as *Whose Justice? Which Rationality?* There MacIntyre holds fast to the historicist, or moral particularist, thesis he advanced in *After Virtue*, and sets about dissolving the apparent paradox. His task has, however, become even more daunting as a result of some important revisions of his understanding of Aquinas, in light of which he now wishes to identify himself not only as Aristotelian but as a Thomist as well. Aquinas's universalism deprives MacIntyre of one possible way out of his dilemma, namely, generating particularism from the notion that justice is necessarily local and therefore altogether variable according to particular local histories, traditions and circumstances.

Whose Justice? comprises some twenty chapters in more than four hundred pages. In the first chapter, entitled 'Rival Justices, Competing Rationalities,' we get a clear statement of the historicist or particularist thesis: 'Since there are a diversity of traditions of inquiry, with histories, there are, so it will turn out, rationalities, rather than rationality, just as it will also turn out that there are justices rather than justice.'[2] But in the last chapter, entitled 'Contested Justices, Contested Rationalities,' just where one might expect a particularist to remind us that justice and rationality are to be understood as plural, rather than singular, concepts, we get, instead, a very different kind of reminder:

This is a point in the argument at which it is important to remind ourselves that the discussion of the nature of tradition-constituted and tradition-constitutive inquiry has been undertaken not for its own sake but to arrive, so far as is possible, at a true account of justice and of practical rationality.[3]

So it appears that MacIntyre believes after all that we can, at least to some extent, develop a *true* account of justice (singular) and practical rationality (also singular). The question then becomes: which account, so far as MacIntyre is concerned, is the true account? Whose justice? Which rationality? In the final two pages of the book we get an unambiguous statement of what has been hinted for three hundred pages: the true—or at least, best—account of justice and rationality, in MacIntyre's judgment, is the Thomistic account.

Is Thomism, however, with its apparently universalistic understandings of justice and practical rationality, compatible with MacIntyre's strong moral particularism? And has MacIntyre, in the three hundred and eighty pages intervening between the two passages I have quoted from *Whose Justice?* dissolved the apparent paradox? The latter question must, in my judgment, be answered negatively. In view of MacIntyre's formidable skills as a dialectician, I am inclined to think that this is only because the former question must be answered negatively as well.

The precise occasion for MacIntyre's acknowledgment of the paradoxical quality of his historicist defense of Aristotle, as well as his promise to dissolve the apparent paradox in a later work, was a reply to Robert Wachbroit's charge that MacIntyre's account of virtues in *After Virtue* leads inescapably to some form of relativism. Now relativism is clearly incompatible with Thomist moral theory. So, in *Whose Justice?* MacIntyre seeks to break the apparent connection between relativism on the one hand, and historicism or particularism, on the other.

MacIntyre presents his particularism as a part of what Russell Hittinger has labeled a 'recoverist' project.[4] MacIntyre does not, that is to say, mean to propose something new; rather he means to recover something that has been lost to post-Enlightenment philosophy. So he asks: 'Of what did the Enlightenment deprive us?' His answer is that the great thinkers of the Enlightenment obscured for their successors the understanding of rational inquiry and justification which has made possible the philosophical achievements of the ancient and medieval philosophers whom MacIntyre so much admires.

What the Enlightenment made us for the most part blind to and what we now need to recover is . . . a conception of rational inquiry as embodied in a tradition, a conception according to which the standards of rational justification themselves emerge from and are part of a history in which they are vindicated by the way in which they transcend the limitations of and provide remedies for the defects of their predecessors within the history of that same tradition.[5]

The inadequate conception of rational inquiry and justification with which the Enlightenment philosophers saddled us, according to MacIntyre, is largely responsible for the conceptual incommensurability of modern moral arguments, which, in turn, accounts for the interminability of contemporary moral disputes. He describes this conception midway through the first chapter of *Whose Justice?*

Rational justification was to appeal to principles undeniable by any rational person and therefore independent of all those social and cultural particularities which the Enlightenment thinkers took to be the mere accidental clothing of reason in particular times and places.[6]

MacIntyre warns us not to 'trap ourselves by, perhaps inadvertently, continuing to accept the standards of the Enlightenment' in the very quest for an adequate alternative.[7] Thus we must not suppose that a better conception of rational inquiry and justification will itself be justified by appeal to principles of pure or abstract rationality independent of distinctive and variable social and cultural understandings.

As an alternative to the Enlightenment conception of rational inquiry and justification, MacIntyre proposes what he calls 'tradition-constituted and tradition-constitutive inquiry.'[8] In drawing a contrast between this conception and the Enlightenment view, MacIntyre says that:

from the standpoint of tradition-constituted and tradition-constitutive inquiry, what a particular doctrine claims is always a matter of how precisely it was in fact advanced, of the linguistic particularities of its formulation, of what in that time and place had to be denied, if it had to be asserted, of what was at that time and place presupposed by its assertion and so on. Doctrines, theses, and arguments all have to be understood in terms of historical contexts.[9]

It is at this point, near the end of the first chapter, that MacIntyre, confronting the objections of an imaginary critic, outlines his strategy for dealing with the problem of relativism:

Acknowledgment of the diversity of traditions of inquiry, each with its own specific mode of rational justification, does not entail that the differences between rival and incompatible traditions cannot be rationally resolved. How and under what condition they can be resolved is something only to be understood after a prior understanding of the nature of such traditions has been achieved. From the standpoint of traditions of rational inquiry the problem of diversity is not abolished, but it is transformed in a way that renders it amenable of solution.[10]

In the following eighteen chapters, MacIntyre seeks to achieve the necessary 'prior understanding of the nature of such traditions.' In good Aristotelian fashion, he executes the task by studying a certain number of actual traditions, and briefly indicating others that should be studied. The four he picks out for detailed treatment are: (*i*) the Aristotelian tradition that 'emerges from the conflicts of the ancient *polis*, but is then developed by Aquinas in a way which escapes the limitations of the *polis*'; (*ii*) the Augustinian tradition that 'entered the medieval period into complex

relationships of antagonism, later of synthesis, and then of continuing antagonism to Aristotelianism'; (*iii*) the Renaissance Aristotelian-Calvinist-
Augustinian tradition that flourished in seventeenth-century Scotland,
only to be 'subverted from within by Hume'; and (*iv*) liberalism—the
paradoxical Enlightenment tradition that while 'born of antagonism to
all tradition, has transformed itself gradually into what is now clearly
recognizable even by some of its adherents as one more tradition.'[11]

These, then, are among the traditions that both constitute forms of
inquiry and are constituted by forms of inquiry. They present competing
conceptions of practical rationality and (relatedly) justice. There are, according to MacIntyre, simply no such things as pure or abstract rationality
and justice—the belief that there are such things is an Enlightenment
illusion. There are, rather, the *rationalities* and *justices* of particular traditions. The concepts of rationality and justice are necessarily embedded in
traditions, apart from which these concepts make no sense. One who
would think about problems of practical rationality and justice must,
therefore, appeal to some tradition to which he, at least tentatively, gives
allegiance.

MacIntyre forcefully and repeatedly claims, however, that one's choice
of a tradition cannot be made from a neutral standpoint from which
the various traditions can be impartially evaluated. It is a central tenet
of MacIntyre's particularism that no such 'tradition-independent' standpoint is available.

> There is no place for appeals to a practical-rationality-as-such or a justice-as-such
> to which all rational persons would by their very rationality be compelled to give
> their allegiance. There is instead only the practical-rationality-of-this-or-that-
> tradition and the justice-of-this-or-that-tradition.[12]

In view of this condition, MacIntyre declares: 'it is an illusion to suppose
that there is some neutral standing ground, some locus for rationality as
such, which can afford rational resources sufficient for inquiry independent of all traditions.'[13]

Still, one must, it seems, choose among traditions; and *Whose Justice?* 'is
primarily addressed [to] someone who [has] not as yet . . . given their
allegiance to some coherent tradition of inquiry.'[14] Must such a person's
choice be arbitrary? Or may such a person appeal to standards or criteria
of rationality by which his choice among traditions may be rationally
guided?

Here MacIntyre faces a dilemma. On his own particularist terms, such
standards or criteria are available only from within traditions. So someone
who has not yet given his allegiance (at least tentatively) to a tradition
apparently lacks standards or criteria of rationality without which his
choice *must* be merely arbitrary. If, however, such choices *are* necessarily

arbitrary, then there seems to be no way of avoiding a fundamental and decisive relativism in practical reasoning and, therefore, in moral and political theory.

MacIntyre's attempt to deal with this dilemma is curious. Surely it was predictable that nonrelativists would join relativists in claiming that his strong particularism is inescapably relativistic. The former critics, unlike the latter, would count this as a reason for him to modify or abandon his particularism, and would demand not a critique of relativism, but a defense of particularism. But instead of answering the objections of the nonrelativists by defending his particularism against the charge of relativism, MacIntyre merely replies to imaginary relativist critics, who, in defense of relativism, claim that MacIntyre's particularism is inherently (and properly) relativistic. He employs his own variant of a familiar retorsive argument to silence relativists:

The person outside all traditions lacks sufficient rational resources for inquiry and *a fortiori* for inquiry into what tradition is to be rationally preferred. He or she has no relevant means of rational evaluation and hence can come to no well-grounded conclusion, including the conclusion that no tradition can vindicate itself against any other. To be outside all traditions is to be a stranger to inquiry; it is a state of intellectual and moral destitution, a condition from which it is impossible to issue the relativist's challenge.[15]

There are two problems with this strategy: (1) although it silences the relativist, it seems to do so at the price of ensuring that the very person to whom MacIntyre says his book is primarily addressed—now described as intellectually and morally destitute—will be in no position to benefit from the advice that it contains; and (2) while it generates the conclusion that an avowed relativist lacks good grounds for attacking MacIntyre's position, it does not show that MacIntyre's position is itself able to avoid a fundamental and decisive relativism. The burden for MacIntyre is to hold on to his particularism while demonstrating that, appearances aside, ultimate choice among traditions need not be arbitrary.

This is a burden MacIntyre is unable to support. When he does confront the problem squarely—asking how it could be rational for someone who has not yet given allegiance to a tradition to deal with the claims of the various rival traditions—his answer seems somewhat evasive:

The initial answer is: that will depend upon who you are and how you understand yourself. This is not the kind of answer which we have been educated to expect in philosophy, but that is because our education in and about philosophy has by and large presupposed what is in fact not true, that there are standards of rationality, adequate for the evaluation of rival answers to such questions, equally available, at least in principle, to all persons, whatever tradition they may happen to find themselves in and whether or not they inhabit any tradition.[16]

Now, I am perfectly willing to entertain the possibility that MacIntyre's answer strikes me as inadequate only because I am among those whose education in and about philosophy is defective in the way he describes. But, if I inhabit a tradition, it is not the Enlightenment tradition that MacIntyre deems responsible for propagating the myth of tradition-independent practical reason. Rather, it is the very tradition of thought about practical rationality and justice to which MacIntyre himself now proclaims allegiance. From the point of view of this tradition, at least, MacIntyre's answer is deeply unsatisfactory.

Thomists maintain that certain fundamental practical truths are available to anyone, regardless of his cultural or intellectual heritage, allegiances, or commitments. These truths find various modes of expression in difference cultures and traditions, but are nevertheless captured in sound practical judgments that may be formed by any thinking person. They are not deduced, inferred or derived from other practical or theoretical truths, but are, rather, *per se nota* (self-evident). Among these truths are those basic practical principles referred to by Aquinas as the 'first principles of practical reason.' Thomists, to be sure, disagree among themselves about the content of these principles—indeed an intramural debate rages among Thomists over the question of whether the set of these principles comprehends within its reference the range of moral and non-moral goods or is limited exclusively to moral realities—but it is a highly heterodox 'Thomism' that denies the universal availability of at least some basic practical truths.

MacIntyre's claim that the rationality of one's choice among traditions will necessarily vary with 'how one understands oneself' represents a decidedly un-Thomistic view. No particular self-understanding is required to understand and affirm the sets of basic practical principles which, according to Thomists, on the one hand underlie all coherent practical thinking, and on the other distinguish fully reasonable from defective practical judgments. One's grasp of these principles does not depend upon any prior commitment to Thomism. On the contrary, one is likely to find Thomism compelling precisely insofar as one consciously and reflectively grasps these principles.

For Thomists, as indeed for many non-Thomists, the rational desire for self-understanding in part motivates the quest for truths about such things as practical rationality and justice. Practical philosophy yields, among other things, self-understanding. The crucial point for the evaluation of MacIntyre's claim here, however, is that 'how one understands oneself' is hardly a separate matter from the quest for truths about practical rationality and justice; nor can self-understanding somehow be achieved prior to reflection on the problems of practical rationality and justice.

If someone standing apart from any tradition cannot, as MacIntyre supposes he cannot, grasp any sound principles of practical rationality and justice, neither, it would seem, could such an individual be capable of sufficient self-understanding to render his choice among the range of traditions confronting him anything other than arbitrary. If knowledge of practical truth cannot be attained apart from a tradition, then surely self-understanding capable of rationally grounding one's choices among traditions cannot be attained apart from a tradition either. So someone not (yet) committed to a tradition who would choose rationally among traditions appears to be caught in a vicious circle. Hence the question MacIntyre rightly identified remains unanswered: how does one choose rationally among traditions?

A possible solution to the dilemma is to allow for a measure of autonomous practical reasoning. This solution, I think, is the authentic Thomist one. MacIntyre's sweeping claims against tradition-independent practical thinking render it unavailable to him, however. His particularism, wielded throughout *Whose Justice?*, but especially in its seventeenth chapter, as a weapon against liberal moral and political thought, stops him from drawing upon the best resources of the tradition he himself views as the most promising alternative to liberalism.

Authentic Thomism is not inconsistent with recognition of the important respects in which traditions supply resources to practical reflection. Thomistic practical philosophy need not, and in fact historically does not, leave out of account the manifold ways in which context affects the rational application of practical principles. MacIntyre could embrace authentic Thomism merely by weakening his particularism to leave room for some autonomous (tradition transcending, universal truth attaining) practical thinking.

Here let me pause to consider the possibility that I have done MacIntyre an injustice in my exposition of his view by conflating two concepts that he would distinguish: (*i*) someone standing apart from any tradition; and (*ii*) someone who has not yet given his allegiance to any coherent tradition. Perhaps MacIntyre means to suggest that while the former person lacks the resources for a nonarbitrary choice among traditions, the latter person, precisely inasmuch as he does not stand outside all traditions (despite not having yet given his allegiance to a coherent tradition), can call upon the resources of the various traditions to choose rationally among coherent traditions.

Even on this reading of *Whose Justice?* however, MacIntyre's dilemma remains. Under the terms of his particularism, the standards by which one would judge a tradition sound or unsound are only available from within one or another tradition. Traditions cannot provide one with such standards unless and until one commits oneself to a particular tradition. Insofar as a choice among traditions must be made in accordance with standards of some sort if it is to be anything other than arbitrary, some such commitment must, it seems, precede it.

MacIntyre's failure to resolve the apparent paradox left over from *After Virtue* should not be permitted to obscure the many successful features of *Whose Justice?* Chief in importance among these, perhaps, is MacIntyre's development of his earlier work on 'epistemological crises' to show how adherents of a tradition can reasonably lose faith in their tradition and, relatedly, how traditions can break down. He argues that traditions can supply rational resources sufficient for their adherents to recognize their own failures. It can become clear, for example, that a tradition has no way of resolving a problem that the tradition itself enables its adherents both to identify and recognize as important. Traditions may, that is to say, fail (and be seen by their adherents to fail) to meet their own standards.[17]

This analysis enables MacIntyre to make a powerful case against an especially strong form of relativism. He demonstrates the falsity of the proposition that each tradition, inasmuch as it sets its own standards of justification, will necessarily be vindicated on its own terms. As he observes, however, this proposition may not be a part of any particular relativist's thesis.[18] I would only add that, by refuting it, MacIntyre does not immunize his own position against weaker forms of relativism.

MacIntyre also gives a good account of how someone whose allegiance to a tradition wavers might recognize the superiority of a competing tradition. In effect, one may judge an alien tradition superior by the very standards that one's own tradition sets but fails to meet.[19] Of course, one's conversion to a new tradition will entail one's adoption of the standards of that tradition in preference to those of one's former tradition. From MacIntyre's point of view, however, the convert will, in a sense, be indebted to the tradition he has abandoned for the rational resources that enabled him to recognize the deficiencies of that tradition and the superiority of its rival. For MacIntyre, even a seriously defective tradition can supply what is needed for someone to engage in effective practical thinking.

Much of MacIntyre's analysis of the role of traditions in practical reflection seem to me not only acceptable, but insightful. In his zeal to topple what he calls the Enlightenment conception of practical reason, however, MacIntyre mars his analysis by claiming too great a role for tradition, and, correspondingly, omitting the important, if limited, role of universally available practical principles in intellectual conversion and achievement in practical philosophy generally. While his argument entitles him to claim a considerable role for traditions in practical thinking, it does not support his radical claim that there can be no resources of practical rationality apart from those supplied by traditions. So long as MacIntyre hangs on to this claim, his analysis will be vulnerable to charges of relativism and vexed by a seemingly indissoluble paradox.

A second notable achievement of *Whose Justice?* is MacIntyre's critique of what he describes as the 'characteristically modern form of practical reasoning.'[20] This mode of reasoning treats first-person expressions of preferences without qualification as statements of reasons for action. MacIntyre argues persuasively that this way of treating preferences or desires breaks not only with ancient and medieval understandings, but also with Hume's philosophy. Hume recognized that 'I want' may express a passion, thus revealing a *motive* for action, but it lacks the impersonality necessary to function as a *reason* for action.

Someone can want something for a reason; but the sheer desire for something is not itself a reason for action. Inasmuch as such a desire is capable of projecting goals and motivating action it may, of course, figure as the ultimate term in an accurate descriptive account of behavior. But a want cannot provide a practical reasoner with an ultimate intelligible ground for a goal such a want might project as an attractive option. In MacIntyre's terms, such a want cannot serve as a *premise* for practical reasoning. Only an end or purpose that is rationally desirable for its own sake, thus providing an ultimate intelligible ground for someone's choosing for its sake, can function as an ultimate *reason* for action. Only such ends or purposes can serve as premises for practical reasoning.

Of course, skeptics deny that there are any such ends or purposes. The skeptical view is that Thomists, and other perfectionists, are simply misguided in supposing the practical intellect can grasp ends or purposes that are *intrinsically* worthwhile. According to skeptics, the belief in ultimate intelligible goods—and thus the belief in ultimate *reasons* for action—is the equivalent in practical philosophy of belief in the tooth fairy.

Contemporary philosophers who subscribe to the mode of practical reasoning that MacIntyre rightly identifies as dominant, however, are not skeptics. If his criticisms of this mode of reasoning are on the mark, as I think they are, then MacIntyre has established something important: the alternative to perfectionist moral and political theory is not anti-perfectionism (as in Rawls's theory of justice, for example) but skepticism. And if we have reason to be skeptical about skepticism, as most contemporary philosophers rightly think we do, then moral and political philosophers ought to turn their attention to the search for a sound perfectionism.

NOTES

1 Alasdair MacIntyre, *After Virtue*, 2nd ed. (Notre Dame, Ind.: University of Notre Dame Press, 1984), 277–8.

2 Alasdair MacIntyre, *Whose Justice? Which Rationality?* (Notre Dame, Ind.: University of Notre Dame Press, 1988), 9.
3 Ibid., 389.
4 Russell Hittinger, *A Critique of the New Natural Law Theory* (Notre Dame, Ind.: University of Notre Dame Press, 1988), 1.
5 MacIntyre, Whose *Justice?*, 7.
6 Ibid., 6.
7 Ibid., 7.
8 This label, which makes no appearances in *After Virtue*, appears first on p. 9 of *Whose Justice?* and is employed throughout the remainder of the text.
9 MacIntyre, *Whose Justice?*, 9.
10 Ibid., 10.
11 Ibid.
12 Ibid., 346.
13 Ibid., 347.
14 Ibid., 393.
15 Ibid., 367.
16 Ibid., 393.
17 Ibid., 361–4.
18 Ibid., 364.
19 Ibid., 364–5.
20 Ibid., 338.

14

Human Flourishing as a Criterion of Morality: A Critique of Perry's Naturalism

In *Morality, Politics, and Law*, Michael Perry adumbrates a 'naturalist' account of moral knowledge.[1] According to Perry, such knowledge is 'primarily about what sort of person a particular human being ought to be—what projects she ought to pursue, what commitments she ought to make, what traits of character she ought to cultivate—if she is to live the most deeply satisfying life of which she is capable.'[2] '[O]nly secondarily . . . [is it about] what choices a particular human being ought to make in particular situations of choice, given the person she is, which means, in part, given the person she is committed to becoming.'[3]

Perry claims that all moral imperatives, though not all moral judgments, are hypothetical.[4] They indicate what a person should do if he wishes to flourish. Why should a person make a commitment to flourishing? Perry's reply to this question is worth quoting at length:

[T]here is no noncircular way to justify the claim 'One ought to try to flourish.' Any putative justification would presuppose the authority of that which is at issue: flourishing. . . . We cannot justify flourishing. Nonetheless, most human beings are committed to (their own) flourishing; they do value it. . . . Just as the commitment to the value of rationality is not at issue for most of us, the commitment to, the value of, flourishing is not at issue either.[5]

So, the question, while neither meaningless nor trivial, cannot be answered; yet it stands in need of no answer. 'Naturalist ought-talk,' he says, 'presupposes that any person to whom an ought-claim is addressed is committed to her own flourishing.'[6]

Perry proposes to distinguish his view of the foundations of moral knowledge from the views of two other contemporary naturalists, Mortimer Adler and John Finnis. These philosophers, as Perry interprets them, correctly judge that ethics is eudaimonistic[7]—that is, has to do with human flourishing—but misguidedly propose to answer the unanswerable question: 'Why flourish?' I shall use the occasion of Perry's criticisms of Adler and Finnis to offer a critique of Perry's own eudaimonistic ethical theory.

My thesis is that Perry's account of the axial foundations of moral knowledge is seriously defective, and that its defects lead him to embrace a correspondingly defective method of normative moral judgment (consequentialism). I shall present my critique in three sections. First, I shall argue that Perry's case against Adler fails because he misunderstands the notion of self-evidence, as it is applied to foundational practical (including axial) principles. Second, I shall argue that Perry's case against Finnis is marred not only by his misunderstanding of claims of self-evidence, but also by a deep confusion about the foundational axial principles that Finnis claims to be self-evident. Finally, I shall argue that Perry fails in his efforts to establish the commensurability of basic forms of human good. Perry needs to establish this commensurability in order to vindicate his consequentialist method of normative moral judgment. If basic human goods as they figure in options for morally significant choice are incommensurable, as Finnis and others claim they are, then comparisons of value, which all forms of consequentialism require, are unworkable.

I. PERRY'S CRITIQUE OF ADLER ON THE SELF-EVIDENCE OF BASIC PRACTICAL PRINCIPLES

Perry dismisses Adler's claim that the categorical injunction, '[w]e ought to desire (seek and acquire) that which is really good for us,'[8] is a self-evident truth on the ground that 'there is something mysterious about an account of truth according to which a proposition can be true—"self-evidently" true—even if it cannot be supported by a noncircular argument.'[9] The only support Perry adduces for this alleged mysteriousness is John Rawls's pronouncement that 'there are great obstacles to maintaining that [first principles] are necessarily true, or even to explaining what is meant by this.'[10] Laying aside distinctions between self-evident and necessary truths,[11] Perry's dismissal of Adler's claim is unwarranted by his arguments.

Adler defends his categorical injunction by claiming that '[i]t is impossible to think the opposite.'[12] But if this is so, he reasons, then one cannot rationally deny it. Perry says—without citation but within quotation marks—that Adler's appeal to self-evidence 'means that it is impossible to think that the proposition [that flourishing is a good] is false.'[13] But this statement misrepresents Adler's position. He argues that because it is impossible to think the opposite, the proposition that we ought to desire that which is really good for us is rationally undeniable. Adler does not believe that this argument proves that the proposition is self-evident; he knows very well that self-evidence cannot be proved. Instead, his argument represents a dialectical defense of a practical proposition that he claims to be self-evident. If the argument is sound, it undercuts counter-arguments intended to cast doubt upon the proposition.[14]

Adler invites his readers to test his claim that it is impossible to think that one ought not to desire that which is really good by attempting such a denial for themselves. His point is that, while one can say the words 'we ought not to desire that which is really good for us,' the obvious incoherence of the proposition renders it impossible to think that proposition. ' "[O]ught to desire," ' Adler says, 'is inseparable in its meaning from the meaning of "really good." '[15] As I interpret it, this proposition means that one can no more think that one ought not to desire that which is really good than one can think that there can be uncles or aunts without nieces or nephews.

This argument is not direct; no direct argument is available.[16] The 'categorical ought' cannot be deduced, inferred or derived from more fundamental propositions. Perry correctly observes that any attempt at such a deduction, inference or derivation is bound to be circular. Perry fails to notice, however, that Adler does not propose a direct argument. He makes no attempt to deduce, infer or derive his proposition. Instead, Adler believes that because his proposition is self-evident, it requires no direct argument. For Perry to supply such an argument, establish its circularity, and declare that 'Adler's argument in support of the truth of the categorical prescription doesn't work,'[17] does Adler an injustice.

Adler clearly eschews direct arguments—presumably because he is perfectly aware that such arguments would be circular—and defends his categorical injunction dialectically. This defense may be flawed; indeed, it might be possible to establish that the proposition stating his categorical injunction is false or meaningless. Propositions claimed to be self-evident are not thereby rendered irrefutable. But Perry's implicit claim that any proposition that cannot be argued for directly is 'beyond justification and, therefore, neither true nor false,'[18] merely begs the question of whether there are self-evident truths. Thus, regardless of whether Adler's categorical injunction is sound, Perry's argument against it is not.

Perry seems to misunderstand the notion of self-evidence, at least as applied to putative foundational practical principles. Inasmuch as such principles are basic, they cannot be deduced, inferred or (in any strict sense) derived from still more fundamental principles. Hence, they cannot—in principle cannot—be argued for directly. They may be defended dialectically (for example, by arguments establishing their rational undeniability or identifying logical errors in counter-arguments). And dialectical arguments in their defense may be refuted. But a claim that a certain proposition states a self-evident basic practical principle (for example, an axial principle or moral norm) cannot be defeated by establishing that any direct argument for that proposition is bound to be circular. Were a direct argument available in support of a putatively self-evident basic practical principle, this would merely indicate that, contrary to what was being claimed for it, the principle in question is neither basic nor self-evident.

If Perry's proposition that there are no self-evident truths is true, then Adler's claim that his categorical injunction is self-evident must be false. But Perry has offered no argument to show that there can be no self-evident truths. (He cannot, of course, claim that it is self-evident that there can be no such truths.) And the authority of even so eminent a philosopher as John Rawls is no substitute for argument in the case of a matter of such import as the (im)possibility of self-evident practical principles. Equally eminent philosophers, such as Thomas Aquinas, have held the contrary view. In the absence of argument, Perry's dismissal of Adler's categorical injunction is mere hand-waving.

II. PERRY'S CRITIQUE OF FINNIS ON FOUNDATIONAL PRACTICAL PRINCIPLES

Perry's critique of John Finnis's theory of the foundations of moral knowledge founders not merely on Perry's misunderstanding of claims of self-evidence, but also on a deep confusion about the foundational axial propositions that Finnis claims are self-evident. Perry says that 'for Finnis . . . flourishing or well-being is good in the sense that it is to be pursued, that we ought to pursue it.'[19] Distinguishing his own position from the one he imputes to Finnis, Perry declares, 'Rather than saying, with Finnis, that the good or value of flourishing is self-evident, we should say that the value of flourishing is not at issue for most of us.'[20] But has Perry represented Finnis's position accurately? Quoting from Finnis's *Natural Law and Natural Rights*, Perry says, 'For Finnis, the truth of the proposition that flourishing is good or valuable is "obvious ('self-evident') and even unquestionable." At another point Finnis says that the truth of that proposition is "underived." '[21] Notice that Perry's quotation of Finnis begins only after Perry states in his own words the proposition that he claims Finnis holds to be self-evident. But that proposition— 'flourishing is good or valuable'—never appears in Finnis's work. It is a proposition that Finnis neither holds nor has any stake in holding.

What Finnis proposes as 'obvious ("self-evident") and even unquestionable' is not the value of flourishing, but rather what he refers to variously as 'basic values,'[22] 'basic forms of human flourishing,'[23] 'basic forms of human good,'[24] 'basic component[s] in our flourishing'[25] and 'basic aspects of human well-being.'[26] Similarly, Finnis nowhere claims that 'the proposition that flourishing is good or valuable' is underived. Rather, he argues, following Aquinas, that what he calls 'the first principles of natural law, which specify the basic forms of good and evil and which can be . . . grasped by anyone of the age of reason . . . are per se nota (self-evident) and . . . underived.'[27]

In interpreting Finnis, Perry seems to assume that the following two propositions are equivalent: (1) that the value of human flourishing is self-evident; and (2) that the constitutive aspects of human flourishing (that is, Finnis's 'basic values') are self-evident. But they are not. Finnis espouses the latter proposition. The putative issue at stake in the former proposition—the value of flourishing—is not, under Finnis's theory, as Perry would have it, a question that need not be answered. Rather, it is a non-question. It is as nonsensical as asking, 'What is the value of value?'

These two propositions do not represent alternative ways of formulating the same proposition. The significance of the difference between the two propositions becomes clear when the focus shifts from the issue of self-evidence to the question of how 'human flourishing,' in Perry's case, and 'basic values,' in Finnis's case, are supposed to function in moral life as reasons for choice and action.

The crucial point is that, for Finnis, the basic values are constitutive aspects of human flourishing. They do not function as reasons for choice and action because they are means to flourishing; they are, rather, ends-in-themselves. They are not instrumental to the production of 'flourishing' (however that term is conceived); they are, instead, intrinsically valuable. They can be intelligibly chosen just for their own sakes. They are ultimate reasons for choice and action.

Finnis does not conceive of flourishing as some deeper reason for action by reference to which basic values, as proximate reasons for action, have their intelligible appeal. There is no flourishing beyond the basic values. They are constitutive, and, thus, fundamental. One can choose precisely and ultimately for the sake of a basic value (or some combination of basic values). One cannot, however, choose precisely and ultimately for the sake of flourishing. Does this mean that, as far as Finnis is concerned, the notion of flourishing is meaningless? No. It means only that the concept of flourishing is intrinsically variegated. Goodness can be predicated of the various basic aspects of human flourishing only in an analogical—not in a univocal—sense. Finnis does not suppose that basic values are good because they have in common some fundamental feature, such as the capacity to produce flourishing, constitutive of their goodness. If their goodness is derived from something more fundamental, they would not be ultimate reasons for action. To be sure, basic values share a formal feature precisely inasmuch as it can be said that each of them is an ultimate reason for action and an aspect of human flourishing. But each is a different reason.

For Finnis, as well as for other authors whom Perry would describe as naturalists, to say that something is a value is to say it provides an intelligible reason for action. It may, perhaps, compete with other reasons.

One may have a reason to do something, yet at the same time have a reason not to do it (or a reason to do something else instead). A reason may be defeated by competing reasons, and yet remain a reason. The point is that a value, understood as providing a reason for action, is capable of grounding the intelligibility of a choice for its sake, even if such a choice is unwise, imprudent or immoral.

To claim, as Finnis does, that knowledge, for example, is a basic value is to say that knowledge is an ultimate intelligible reason for action. A basic value does not have its intelligibility by reference to something beyond itself (the way a purely instrumental value, for example, money, has its intelligibility as a reason for action by reference to values other than itself, such as the things that money can buy). Thus, the basic value of knowledge cannot be deduced, inferred or derived. The premises needed for such deductions, inferences or derivations are unavailable. If the intelligibility of knowledge as an ultimate reason for action is to be grasped, that intelligibility must be picked out of the data by non-inferential acts of understanding.[28]

We may now easily distinguish Finnis's view of the axial foundations of moral knowledge from Perry's view. Perry seems to understand 'value(s)' as providing reasons for action, but he differs from Finnis in treating flourishing as a value. Underlying this difference is a radically different conception of flourishing. Perry conceives of flourishing not as consti-tuted by irreducible values (for example, friendship, knowledge, life, health and beauty), but rather as itself the ultimate value. Under his conception, Finnis's 'basic' values are proximate reasons for choice and action. They are means of flourishing, rather than ends-in-themselves. As means, they are instrumentally, rather than intrinsically valuable. Their choiceworthiness derives from their capacity to produce flourishing. Con-trary to Finnis's view, they are neither underived nor self-evident; their value can be inferred from their capacity to produce flourishing. The proposition that knowledge conduces to flourishing may function as a minor premise that leads to the conclusion that knowledge is a value.

Of course, values such as knowledge may, for Perry, still be described as basic in one sense: All commitments, projects and choices must be made for the sake of one or another such value. One flourishes by gaining knowledge, having friends, enjoying good health. Still, these values are understood not as ends-in-themselves (and thereby constitutive of flourishing), but rather as means to flourishing. They are reasons for action, but they are not ultimate reasons. Flourishing is the ultimate reason. Other values are intelligibly choiceworthy insofar as they conduce to flourishing.

Under this conception, value can be predicated of knowledge, friend-ship and health, univocally. Thus, these ends are all valuable in the same sense. They all conduce to flourishing. The capacity to produce flourishing is what they have in common and, indeed, what constitutes their value.

In this case, however, an account of flourishing must be given independently of the values through whose realization one may flourish. It is not enough to say that the meaning of flourishing is to possess and employ wisdom, participate in friendships, or enjoy good health, because these values have their ultimate intelligibility not in themselves (as under Finnis's view), but by reference to something else, namely that to which they conduce. Thus, it makes sense to formulate propositions about 'the value of flourishing' (whether one claims that this value is self-evident, or a necessary truth, or, as in Perry's case, 'not an issue').

What, then, is Perry's account of flourishing? What account can be given of that putative, ultimately valuable reality to which knowledge, friendship, life, health and beauty may conduce? If flourishing is not constituted by these values but, rather, is itself the ultimate value, then two questions arise: (1) what is flourishing?; and (2) what is the value of flourishing?

We have already encountered Perry's answers to these questions. His answer to the second question—the question he wrongly assumes that Finnis tries to answer—is that it can be ignored: 'the value of flourishing is not at issue for most of us.'[29] His answer to the first question is that to flourish is 'to live the most deeply satisfying life of which one is capable (or at least as deeply satisfying a life as any of which one is capable).'[30]

For Perry, the ideal of 'the most deeply satisfying life of which one is capable' is the ultimate reason for action and criterion of morality. Other values have their intelligibility by reference to the value of such a life. They are valuable inasmuch as they contribute to the satisfactions constitutive of such a life. How, for example, do we judge knowledge to be a valuable pursuit? Not, as Finnis would have it, by virtue of one's grasp of the value of knowledge as something worthwhile for its own sake. Rather, it is because knowledge conduces to the most deeply satisfying life. What is ultimate and intrinsically valuable is not knowledge itself as an irreducible aspect of human well-being, but the deep satisfactions that knowledge is capable of producing in the psyche of one who engages in the activity of knowing. The satisfactions attainable in developing and fulfilling one's capacities for knowing may be essential ingredients in the most deeply satisfying life of which one is capable.

The difference between Perry and Finnis is not, as Perry imagines, about whether 'the value of flourishing' is 'not an issue' or 'self-evident' (as he wrongly believes Finnis to suppose). Rather, Perry and Finnis hold radically different conceptions of human flourishing. As a result, they differ about the role of flourishing as an ideal in practical reasoning and moral life. In Finnis's conception, a consequentialist method of moral judgment is ruled out because of the incommensurability that must attend the basic aspects of human flourishing if they are irreducible.[31] In Perry's view, by contrast, apparently diverse values can be commensurated by appeal to the underlying common feature constitutive of the 'value,' that is, their capacity to produce the satisfactions that contribute to 'the most deeply satisfying life.' For Perry, then, sound moral judgments will require a consequentialist method by which the value available in one project, commitment, character or (other) choice may be rationally compared with the value available in others.

III. PERRY'S CONSEQUENTIALISM AND THE INCOMMENSURABILITY OF VALUES

Perry's conception of human flourishing is, it seems, psychologistic. Human choice and action are ultimately intelligible by reference to satisfaction. Values are reasons for action insofar as they tend to produce satisfactions. Values generate moral imperatives by contributing to the most deeply satisfying life of which one is capable. The ideal of 'the most deeply satisfying life,' then, serves as Perry's criterion of normative moral judgment.

Perry's ethical theory is unique neither in adopting a psychologistic conception of human flourishing nor in identifying flourishing as the criterion of morality. This is typical of a utilitarian approach. Perry wishes, however, to distinguish his position from at least two versions of utilitarianism: preference–utilitarianism and experience–utilitarianism.

He dismisses preference–utilitarianism with a succinct argument: people may simply be mistaken about their preferences. By what standard does Perry suppose we may judge a person's preferences to be mistaken? The standard of what that person would find most deeply satisfying. 'It simply makes no sense,' Perry declares, 'to give priority to satisfaction of a person's mistaken preferences rather than to strategies for correcting her mistaken vision of her possibilities and of what she would find most deeply satisfying.'[32]

The apparent ground of Perry's rejection of experience–utilitarianism is its identification of value with happiness. He says that, '[a]ccording to experience–utilitarianism, the fundamental good for human beings is a mental state, or experience, sometimes called "happiness." '[33] Quoting Dan Brock's description of this version of utilitarianism, Perry describes its conception of ultimate value as 'conscious experience enjoyed for its own sake.'[34] Perry then claims that '[t]his conception of human good or well-being is utterly implausible.'[35] His argument is worth quoting at length:

> To achieve the mental state in question is not necessarily to have achieved well-being or even to have come close. It is not necessarily to be flourishing. For example, a person may have masochistic or even sadistic sensibilities and thus be 'happy' when she is engaged in masochistic or sadistic activities. . . . However, such 'happiness' does not entail that she is necessarily living anything close to a life as deeply satisfying as any of which she is capable. . . . The fundamental problem with the experience–utilitarian standard of value is that it takes as given—it presupposes the authority of—existing sensibilities. What makes a person 'happy' depends on her sensibilities, yet a person's sensibilities might be antithetical to, subversive of, her flourishing.[36]

Perry does not condemn experience–utilitarianism, as Finnis surely would, for its psychologistic conception of flourishing; rather, it is identifying flourishing with the mental state in question that he opposes. He wishes to distinguish the concept of happiness, at least as it functions in experience–utilitarianism, from that of a deeply satisfying life. Presumably, if one defines happiness as deep satisfaction, Perry would have no objection to the use of the term in moral theory. His concern, it seems, is to establish that when being supremely happy differs from living the most deeply satisfying life, it is the latter ideal that matters for practical reasoning and moral judgment.

I contend that Perry's ethical theory is best understood not as an alternative to experience–utilitarianism, but as a more sophisticated version of it. Perry's ideal of human flourishing, no less than the ideal proposed in the version of experience–utilitarianism he criticizes, is a psychological or mental state; it consists of an experience: profound satisfaction.[37]

Perry's argument against experience–utilitarianism reveals the lack of subtlety of the version of experience–utilitarianism he criticizes. One might, he argues, be as satisfied as possible given one's sensibilities; yet, one might still be more deeply satisfied if one altered one's sensibilities. One should not, therefore, presuppose the authority of the sensibilities that one happens to have. For instance, a perfectly satisfied pig probably does not enjoy the profundity of satisfaction of a perfectly satisfied man. Likewise, a perfectly satisfied man of limited sensibilities does not enjoy the profundity of satisfaction of a perfectly satisfied man of more eminent sensibilities. One's flourishing, therefore, can be achieved only to the extent that one both acquires the finest sensibilities of which one is capable, and experiences the highest degree of satisfaction of which one equipped with such sensibilities is capable.

Morality, therefore, requires one to do more than seek the happiness of which one is capable given one's sensibilities. It requires one to seek to acquire the most eminent sensibilities of which one is capable. Only by acquiring such sensibilities can one hope to lead the most deeply satisfying life of which one is capable. A drink of water may perfectly satisfy one's thirst. But surely it does not yield the depth of satisfaction that an opera lover would experience in listening to Don Giovanni. Someone capable of acquiring the sensibilities that make possible such profound satisfactions, but who nevertheless settles for a life of comparatively trivial satisfactions, fails in regard to the moral imperative requiring one to seek the most deeply satisfying life of which one is capable.

Of course, not everyone can acquire, or should seek to acquire, the opera lover's sensibilities. It would be foolish to attempt to acquire sensibilities one is incapable of acquiring, even if someone else would find life more deeply satisfying by virtue of their acquisition and fulfillment. Similarly, it would be misguided to seek to acquire sensibilities that one could never begin to fulfill, even if such sensibilities would make one's life more deeply satisfying in circumstances in which they could be fulfilled. The opposite of a deeply satisfying life is a profoundly frustrated life. Inasmuch as individuals differ in their circumstances and natural capabilities, prudence is required if individuals are to avoid profound frustration in the very quest for the most deeply satisfying life. Perry is careful to say that to flourish is to 'live the most deeply satisfying life of which one is capable.' Different individuals will differ in the depths of satisfaction of which they are capable.

Perry generally avoids speaking of 'desires' as the realities whose satisfaction comprises flourishing. Instead, he speaks of the satisfaction of 'interests.'[38] Indeed, he points out that one's interests and desires may diverge—giving one an interest in the 'nonsatisfaction' of some desires: '[T]o have a preference (or want or desire) . . . is not necessarily to have an interest in the satisfaction of that preference. A person has an interest (if she is committed to flourishing) in the satisfaction of preferences the satisfaction of which is constitutive of her flourishing.'[39] Thus, one has an interest in satisfying certain desires, preferences or wants. Which ones? Those 'the satisfaction of which is constitutive of one's flourishing.' In other words, those the satisfaction of which constitutes the most deeply satisfying life of which one is capable. Flourishing does, therefore, consist of satisfying desires. One's 'interests' are constituted by satisfactions of a discriminating sort. Satisfying some desires is not in one's interest to the extent that it impedes deeper satisfactions of which one is capable. Not all satisfactions are equal. A wife-abuser acts contrary to his own flourishing, and thus behaves immorally, when he elects the lesser satisfactions available to him in beating his wife over the truly profound satisfactions he could experience were he to cultivate a gentle, loving relationship with her.[40]

As Perry explicitly recognizes, a feature that his ethical theory shares with all forms of utilitarianism is its consequentialism. In an article based on notes developed in the preparation of *Morality Politics and Law*, he attempted to refute the claim made by Finnis, among others, that the incommensurability of basic forms of human good renders impossible those comparisons of the 'value' to be realized by human choices that are required by the consequentialist method of moral judgment. Perry does not repeat his arguments against the incommensurability thesis in his book. Instead, he cites this article and incorporates its arguments by reference.[41]

Among the issues at stake in the dispute about consequentialism is the existence of moral absolutes, which are specific exceptionless moral norms that exclude classes of behavior described in nonevaluative terms (for example, never directly kill an innocent human being). Perry takes the view that 'no determinate rule of conduct is absolute.'[42] He recognizes that this view depends upon the truth of the proposition that values are commensurable. 'Can one ever justify a choice that of itself does nothing but damage a basic human value on the ground that that damage is outweighed by benefit to a different basic human value? Not if the values in question are incommensurable.'[43]

Perry offers two arguments against Finnis's incommensurability thesis. First, following Kent Greenawalt, among others, Perry maintains that Finnis overlooks a situation of moral choice in which one and the same value is at stake, and in which no incommensurability problems arise. Consider, for example, a case in which a 'hundred lives can only be saved by intentionally killing an innocent person.'[44] One cannot object to a consequentialist argument that the slaying of an innocent may be justified on the ground that different values are incommensurable. Different values are not involved. What consequentialists would have us compare here are not different values, but rather different manifestations of one and the same value, human life. It is a matter of comparing the value of one life with that of a hundred. And surely here, Perry argues, we have commensurability. So he asks: 'What difference does it make that an act will do nothing of itself but damage a basic human good, so long as the indirect consequences of the act will be to salvage, in spades, that same human good?'[45]

This common objection to the incommensurability thesis rests on a misunderstanding.[46] Those who defend the thesis, including Finnis, argue that values are incommensurable; they do not maintain merely that categories of value are incommensurable.[47] David's life and Rachel's life are both lives, and therefore are instantiations of the basic value of life. But the life of each, independently of the life of the other, is an ultimate intelligible reason for action. As ultimate reasons, their lives are incommensurable with one another. The value of each individual's life is not derivative of some still deeper value in which different individuals share, and by reference to which individual lives have their intelligibility as reasons for action. David's life is intrinsically valuable. So is Rachel's. As intrinsic values, their lives are incommensurable. As persons constituted by incommensurable values, they are incommensurable persons. The upshot of this incommensurability is that no valid moral norm may direct someone making a choice whether to kill to weigh the life of one person against the life of another or the lives of any number of others.[48]

For purposes of his second and more comprehensive argument against the claim that basic values are incommensurable, Perry considers choices that implicate different categories of values. Choices of this sort, he argues, present the most plausible case for the incommensurability thesis. Even so, he maintains, the thesis fails. He observes that ' "commensurable" means "able to be measured by the same standard." '[49] He then deploys the following argument: 'I cannot think of any two things that are not commensurable—that cannot be compared in terms of the same standard. Think of any two things—any two things at all—and then consider this standard: which of the two things would you prefer to talk about right now.'[50]

The problem with this argument is that preferences cannot supply the sort of standard of comparison required to vindicate consequentialism as a method of choosing *rationally* among possibilities. The consequentialist does not say, 'Choose whatever option you prefer.' Rather, he proposes his method as a way of deciding which option is *rationally* preferable. It directs someone faced with a set of options to identify, and choose, the option likely to produce the objectively best proportion of good to bad consequences in the long run. It thus presupposes that values are commensurable prior to choice and independent of preferences. To observe that values can be compared by reference to a purely subjective standard, such as one's preferences, does not help the consequentialist. When critics of consequentialism characterize it as a technique of rationalizing preferences adopted prior to applying its method, rather than a method of deciding rationally among available options,[51] consequentialists *deny* the charge.

Perry implicitly admits that comparing values by appeal to preferences does not render the consequentialist method workable. After quoting Finnis's claim that adopting a set of commitments is nothing like carrying out a computation of allegedly commensurable goods, Perry says:

Finnis is right. We cannot justify, in consequentialist terms, those of our commitments and projects that supply us with our fundamental standards of comparison, because we need those standards of comparison before we can undertake any consequentialist weighing. Any effort to justify, on consequentialist grounds, such commitments and projects would end up being circular, in that the consequentialist justification would have to presuppose the very commitments/projects/standards to be justified.[52]

Exactly. Perry fails, however, to grasp the implications of this admission. If basic human values cannot be compared prior to commitments, it is because they are not reducible to each other or to some common feature constitutive of their value.[53] They are, rather, intelligibly choiceworthy in themselves. Their intelligible appeal, as ultimate reasons for action, neither derives from, nor depends upon, their common capacity to produce satisfactions that ordinarily supervene upon their realization.[54] Thus, they may properly be characterized as constituting human flourishing.

What, then, are the standards that should guide choice and action in respect of basic values? If there were no such standards, basic commitments would be arbitrary. Perry and Finnis agree that nonarbitrary standards are available. Perry, hanging on to the belief that values are commensurable (presumably by resort to preferences), imagines that the standards are 'standards of comparison,'[55] against which the 'value' of different possibilities can be measured. But his position is paradoxical because the standards needed to guide basic commitments can only be supplied by the commitments that they are needed to guide.

He assumes that Finnis's standards must also be standards for comparing values, and argues, therefore, that Finnis must allow commitments to supply standards. On the basis of this supposition, he easily draws the conclusion that Finnis has no ground for claiming that there are exceptionless specific moral norms. Perry asks:

If our commitments and projects and the standards of comparison they supply us with are not necessarily arbitrary, then why isn't it open to us to use those standards when we must decide whether to commit an act that of itself does nothing but damage a basic human value, just as it is open to us (as Finnis acknowledges) to use them in other situations of choice?[56]

But Perry's supposition that Finnis's standards are standards of comparison is wrong. Because Finnis understands human flourishing as constituted by incommensurable values, he does not suppose that choice and action can be guided by comparisons of value. He therefore has no stake in looking to commitments to provide such comparisons.

Human flourishing, according to Finnis, provides standards for choice and action because the integral directiveness of basic practical principles enables us to identify intermediate moral norms[57] that exclude ways of choosing that are incompatible with a will towards integral human fulfillment.[58] Inasmuch as the human values that constitute such fulfillment are incommensurable, these intermediate norms[59] will exclude, among other possible choices, choices that integrate evil into the chooser's will by way of an intention to destroy, damage or impede any such human value. Practical reason requires that basic goods be treated as ends-in-themselves, because that is what they are if the incommensurability thesis is valid.

It is a form of practical unreasonableness to reduce ends-in-themselves to mere means. The temptation to do so arises as a result of our desires; but these desires trade upon, and are often rationalized in terms of, the intelligible (non-desire-based) appeal of goods involved in the tempting option. An implication of the incommensurability of values is that even immoral options retain an intelligible appeal. Circumstances can arise in which certain genuine (incommensurable) values can be advanced only by treating other ends-in-themselves as mere means. But this same incommensurability supports the principle that the ends do not justify the means. Genuine, foreseeable evils (the death of a hundred, as in Greenawalt's example) must, in these circumstances, be accepted as side effects of one's morally required choice not to do evil by engaging in acts that set the will directly against a basic human good.[60]

The incommensurability of basic values as they figure in options for morally significant choosing does not mean that human flourishing—considered as the guiding ideal of integral human fulfillment—can be dispensed with in formulating the ultimate criterion of moral rectitude. It only means that it cannot provide such a criterion in the direct and straightforward way that Perry imagines. Human flourishing, understood as incommensurable people participating in incommensurable basic values, can provide standards capable of guiding choice and action despite the impossibility of comparisons of value. Taken together, the basic forms of human good comprise an ideal of integral human fulfillment. To the extent that one's choices are made compatibly with a will towards this ideal—as specified by the intermediate moral norms it generates—they may be judged morally upright.

NOTES

1 Michael Perry, *Morality, Politics, and Law* (NY: Oxford University Press, 1988), 10. The aggressive tone of my critique of this account should not be taken to reflect a judgment on my part that Perry's thought is without merit. He has astutely perceived that '[n]eo-Kantian talk about "autonomy" or "freedom" doesn't begin to compensate for the studied inattention to the question of the authentically human' that characterizes much Anglo–American thought about law and morals. Ibid., 182. By introducing a neo-Aristotelian perspective into the current debate concerning these matters, Perry makes a substantial contribution to remedying this lack of attention to the human good.
2 Ibid., 11.
3 Ibid., 12.
4 Ibid., 18.

5 Ibid., 15 (emphasis in original).
6 Ibid., 18 (footnote omitted).
7 Ibid., 12–16.
8 Ibid., 13 (quoting Mortimer Adler, *Six Great Ideas* (NY: Collier Books, 1981), 79).
9 Ibid., 14 (footnote omitted).
10 Ibid., 14, 217, n. 28 (quoting John Rawls, *A Theory of Justice* (Cambridge, Mass.: Harvard University Press, 1971), 578) (emphasis added by Perry).
11 Let us assume with Perry that Rawls means to deny the possibility of self-evident practical principles.
12 Michael Perry, *Morality*, 13 (quoting Mortimer Adler, *Six Great Ideas*, 80).
13 Ibid., 14.
14 For an analysis of the ways that dialectical arguments may support or cast doubt on propositions claimed to be self-evident, see Robert P. George, 'Recent Criticism of Natural Law Theory,' *University of Chicago Law Review*, 55 (1988), 1371, 1410–1412, reprinted herein as Chapter 2.
15 Michael Perry, *Morality*, 13 (quoting Mortimer Adler, *Six Great Ideas*, 80).
16 Were it otherwise, we could judge the proposition true, but not self-evident.
17 Michael Perry, *Morality*, 14.
18 Ibid., 13–14 (emphasis omitted). Perry claims that Adler's categorical injunction is 'beyond justification in the sense that any effort to justify it would be circular.' Ibid., 14 (citing Peter Singer, *Practical Ethics* (NY: Cambridge University Press, 1979), 203).
19 Ibid.
20 Ibid., 15–16.
21 Ibid., 14 (footnotes omitted; emphasis added).
22 John Finnis, *Natural Law and Natural Rights* (NY: Oxford University Press, 1980), 59, quoted in Michael Perry, *Morality*, 14.
23 See John Finnis, *Natural Law*, 22.
24 Ibid., 85.
25 Ibid., 87.
26 Ibid., 94.
27 Ibid., 33–4.
28 See, ibid., 34.
29 Michael Perry, *Morality*, 15–16.
30 Ibid., 19.
31 To say that basic human goods are irreducible to satisfactions is not to deny that the satisfactions which ordinarily, though not always, supervene upon the realization of such goods are intrinsic aspects of their perfection.
32 Michael Perry, *Morality*, 80 (footnote omitted).
33 Ibid., 79 (footnotes omitted).
34 Ibid. (quoting Brock, 'Utilitarianism,' in *And Justice for All*, Tom Regan and Donald Van DeVeer, eds. (Totowa, NJ: Rowman and Littlefield, 1982), 222).
35 Ibid.
36 Ibid., 79–80 (footnotes omitted; emphasis added).
37 Can Perry respond by claiming that I misrepresent him in identifying his ideal of the most deeply satisfying life with a psychological or mental state, e.g., deep satisfaction? Can he argue that a deeply satisfying life is a life of fulfillments not reducible to mere (or even deep) satisfactions? No one whom Perry would identify as a naturalist denies that the realization of values is usually satisfying. The advantage for a consequentialist of identifying the value of a project, commitment or choice with the (depth of) satisfaction it promises (or with some such psychological phenomenon) is that satisfaction

can then, one might suppose, function as the underlying common feature in terms of which basic human goods can be commensurated. In the absence of such an identification, basic human goods seem to be what Finnis claims they are: ultimate, irreducible and constitutive aspects of human flourishing—in short, incommensurable.

38 See, e.g., Michael Perry, *Morality*, 19.

39 Ibid., 20.

40 I am not importing an ultimately egoistic criterion of morality into this example (which is mine, not Perry's). Perry is explicit—indeed emphatic—in his endorsement of such a criterion: 'The commitment to flourishing presupposed by naturalist ought-talk . . . is a person's commitment to *her own* flourishing.' Ibid., 21 (emphasis in original). I dissent, as would many contemporary interpreters of Aristotle, from Perry's claim that this egoism is something that his view has in common with Aristotle's practical philosophy. Ibid., 23.

41 Ibid., 79, 262, n. 14 (citing Perry, 'Some Notes on Absolutism, Consequentialism, and Incommensurability,' *Northwestern University Law Review*, 79 (1985), 967).

42 Ibid., 187, 310, n. 17. Perry says that he has 'argued elsewhere that no determinate rule of conduct is absolute.' Ibid. (citing Perry, 'Some Notes'). In fact, what he defended in 'Some Notes on Absolutism, Consequentialism, and Incommensurability' is the somewhat weaker proposition that if a moral theory contains an absolute determinate rule of conduct, then that rule must be justified on consequentialist grounds. He noted in his article the difference between this claim and the stronger claim that no determinate rule of conduct is absolute. Perry has nowhere, so far as I am aware, actually argued for the stronger claim.

43 Perry, *supra*, n. 41, at 979.

44 Ibid., 975 (quoting Greenawalt, 'Book Review,' *Political Theory*, 10 (1982), 133, 135, reviewing John Finnis, *Natural Law*).

45 Ibid., 977 (emphasis added).

46 This misunderstanding is altogether avoidable in Finnis's critiques of consequentialism published since *Natural Law and Natural Rights*. See, e.g., John Finnis, *Fundamentals of Ethics* (Oxford: Clarendon Press, 1983), where he argues explicitly for the incommensurability of particular instantiations of basic human goods as they figure in options for morally significant choice.

47 This is especially clear in Joseph Raz's powerful defense of the incommensurability thesis. See Joseph Raz, *The Morality of Freedom* (NY: Oxford University Press, 1986), ch. 13 (Incommensurability).

48 The incommensurability thesis, if sound, undercuts consequentialist reasoning generally and thus, as Perry concedes, leaves reason free to identify specific absolute norms such as that against direct killing. But the incommensurability thesis does not imply that considerations of consequences are irrelevant to moral choosing. (On some of the various ways in which consequences can and should be taken into account, consistently with the incommensurability thesis and with moral norms, see John Finnis, *Natural Law*, 111–18.) What it does imply is that such considerations cannot negate moral norms. It is also worth pointing out that, when the question is not one of direct killing, various non-absolute moral norms are relevant to decisions about causing death or saving lives. In certain situations, a norm (e.g., that requiring fairness in the distribution of the benefits and burdens of communal life) may permit, or even require, an action that, as a consequence, will cost more lives

than it saves. In other circumstances, a norm (perhaps the same norm) will require an action directed to saving as many lives as possible.

49 Perry, 'Some Notes,' 979.

50 Ibid., 980 (emphasis in original).

51 See, e.g., John Finnis, *Fundamentals*, 94.

52 Perry, 'Some Notes,' 980.

53 Thus, Finnis's observation, '[N]one can be analytically reduced to being merely an aspect of any of the others, or to being merely instrumental in the pursuit of any of the others.' John Finnis, *Natural Law*, 92.

54 See *supra*, n. 31.

55 Perry, 'Some Notes,' 981.

56 Ibid., 981–2 (footnote omitted; emphasis added).

57 These norms are 'intermediate' between: (1) the most general moral norm, which requires the willing and choosing of those, and only those, possibilities whose willing is compatible with a will toward integral human fulfillment, and from which are derived general (but less general) norms (e.g., those against willing directly contrary to basic human goods or arbitrarily favoring some people over others in distributing common burdens or benefits); and (2) fully specific moral norms (e.g., those against direct killing or racism) that may be derived from these.

58 For detailed accounts of the ways in which the ideal of integral human fulfillment, understood in light of the incommensurability of basic human goods, can generate intermediate moral norms capable of serving as standards for choice and action in respect of incommensurable goods, see John Finnis et al., *Nuclear Deterrence, Morality, and Realism* (NY: Oxford University Press, 1987), 281–8; Germain Grisez et al., 'Practical Principles, Moral Truth, and Ultimate Ends,' *American Journal of Jurisprudence*, 32 (1987), 121–129. Anyone interested in understanding the relationship between flourishing and morality in Finnis's ethical theory should consult these texts. My brief sketch in this chapter is meant to do no more than indicate the scope of Perry's misunderstanding of that theory and the inadequacies of the case he presents against those dimensions of the theory that he rejects (e.g., anti-consequentialism).

59 There are many other intermediate norms. See, e.g., John Finnis, *Natural Law*, 100–27. I focus here on the one such norm capable of generating moral absolutes because of its centrality in the debate over consequentialism.

60 For a defense of the theory of human action implicit in this proposition, see John Finnis et al., *Nuclear Deterrence*, 288–91. A theory of action along these lines, though unacceptable to consequentialists, is required once basic human goods are understood not as definite goals instrumental to the production of 'value,' but rather as incommensurable, constitutive aspects of human flourishing.

15

Nature, Morality and Homosexuality

In *Virtually Normal: An Argument About Homosexuality*,[1] Andrew Sullivan, the young, 'gay,' British, Roman Catholic former editor of the *New Republic*, has argued eloquently and intelligently for dramatic revisions of natural law thinking and public policy regarding sexual morality and marriage. It is incumbent upon natural law theorists and, indeed, anyone who is inclined to support traditional ideas about sex and marriage, to take Sullivan's challenge to the natural law tradition very seriously. My aim in this chapter is to engage his arguments about nature, morality and homosexuality.

Homosexual acts have long been condemned as immoral by the natural law tradition of moral philosophy as well as by Jewish and Christian teaching. Sullivan argues that these condemnations are rooted in a failure to recognize that, for somewhere between two and five per cent of the population, homosexuality is, in a sense decisive for the moral evaluation of homosexual conduct and relationships, 'natural.' But (as Sullivan asks) what is a 'homosexual'? And what, precisely, is the sense in which homosexuality is 'natural'?

Sullivan approaches the first question autobiographically. At about age ten he began to feel what he describes as a 'yearning' which 'was only to grow stronger as the years went by' (p. 4). Although initially 'not sexual,' it was, nevertheless, 'a desire to unite with another: not to possess but to join in some way; not to lose myself but to be given dimension' (p. 6). This is, of course, a perfectly normal experience. In Sullivan's case, however, there was something not entirely normal about the way this yearning developed, namely, as a desire to be united not only emotionally but also physically with a person of his own sex.

Sullivan recognizes that his experience may differ in various respects from that of other homosexuals. In particular, he observes that the experience of female homosexuals tends to differ from that of males in that 'it is more often a choice for women than for men; it involves a communal longing as much as an individual one; and it is far more rooted in moral and political choice than in ineradicable emotional or sexual orientation' (p. 16). Nevertheless, he says, even many lesbians report experiences not entirely unlike his own. He concludes that homosexuality, whatever the form of its expression, 'is bound up in that mysterious and unstable area where sexual desire and emotional longing meet; it reaches into the core of what makes a human being who he or she is' (p. 17).

Thus, Sullivan puts into place a crucial premise of his argument for the value and moral validity of homosexual conduct, namely, that for people like him the fulfillment of a longing for emotional and physical union with someone of the same sex is critical to the success of their lives. For a homosexual, such fulfillment is, Sullivan goes so far as to suggest, the very thing 'which would most give him meaning' (p. 12). It is in this sense that homosexuality is 'natural' for homosexuals.

So, Sullivan reasons, homosexual genital acts, far from being 'unnatural,' are, or at least can be, naturally fulfilling for people whose fundamental yearning is to unite with someone of the same sex. Such acts, Sullivan supposes, can be truly unitive, and, thus, valuable, in the same way that heterosexual intercourse can be unitive and valuable.

Of course, many people believe that sexual intercourse has value only in the context of marriage, or, at least, that marital intercourse has special meaning and value. Sullivan himself holds this view.[2] When combined, however, with his proposition that some people are homosexual 'by their nature,' and with the proposition which he thinks follows from it, namely, that for such people homosexual genital acts can be unitive and fulfilling, it leads to the social and political conclusion that society should accept and provide for marriages between same-sex couples. And this conclusion is one that Sullivan presses with particular vigor.

If homosexuality is 'natural,' in a morally normative sense, then homosexuals are, as Sullivan says, 'virtually normal': 'virtually' in the sense that homosexual orientation is comparatively rare—certainly no more than one person in twenty, and perhaps as few as one person in fifty, is homosexual (so, in a merely statistical sense, heterosexuality is the 'norm'); 'normal,' because being homosexual is no more *ab*normal than, say, being black, or Jewish, or having red hair.

If, as Sullivan argues, homosexual relationships and conduct are naturally fulfilling and, as such morally good, then it follows not only that 'marriage should be made available to everyone, in a politics of strict neutrality,' (p. 203), but also that military positions should be made available to homosexuals and heterosexuals on a nondiscriminatory basis, as should positions as teachers, coaches and counselors in public schools. In Sullivan's view, law and government may no more legitimately draw distinctions between homosexuals and heterosexuals than they may distinguish between blacks and whites, Jews and gentiles, or redheads and brunettes. Thus, Sullivan calls for more than the mere *toleration* of homosexuality in and by the institutions of public life; as his demand for 'gay marriage' makes clear, he believes that these institutions are morally obliged to treat homosexual relationships as equal in worth and dignity to socially approved (i.e., marital) heterosexual relationships.

At the same time, Sullivan opposes extending civil rights laws to forbid discrimination based on sexual orientation into the private realms of housing and employment. He argues that 'liberals,' who would bring the coercive force of law to bear to overcome intolerance of homosexuality in the larger society, have strayed from liberalism's own principles. 'Liberalism,' he declares, 'is designed to deal with means, not ends; its concern is with liberty, not a better society' (p. 159). Contemporary liberals, in their zeal to free homosexuals (and members of other minority groups) from the consequences of prejudice, have, Sullivan suggests, 'created a war within [liberalism] itself' (p. 147). They have breached the traditional liberal commitment to public neutrality between competing visions of what makes for, and detracts from, a valuable and morally worthy way of life. In practice, then, liberalism has become a threat to the very idea of private liberty it celebrates in theory.

Sullivan's argument proceeds by engaging ideas and arguments about the morality and politics of homosexuality advanced not only by 'liberals' and 'conservatives,' but also by more extreme parties on each side, viz., 'prohibitionists' and 'liberationists.' While acknowledging that his categories are 'ideal types' whose tenets few people subscribe to in pure form, he subjects each to detailed criticism. His own view, unsurprisingly, fits into none. Sullivan is, in the end, not so much a 'neo-conservative,' as he is sometimes said to be, as a sort of conservative liberal, saying 'yes' to 'gay marriage' and to open homosexuals in the military and schools, and 'no' to state-sponsored affirmative action and the legal prohibition of private discrimination based on sexual orientation.

Liberalism, whether in the form Sullivan criticizes or in his own 'conservative' version of it, contrasts sharply with 'gay liberationism' which scoffs at bourgeois values and seeks to subvert mainstream institutions (such as marriage and the family) as opposed to integrating homosexuals fully into them. Sullivan's 'liberationists' eschew the argument that homosexuality, and homosexual conduct, are natural. They refuse to grant to 'conservatives' the proposition that human nature has determinate content or any sort of moral normativity. They celebrate the plasticity of human nature and practice a 'queer politics' which goes in for 'outings,' 'speech codes,' 'censorship' and 'intimidation' (p. 93). As Sullivan depicts it, liberationism tends to philosophical nihilism and political authoritarianism. Gay liberationists are the sort of people who give homosexuality a bad name.

'Prohibitionists' and 'conservatives' are Sullivan's classifications for people who judge that homosexual conduct is morally bad and believe that social policy ought to reflect that judgment. Conservatives differ from prohibitionists mainly in their tolerant attitude toward acts of 'private' immorality. They strongly oppose the vilification of homosexuals and typically favor the repeal of laws against sodomy. Moreover, conservatives tend not to be especially uncomfortable in dealing with homosexual friends and acquaintances who do not flaunt their homosexuality. The only real demand they make is that active homosexuals respect the sensibilities of others and be discreet about their sexual relationships to a degree that married people need not be. At the same time, conservatives oppose 'gay marriage' and other forms of official recognition and approbation of homosexual conduct and relationships. Although they tend to avoid the moralistic rhetoric of prohibitionists, conservatives share the moral belief that a life of active homosexuality should not be put forward as any sort of model of virtue.

Sullivan attacks the conservative view on two fronts. First, he challenges, as we have seen, the premise that homosexual acts, and relationships integrated around those acts, are morally bad or, indeed, morally inferior in any way to upright heterosexual conduct. (This challenge, obviously, cuts equally against the prohibitionists, who favor a more aggressive policy of discouraging homosexual activity. I shall therefore defer discussion of it until I turn to Sullivan's engagement with prohibitionism.) Second, he challenges the conservative belief that homosexuality can, much less should, be kept private. He claims that 'the old public–private distinction upon which the conservative politics is based,' (p. 130) has been eviscerated by the rise of the 'gay rights' movement. With large numbers of homosexuals 'out of the closet,' the cultural basis of conservative politics is collapsing; 'its bluff is being slowly but decisively called' (ibid.).

What is the conservative to do? One possibility is to join Sullivan and other non-liberationist proponents of 'gay rights' (such as Bruce Bawer, Gabriel Rotello and Stephen Macedo) in encouraging 'conservative trends among homosexuals and a co-optation of responsible gay citizenship' (p. 132). To do this, however, the conservative must, in effect, lay aside his moral qualms about homosexual conduct and accept something like Sullivan's ideal of the 'virtuous homosexual' who reserves sex for stable, loving, monogamous relationships and embraces other 'family values.' Above all, according to Sullivan, the conservative who takes this route should support the campaign for same-sex marriage as the best way to channel homosexual desire in the proper direction and encourage 'a responsible homosexual existence' (p. 107). His only other option, Sullivan believes, is to join the prohibitionists and, especially, 'the religious fundamentalists who do not share conservatism's traditional support of moderate and limited government.'

Contrary to what this last comment, shorn of its context, may suggest to the reader, Sullivan's chapter on prohibitionists is mainly concerned with Catholic appeals to rational moral principles of natural law, rather than evangelical arguments from revealed truth. Sullivan treats these appeals with respect, noting that the tradition of thought about natural law (of which the Church is today the principal institutional exponent) 'has a rich literature, an extensive history, a complex philosophical core, and a view of humanity that tells a coherent and at times beautiful story of the meaning of our natural selves' (p. 23). To his credit, Sullivan denies that prohibitionism's principled moral opposition to homosexual conduct can be dismissed as a 'phobia' or written off as 'bigotry.' At the same time, he argues that neither philosophical nor theological arguments against homosexual acts can survive criticism.

Sullivan concedes that both the Jewish and Christian scriptures appear to condemn homosexual genital activity. As he points out, however, in our own time, pro-'gay' critics have 'reinterpreted' the relevant scriptural passages in efforts to show either that what is being condemned is something other than sexual misconduct, or that the condemnation pertains only to ritual impurity and not to morality as such. Sullivan relies on the work of some of these critics, though he is forthright in acknowledging his own lack of professional competence to judge their claims. I, too, am no expert in biblical interpretation. Still, I would point out that some of the work on which he relies, particularly certain arguments advanced by the late John Boswell, has come in for scathing criticism from distinguished scholars (including some who share Boswell's and Sullivan's moral and political views about homosexuality) for 'politically correcting' the Bible and Jewish and Christian history.[3]

Where Sullivan is prepared to concede that a biblical text condemns homosexual conduct on moral grounds, as in the case of St Paul's Letter to the Romans, he argues that what is being condemned is not anything related to *homosexuality*—as we now know and understand it—but, rather, 'the perversion of heterosexuality' (p. 29). According to this argument, St Paul, being ignorant of the fact that some people are 'by their nature homosexual' (this presumably having been a discovery of modern psychologists), perceives perversion in all homosexual acts, whereas, in truth, there is perversion only in the homosexual acts of persons who are by their nature heterosexual.[4]

This argument is dubious. Its premise, that Paul and the people of his time simply 'assume that every individual's nature is heterosexual' (p. 29), trades on an equivocation on the meaning of the term 'nature' and its cognates. It is implausible to suppose that Paul, as a Pharasaical Jew and a Christian, understood people's natures to be constituted, in any sense relevant to moral judgment, by their *desires* (even those deep and more or less stable emotional desires Sullivan calls 'yearnings'), sexual or otherwise. (This is not to deny that Paul considered it 'natural' for people to experience bad as well as good desires, including sexual desires.) The view that human nature *is* ultimately constituted by emotional desires, while not unknown in the ancient world, is prominent today largely because of the profound influence of Thomas Hobbes[5] and, especially, David Hume[6] on the intellectual life of our culture. It was, however, rejected by the greatest pre-Christian philosophers, and I see no evidence of it in Paul's letters or in the writings of other Jews and Christians in the premodern world. So it is anachronistic for contemporary critics, such as Sullivan, to suppose that writers like Paul understood human nature to be constituted more or less as they believe it is—namely, by deep and fairly stable emotional desires—and then to claim that the early writers simply failed to understand that some people are 'by their nature' homosexual.

In fact, Sullivan's whole argument against 'the prohibitionists,' and, by implication, much of his argument against 'the conservatives,' assumes that they understand people's 'natures' to be constituted in the essentially Humean way that Sullivan and other liberals believe human nature(s) to be constituted. But, in fact, they reject the Humean understanding of how human nature is constituted as a *mis*understanding. Thus they need not, and—in my own case and in the cases of 'prohibitionists' and 'conservatives' cited by Sullivan with whose work I am familiar—do not, deny, as Sullivan thinks we must deny, that genuine homosexual orientation exists.[7]

But, if one's nature is not constituted by one's basic emotional desires, what is it constituted by? What is it that is fundamental about each of us as human persons and rightly motivating of us?

Let us get at these questions by considering Sullivan's analysis of natural law argumentation, particularly as it has been advanced in recent statements of the Catholic Church on homosexuality and homosexual genital acts. He thinks that he has caught the *magisterium* of the Church in a contradiction. Unlike St Paul (as Sullivan, Boswell and others read him), contemporary churchmen recognize that homosexually oriented persons exist; such persons are not merely heterosexuals who, for whatever reasons, choose to engage in homosexual acts. But, Sullivan suggests, if the Pope and Cardinal Ratzinger acknowledge that some people's 'natures' are homosexual, how can they continue to insist that homosexual acts violate natural law?

The answer is that the Church has a view about human good and the constitution of human nature which is much more like St Paul's (as I read him)—and Aquinas's and, for that matter, Plato's—than it is like Sullivan's, or Hobbes's or Hume's. The Church teaches that a person's nature, in the sense relevant to moral judgment, is constituted by human goods which give him *reasons* to act, and to refrain from acting, and not by *desires* which may, rightly or wrongly, also motivate him.[8] These 'natural goods' are 'basic' inasmuch as they are ends or purposes which have their intelligibility not merely as means to other ends, but as intrinsic aspects of human well-being and fulfillment. Far from being reducible to desires, basic human goods give people *reasons to desire things*—reasons which hold whether they happen to desire them or not, and even in the face of powerful emotional motives which run contrary to what reason identifies as humanly good and morally right.[9]

This understanding of human nature and the human good has been applied to questions of homosexual conduct by John Finnis, whose views Sullivan classifies as 'conservative.' For Finnis, as for the broader natural law tradition, the immorality of homosexual genital acts follows by implication from the intrinsic immorality of all forms of non-marital sex.[10]

Marriage, according to Finnis, is one of the basic human goods. As such, it provides a non-instrumental reason for spouses to unite bodily in acts of genital intercourse. This bodily union is the biological matrix of the multilevel (bodily, emotional, dispositional and even spiritual) relationship which is their marriage. Marital acts, while (necessarily) reproductive in type, are not merely instrumental, as St Augustine seems to have supposed, to the good of having children (or avoiding sin).[11] Nor are they mere means of sharing pleasure or even promoting feelings of closeness, as many contemporary liberals think. Rather, such acts realize the intrinsic good of marriage itself as a two-in-one-flesh communion of persons:

The union of the reproductive organs of husband and wife really unites them biologically (and their biological reality is part of, not merely an instrument of, their *personal* reality); reproduction is one function and so, in respect of that function, the spouses are indeed one reality, and their sexual union therefore can *actualize* and allow them to experience their *real common good—their marriage*.[12]

If this view, or something like it, is sound, then it is plain that oral or anal sex acts, whether engaged in by partners of the same sex or opposite sexes, and, indeed, even if engaged in by marriage partners, cannot be marital. (This moral insight, if such it is, accounts for provisions of both civil and canon law according to which marriages cannot be consummated by such acts.[13]) Only acts of the reproductive type (whether or not, as Finnis explains, they are intended to be, or even can be, reproductive in effect) can actualize (and, in law, consummate) marriage. Other sexual acts cannot be truly unitive because they do not unite the partners biologically, making them truly two-in-one-flesh.[14]

Moreover, masturbatory and sodomitical acts, by their nature, instrumentalize the bodies of those choosing to engage in them in a way which cannot but damage their integrity as persons. Inasmuch as non-marital sexual acts cannot realize any intrinsic common good, such acts cannot but be willed for instrumental reasons. And in such willing, 'the partners treat their bodies as instruments to be used in service of their consciously experiencing selves; their choice to engage in such conduct thus dis-integrates each of them precisely as acting persons.'[15]

Of course, this will not be considered morally problematic by people who hold an essentially dualistic conception of human beings as non-bodily persons who inhabit nonpersonal bodies which they 'use' as 'equipment.'[16] (And dualists of a conservative bent will be quick to point out that they support not just any instrumentalized sex, but only that directed toward such valuable ends as emotional closeness and intimacy.) But those who reject the idea that the nature of human beings is consti-tuted by their basic emotional desires tend to be the very people who reject person/body dualism. Start the list with John Finnis and Cardinal Ratzinger.

Sullivan devotes two or three pages to criticizing Finnis, whose bravery, honesty and intelligence in arguing about homosexuality he praises. His focus, however, is on what Finnis says about the social and political implications of homosexuality and its legal treatment, rather than his more fundamental argument that homosexual conduct is intrinsically non-marital and immoral. I have sketched that argument (all-too-briefly) here, not to defend it from its liberal critics—which I and others have done elsewhere[17]—but simply to show how it rejects—from start to finish—the conception of human nature as constituted by emotional desires which Sullivan wrongly believes is shared by natural law theorists who claim that homosexual acts are morally bad.

Once we see that 'prohibitionists,' such Cardinal Ratzinger, and 'con-servatives,' such as John Finnis, in fact reject the Humean conception of how human nature is constituted, Sullivan's charge that the Church's recognition of the reality of homosexual orientation is inconsistent with its continued condemnation of homosexual acts loses its force. Indeed, it becomes clear that the Church's view of homosexual desire (and the homosexual condition) as 'disordered' (in that it *inclines* people to sin) is perfectly consistent with its ringing affirmation of the intrinsic worth and dignity of *all* persons, not excluding those who happen to be homosexual. In this light, Cardinal Ratzinger's 1986 statement deploring 'violence and malice in speech or action' against homosexual persons is hardly the 'stunning passage of concession' Sullivan describes it as being. Rather, it is a simple reminder of the all-embracing scope of Christ's command: 'Love thy neighbor.'

In the end, I think, Sullivan rejects the teaching of his Church (and mine) that homosexual acts are intrinsically immoral, because he has come to believe that the sublimation of sexual desire to which the Church calls those whose homosexual inclinations make marriage a psychological impossibility alienates people from themselves and 'leads to some devastating loneliness' (p. 189). For Sullivan, it is celibacy that is 'unnatural,' at least for people from whom it is demanded because of a sexual orientation they did not choose, rather than, say, a religious vocation they did choose.

Of course, different people will consider (and even experience) the onerousness of sexual abstinence differently depending upon their grasp of the reasons for exercising sexual self-restraint. And people's judgments as to whether such reasons obtain will likely vary depending on their understanding, however informal and implicit, of the human good, of what is truly and integrally fulfilling of human persons.

It is entirely understandable that someone whose self-understanding is formed in accordance with the characteristically modern conception of human nature and the human good would be dubious about the proposition that there are morally compelling reasons for people who are not married, who cannot marry, or who, perhaps, merely prefer not to marry, to abstain from sexual relations. For Sullivan and others who share this self-understanding, sexual abstinence seems not only pointless, but emotionally debilitating and even, in some sense, dehumanizing.[18] They should at least consider, however, that the modern conception does not hold a monopoly on the allegiance of thoughtful men and women. The alternative conception of human nature and its fulfillment articulated in the natural law tradition (and embedded in one form or another in historic Jewish and Christian faith) enables people who critically appropriate it to understand themselves and their sexuality very differently. Of course, the adoption of this (or any other) view, even if sound, cannot by itself effect a change of sexual orientation or simply eradicate homosexual or other morally problematic sexual desires. It can, however, and does, render intelligible and meaningful the struggle to live chastely, irrespective of the strength of such desires and regardless of whether one is 'gay' or 'straight,' married or single.

NOTES

1 Andrew Sullivan, *Virtually Normal: An Argument About Homosexuality* (NY: Alfred A. Knopf, 1995). All page references in the text are to this work.
2 See Sullivan's letter to the editor in *Commentary*, Mar. 1997, responding to Norman Podhoretz's article 'How the Gay Rights Movement Won.'
3 Daniel Mendelsohn demolishes many of the claims made by John Boswell in the latter's *Same-Sex Unions in Premodern Europe* (NY: Villard Books, 1994) in 'The Man Behind the Curtain,' *Arion*, III: 3 (1996), 241–273. See also Brent Shaw, 'A Groom of One's Own,' *The New Republic*, July 18/25, 1994, 33–41; and Robin Darling Young 'Gay Marriage: Reimagining Church History,' *First Things*, No. 47, Nov. 1994.

4 On St Paul's teaching regarding the 'unnaturalness' of homosexual acts see Jeffrey Satinover, *Homosexuality and the Politics of Truth* (Grand Rapids: Baker Books, 1996), 151–2.

5 'The Thoughts are to the Desires as Scouts and Spies to range abroad, and find the way to the things desired.' Thomas Hobbes, *Leviathan*, pt. 1, ch. 8 (1651).

6 'Reason is, and ought only to be, the slave of the passions, and can never pretend to any office, other than to serve and obey them.' David Hume, *A Treatise of Human Nature*, bk. 2, pt. 3, s. III (1740).

7 At the same time, because the phrase 'homosexual orientation' is used in ways that render its connotations uncertain, I think it generally preferable to speak of homosexual attraction, desires, tendencies or dispositions. On the 'radically equivocal' character of the phrase as it is deployed in contemporary political debate, see John Finnis, 'Law, Morality, and "Sexual Orientation,"' *Notre Dame Law Review*, 69 (1994), s. I.

8 Thus, Aquinas says that 'the good of the human being is in accord with reason, and human evil is being outside the order of reasonableness.' *Summa Theologiae*, 1–2, q. 71, a. 2c, on which see John Finnis, *Natural Law and Natural Rights* (Oxford: Clarendon Press, 1980), 36.

9 On basic human goods as reasons for action see Robert P. George, 'Recent Criticism of Natural Law Theory,' *University of Chicago Law Review*, 55 (1988), 1371–1429, reprinted herein as Chapter 2. For my critique of the 'naturalism' of Michael Perry—a prominent Catholic thinker who, I maintain, reduces human goods to matters of psychological satisfaction—see Robert P. George, 'Human Flourishing as a Criterion of Morality: A Critique of Perry's Naturalism,' *Tulane Law Review*, 63 (1989), 1455–1474, reprinted herein as Chapter 14.

10 See John Finnis, 'Law, Morality, and "Sexual Orientation,"' s. III.

11 See St Augustine, *De bono coniugali* (9.9). For a critique of the Augustinian view, see Robert P. George and Gerard V. Bradley, 'Marriage and the Liberal Imagination,' *Georgetown Law Journal*, 84 (1995), 301–320, reprinted herein as Chapter 8.

12 Finnis, 'Law, Morality, and "Sexual Orientation,"' 1066.

13 See George and Bradley, 'Marriage and the Liberal Imagination,' 307–9, and the authorities cited therein.

14 For a further explanation and defense of this claim, see George and Bradley, 'Marriage and the Liberal Imagination.' Please note that a sexual act's being reproductive in type is a necessary, though not a sufficient, condition of its being marital. Adulterous acts, for example, can be reproductive in type, and even in effect, but (obviously and by definition) are non-marital.

15 Finnis, 'Law, Morality, and "Sexual Orientation,"' 1066–7. See also, George and Bradley, 'Marriage and the Liberal Imagination,' 313–18. The argument is further developed in Patrick Lee and Robert P. George, 'What Sex Can Be: Self-Alienation, Illusion, or One-Flesh Union,' *American Journal of Jurisprudence*, 42 (1997), reprinted herein as Chapter 9.

16 On the reliance of liberal sex ethics on person–body dualism, see George and Bradley, 'Marriage and the Liberal Imagination,' 311, n. 32. For arguments that dualism of this sort is philosophically untenable, see the works cited therein.

17 See George and Bradley, 'Marriage and the Liberal Imagination'; Lee and George, 'What Sex Can Be'; and John Finnis, 'The Good of Marriage and the Morality of Sexual Relations,' *American Journal of Jurisprudence*, 42 (1997).

18 By the same token, many people who share this understanding find not just abstinence but also sexual *fidelity* to be pointless, debilitating, etc. It is a standing challenge (coming from both 'liberationists' and 'conservatives')

to Sullivan and others who maintain that advocacy of same-sex 'marriage' can be consistent with belief in the requirement of marital fidelity to identify a rational principle (or set of principles) consistent with this understanding which condemns 'open' marriages and promiscuity in general as immoral. Of course, it is clear that some supporters of same-sex 'marriage' do not, in fact, oppose promiscuity. After interviewing Sullivan, the editor of *The Harvard Gay and Lesbian Review* stated his own opinion on these matters: 'The attempt to sanitize same-sex marriage for tactical reasons has resulted in a kind of studied silence on the subject of sex. . . . We end up soft-pedaling sex in favor of "commitment." And while the discussion of sex within marriage has been avoided, the discussion of non-marital and extra-marital sex has also largely been missing. . . . And yet, in talking about an institution that most Americans define as fidelity to a single partner for a lifetime, how can we avoid discussing sexual promiscuity and serial monogamy and the myriad ways that long-term gay couples have defined their relationships. I for one know relatively few gay male couples whose relationship is not "open" to some extent. Gabriel Rotello and Andrew Sullivan . . . have regarded same-sex marriage as a possible antidote to gay male promiscuity and wildness—which it may well be, though I think it's just as likely that gay marriages would liven up the institution [of marriage] as submit to its traditional rules (which suits me fine).' *Harvard Gay and Lesbian Review: A Quarterly Journal of Arts, Letters and Sciences*, 4 (1997), 4.

16

Can Sex Be Reasonable?

Reason is, and ought only to be the slave of the passions, and can never pretend to any other office than to serve and obey them.

David Hume

In his Introduction to *Sex and Reason* (Harvard University Press, 1992), Richard A. Posner says that his 'ambition is to present a theory of sexuality that both explains the principal regularities in the practice of sex and in its social, including legal, regulation and points the way toward reforms in that regulation' (pp. 2–3). Although he states that his emphasis is on positive, rather than normative analysis, his book is filled with policy recommendations and other prescriptions. He describes the normative side of his theory as 'a libertarian—not to be confused with either libertine or modern liberal—theory of sexual regulation' (p. 3). Libertines and liberals will not, however, find much to complain about in Posner's libertarianism. He would permit law no role in maintaining a community's moral ecology: 'Government interference with adult consensual activities is unjustified unless it can be shown to be necessary for the protection of the liberty or property of other persons' (p. 3).[1] And, as Elizabeth Kristol observes, '[o]ver and over . . . Posner extols the virtues of the [permissive or "morally indifferent"] Swedish approach to sex.'[2] Furthermore, orthodox liberals will be pleased (and perhaps a bit surprised) to find that Judge Posner seems perfectly comfortable with the active role played by the courts in advancing significant aspects of the sexual revolution in the United States; indeed, he is, if anything, critical of the Supreme Court for not going far enough (e.g., pp. 324–50).[3]

It will come as no surprise to readers, however, that this libertarianism hinges on what Posner labels and 'economic' theory of sexuality. '[E]conomics,' he says, is 'the science of rational human behavior' (p. 4). An economic theory of sexuality, therefore, 'asserts the paramountcy of rational choice in volitional human behavior, which sexual behavior is' (p. 3). Immediately, however, he anticipates and attempts to answer a possible objection to his project:

The effort may seem quixotic, for it is a commonplace that sexual passion belongs to the domain of the irrational; but it is a false commonplace. One does not will sexual appetite—but one does not will hunger either. The former fact no more excludes the possibility of an economics of sexuality than the latter excludes the possibility of an economics of agriculture (pp. 4–5).

According to Posner, then, an economics of sexuality is possible because, whatever the role of 'passion' and 'appetite,' sexuality does not belong exclusively to the 'domain of the irrational.' Sexual choices are, to some extent at least, 'rational choices.'

Does Posner thus explicitly deny the proposition Hume asserts in the passage quoted above? Does he hold that reason can judge and direct sexual and other passions by determining what one *ought* to want, rather than functioning merely as passion's ingenious servant by determining (only) how one can get what one *happens* to want? In what sense does Posner suppose that sex is or can be a matter of '*rational* choice'? The exact sense in which Posner supposes that sex can be rational is critical to pin down, for depending on whether he accepts or rejects the Humean view of rationality as purely instrumental, important challenges to his presuppositions about human goods, human action and morality will be available to Posner's critics.

To reach such fundamental philosophical issues, however, it will be necessary to cut through the ambiguity of the term 'rational choice.' John Finnis has usefully identified three distinct senses of this term in contemporary philosophical discussion: (1) decision and action which is technically right, i.e., is identifiable according to some art or technique as effective for attaining a certain technical objective; (2) choice which is rationally motivated, i.e., choice whose object has been shaped by practical intelligence and has rational appeal, even if it is in certain respects motivated ultimately by *feelings* (as opposed to *reasons*) which have to some extent fettered and instrumentalized reason, thus rendering the choice unreasonable and immoral, though rational; and (3) choice which is fully reasonable, i.e., choice which is not merely rationally motivated, but complies with all relevant requirements of practical reasonableness and is thus morally right.[4]

It is only in sense (1) that a Humean can affirm the possibility of 'rational choice.' According to Hume, one's non-instrumental ends are given by 'the passions,' not identified and willed for reasons; thus one chooses rationally only to the extent that one pursues those preordained ends intelligently and efficiently. Under a Humean account, what Posner refers to as 'volitional human behavior' (p. 3) is intelligible, and therefore rational, when it is intelligibly directed to the efficient satisfaction of an agent's desires. Rationality, as Humeans understand it, is purely instrumental to maximizing goods or ends whose appeal to the agent is exclusively sub-rational.

The non-instrumental[5] conception of rationality embodied in senses (2) and (3) constitutes a significant challenge to this Humean view of practical reason and human motivation. Defenders of the non-instrumental conception argue that there are ends or goods that provide *ultimate reasons* for choice and action. These ultimate reasons are intelligible not merely as means to the achievement or realization of ends that appeal exclusively to some sub-rational aspect of the acting person (for example, feelings of desire or aversion); rather, their intelligibility as reasons is, at least in part, intrinsic. Hence, rational choices, in senses (2) and (3) are choices for the sake of, and are motivated in part by, ends that are not merely *desired* by some agent as *means* to other ends, but *rationally desirable ends in themselves.*[6] Some philosophers refer to such ends as 'basic human goods.'[7]

The non-instrumental conception of rationality presupposes a multiplicity of basic human goods and the need for free choices among incompatible options for which one has ultimate reasons.[8] Moral norms guide such choices by providing 'second-order' reasons for action[9] that may defeat—though they cannot destroy[10]—'first-order' reasons provided by basic human goods, thus narrowing the possibility for fully reasonable choice (that is, rational choice in sense (3)).[11] In the limiting case, one's fully reasonable and therefore morally upright options would be narrowed to one.

Despite Posner's affirmation of the 'paramountcy of rational choice' in sexual behavior (p. 3), his economic theory of sex neither implies nor entails a denial of Hume's proposition. The 'reason' with which *Sex and Reason* is concerned is, in fact, 'technical' or 'instrumental' reason—reason in a sense akin to sense (1). Thus Posner accurately describes his theory of sex as '[f]unctional, secular, instrumental, [and] utilitarian' (p. 3). By focusing on instrumental rationality, Posner seeks to explain, and *in that sense* to identify, the 'reasons for' (that is to say, the causes of)[12] a wide range of phenomena, including sexual habits, customs, mores, taboos, laws and regulations in various societies at various times in their histories.[13]

Given the kind of economic theory Posner wishes to vindicate in this work and others, it seems clear that he must, like Hume, deny the possibility of non-instrumental rationality. According to what he considers the 'rational' model of human action, 'people act in accordance with the balance of pleasures and pains' (p. 386). If Posner is wrong and reason is capable of mastering passion, then phenomena that are constituted in part by free choices (that is to say, choices that people make for non-instrumental reasons and not merely for the sake of satisfying desires) would defy comprehensive explanation by a theory that is purely 'functional,' 'instrumental' and 'utilitarian.' The affirmation of non-instrumental rationality is incompatible, then, with the kind of economic analysis of sex[14] that Posner proposes.[15] In this sense, at least, Posner is indeed a Humean and as such opens himself up to traditional challenges to the Humean conception of rationality.

Indeed, Posner himself acknowledges as the principal alternative to his economic theory of sex the moral approach to sexual choice, which rejects the Humean conception of rationality as purely instrumental:

> The uncompromising, the truly unassimilable rival of the economic theory . . . is not scientific or social scientific; it is a heterogeneous cluster of moral theories. These theories, the work of Catholic theologians such as Thomas Aquinas, Catholic philosophers such as Elizabeth Anscombe, lawyers such as James Fitzjames Stephen and Patrick Devlin, neoconservatives such as Irving Kristol, and philosophers of liberalism from Immanuel Kant to Joel Feinberg and Ronald Dworkin, are not convergent—far from it. But they are at one in regarding moral and religious beliefs that are irreducible to genuine social interests or practical incentives as the key to both understanding and judging sexual practices and norms. This makes them incompatible with the broadly scientific outlook that informs the approaches I seek to recast in the mold of economics . . . (pp. 3–4).

Posner describes his 'functional approach' to sexuality as 'resolutely secular, scientific . . . and disinclined to view sexual activity in moral terms' (p. 220). In this respect, as Posner himself remarks, his economic theory has much in common with the approaches to sex of Freud, Marcuse and a variety of contemporary feminist, sociobiological and anthropological writers (p. 220). 'To find a real, no-holds-barred rival to the economic approach,' he says, 'we must look outside functionalism to . . . moral theories of sex' (p. 221). In criticizing such theories, Posner pays particular attention to Catholic sexual ethics, in part because 'Catholics are more prone than Protestants to offer *reasons* for religious beliefs and practices' (p. 225).

In contrast to Hume and the purely instrumental conception of reason, Catholic thinkers have held that non-instrumental rationality is indeed possible. What I have labeled the first-order reasons for action provided by intrinsic human goods are, according to Aquinas, 'the first principles of practical reason and basic precepts of natural law.'[16] Moral norms, which provide second-order reasons that guide choice and action with respect to incompatible options provided by the multiplicity of first-order reasons, are themselves principles of natural law. As principles of natural law, both kinds of reasons are accessible to the inquiring human intellect (operating in what Aquinas, following Aristotle, called its 'practical' mode[17]) even apart from revelation or appeals to religious authority.[18]

According to Catholics and other natural law theorists, sex is morally significant because people can choose to have sex for non-instrumental *reasons*, not merely because they have non-rationally grounded *desires* for sexual satisfaction, and can have reasons (including, but not limited to, *conclusive* reasons provided by moral norms) not to have sex, their desires for sexual satisfaction notwithstanding. Decisions to engage or not engage in sexual acts, like other morally significant choices, can therefore be 'rational choices' and, as such, intelligible not merely in the instrumental, but also in the non-instrumental sense. Such choices are morally upright precisely to the extent that they are fully reasonable; they are immoral, even when rationally grounded, when they are excluded by relevant moral norms that defeat one's reasons for making such choices.

Under the Catholic and natural law understandings, for example, the basic human good of transmitting life to new human persons, together with the basic human good of marital union itself (the intelligibility of which partly depends on, and is partly specified by, its unique role and value in transmitting life to, nurturing, and educating new human persons), give partners in marriage basic reasons to engage in sexual intercourse. These reasons may, of course, compete on any particular occasion with reasons the partners have *not* to engage in intercourse. When no moral norm defeats a reason for the spouses to have sex, the choice whether to have sex or not is a choice between morally acceptable options and is, in that sense, underdetermined by reason. To be sure, though, the choice remains rationally grounded, as a choice either way is made for a basic reason.[19]

According to a common misunderstanding, Catholic teaching condemns sexual relations, even between spouses, except for the purpose of procreation. In fact, Catholic teaching affirms and indeed recommends sexual relations for the sake of expressing and making experienced and concrete the marital union of the spouses, even when one or both partners are temporarily or permanently sterile or when they have a reason to avoid procreation. The teaching denies, however, that the partners may reasonably act contrary to the procreative good by sterilizing a sexual act (and thereby committing an *anti*-procreative act and not merely choosing to engage in chaste *non*-procreative sex), as opposed to timing their intercourse to occur during infertile periods thus enabling them to act for the sake of one good (marital union) without acting directly against another (procreation).[20] The tradition thus affirms marital sex even when it is 'just for fun,' so long as it actualizes and expresses their marital love and commitment. The tradition holds that sex is unreasonable, and that therefore people should abstain from sex, when they have no basic reasons to engage in sexual activity or relations, as well as when their reasons to engage in such relations are defeated by countervailing reasons. Thus, the Catholic tradition rejects masturbation, including mutual masturbation, and other acts that aim at orgasm other than for the non-instrumental reasons provided by the goods of procreation and the (genital) expression of marital union.[21]

In rejecting Posner's Humean propositions about reason, the Catholic tradition challenges the premises of Posner's economic theory of sex. In maintaining that people can have sex for non-instrumental reasons, and can have non-instrumental reasons not to have sex, the Catholic tradition directs reason to master passion even in the domain of sexuality.[22] This is not to suggest, however, that reasons is to obliterate desire, as in certain Stoic theories of natural law. On the contrary, reason's role, under the Catholic understanding, is to integrate and channel sexual desires in the service and support of the basic human goods that provide ultimate reasons for people to have sex so as to instantiate and express those goods, or to refrain from having sex out of respect for those goods and the relationships, activities and dispositions which really instantiate and express them. Sexual desire makes an important contribution to human well-being when integrated into human lives, relationships and chosen activities and dispositions in such a way as to serve the procreative and unitive goods of marriage. Sexual desire is morally problematic only to the extent that it is allowed the Humean role of shaping dispositions and choices unintegrated with reasons for action provided by basic human goods. Such desires provide sub-rational motives for acting in ways that compromise individual integrity and/or falsify or damage human relationships.

Moreover, according to the Catholic understanding, sexual choices, like other free (i.e., morally significant) choices, have a 'reflexive' or 'intransitive' significance in addition to their 'transitive' or instrumental significance in bringing about new states of affairs in the world beyond the choosing person's will or character. For free choices *endure* in the character and personality of the choosing subject unless and until they are reversed by some incompatible choice or by the firm resolve to choose differently should one confront the same or relevantly similar options in the future.[23] This durability of choices is possible because in choosing one integrates the objects of one's choices (that is, the intelligible contents of the proposals one's choices *adopt*) into one's will, thus unavoidably effecting a kind of synthesis between oneself as an acting person and the human goods or evils one intends as ends in themselves or means to other ends.[24] Hence, one's sexual and other morally significant choices go to the self-constituting of one's *character*.

Although Posner recognizes that the Catholic approach to sexuality represents a substantial alternative that challenges his 'economic' approach and other 'functional' approaches at the most fundamental level, he displays an inadequate understanding of Catholic sexual ethics and thus fails to appreciate the power and significance of the challenge. His exposition of the modern Catholic understanding of sexual morality and immorality is simplistic and, in certain respects, inaccurate. As a result, he never clearly confronts the challenge posed by Catholic moral teaching to the Humean reduction of all practical reasoning to purely instrumental rationality.

In fact, Posner seems to suppose that all or almost all of Catholic sexual ethics turns on the so-called 'perverted faculty argument'—that is, the claim that sexual acts are immoral when they are 'unnatural' and 'unnatural' when they employ a sexual organ for a purpose other than the one nature intended. After briefly defending this argument against 'the traditional objections' that he describes as 'shallow,' Posner criticizes it for its 'incomplete understanding of the natural functions of human sexuality' (p. 227). 'The point,' he says, 'is not that the idea of a distinctly human nature is wrong or empty but that it no longer points inexorably to Christian sexual morality' (p. 228).

The problem with Posner's analysis and critique of modern Catholic sexual ethics is that most influential Catholic moralists and other sophisticated natural law theorists who defend traditional ideas about sexuality do not rely on the 'perverted faculty argument' or other putative derivations of moral norms from facts about human nature or human functions.[25] In fact, such leading Catholic natural law theorists as Germain Grisez and John Finnis explicitly reject naturalism of this sort as logically untenable.[26] It does not figure in the teachings of modern Popes, nor is it even mentioned in the work of the one contemporary Catholic defender of traditional sexual morality that Posner mentions, Elizabeth Anscombe. In his single comment on Anscombe, he praises her 'powerful defense' of Pope Paul VI's rejection of contraception in his 1968 encyclical *Humanae Vitae*, but fails to observe that neither Anscombe's defense, nor the encyclical itself condemned contraception *on the ground* that it perverts the sexual faculty or is 'unnatural' in the sense of being contrary to a 'natural function.' Although this is not the place to rehearse in detail the arguments advanced by Paul VI and by philosophers such as Anscombe, Grisez and Finnis who defend his teaching,[27] it is worth observing that these moralists reject certain sexual and non-sexual acts as 'unnatural' and 'contrary to natural law' only insofar as they judge them to be *unreasonable*—that is, contrary to moral norms that provide conclusive reasons not to perform such acts.[28]

Despite what Posner suggests, proponents of the Catholic or natural law approach to sexual ethics and to ethics generally do not understand the key to judging human acts and the norms governing those acts to be moral or religious beliefs that are irreducible to genuine human or social interests. According to the Catholic and natural law traditions, no such moral belief could be sound. *All* of morality is concerned with the true good(s) of flesh and blood human beings, and all moral norms attain their force and have their truth by directing the will of the choosing subject in conformity with the ideal of integral human well-being and fulfillment. Morality is about rectitude in willing: one chooses uprightly by willing compatibly with every intrinsic human good as it is, or could be, instantiated in every human person and community. In acting for such goods in morally upright ways, regardless of one's ultimate success in bringing about the results one seeks, one establishes or reinforces a morally upright character. By the same token, immoral actions corrupt one's character, their good consequences, if any, notwithstanding. Immorality—whatever its good and bad consequences for other or for oneself with respect to other interests—is therefore always contrary to the concrete interests of the immoral actor in establishing and maintaining a morally good character.

Of course, the natural law tradition holds that the human good is intrinsically variegated and that, given finitude and other human limitations, people must choose between incompatible options offering different, or different possible instantiations of, basic human goods. One cannot, then, act on every reason provided by every possible instantiation of every basic human good. However, Catholics and other natural law theorists hold that one can and should avoid choosing deliberately to destroy, damage or impede any basic good. In other words, one can and should avoid acting *against* a basic reason (and thus *unreasonably*), even when one chooses to act on another basic reason that is incompatible with the forgone reason.[29] (Of course, the norm that excludes acting directly against a basic human good is not the only moral principle recognized by Catholics and other natural theorists. Other norms, such as the Golden Rule of fairness, are often relevant to sexual and other morally significant choices.)

Posner's failure to engage the most sophisticated defenders of 'moral theories' of sex deprives him of the occasion to defend his economic approach against the most fundamental challenge to its Humean premises, that is, its implicit denial of the possibility of non-instrumental rationality. And this challenge is formidable not only for the economic analysis of sex, but also for the economic analysis of law for which Posner is justly famous. The intrinsically related[30] possibilities of free choice and rationally motivated action point as much to the need for a moral approach to law—and thus to the limitations of economic and other functional approaches—as they do to a moral approach to sex.[31]

NOTES

1 I defend, against familiar liberal and libertarian criticism, the sort of 'moral environmentalism' Posner would exclude in Robert P. George, *Making*

Men Moral: Civil Liberties and Public Morality (NY: Oxford University Press, 1993).

2 Elizabeth Kristol, Book Review, *American Spectator* (May 1992), 68, 70, reviewing Richard A. Posner, *Sex and Reason* (Cambridge, Mass.: Harvard University Press, 1992).

3 Posner is also critical of the Supreme Court for not having offered more persuasive justifications for its decisions in those cases that extended 'sexual freedom' (pp. 324–41).

4 See John Finnis, 'Natural Law and Legal Reasoning,' in *Natural Law Theory: Contemporary Essays*, Robert P. George, ed., (NY: Oxford University Press, 1992), 134, 140–141. Finnis presents these different senses in the reverse of the order in which I have presented them here.

5 I shall employ this term for rationality in senses (2) and (3), i.e., more-than-merely-instrumental rationality.

6 Something is 'rationally desirable' when it is not merely wanted, but wanted *for a reason*. Purely instrumental goods, such as money, are rationally desirable, but not for their own sakes; one's reason for wanting instrumental goods is provided by an end or good other than that good itself. The end or good served by a purely instrumental good provides one's reason for wanting and acting for that good. By contrast, intrinsic or 'basic' goods are rationally desirable for their own sakes, not merely as a means to other ends or goods; one's reason for wanting an intrinsic good is provided by that good itself. It is in this sense that such goods, and only such goods, provide *ultimate reasons* for choice and action. I explain further the idea of basic human goods as providing ultimate reasons for action in Robert P. George, 'Recent Criticism of Natural Law Theory,' *University of Chicago Law Review*, 55 (1988), p. 117, reprinted herein as Chapter 2.

7 See, e.g., John Finnis et al., *Nuclear Deterrence, Morality, and Realism* (NY: Oxford University Press, 1987), 277–81. Among the basic human goods, according to these philosophers, are life and health, knowledge and aesthetic experience, excellence in work and play, and various forms of 'harmony' ((1) within each person, (2) among persons, (3), between persons and their communities, and (4) between persons and the wider reaches (sources, principles, grounds) of reality).

8 On free choice and its relationship to rationally motivated action, see generally Joseph M. Boyle, Jr. et al., *Free Choice: A Self-Referential Argument* (Notre Dame, Ind.: University of Notre Dame Press, 1976), (noting that free choice between possibilities presupposes reasons for action).

9 In situations in which one faces a choice between or among rationally grounded but incompatible possibilities, moral norms sometimes provide conclusive 'second-order' reasons for action that defeat certain 'first-order' reasons provided by basic human goods. One's options for fully reasonable (and not merely rationally grounded) choice are thus narrowed. Where two or more possibilities remain undefeated, one faces a choice between or among morally acceptable options. See Robert P. George 'Does the "Incommensurability Thesis" Imperil Common Sense Moral Judgments?', *American Journal of Jurisprudence*, 37 (1992), reprinted herein as Chapter 4.

10 If a moral norm or other principle were to *destroy* one's reason to perform a certain act or not, then a decision to perform or not to perform that act despite the norm would not merely be unreasonable, but irrational and therefore unintelligible except as an action motivated purely by feeling or some other sub-rational factor.

11 The crucial difference between senses (2) and (3) is that a choice is 'rational' in sense (2) *whenever* it is rationally grounded—that is to say, whenever it is *for a reason* provided by a basic human good—notwithstanding its morality or immorality, whereas a choice is 'rational' in sense (3) only if it is rationally grounded *and* compatible with all relevant moral norms. Thus an immoral choice is not a 'rational choice' in sense (3)—despite a non-instrumental first-order reason for that choice—inasmuch as one has a conclusive second-order reason not to choose that option. The moral norm that provides one's second-order reason not to choose the option in question defeats one's reason for choosing it. A choice that is 'rational' merely in sense (2) is a choice in which one's emotional desire for, commitment to, a particular basic good cuts back on or fetters reason, typically harnessing it to produce rationalizations for discounting moral reasons (for example, considerations of fairness) and thus for immoral behavior. Such a choice, despite its rational ground, is 'motivated ultimately by . . . feelings that have to some extent . . . instrumentalized reason.' Finnis, 'Natural Law and Legal Reasoning,' 140.

12 On the important distinction between *reasons*, strictly speaking, and *causes*, see Daniel N. Robinson, *Philosophy of Psychology* (NY: Columbia University Press, 1985), 50–7. See also George, 'Recent Criticism,' at 1403–4.

13 The considerable strengths of *Sex and Reason* lie in Posner's fascinating speculations about how to account in functionalist terms for everything from differential rates of rape between societies and among different groups within societies, to the relationship of women's income to sexual mores in different societies, to the connection between polygamy and the phenomenon of clitoridectomy ('female circumcision') in certain cultures. The most controversial elements of Posner's book, particularly his treatment of 'rape as if it were a form of theft, and seduction of children as if it were a from of larceny by trick' (p. 183), while certainly interesting, are not especially provocative when considered in light of the careful qualifications he builds into his analyses of these issues. But see Kristol, Book Review, at 68–9.

14 By the same token, the affirmation of rationality in these senses is incompatible with Posner's brand of economic analysis of law or other social phenomena constituted in part by people's free choices. See Finnis, 'Natural Law and Legal Reasoning,' 150.

15 Philosophers who believe in the possibility of rationality in senses (2) and (3) need not and do not deny the possibility and, in many circumstances, the appropriateness of instrumental or technical reasoning-rationality in sense (1). Finnis, for example, argues that '[l]egal reasoning . . . is (at least in large part) technical reasoning not moral reasoning.' Ibid., 142.

16 St Thomas Aquinas, *Summa Theologiae*, 1–2, q. 94, a. 2, William P. Baumgarth and Richard J. Regan, eds. (Indianapolis, Ind.: Hackett Press, 1988) (author's translation).

17 Fundamental to a sound understanding of Aquinas on 'practical' reason and its distinction from 'speculative' (or 'theoretical') reason is Germain Grisez, 'The First Principle of Practical Reason: A Commentary on the *Summa Theologiae*, I–II, Question 94, Article 2,' *Natural Law Forum*, 10 (1965), 168; see also Germain Grisez et al., 'Practical Principles, Moral Truths, and Ultimate Ends,' *American Journal of Jurisprudence*, 32 (1987), 99, 105–6, 115–20. ('[T]he truth of theoretical knowledge is in the conformity of propositions to prior reality . . . [P]ractical knowledge has its reality, not prior to the knowledge, but through it.').

18 This is not to say that revelation cannot illuminate, enrich or buttress our understanding of the requirements of morality, or that religious authority cannot teach these requirements reliably.

19 On the precise sense in which choice between rationally grounded possibilities may nevertheless be rationally underdetermined, see Joseph Raz, *The Morality of Freedom* (NY: Oxford University Press, 1986), 388–9.

20 Thus, Catholic teaching draws a moral distinction between contraception and non-contraceptive ('natural') family planning. The precise object of a contraceptive choice is to impede the transmission of life to a possible new human person, either as an end in itself or as a means to some other end. Hence, contraception as such necessarily involves the formation of a contralife will. Non-contraceptive forms of family planning are those which do not involve the formation of such a will. For a powerful moral critique of contraception and a defense of the proposition that 'natural family planning' can be non-contraceptive and morally legitimate, see Germain Grisez et al. '"Every Marital Act Ought to be Open to a New Life:" Toward a Clearer Understanding,' *The Thomist*, 52 (1988), 365. Apparently, many people wrongly infer from the Catholic rejection of contraception a condemnation of all non-procreative sex. In fact, the Catholic teaching is that spouses can have a non-instrumental *reason* to have sexual intercourse (which will necessarily, of course, be integrated with and supported by sexual *desire*) even when they do not intend the procreative good. See generally John Finnis, 'Personal Integrity, Sexual Morality, and Responsible Parenthood,' *Anthropos*, 1 (1985), 43, 49 (explaining that spouses may engage in intercourse, according to the Catholic tradition, even when there is no chance of procreation, so long as the sexual act 'is appropriate to make concrete and experienced the real marital good').

21 For a careful explanation and philosophical defense of the Catholic rejection of such sexual choices as immoral, see Germain Grisez, *The Way of Lord Jesus, Vol. 2: Living a Christian Life* (Quincy, Ill.: Franciscan Press, 1993), (arguing that masturbatory acts damage the good of self-integration by instrumentalizing the body in the service of producing subjective satisfactions for the conscious self; and that acts of fornication and sodomy, even when their motives do not include a masturbatory component, achieve at best only the illusion of marital intimacy, and, like masturbatory acts, damage self-integration). Any credible critique of Catholic sexual ethics will have to come to terms with the arguments developed by Grisez in this and other works.

22 The very idea of self-mastery presupposes the possibility of free choice and rationally motivated action. Under a Humean account of choice and action, concepts such as self-mastery, self-possession and self-constitution have at best only weak senses.

23 The Catholic tradition is hardly the first to notice the reflexive or instransitive significance of human choosing. Aristotle points to this significance in distinguishing *making* (poiesis) from *doing* (praxis) and arguing that the decisive point of human acting is the activity in its own right. See *Nicomachean Ethics*, Terrence Irwin trans. (Indianapolis, Ind.: Hackett, 1985), 154, on which see John M. Cooper, *Reason and Human Good in Aristotle* (Cambridge, Mass.: Harvard University Press, 1975), 2, 78, 111. Christian reflection on this significance draws considerably from Old Testament sources, especially Deuteronomy 30:19 and Sirach 15:11–20.

24 Cf. Hume who, denying in effect the possibility of free choice and ultimately-rationally motivated action, concluded that human acts 'are by their very

nature temporary and perishing; and where they proceed not from some cause in the characters, and disposition of the person, who perform'd them, they infix not themselves upon him, and can neither redound to his honour, if good, nor infamy, if evil.' See Hume, *Treatise*, 458–9. It is difficult to see how anyone who accepts Hume's view of rationality can avoid this conclusion.

25 Compare Posner's exposition with the far more nuanced and reliable presentation of Catholic teaching on sexual morality in Ronald Lawler et al., *Catholic Sexual Ethics: A Summary Explanation and Defense* (Huntington, Ind.: Our Sunday Visitor, 1985).

26 See Grisez et al., 'Practical Principles,' 1171, John Finnis, *Natural Law and Natural Rights* (NY: Oxford University Press, 1980), 48. In his powerful restatement and defense of traditional natural law theory, Finnis says of the perverted faculty argument that 'as a general premise, in any form strong enough to yield the moral conclusions it has been used to defend, this argument is ridiculous.' Ibid.

27 Readers who are inclined to dismiss the possibility that a credible philosophical case can be made for contraception's immorality would do well to read G. E. M. Anscombe, 'Contraception and Chastity,' in *Ethics and Population*, Michael D. Bayles ed. (Cambridge, Mass.: Shenkman Publishing Co., 1976) 134, 134–53, and Grisez et al., 'Every Marital Act,' 369–90. People commonly suppose that contraception can be rendered morally problematic only on the basis of 'theological' assumptions. On the contrary, contraception can be rendered morally *un*problematic only on the basis of assumptions about human goods, human action, and morality that, however widely held today, are themselves *philosophically* problematic.

28 According to Aquinas, '[t]he good of the human being is in accord with reason, and human evil is being outside the order of reasonableness.' Aquinas, *Summa Theologeaie*, 1–2, q. 71, a. 2c (author's translation). Thus, as Finnis points out, 'for Aquinas, the way to discover what is morally right (virtue) and wrong (vice) is to ask, not what is in accordance with human nature, but what is reasonable,' Grisez, 'Every Marital Act,' 36. In fairness to Posner, it is true that certain neo-scholastic natural law theorists, claiming (incorrectly in my view) the patronage of Aquinas, advance some version of the 'perverted faculty argument' and commit the 'naturalistic fallacy' of purporting to deduce moral norms and other practical principles from purely theoretical premises such as facts about human nature.

29 The theory of human action at work in this analysis distinguishes various modes of voluntariness with different moral implications. Chief in importance is the distinction between *intending* the destruction, damage or non-realization of a basic human good, whether as an end-in-itself or as a means to some other end, and *accepting* such destruction, damage or non-realization, *as a foreseen, but unintended, side effect* of one's choosing. According to traditional natural law theorists, a stringent moral norm always excludes *intending* evil— even for the sake of bringing about good consequences. *Accepting foreseen evils as an unintended side effect*, on the other hand, is morally permissible when, but only when, it violates no other moral norm, such as the norm requiring agents to observe the Golden Rule of fairness in accepting side effects that harm the interests of others. Of course, consequentialists and certain other critics of natural law theory and traditional ethics reject as morally irrelevant the distinction between intending and accepting side effects. For a response to these critics, see John Finnis, 'Intention and Side-Effects,' in *Liability and*

Responsibility: Essays in Law and Morals, R. G. Frey and Christopher Morris, eds. (NY: Cambridge University Press, 1991), 32, 32–44.
30 I explore this relationship and some of its implications for social inquiry in Robert P. George, 'Free Choice, Practical Reason, and Fitness for the Rule of Law,' in *Social Discourse and Moral Judgment*, Daniel N. Robinson, ed. (San Diego, Calif.: Academic Press, 1992), 123–32, reprinted herein as Chapter 6.
31 One can advocate a moral approach to sex, law and other social phenomena constituted in part by free choices without denigrating or denying the value and validity of other approaches, including functional approaches, to such phenomena. These phenomena are also constituted in part by factors other than people's acting for non-instrumental reasons. The moralist cannot therefore say all there is to be said about them. There is plenty of room (and need) for sociological, psychological and, to be sure, economic analyses of these factors.

17

Moralistic Liberalism and Legal Moralism

What may the criminal law legitimately do about vices that do not directly harm anyone not engaging in, or consenting to, them? In *Harmless Wrongdoing*, Joel Feinberg defends what has become the orthodox liberal answer to this question, namely, that the law may take (limited) steps to prevent offense to nonconsenting parties, but may not forbid consenting parties from engaging in victimless immoralities.

Harmless Wrongdoing is the final installment in Feinberg's four-volume series, *The Moral Limits of the Criminal Law.*[1] Like the three volumes that preceded it, it is a model of clear, rigorous and fair-minded philosophical argument. Feinberg carefully frames the propositions that he believes must be established if the liberal critique of 'morals legislation' is to prevail; he defends those propositions by stating with particularity the reasons for believing them to be true; and he fairly considers any reasons he can think of against them or in favor of incompatible alternative propositions.

Feinberg's overarching goal is to vindicate 'the liberal position,' which he defines as the view that '[t]he harm and offense principles, duly clarified and qualified, between them exhaust the class of good reasons for criminal prohibitions' (p. xix). The 'harm principle' states that '[i]t is always a good reason in support of penal legislation that it would be effective in preventing (eliminating, reducing) harm to persons other than the actor (the one prohibited from acting) and there is no other means that is equally effective at no greater cost to other values' (p. xix). The 'offense principle' says that '[i]t is always a good reason in support of a proposed criminal prohibition that it is necessary to prevent serious offense to persons other than the actor and would be an effective means to that end if enacted' (p. xix).

In *Offense to Others*, an earlier volume in the series,[2] Feinberg rejected 'the extreme liberal position' that only the harm principle can justify criminal prohibitions. That rejection enables him to draw on the 'offense principle' to support laws that would forbid pornographers, for example, from displaying their wares in public places. But his 'moderate liberalism' nevertheless enables him to oppose laws that seriously impede, and *a fortiori* those that forbid, distribution of even the most sordid pornographic materials.

In *Harmless Wrongdoing*, Feinberg warns his readers not to confuse the distinction between 'moderate' and 'extreme' liberalism with the distinction between 'cautious' and 'bold' liberalism. Cautious liberals hold that 'only the harm and offense principles state reasons that are always good and frequently decisive for criminalization, while conceding that legal moralism states reasons that are sometimes (but rarely) good' (p. 324). Bold liberals believe that 'the harm and offense principles state reasons that are not only always good and frequently decisive, but also that they are the only kinds of reasons that are ever good or decisive. . . .' (p. 324). While Feinberg has no interest in defending 'extreme' liberalism, he did set out to defend a 'bold,' albeit 'moderate,' liberalism; and he strenuously attempts to hold on to the bold position in the face of criticisms marshaled by opponents of liberalism. He admits, however, that 'some of the legal moralist's counterexamples [may] prove too difficult to handle satisfactorily.' In that case, he is willing to retreat to 'cautious' liberalism as 'the fallback position' (p. 324).

Cautious or bold, Feinberg's liberalism is, by his own reckoning, universalistic and, indeed, 'dogmatic.' Unlike the more circumspect liberalism of, say, Joseph Raz,[3] Feinberg's liberalism is not meant to apply only in modern pluralistic or secular societies. Rather, it is proposed and defended as the one true (political) faith. Although it is in many ways a doctrine of tolerance, it is self-consciously intolerant of non-liberal cultures. In *Harmless Wrongdoing*, Feinberg concludes the *Moral Limits of the Criminal Law* series with a stirring declaration on precisely this point: '[I]f there is personal sovereignty anywhere, then it exists everywhere, in traditional societies as well as in modern pluralistic ones. Liberalism has long been associated with tolerance and caution, but about this point it must be brave enough to be dogmatic' (p. 338).

While he defends a 'dogmatic' liberalism, Feinberg does not offer a dogmatic defense of that liberalism. He does not assume the truth of liberalism in advance. He recognizes that 'the liberal position' on the moral limits of the criminal law is not self-evidently true, and that its truth must therefore be established by argument. Despite this recognition, however, he offers little direct or affirmative argument to establish its truth. His method is one of dialectical, rather than direct, argumentation. He seeks to demonstrate that: (1) the liberal position can withstand arguments meant to establish its falsity; and (2) alternatives to liberalism suffer debilitating defects.

In *Harm to Self*,[4] the third volume in the series, Feinberg indicated that his commitment to liberalism followed in part from his view that 'personal sovereignty' almost always outweighs considerations that support criminalizing behavior that, if it harms anyone, harms only parties consenting to it. And, as he reminds his readers in *Harmless Wrongdoing*, in the very first book of the series, *Harm to Others*,[5] he concluded that the concept of 'moral harm' (or corruption of oneself) is not a legitimate concern of the law because '[h]arm to character . . . need not be a setback to one's interests . . . and when it is not, it cannot be a harm in the primary sense unless the person has a prior interest (and again he need not) in the excellence of his character' (p. 17).

Feinberg's rejection of the concept of moral harm is important because the widely shared Aristotelian belief that a morally upright character is intrinsically valuable is central to the traditional (and, in my view, best) defense of the moral validity of morals laws. The view that personal sovereignty almost always outweighs considerations supporting laws that protect the moral environment in which people form their characters will seem far less plausible to someone who believes, as I do, that a good character is an objective, rather than a mere subjective, interest or value, than it does to Feinberg. Nonetheless, since Feinberg's arguments in *Harmless Wrongdoing* rarely presuppose that his readers share his views about personal sovereignty and moral harm, I shall not take issue with these views here.

Feinberg's defense of the liberal position is moralistic: his reasons for rejecting morals laws are moral reasons. None of the participants in the modern philosophical debate over morals legislation deny that the proper scope of the criminal law is limited. No one believes that the law can or should enforce every moral obligation. Even Feinberg's fiercest opponents acknowledge practical or prudential reasons for restricting the reach of the criminal law. What Feinberg wishes to show is that there are compelling moral reasons as well. He insists that laws forbidding activities that neither harm nor seriously offend others are immoral laws, notwithstanding the immorality of the activities they forbid.

Of course, some liberals argue against morals legislation on the ground that the activities typically forbidden by morals laws are not really immoral. The radical version of this argument appeals to general moral subjectivism or relativism. Consider the following chain of reasoning:

(i)   All moral views are relative.
(ii)   Thus, no one has the right to impose his view of morality on anyone else.
(iii) Therefore, laws forbidding allegedly immoral activities on the ground of their immorality are wrong.

The glaring defect in the logic of this argument has been pointed out by virtually every serious writer on the subject, including Joel Feinberg. Propositions (ii) and (iii) express moral judgments. These judgments are either relative or non-relative. If they are relative, as (i) says that all moral judgments are, then there is no reason for someone who happens not to share them to revise his view in favor of the liberal position. If they are non-relative, then proposition (i) is false and cannot provide a valid premise for propositions (ii) and (iii). Feinberg makes the point in the form of a warning to his fellow liberals:

The liberal . . . had better beware of ethical relativism—or at least of a sweeping ethical relativism, for his own theory is committed to a kind of absolutism about his favorite values. If his arguments conveniently presuppose ethical relativism in some places yet presuppose its denial elsewhere, he is in danger of being hoist with his own petard [p. 305; emphasis in original].

A less radical version of the relativistic argument for liberalism avoids this self-contradiction by affirming the existence of a certain class of objective moral judgments while denying that judgments about the sorts of activities forbidden by morals laws are within this class. Liberals who rely on this argument typically claim, not that all moral judgments are relative, but only that moral judgments condemning activities that do not harm or unreasonably offend others are relative. The relativism of this form of liberalism is what Feinberg might call a less 'sweeping' form of relativism.

This form of liberalism identifies as a central non-relative truth the proposition that it is morally wrong—because it violates people's rights to autonomy or personal sovereignty—for the law to forbid people from doing as they please in matters that concern only themselves and their consenting partners. Moral judgments about such matters—the very stuff of autonomy or sovereignty—are subjective or relative. This form of liberalism identifies the whole of objective morality with the morality of interpersonal conduct. It acknowledges the existence of objective reasons for action (or forbearance) only where the rights or interests of others are at stake. It makes political theory the central concern of moral philosophy, and the requirements of justice the sole concern of political theory.

Feinberg, however, does not wish to argue on the basis of even so limited a form of relativism. He boldly suggests that liberal principles of political morality ought to be persuasive even to people who believe that objective moral norms govern self-regarding, as well as other-regarding, conduct. Thus, he is willing to grant, at least for the sake of argument, that the activities typically forbidden by morals laws really are immoral. The burden of his argument is to show that morals laws are seriously wrong even when the moral norms they enforce are objectively true.

Thus, Feinberg's liberalism accords the legislator the same role as does the liberalism of the moderate relativist who denies that there are self-regarding immoralities. The task of the conscientious legislator, in either form of liberalism, is easier than the traditional moralist imagines; for the legislator can exclude some morally controversial activities from the domain of criminal prohibition without undertaking the daunting task of inquiring into their moral status. The legislator need only inquire whether an act or practice proposed as a candidate for criminalization is likely to prove harmful or unavoidably offensive to non-consenting parties. Of course, that is often a difficult question requiring skill and knowledge in various areas of social (and sometimes natural) science. Consider the question of whether the widespread availability of pornography leads to violence against women. Some competent researchers say 'yes,' others say 'no.' A liberal legislator trying to decide on a bill that would restrict the availability of pornography would have no easy job in sorting through the evidence and deciding which way to vote. But Feinberg's and the moderate relativist's liberalism would free him from the additional task of moral reflection that would otherwise be imposed on him by the traditional moralist who believes that the morality of pornography ought to be relevant to the legislator's judgment.

While declining to identify the whole of objective morality with the morality of interpersonal conduct, Feinberg does share with moderate relativist liberals a conception of liberalism as a purely political doctrine. Unlike competing political doctrines, it is not, nor is it even continuous with, a doctrine of personal morality. It says what society, or the state or the criminal law, must do, may do and may not do. Although Feinberg does not deny that there can be objectively true judgments of personal morality, his liberalism claims to presuppose no particular judgments of personal morality, and is, indeed, meant to be consistent with widely divergent views on the moral permissibility of the activities typically prohibited by morals laws.

Although this conception of liberalism as a purely political doctrine—in no way dependent upon or continuous with a doctrine of personal morality—is the prevailing view among liberal political philosophers, some contemporary liberals dissent from it. Recently some liberal political philosophers have challenged the belief that liberalism consists of a 'relatively independent body of moral principles, addressed primarily to the government and constituting a (semi-)autonomous political morality.'[6] These 'perfectionist'[7] liberals take the view that the values and moral principles that govern practical rationality in the area of personal moral judgments are the same as those that govern in the area of political judgments. Accordingly, they reject the 'anti-perfectionism' of John Rawls and his followers, and ground the liberal concern for individual freedom, not in an autonomous principle of political morality that directs the state to refrain from imposing any controversial conception of human well-being or flourishing on individuals who may not share that conception, but rather in a distinctively liberal conception of human well-being or flourishing.[8] Although perfectionist liberals share Feinberg's aversion to morals legislation, they typically allow the law greater scope to combat vice through non-coercive means than do anti-perfectionist liberals.

Sometimes Feinberg's liberal premises generate conclusions that are unacceptable even to those generally favoring a permissive regime of criminal law. In most of these cases, he is admirably willing to face up to the implications of his fundamental principles and embrace unpopular conclusions openly. For example, instead of fabricating ad hoc reasons to justify widely accepted laws forbidding bigamy and usury, Feinberg straightforwardly declares these practices (when engaged in by consenting parties) to be beyond the morally legitimate reach of the criminal law (p. 166).

In most of the cases in which he would permit the legal prohibition of acts that in themselves harm no one apart from parties consenting to them—consensual dueling and slavery are two examples—he makes it clear that the ground for criminalization is purely pragmatic and has nothing to do with the wickedness of fighting duels or selling oneself into slavery. His sole reason for supporting laws against these sorts of immoralities is that there are 'insolvable problems of verifying voluntariness' (p. 166). His justification, then, for criminalization in these areas is to protect nonconsenting parties from being forced into fighting duels or slavery.

Feinberg does, however, identify one or two cases—which he assures us are strictly hypothetical—in which he finds himself unable, in good conscience, to oppose the criminalization of verifiably voluntary immoralities whose prohibition cannot be justified under an honest application of his liberal principles. An example is a hypothetical case originally proposed by Derek Parfit: a couple deliberately act to conceive a child at a time when they know the child will be born with serious permanent impairments, and when they could have waited a month and conceived a child likely to enjoy perfect health. Now, the couple's action violates neither the harm nor offense principles; so, under a strict application of Feinberg's liberalism, it is, as he admits, beyond the morally permissible scope of the criminal law. Nevertheless, Feinberg is willing to 'carve out a clear categorical exception to [his] liberalism' (p. 327) and permit the law to punish the parents for their cruelty. While not attempting to hide the fact that he is making an exception, he defends his willingness to permit the criminalization of such gratuitous cruelty by appealing to the 'humane spirit' of liberalism. He describes his position as 'reluctantly departing from the letter of liberalism but not from its spirit' (p. 327).

In treating arguments against the liberal position or in favor of the legal enforcement of morality, Feinberg refrains from distorting his opponents' claims or presenting their arguments in an unfairly unfavorable light. He rarely criticizes a view before taking pains to present the strongest argument he can muster on its behalf. He does not pretend that the sole alternative to the libertarian permissiveness he espouses is an authoritarian oppression that no honorable critic of liberalism would endorse or even tolerate. Nor does he resort to questioning the motives or character of those who do not share his liberal faith. In the most ancient and best tradition of philosophy, he treats his interlocutors as partners with him in the quest for truth.

Occasionally, however, he fails, despite a bona fide effort, to understand or adequately represent a non-liberal author, position or argument. For instance, at one point, he mistakenly interprets St Thomas Aquinas as an opponent of victimless crimes and thus as someone who strictly subscribed to the liberal position on the moral limits of the criminal law. What Aquinas actually held in his famous discussion about whether human law should repress all vices, is that the law should be concerned mainly with those vices that cause harm to others. He did not hold the view that the law must, as a matter of principle, refrain from prohibiting victimless immoralities.[9] In fact, Aquinas's position, which is the one I believe to be correct, is the position of most defenders of morals legislation, namely, that, while the main concern of the criminal law ought to be the prevention of murder, rape, theft, fraud and the like, the law may also legitimately protect the community's moral environment by forbidding what James Fitzjames Stephen, the nineteenth-century defender of morals laws, referred to as 'the grosser forms of vice.'[10]

Elsewhere, in attempting to rebut Ernest Nagel's claim that some laws that liberals would justify by reference to the offense principle are really morals laws inasmuch as people find the activities they prohibit offensive precisely because they consider them to be immoral,[11] Feinberg argues:

[I]f public nudity . . . or public married intercourse are judged immoral by most people, it is obviously not because they are thought to be inherently wicked wherever and whenever they occur, but rather precisely because they offend those who witness them. In these cases the actions are immoral (better 'indecent') because they offend; they do not offend because they are judged to be, in their essential nature, immoral. Thus one can urge their prohibition entirely on the liberal ground of the offense principle, without recourse to legal moralism at all [pp. 15–16].

But Feinberg is mistaken in supposing that most people consider public nudity or public married intercourse immoral 'precisely because they offend those who witness them.' Moral conservatives, and other non-liberals, do, in fact, consider public nudity and public married intercourse to be 'inherently wicked' regardless of whether they offend anyone. Of course, they do not consider nudity or marital intercourse to be inherently wicked. But they do consider *public* nudity and *public* intercourse to be wicked—even in circumstances where all the members of the relevant public hold 'sexually liberated' attitudes and are therefore unoffended by public nudity and intercourse. Thus, moral conservatives consider public nudity immoral even on designated nude beaches where, presumably, no one present is in danger of being offended. The reason they consider public nudity immoral—regardless of whether it gives offense—is that it is, 'in its essential nature,' immodest. And immodesty is, in their view, immoral.

At another point, Feinberg ventures to meet a theological argument that seeks to justify the legal enforcement of morals on the ground that all immoralities, including victimless immoralities, are direct wrongs against God and should therefore be punished. According to Feinberg:

[T]here . . . seems [to be] little point, and no justification, for using the resources of the all-too-human political state for such purposes. Just as God's authority over human beings must be thought of in highly personal terms, so must His 'retribution.' No merely political leader has ever made a persuasive claim to speak, qua political leader, for God, and the claim to be an instrument of God's highly personal purposes is a piece of swaggering presumption, not to say insolent usurpation. If God decrees 'retribution' for all private acts that are incidentally non-compliant with His own Will, He has his own resources. The human criminal law is hardly necessary [p. 163].

Here Feinberg fails to appreciate, much less credit, the theology of those who make the argument he attempts to refute. His theological counterargument presupposes an understanding of the relationship between human and divine causality, and between religious and secular authority, that many—perhaps most—religious people simply do not share. They believe that there is nothing in principle presumptuous or insolent about trying to be an 'instrument of God's highly personal purposes.' According to most theological views, God's mercy is as 'highly personal' as his judgment; but people who hold these views do not believe that that fact absolves human beings from the responsibility to serve as instruments of divine mercy. By her own account, Mother Teresa, for example, sought precisely to serve as such an instrument. Thus, it begs the question to say against the Ayatollah, for instance, that his aspiration to be an instrument of another of God's highly personal purposes—namely, his retribution—is 'a piece of swaggering presumption, not to say insolent usurpation.' It is very well to observe that 'God has his own resources' and therefore has no need to employ fallible human institutions like the criminal law. But the fact that an omnipotent God could effect his will in other ways hardly refutes the claim that he has chosen to effect it through any particular agency—even a fallible human agency. After all, God could comfort dying beggars without the help of Mother Teresa. But many religious people suppose that, in his inscrutable wisdom, he has chosen to deliver that comfort precisely through her agency.

It is, to say the least, unusual to encounter explicitly theological argumentation in a work of liberal political theory. Perhaps Feinberg's venture
into theology is merely a stray bullet. I doubt it, though. One of the points
that Feinberg wishes to establish is that the liberal position on the limits of
the criminal law does not depend on any particular view of the source or
content of judgments of personal morality. As I have observed, Feinberg
thinks that people holding widely varied moral (and, we can now add,
religious) views nonetheless have reason to subscribe to liberal political
views. I doubt, however, that his position can be sustained. At critical
points, one will find Feinberg's rejection of particular morals laws more or
less persuasive, depending on one's judgments of personal morality.

Let me give an example of a case in which Feinberg's rejection of a
morals law clearly depends on a judgment of personal morality widely
shared by people who happen to be liberals and widely rejected by people
who hold more traditional ideas. Along with 'Parfit's misconceived baby,'
Feinberg cites as an especially difficult case for liberal opponents of morals legislation Irving Kristol's hypothetical example of a 'gladiatorial con-
test[] in Yankee Stadium before [a] consenting adult audience . . . between
well-paid gladiators who are willing to risk life or limb for huge stakes' (p.
128). A strict liberal will not want the law to prohibit such contests, for
there is no non-consenting victim. Yet, as Feinberg says, '[i]t is morally
wrong for thousands of observers to experience pleasure at the sight of
maiming and killing' (p. 139). As in the 'misconceived baby case,' the
'humane spirit' of liberalism seems to be in conflict with its 'letter.'

Feinberg outlines three possible liberal responses to the gladiatorial
contests. The one that he considers least satisfactory is the very strategy
that worked in the case of dueling and voluntary slavery, namely, to
support a ban on gladiatorial contests on the ground that it is too difficult
to ascertain whether the gladiators' participation is voluntary. Alternatively, a liberal could support a ban on the ground that the gladiatorial
spectacle will brutalize the audience and lead to an increase in violent
crimes. Thus, a legitimate concern to prevent harm to others would
provide the rationale for legal prohibition. Of course, it might be very
difficult to establish that the gladiatorial contests would lead to more
violence. The difficulty of proving that pornography leads to crimes
against women may be replicated in the case of the gladiatorial contests.

A third possibility, which Feinberg describes as 'a rather uncomfortable
fallback position for the liberal who wishes to preserve without hypocrisy
what he can of his liberal principles in the face of Kristol's vivid
counterexample' (p. 131), would be to 'concede that the case is close,' but
distinguish it from the actual examples that people quarrel over: 'pornographic films, bawdy houses, obscene books, homosexuality, prostitution,
private gambling, soft drugs, and the like, [which] are at most very minor

free-floating[12] evils, and at the least, not intuitively evils at all. The liberal can continue to oppose legal prohibitions of them, while acknowledging that the wildly improbable evils in [Kristol's] hypothetical example[] ... are [an]other kettle[] of fish' (p. 131).

The liberal can, to be sure, support the legal proscription of gladiatorial contests without hypocrisy or inconsistency by modifying his position to permit the prohibition of evils that are truly grave. But any judgment of the gravity of evils like those involved in gladiatorial spectacles, and any judgment that compares the gravity of these evils to the gravity of other evils (like those involved in pornographic films, bawdy houses, obscene books, etc.), will be a judgment of personal morality, not a judgment one can make on the basis of liberal principles of political morality.

While liberals will likely judge the evils of gladiatorial contests to be particularly grave, non-liberals are just as likely to judge other evils, including some of those on Feinberg's list, to be equally or even more serious. Many non-liberals consider the sorts of activities that Feinberg assures us are 'at most very minor evils' to be at least very serious evils. Thus, the very considerations of personal morality that may lead Feinberg to favor the banning of gladiatorial contests may lead his philosophical opponents to support the criminalization of, say, pornography, prostitution and the recreational use of drugs.

Liberals may find such judgments baffling; but traditional moralists do not. Traditional morality takes sexual immorality, for example, to be a deadly serious business. Traditional moralists believe that there are intrinsically evil acts—including intrinsically evil sexual acts—and that these acts disintegrate the individual personality and often threaten the integrity of critical human relationships. (In the traditional language, they 'tend to corrupt and deprave.') Of course, traditional moralists might be wrong on these points. Liberals might be correct in supposing that sexual immoralities are 'at most very minor evils.' But, regardless of which side has the superior understanding of sexual morality and immorality, the point remains that if the validity of the liberal position on the moral limits of the criminal law depends on a denial that there are intrinsically evil sexual acts, or that such acts can be seriously evil, then liberalism is not quite as independent of a doctrine of personal morality as Feinberg imagines.

I shall conclude by considering an argument by which Feinberg seeks to show that traditional moralists, who typically subscribe to retributivist justifications of criminal punishment, cannot square their retributivism with their willingness to criminalize 'victimless' immoralities.[13] If successful, the argument tells against what I consider to be the most plausible alternative to the liberal position. But even if the argument ultimately fails, as I think it does, it is nevertheless illuminating. For, to answer Feinberg's argument, the traditional moralist must defend a third

controversial position in addition to his legal moralism and his retributivism, namely, his belief in a prima facie (defeasible) moral obligation
to obey the law as such.

Retributivism holds that punishment is justified for the sake of restoring an order of fairness, particularly in respect of the distribution of the
benefits (including liberty) and burdens (including sacrifices of liberty) of
common life, when this order of fairness has been disturbed by criminal
wrongdoing. For example, a criminal may justly be deprived of liberty
commensurate with the liberty he wrongfully seized in breaking the law.
The retributivist wishes the law to maintain a state of affairs in which a
law-abiding individual, looking back over a period of time, will have no
reason to consider himself to have been a sucker for obeying the law when
others were disregarding it with abandon. Retributivism thus considers
(just) punishment to instantiate—immediately and in itself—the good of
justice because it restores the order of fairness.

Traditional moralists also hold that morals laws may legitimately be
enacted and enforced for the sake of establishing and maintaining a cultural milieu conducive to virtue and inhospitable to vice. And they believe
that morals offenders may legitimately be punished. To some extent, they
understand the moral obligations not to engage in the activities prohibited
by morals laws to be obligations in justice. They hold that it is wrong to
manufacture or distribute or even purchase pornography, for example,
not only because such activities are intrinsically immoral, but also because
one has an obligation to one's fellow citizens not to do things that make
pornography more widely available, or acceptable, or that may tempt or
induce others to produce or distribute or use the stuff. Such an obligation
to others is an obligation in justice. To the extent that antipornography
laws restrict liberty and provide for punishment for the sake of preserving and restoring a just social order, they present no problem for
retributivists.

Of course, Feinberg, who rejects the very concept of moral harm, denies
that people have obligations not to corrupt the characters of others. So he
perceives no injustice in efforts to induce people to use pornography, even
if pornography does tend to corrupt and deprave. But his point against
legal moralists here does not depend on joining the issue with them over
the concept of moral harm. He has noticed that the traditional case for
enforcing morality does not rest exclusively on an appeal to justice, understood as the restoration and preservation of an order of fairness (or a just
social order). The traditional case has a morally paternalistic dimension as
well. But just to the extent that the point of a law is paternalistic—and is
thus motivated by something other than a concern to prevent injustice—
punishment for breaking that law seems to be unjustifiable. If the point of
punishment, according to the retributivist view, is to restore an order of

justice disturbed by criminal wrongdoing, how can punishment be justified for an act which in no way disturbed that order? In Feinberg's terms: how can there be retribution for crimes without victims?

Another way of stating the dispute between liberal and traditional moralists is that they disagree about whether there are ever valid reasons other than the prevention of injustice for restricting people's liberty to do as they please. The liberal position is that there are no such reasons; traditional moralists, on the other hand, hold that preventing people from hurting themselves (physical paternalism) or corrupting themselves (moral paternalism) can be valid reasons for restricting liberty. It is important to notice that Feinberg's argument does not assume the liberal position to be true in advance. Rather, it seeks to exploit what he takes to be a contradiction between retributivism and legal moralism to show that if the traditional moralist wishes to retain his view that what justifies punishment is the good of restoring the disrupted order of justice, then he must abandon his view that the law may justly criminalize acts that do not disrupt that order.

To meet Feinberg's argument, the traditional moralist must indeed claim that 'victimless' crimes involve some injustice. But he need not claim that the injustice inheres in the underlying immoralities of the victimless class that are prohibited under the criminal law. He can claim instead that the morals offender's injustice is the breach of a duty not to break laws that are not unjust—regardless of whether the law is motivated by a concern to prevent injustice and irrespective of whether the activity forbidden by the law is unjust. It is the breach of the duty not to break laws that are not unjust that is itself unjust and, thus, warrants punishment.

Feinberg's argument overlooks the claim of traditional moralists that people have a prima facie moral obligation to obey the laws of a basically just society. Traditional moralists understand this obligation to be an obligation that every member of the community owes to all other members; it is an obligation in justice. They hold that the prima facie obligation may be defeated in the case of seriously unjust laws; and that it is always defeated when the law requires a citizen to perform an unjust or otherwise immoral act. They maintain, however, that where the law is not unjust—whether or not its purpose is to prevent injustice—it creates a moral obligation, even where no such obligation existed prior to the law's enactment. The sheer fact of legislation creates an obligation. People who violate the law breach this obligation and disrupt the order of justice. A concern to restore that order provides a valid retributive reason for punishment.

Thus, traditional morality considers punishment justifiable even in cases where an act forbidden under the law is neither inherently unjust nor intrinsically immoral. Consider, for example, laws based on physical, rather than moral, paternalism. Riding a motorcycle while not wearing a helmet may be dangerous and foolish, but it is neither unjust nor otherwise immoral. It may cost the cyclist his life in an accident, but it will not harm others or corrupt his own character. (In any event, let us stipulate these things for the sake of argument.) Prior to the enactment of a law requiring helmets, cyclists have safety reasons to wear helmets; but it would be unjust to punish them for not wearing helmets, not only because the principles of the rule of law would forbid punishment for a perfectly lawful—even if dangerous and foolish—act, but also because the failure to wear a helmet does not disrupt the order of justice. But, according to traditional moralists, the situation changes the moment a law on the subject goes into force. Where legitimate public authority has acted without injustice to remove from private judgment the choice of whether to wear a helmet while riding a motorcycle, it is unjust for an individual to seize back that choice. Someone who does so—who breaks the law— may justly be punished precisely for the injustice involved in failing to obey a just law.

Of course, the libertarian critic of paternalism will claim that the law's paternalism renders it unjust. But this claim, even if it were true, will not restore the force of Feinberg's argument against retribution for victimless immoralities. That argument is supposed to show that acts which are not unjust in themselves should never be made illegal because there can be no valid retributive reason for punishing people who commit victimless crimes. The argument cannot, however, assume in advance that people cannot be punished for performing acts not in themselves unjust because it is (for some other reason) in principle wrong to criminalize acts except for the sake of preventing injustices. To make this illicit assumption would be to confuse the issue of the proper basis of criminalization with the issue of the legitimacy of punishment for violations of a criminal law.

Feinberg's argument seems to assume that the reason for making an act illegal must be the same as the reason for punishing someone who commits the illegal act. Traditional moralists do not share this assumption. If, as they believe, there is a prima facie moral obligation to obey the law, and if this obligation is an obligation in justice, then a valid retributive reason exists for punishing someone who breaks the law, even where the act forbidden by the law is not inherently unjust. To salvage his argument against retribution for victimless crimes, Feinberg must, therefore, show that traditional morality is mistaken in supposing that there is a prima facie obligation to obey the law, or, at least, mistaken in supposing that the obligation to obey the law is an obligation in justice.

Even if Feinberg ultimately fails to give compelling reasons for traditional moralists to abandon their legal moralism and adopt the liberal position, his project can hardly be described as a failure. The arguments he marshals against legally prohibiting victimless immoralities are far from trivial; and even their failings are illuminating. Moreover, his able defense of liberalism shows that obituaries generated by the recent barrage of criticism of liberal moral and political thought are, at best, premature. Dead traditions of thought do not produce achievements on the order of Joel Feinberg's *Moral Limits of the Criminal Law* series.

NOTES

1 Joel Feinberg, *The Moral Limits of Criminal Law* (NY: Oxford University Press, 1984–88), vol. 1, *Harm to Others*, vol. 2, *Offense to Others*, vol. 3, *Harm to Self*, vol. 4, *Harmless Wrongdoing*.
2 See *supra*, n. 2.
3 See Joseph Raz, 'Liberalism, Skepticism, and Democracy,' *Iowa Law Review*, 74 (1989), 761, 785, n. 31.
4 See *supra*, n. 2.
5 See *supra*, n. 2.
6 Joseph Raz, *The Morality of Freedom* (NY: Oxford University Press, 1986), 4.
7 'Anti-perfectionists' hold that governments are either: (i) required to remain neutral on controversial questions of what makes for, or detracts from, a morally good life; or (ii) forbidden to act on the basis of controversial ideals of moral goodness. They typically defend strict versions of the harm principle as an implication of the requirements of governmental neutrality and the exclusion of ideals. 'Perfectionists' believe that governments may legitimately act on the basis of judgments about what is humanly good and morally right, even when these judgments are controversial. Traditional moralists are perfectionists. They typically reject the harm principle and permit the legal prohibition of some victimless immoralities. But some contemporary liberals are also perfectionists. They reject government neutrality and the exclusion of ideals; but, at the same time, they maintain that a due regard for the human good of individual autonomy limits the means by which governments may pursue controversial moral ideals. They typically accept a version of the harm principle that forbids, or sharply limits, the use of coercive measures to combat victimless immoralities.
8 See generally Vinit Haskar, *Equality, Liberty, and Anti-Perfectionism* (NY: Oxford University Press, 1979); Joseph Raz, *The Morality of Freedom* (Oxford: Clarendon Press, 1986); Galston, 'Liberalism and Public Morality,' in *Liberals on Liberalism*, Alfonso Damico, ed. (Totowa, NJ: Rowman and Littlefield, 1986), 129; William Galston, 'Defending Liberalism,' *American Political Science Review*, 76 (1982), 621.
9 St Thomas Aquinas, *Summa Theologiae*, 1–2, q. 96, a. 2, Reply.
10 James Fitzjames Stephen, *Liberty, Equality, Fraternity* (Chicago, Ill.: University of Chicago Press, 1991).
11 P. 15 (citing Nagel, 'The Enforcement of Morals,' *The Humanist* (May/June 1968), 19, 26).
12 A 'free-floating' evil, in Feinberg's taxonomy, is an evil that exists independently of its effect on anyone's interests. 'Free-floating evils' are a sub-class of

'non-grievance evils,' that is, evils that do not give grounds for personal griev-
ances. For Feinberg's very useful taxonomy of evils, see 17–20.
13 Feinberg sets out this argument on pp. 159–65 of *Harmless Wrongdoing* under
the section title "Retribution" for wrongs without victims.'

18

Law, Democracy and Moral Disagreement

One hears much these days about the decline of civility, decorum and respect among adversaries in public discourse and civic affairs in the United States and elsewhere. Some find the possibility of a palliative in variously articulated notions of why it is important, on many morally divisive issues, to 'agree to disagree.' Many of these notions tend in the direction of skepticism about the possibility of objective truth, practical consensus, or both on such issues. Others tend toward the formal exclusion of substantive moral debate from the realm of politics, lest the passions inevitably unleashed in morally charged political disputation jeopardize social stability. A different tendency is evident, however, in *Democracy and Disagreement: Why Moral Conflict Cannot Be Avoided in Politics, and What Should Be Done About It*, by political theorists Amy Gutmann and Dennis Thompson,[1] and *Legal Reasoning and Political Conflict*,[2] by legal scholar Cass Sunstein. These works offer thoughtful reflections on the implications of moral disagreement for the conduct of civic life and concrete advice about how our polity can best cope with entrenched moral disagreement.

I. RAWLS AND THE FACT OF REASONABLE DISAGREEMENT

Anyone who has ever attended a cocktail party or taught a college course in ethics or political theory is likely to be familiar with the following line of argument. People in our society disagree about the morality of, for example, abortion, pornography or homosexual conduct. The fact of moral disagreement shows that that there is no objective moral truth about these matters; there is merely subjective opinion. Further, no one has a right to impose his merely subjective moral opinions on those who happen not to share them. Therefore, laws prohibiting, discouraging or even disfavoring abortion, pornography or homosexual acts unjustifiably violate people's freedom.

A moment's reflection, however, brings to light a host of fallacies in this line of reasoning. Perhaps the most damning is its illicit inference of an absence of objective moral truth from the existence of moral disagreement. If Alex claims that slavery, for example, is morally wrong, and Bertha disagrees, then the fact of Bertha's disagreement does not mean that Alex's claim is false. True, Alex might be mistaken about the moral wrongness of slavery, but the mere fact of Bertha's disagreement is not a sufficient reason for thinking that he is mistaken. After all, Bertha also might be mistaken. If Charlie comes along, not yet having formed his own opinion about slavery but wishing to form a sound opinion, he will want to consider Alex's arguments for slavery's immorality, together with Bertha's counterarguments, before reaching a judgment. Charlie could not reasonably conclude from the sheer fact of disagreement between Alex and Bertha that the matter admits of no objective moral truth. Moreover, such a conclusion remains unreasonable if Alex and Bertha shift from debating slavery to arguing about abortion, homosexual conduct, pornography, recreational drug use or any other currently contested moral issue.

But what if Alex and Bertha are both 'reasonable people'? If reasonable people disagree about whether an act is immoral, does that mean that no objective truth exists about the matter, that there is only subjective opinion? Not necessarily. Their disagreement may simply mean that either Alex or Bertha is mistaken, or that both are. Even reasonable people are fallible and sometimes are less than fully informed.[3] Alex or Bertha might be partially or wholly ignorant of, or insufficiently attentive to, some relevant fact or value. One or the other (or both) might be making a logical mistake or some other error in reasoning. Prejudice of one sort or another might be impeding a crucial inference or other insight.

Of course, people who believe (as I do) in objective moral truths do not suppose that those truths are always obvious and that moral questions are never difficult. On the contrary, certain moral questions are exceedingly difficult. Some moral questions are intrinsically difficult; others are difficult for people in cultural circumstances in which ignorance, prejudice, self-interest or other factors tend to obscure relevant facts or values and impede critical insights, even for reasonable people. To say that a moral question is difficult, however, is in no way to suggest that it admits of no right answer. Even reasonable disagreement does not indicate an absence of objective truth.[4]

Thus far, I have been concerned with showing that, contrary to what one hears at cocktail parties and in undergraduate classrooms, the absence of objective moral truth does not follow from the existence of disagreement—even 'reasonable disagreement,' that is, disagreement about moral issues of sufficient difficulty that reasonable people, in a prevailing set of circumstances, can find themselves disagreeing about them. There is, however, a less direct, but considerably more sophisticated, way of arguing from the fact of moral disagreement among reasonable people to liberal conclusions about certain morally charged issues of law and public policy. John Rawls's most recent work appeals to what he calls 'the fact of reasonable pluralism' as a premise for a form of liberal constitutionalism[5] that includes, among other things, a 'duly qualified' right to abortion.[6] In constructing his argument, Rawls eschews any appeal to moral subjectivism or relativism, even of a limited type.[7] At the same time, he offers no refutation of the arguments advanced by opponents of abortion in support of their belief in the fundamental equal dignity of unborn human beings. His strategy is not to identify false premises or errors of reasoning in the case that opponents of abortion publicly advance. Rather, he suggests that their claims, even if true, cannot be defended except by appeal to principles drawn from what he calls 'comprehensive doctrines.'[8] He maintains that principles drawn from such doctrines—whether secular, such as Marx's communism or the 'comprehensive' liberalism of Kant or Mill (as opposed to Rawls's noncomprehensive or 'political' liberalism),[9] or religious, such as Judaism or Catholicism—cannot serve as legitimate grounds for making public policy on issues, such as abortion, that touch upon what he calls 'constitutional essentials' and 'matters of basic justice.'[10]

Rawls's argument applies what he calls the 'criterion of reciprocity': namely, the idea that 'our exercise of political power is proper only when we sincerely believe that the reasons we offer for our political action may reasonably be accepted by other citizens as a justification of those actions.'[11] He maintains that when it comes to the issue of abortion, for example, reasonable people who subscribe to certain comprehensive forms of liberalism, or other comprehensive doctrines that also support a woman's right to abortion (in the first trimester of pregnancy, at least, and possibly beyond), cannot be expected to accept the reasons for prohibiting abortion advanced by those who subscribe to competing comprehensive doctrines, which include the belief that the unborn have a right not to be aborted. The arguments advanced by opponents of abortion—even if those arguments appeal to reason alone and not to revelation or other forms of religious authority, and indeed, even if the position they are advanced to support is true—therefore fail to qualify as 'public reasons,' as Rawls conceives them:[12] that is, as reasons that provide legitimate grounds for making public policy when it comes to fundamental political questions. Public policies based on such arguments and reasons violate what Rawls calls 'the liberal principle of legitimacy.'[13]

Therefore, to analyze the problem of abortion in Rawlsian terms, people who believe that abortion is wrongful killing (and as such a violation of human rights), and who are prepared to defend this belief, not (or not exclusively) by appeal to authority or revelation, but by appeal to scientific facts and to moral principles accessible to rational persons as such, should nevertheless desist from the exercise of political power to secure legal protection for abortion's unborn potential victims. As a violation of the liberal principle of legitimacy, advocacy and action to restrict abortion are contrary to political justice and, in that way, unreasonable.

But we must ask: how can it be unreasonable for people to seek legal protection for the unborn if they are prepared to provide rational arguments (which may well be sound) for believing that the unborn are human beings with human rights? Precisely because the issue is fundamental—going to the question of who is to count as a member of the human community whose rights must therefore be respected and protected—it would seem important for any nation to settle its law and public policy on the subject of abortion in accordance with the best moral judgment of its policymakers and citizens.

It is true that arguments in favor of a fetal right to life cannot avoid appealing to certain metaphysical and moral propositions that are currently in dispute among reasonable people. But the same is true of arguments for a right to terminate pregnancy and deliberately bring about fetal death. Rawls's treatment of abortion provides an apt example. He declares that 'any reasonable balance' of the values at stake in the debate about abortion 'will give a woman a duly qualified right to decide whether or not to end her pregnancy during the first trimester . . . [Moreover, it] may allow her such a right beyond this, at least in certain circumstances.'[14] Yet a great many thoughtful people, including most opponents of abortion, reject Rawls's idea that the right to life is properly subject to 'balancing' against competing values in the making of public policy. Is the rejection of this idea somehow unreasonable? Certainly on its face it is not, and Rawls provides no argument for believing it to be so. Indeed, any argument that Rawls, or someone sharing his view, might make in support of the idea that the question of abortion is properly resolved by balancing, let alone the particular conclusions that he claims follow from a proper balancing, will unavoidably appeal to principles drawn from comprehensive liberalism or for some other comprehensive view that many reasonable people reasonably reject.[15] Consequently, Rawls's argument, in the end, offers reasonable citizens who happen not to share his belief in a right to abortion no reason that they can reasonably accept to refrain from acting in the political sphere to vindicate the basic human rights of unborn human beings whom they reasonably believe to be potential victims of unjust killing in abortion.

Should we conclude, then, that the fact of moral disagreement has no relevance whatsoever to the deliberations of citizens, legislators and judges who must make decisions about abortion and other morally charged issues of law and public policy? The two works examined in this chapter argue powerfully for a more limited, although far from trivial, relevance of the fact of moral disagreement to democratic deliberation and legal reasoning. Although both fit comfortably into the liberal tradition of thought about morality, politics and law that has been so powerfully shaped in our time by Rawls's writings, their authors are centrally concerned with the implications of the fact of moral disagreement for the manner in which morally charged issues should be debated and resolved in politics and in the courtroom, instead of with the substantive outcomes that ought to be reached by such deliberations.

II. DELIBERATIVE DEMOCRACY IN THE FACE OF REASONABLE DISAGREEMENT

Gutmann and Thompson develop and defend the ideal of 'deliberative democracy,' which they describe as 'a conception of democracy that secures a central place for moral discussion in political life' (p. 1). Its 'core idea' is that 'when citizens or their representatives disagree morally, they should continue to reason together to reach mutually acceptable decisions' (p. 1). Thus, the deliberative conception of democracy differs from non-deliberative conceptions. For example, a non-deliberative conception of democracy is understood to constitute nothing more lofty than a desirable means of resolving conflicts among citizens who are motivated, for example, purely by self-interest or ideological commitments. The deliberative conception of democracy, on the other hand, has the more elevated goal of also attempting to promote reasonable discussion and mutual respect, even when consensus is unlikely to be achieved.

The 'constitution' of deliberative democracy, as Gutmann and Thompson conceive it, includes as its central principles 'publicity,' which requires that citizens and public officials justify their actions publicly (p. 95), the 'accountability' of members of the democratic polity to their fellow citizens and others who live under their rule (p. 128), and the need for law and public policy to respect 'basic liberty' and to afford to all 'basic opportunity' and 'fair opportunity' (p. 12). The 'first principle' of deliberative democracy, however, is 'reciprocity,' which Gutmann and Thompson define as citizens 'seeking fair terms of social cooperation for their own sake' (p. 2). They add to this requirement the need to try 'to find mutually acceptable ways of resolving moral disagreements' (p. 2). In sum, citizens who are faithful to the ideal of deliberative democracy and who find themselves in fundamental, albeit reasonable, disagreement with their fellow citizens over important moral issues must, in attempting to resolve the conflict, make their arguments in ways that respect their opponents as fellow citizens and reasonable people.

This mutual respect among citizens has intrinsic as well as instrumental value. Reciprocity is more than merely a requirement of prudence for the sake of social peace or even sound public policy, though it will certainly advance the former goal and may even conduce to the latter. Reciprocity is above all a constitutive moral value of deliberative democracy, something that democratic citizens owe to one another as a matter of justice. It is what might be called a 'common good' of the political community, a mutual moral benefit to all concerned, even (or perhaps especially) when people find themselves in irresolvable disagreement over fundamental moral issues. As such, the mutual respect citizens owe to one another provides a kind of moral bond between them, their substantive moral disagreements notwithstanding; and it requires them to search for moral accommodation whenever possible.

The politics of moral disagreement in a deliberative democracy is not, then, simply a matter of putting together a majority for one's position; and it is certainly not a matter of gaining a majority by whatever rhetorical or other means necessary. The ideal of reciprocity is realized in practice when, or to the extent that, citizens understand and accept the obligation to justify their positions to those fellow citizens who reasonably disagree. If democracy is, as Justice Antonin Scalia says, the idea that 'the majority rules,'[16] deliberative democracy, as Gutmann and Thompson conceive it, adds the demand that the winners do their best to justify their position to the losers, thus giving them the respect to which they are justly entitled. In the less than ideal circumstances of real life politics, Gutmann and Thompson maintain, 'citizens who reason reciprocally can recognize that a position is worthy of moral respect even when they think it morally wrong' (pp. 2–3).

To flesh out their conception of deliberative democracy and to illustrate some of its implications, Gutmann and Thompson explore a wide range of currently morally charged political questions, including surrogate motherhood (ch. 7), welfare reform (ch. 8), and affirmative action (ch. 9). Their leading and most frequently invoked example, unsurprisingly, is that of abortion. They distinguish abortion and other moral questions that give rise to true 'deliberative disagreements' from moral questions about which people may happen to disagree, but that do not qualify as matters of deliberative disagreement (pp. 73–4).[17] They cite, as an example of a possible disagreement that is not deliberative, a dispute 'about a policy to legalize discrimination against blacks and women' (p. 3). The difference, they say, is that the claims on both sides of the debate about abortion 'fall within the range of what reciprocity respects' (p. 74).

Although their sympathies seem plainly to fall on the pro-choice side of the debate over abortion, Gutmann and Thompson forthrightly observe that the pro-life position cannot be dismissed, as it often is by their fellow liberals, on the ground that it represents an attempt to impose a religious view on citizens who do not accept it.[18] 'Although pro-life advocates sometimes invoke a religious conception of human life, the belief that the fetus is a human being with constitutional rights does not depend on a distinctively religious conception of personhood' (p. 75). The pro-life view, they say, 'may also derive its plausibility from secular considerations such as the similarity of successive stages in the natural development from fetus to infant,' whereas the pro-choice position 'gains some credibility from the striking differences among a zygote, a five-month-old fetus, and an infant' (p. 75). Gutmann and Thompson conclude that 'in these respects both [the] pro-life and pro-choice positions seem reasonable' (p. 75).

Indeed, Gutmann and Thompson seem to maintain that the pro-life and pro-choice positions are more or less equally reasonable, which means that 'the disagreement is fundamental and irresolvable, at least within the limits of our present moral understanding' (p. 75). The debate over the humanity and moral status of the unborn is, they conclude, a 'deadlock'— for now, at least (pp. 76–7). In defending this obviously highly controversial claim, they say that when it comes to the debate about abortion, 'the effect of reading and listening to the arguments on both sides, at least for citizens who are open to opposing views, has been to conclude that neither side has yet refuted its rival' (p. 75). Here, surely, the authors are illicitly generalizing their own conclusion. The fact is that thoughtful people 'open to opposing views' who have examined the issue have reached various conclusions. Some, to be sure, have drawn Gutmann and Thompson's conclusion that the matter is rationally deadlocked. A great many others, however, have concluded that one side or the other has the stronger (even much stronger) rational case.

Obviously, the sheer fact that reasonable people disagree about the issue of abortion is no warrant for believing that the pro-life and pro-choice positions are roughly equal in rational strength. After all, the fact that reasonable people on both sides of the debate disagree with Gutmann and Thompson's conclusion that the issue is rationally deadlocked does not mean that their conclusion is incorrect. The proposition that the issue of abortion is rationally deadlocked is just one controversial view among a range of controversial views about abortion. In trying to decide which view is correct, the fact of disagreement settles nothing. Anyone who wishes to form a sound judgment has no choice but to examine critically the arguments and counterarguments put forward by champions of the various positions.

To their credit, Gutmann and Thompson present and carefully criticize arguments advanced by several leading proponents of the pro-choice position, including Ronald Dworkin[19] (pp. 75–7) and Cass Sunstein[20] (p. 375, n. 21). Unfortunately, however, they do not present and criticize arguments advanced by pro-life thinkers.[21] In fact, their presentation of the pro-life case suffers from inadequacies that obscure its rational strength. What Gutmann and Thompson describe entirely abstractly as 'the natural development of fetus to infant' (p. 75) is concretely something's (or, more precisely, some being's) natural development from the fetal stage of its life into its infancy. It is the natural development of a distinct, unitary substance—a human being—who begins as a zygote and develops without substantial change through the embryonic and fetal stages of its life, then through its infancy, childhood, adolescence and finally into adulthood. The 'similarity' of the 'successive stages' in a human being's development consists of nothing less than the fact that these stages are stages in the life of a particular human being, with its unity, distinctness, and identity remaining intact through the successive stages of its development.[22] Each of us who is now an adult is the same human being who was at an earlier time an adolescent, a child, an infant, a fetus, an embryo and a zygote. Thus, however striking one finds the differences between zygote, fetus and infant, these differences cannot bear the moral weight necessary to warrant the conclusion that killing X at an early enough stage of X's development is not killing a human being, or indeed is not killing X.

In view of these considerations, it seems difficult to resist John Finnis's conclusion that people who 'attend[] strictly to the arguments and [are] not distracted by the numbers and respectability of those who propose them . . . will find that (apart from the question whether killing is intended in cases where the pregnancy itself threatens the mother's life) the issue is not even a close call.'[23] If Finnis is right (or, for that matter, if he is very badly wrong and the pro-choice argument is the clear winner), does this mean that abortion does not qualify for treatment as a matter of deliberative disagreement as Gutmann and Thompson conceive it?

In my view, people ought to respect the principle of reciprocity whenever they find themselves in disagreement with reasonable people of goodwill, regardless of whether they find the position (or even the arguments) advanced by such people to be worthy of respect. It is not the worthiness of a position (or argument) that makes this principle applicable. Rather, it is a matter of respecting people's reasonableness (even when they are defending a view that one can only judge to be fundamentally unreasonable) and their goodwill (even when they are defending practices or policies that one can only judge to be gravely unjust or in some other way immoral). By observing the principle of reciprocity in moral and political debate, one is not necessarily indicating respect for a position (which one perhaps reasonably judges to be so deeply immoral as to be unworthy of respect), but for the reasonableness and goodwill of the person who, however misguidedly, happens to hold that position. The point of observing the requirements of reciprocity is to fulfill one's obligations in justice to one's fellow citizens who are, like oneself, attempting to think through the moral question at issue as best they can.

However, reciprocity does not necessarily require compromising with one's opponents in circumstances in which political compromise is not a matter of practical necessity; for when it comes to issues such as abortion, no moral compromise is possible without doing injury to someone's rights (that is, the rights of the fetus if, in truth, abortion violates fetal rights, or the rights of the woman if, in truth, women have a right to abortion). Reciprocity does entail, however, that supporters of a right to abortion are entitled to a respectful hearing for their arguments, that opponents of abortion have an obligation to consider these arguments and meet them with counterarguments, and vice versa. It follows, then, that the obligations of the principle of reciprocity will, under certain circumstances, apply even in disagreements in which one side cannot but view the other as denying the equal dignity of a class of their fellow human beings.

Here the test case is surely the issue of slavery. Prior to its abolition, clearheaded people whose understanding was not impeded by prejudice, self-interest, pseudoscience or other prevalent cultural conditions (of which slavery was itself partially a cause and partially an effect) saw slavery for the intolerable moral evil that it was (and is). Almost everybody today thinks of these 'abolitionists' as moral heroes. Many of us imagine that had we been around in those days we would have stood with them. We should allow, however, that some defenders of slavery, although tragically mistaken and objectively guilty of grave injustice toward the enslaved, were not people of bad will. Opponents of slavery, however much they (rightly) held in contempt the pro-slavery position and pro-slavery arguments, had reason to respect the principle of reciprocity in dealing with those persons who, misguidedly but in good faith, held that position and made those arguments,[24] even as they forcefully rebutted those claims and struggled in the political sphere for slavery's abolition. Today, however, in a society in which the institution of slavery has long been abolished, and which is fortunately largely free of the fundamental misconceptions and prejudices that made it possible for reasonable people—even people of goodwill—to rationalize so monstrous an evil, it would be wrong to say that those who would enslave others or rationalize their enslavement deserve treatment in accordance with the principle of reciprocity. Thus, there is no reason to give a respectful hearing to those who would revive those prejudices or stir up the residue of racial prejudice that, alas, remains.

Gutmann and Thompson are therefore right to treat arguments for the reinstitution of slavery or policies of racial discrimination as unworthy of reciprocity. However, I think the reasons they are right go beyond their belief that citizens have greater reasons for certainty on the subjects of slavery and discrimination than on abortion (p. 77). In my view, the key distinction between slavery and racial discrimination, on the one hand, and abortion, on the other, to the extent that the requirements of reciprocity are concerned, is that, whereas ours is (thank God) no longer a society in which it is difficult sometimes even for honorable people to see the wickedness of slavery, it is a society that tends to obscure even for many reasonable people of goodwill the injustice of abortion. Therefore, even those who share my view that abortion is an evil parallel to that of slavery in its denial of the equal dignity of a particular category of human beings can reasonably judge the disagreement about abortion to require them to respect the principle of reciprocity in debating the issue with their opponents, under current circumstances, even as they hope and pray that the day is not far off when people will look back on the era of abortion on demand the way we now look back on the era of chattel slavery.

To be clear, I am not suggesting that the people who perceived the enormity of the evil of slavery prior to its abolition should not have opposed it with resolution and determination, or that they should have refrained from protest and civil disobedience in the cause of ending it. The opposite is true. I also do not suggest that slavery was somehow less evil when it had respectable advocates than it would be today when no respectable person would defend it. What I propose is that a certain sensitivity to the ways in which cultural factors in some cases facilitate, and in others hinder, sound moral understanding can legitimately enter into assessing whether those who perceive and oppose a grave moral evil are obliged to adopt a stance of civility toward their opponents and even a certain (if limited) attitude of respect toward their arguments (namely, a willingness to give their arguments an honest hearing, and a felt obligation to meet them with counterarguments, rather than dismissing them as mere rationalizations for positions adopted in bad faith).

I am not suggesting, however, that the evil of slavery (or abortion) is culturally relative. Slavery was no less unjust in the United States in 1857 than it would be here (and is in the Sudan, where it still exists)[25] in 1997. What can be culturally relative, however, is whether advocates of what one judges to be a grave injustice deserve to be treated in accordance with the principle of reciprocity. My suggestion is that the principle of reciprocity should govern moral debate whenever cultural circumstances or other factors make it possible for reasonable people of goodwill to be mistaken about a putative moral evil; and reasonable people of goodwill can be mistaken about even serious moral evils when ignorance, prejudice, self-interest and other factors that impair sound moral judgment are prevalent in a culture or subculture.[26]

III. REASONABLE DISAGREEMENT AND JUDICIAL REVIEW

One might ask, however, whether great issues of morality and social justice, such as slavery and abortion, are fit subjects for democratic deliberation and resolution at all. Given their fundamental importance, and in view of the intensity of the passions and divisions such issues provoke, would it not be more appropriate to resolve them (or at least attempt to resolve them) judicially rather than democratically? Further, is it not the genius of the American political system often to remove many of the most profoundly divisive issues from what can be viewed as the morally ambiguous and untidy world of democratic politics (in which political compromises often produce results that are flatly inconsistent with anybody's principles) to what Ronald Dworkin describes as the 'forum of principle'[27] provided by appellate courts?

In *Legal Reasoning and Political Conflict*, Cass Sunstein pleads powerfully, and in my view persuasively, for resistance to these sentiments. They are rooted, he suggests, in too optimistic a view of the wisdom, foresight and prudence of judges, and too pessimistic a view of the capacity of people in democracies to settle upon, and live by, sound principles of political morality and to live with the moral and political conflict that is an unavoidable feature of the modern democratic enterprise.[28] In response to what he rightly takes to be Dworkin's overblown claim on behalf of the courts,[29] Sunstein declares that 'the real forum of high principle is politics, not the judiciary—and the most fundamental principles are developed democratically, not in courtrooms' (p. 7).

At the same time, Sunstein eschews the wholesale condemnation of judicial intervention in important moral disputes, such as the conflicts over abortion, pornography and homosexuality. He does not join Justice Scalia, Robert Bork and other advocates of strict judicial restraint, who argue that such interventions amount to a usurpation of democratic authority and a betrayal of constitutional principle. He rejects the 'originalism' through which these jurists seek to establish principled, and not merely pragmatic, limits to the authority of judges to invalidate legislation as unconstitutional. Sunstein argues that the originalist interpretative method cannot justify or accommodate certain 'fixed points' in our constitutional law in areas such as freedom of speech, racial discrimination and sex equality (pp. 173–5).[30] Moreover, he maintains that any interpretative theory, including originalism, cannot be justified except to the extent that it can be credibly presented by its proponents as likely to lead, 'all things considered, . . . to a good system of constitutional law' (p. 175).

Sunstein's approach, then, to the problem of democracy and judicial review is, in a certain sense, pragmatic: he rejects, on the one hand,

Dworkin's idea of courts as 'forums of principle' that are uniquely suited to resolve disputes about matters of political morality that are too fundamental and important to be left to the institutions of democratic rule, and also rejects, on the other hand, the originalists' belief that the judicial invalidation of democratically produced outcomes is in principle illegitimate, except to the extent that it can be justified by appeal to the text, internal logic, structure or original understanding of the Constitution. Where, then, does Sunstein's pragmatism leave us?

It leaves us with case-by-case evaluation, in light of our substantive views about the moral issues at stake in each case together with our best judgments about the likely consequences, all things considered, of their judicial as opposed to democratic resolution. The existence of moral disagreement is by no means irrelevant to such evaluation. Among the things to be considered is the fact that judges who contemplate wading into major moral controversies 'have a weak democratic pedigree and limited fact-finding capacity,' (p. 6) along with the same fallibility and susceptibility to serious moral error as everybody else. These factors suggest the need for 'a special strategy for producing stability and agreement in the midst of social disagreement and pluralism: Arbiters of legal controversies try to produce incompletely theorized agreements' (p. 4).

The idea of 'incompletely theorized agreements' is the central contribution of Sunstein's book.[31] It is, both substantively and procedurally, a pragmatic counsel of judicial restraint. Substantively, it militates against, without definitively precluding, judicial interventions in morally charged disputes, such as those concerning affirmative action, homosexuality and euthanasia.[32] Thus, it cuts against both conservative (as in the case of 'racial preferences')[33] and liberal (as in the case of 'same-sex marriage')[34] judicial activism. Such disputes turn on large-scale moral-theoretical issues about which reasonable people in our society disagree. Judges have opinions on these issues, but their opinions are no more likely to be sound than are the opinions of people in other branches of government (or even those of citizens generally), and no less likely to reflect the values, interests and even prejudices of their class or peer group (p. 177). Procedurally, the idea of 'incompletely theorized agreements' favors limited, incremental judicial interventions when judges embark upon such interventions. In situations in which people agree on a particular result but diverge in their theoretical justifications, Sunstein advocates narrow agreements rather than attempts to appeal to controversial theoretical justifications.

Sunstein illustrates the implications of the idea of 'incompletely theorized agreements' by examining the case of abortion. He reiterates the pro-choice argument he advanced in his 1993 book, *The Partial Constitution* (Cambridge, Mass.: Harvard University Press, 1993), pp. 270–85, which claims that laws forbidding abortion are constitutionally suspect on equal protection grounds because they constitute an impermissibly selective co-optation of women's bodies.[35] This contention is one of the pro-choice arguments criticized by Gutmann and Thompson, and the points they make against it strike me as decisive (p. 375, n. 21). Whether or not the argument is viable does not matter here, however, for Sunstein's purpose in introducing it in *Legal Reasoning and Political Conflict* is not to congratulate the Court for its decision in *Roe* v. *Wade*,[36] or to encourage the Justices to reaffirm its central holding, as they did in *Planned Parenthood* v. *Casey*,[37] only this time on equal protection rather than due process grounds. On the contrary, Sunstein's point is that, even if one accepts his equal protection argument (or some other argument meant to show that laws prohibiting abortion are inconsistent with the Constitution), 'it does not follow that the Supreme Court was correct to invalidate such laws in 1973 in *Roe* v. *Wade*' (p. 180). Had the Court paid heed to the ways in which socially divisive moral issues demand 'incompletely theorized agreements' in law as well as in politics, the Justices would have restrained themselves from attempting to impose upon the nation a comprehensive and definitive resolution of the abortion controversy:

> The Court would have done far better to proceed slowly and incrementally, and on grounds that could have gathered wider social agreement and thus fractured society much less severely. The Court might have ruled that abortions could not be prohibited in cases of rape or incest, or that the law at issue in *Roe* was invalid even if some abortion restrictions might be acceptable. Such narrow grounds would have allowed democratic processes to proceed with a degree of independence— and perhaps to find their own creative solutions acceptable to many sides. In this way a narrow, incompletely theorized agreement could have been possible in the Court, in a way that would have been much healthier for democratic processes in the United States. And in this fashion other branches of government might have participated in the evolving interpretation of the Constitution . . . [pp. 180–1].

The pragmatism evident in this passage will likely strike many of Sunstein's readers as unprincipled. Critics will say that fidelity to constitutional principle surely requires justices who genuinely believe that most or all laws restricting abortion violate the Constitution to invalidate such laws. Moreover, the critics will observe, Justices have sworn an oath to uphold the Constitution; do they not violate that oath in declining, for extraconstitutional reasons, to strike down laws that they believe to be unconstitutional?

Sunstein might well respond to these criticisms simply by reasserting his view that the Constitution should be viewed instrumentally, as a means to certain ends, and that the judiciary is justified in standing back and allowing the machinery of democratic deliberation to work whenever, all things considered, those ends are likely to be better served by judicial abstention or, at least, by circumspection. A more satisfactory defense of Sunstein's position, however, would attack the widely held assumption that the courts, and ultimately the Supreme Court, are always the final authoritative interpreters of the Constitution.[38] After all, federal and state executives and legislators also swear an oath to uphold the Constitution. And they too have roles to play in its interpretation— including the interpretation of its morally significant guarantees. Sunstein's idea of 'incompletely theorized agreements,' if taken seriously by courts, would serve as something of an antidote to the tendency of judges to treat themselves—and, even more importantly, for other actors in the political system (including citizens) to treat them—as enjoying supremacy in matters of constitutional interpretation. As Jeremy Waldron argues, 'legislatures and governors should show the same healthy disrespect for the Supreme Court's general view of the Constitution as the Supreme Court justices characteristically show for what they take to be the general view of the legislatures.'[39] For judges finally to give some considered deference to the opinions of legislators and voters on matters of moral consequence, far from constituting an abdication of fidelity to constitutional principle, would represent a salutary judicial acknowledgment of the moral value of democratic deliberation. Moreover, such deference would constitute a long overdue admission of the fact that judges, as such, have no special powers of moral insight that make it consistently more likely that they will do better than citizens and their elected legislators and executives when it comes to discovering the right answers to controversial moral questions.

Here, perhaps, the test case is school desegregation. *Brown* v. *Board of Education*[40] is a case in which the courts, particularly the Supreme Court, are widely given credit for intervening decisively in a major moral controversy and vindicating basic moral and constitutional rights against racial discrimination. As such, it seems to stand as an example of judges doing successfully what Sunstein's idea of incompletely theorized agreements would discourage them from doing. Whether or not *Roe* v. *Wade* was correctly decided remains a matter of intense disagreement; almost nobody today, however, considers *Brown* to have been a mistake (p. 16). Is it not a good thing that the judiciary, when it came to school desegregation, declined to defer to the contrary constitutional interpretations (if such they were) of state legislators and executives?

Sunstein would be perfectly entitled to argue in self-defense that *Brown* is an entirely laudable exception to what is, after all, nothing more than a general rule that, all things considered, it is better for the health of a democratic society if its courts decline to intervene, or at least decline to intervene in comprehensive and decisive ways, in large-scale moral controversies. He could observe that for every *Brown* in which the courts get it right there is a *Dred Scott*[41] in which they get it grotesquely wrong. In fact, though, in commenting on *Brown* in *Legal Reasoning and Political Conflict*, Sunstein makes no concession to those who would cite that case in support of judicial intervention in morally charged political controversies. Although he treats *Brown* as among the 'fixed points' in constitutional law (p. 16),[42] he questions the success of the Supreme Court's intervention in the school segregation controversy and in related issues of racial discrimination. According to Sunstein, 'real desegregation began only after the democratic branches—Congress and the president— became involved' (p. 176). Further, there is, he says, 'little evidence' that democratic action in the cause of desegregation was the result of the Court's leadership (p. 176).[43] In short, although Sunstein explicitly declines to say that *Brown* was wrongly decided (p. 176), he concludes that, even in that case, judicial intervention cannot be credited with doing much good. The history of desegregation, he suggests, should be counted as evidence of the ability of the people, acting through democratic procedures, to handle serious political conflict, undo substantive injustices, and bring their institutions into line with moral and constitutional principles.

IV. CONCLUSION

Democracy, in practice, often seems incapable of being morally deliberative; courts, by contrast, create the impression of being forums of genuine deliberation about matters of the most profound moral consequence. Sunstein's *Legal Reasoning and Political Conflict* provides strong reasons to question these perceptions, and Gutmann and Thompson's *Democracy and Disagreement* shows how genuine deliberation is possible in a democracy even in the face of serious and protracted moral disagreement. Together, these works provide reasons for Americans to become a bit less cynical about democratic politics and a bit more skeptical of judicial interventions that displace or short-circuit the processes of democratic deliberation.

In commenting on Gutmann and Thompson's work, I have not so much dissented from their view of the importance of reciprocity to proper democratic deliberation as I have attempted to reinforce and extend it, by suggesting that the applicability of the principle of reciprocity can be affected by the bearing of cultural circumstances upon people's abilities to recognize serious evils for what they are.

In Sunstein's work, I find important reasons for doubting the wisdom of attempting to resolve morally charged political conflicts through sweeping judicial intervention. His willingness to expose the weaknesses of arguments for such intervention despite the tendency of courts in recent decades to intervene on behalf of the liberal causes he favors lends particular credibility to the case he makes for 'incompletely theorized agreements.'

More than a few people today wonder how the institutions of American constitutional democracy can meet the challenges presented by profound and seemingly intractable moral disagreement. These works go far toward providing an answer. At the same time, they make it clear that much depends on the willingness of participants in public debates, at every level, to renew their dedication to honesty, self-criticism, civility, good faith and respect for their opponents, however misguided they may believe them to be.

NOTES

1 Amy Gutmann and Dennis Thompson, *Democracy and Disagreement: Why Moral Conflict Cannot Be Avoided in Politics, and What Should Be Done About It* (Cambridge, Mass.: Harvard University Press, 1996).
2 Cass Sunstein, *Legal Reasoning and Political Conflict* (NY and Oxford: Oxford University Press, 1996).
3 John Rawls, *Political Liberalism* (NY: Columbia University Press, 1993), 54–8 (discussing the 'burdens of judgment' that may generate disagreement between 'reasonable persons').
4 Of course, to show that the mere fact of moral disagreement does not logically entail the absence of moral truth is by no means to disprove the moral subjectivist's claim that there are no objective moral truths. The question whether morality is objective or merely subjective is itself a difficult one. The argument from disagreement is perhaps the weakest in the arsenal of moral subjectivists. I shall not address their stronger arguments here, however, because the topic of this chapter is not subjectivism as such, but rather the question of what, if anything, follows from the fact of moral disagreement. For a powerful defense of moral subjectivism, see Jeffrey Goldsworthy, 'Fact and Value in the New Natural Law Theory,' *American Journal of Jurisprudence*, 41 (1996), 21, 38–45. For my criticisms of Goldsworthy's arguments for subjectivism, see Robert P. George, 'A Defense of the New Natural Law Theory,' *American Journal of Jurisprudence*, 41 (1996), 47, 56–61, reprinted herein as Chapter 1.
5 Rawls, *Political Liberalism*, 36.
6 Ibid., 243, n. 32. I should point out that Rawls's formal treatment of abortion is brief and is proposed as a mere illustration of his general argument. However, in his Introduction to the Paperback Edition of *Political Liberalism*, Rawls appears to endorse, subject to several (unspecified) addenda, an argument for a right to abortion advanced in Judith Jarvis Thomson, 'Abortion,' *Boston Review* (Summer 1995), 11, 11–15. See John Rawls, *Political Liberalism*, lvi, n. 31 (paperback ed., 1996). For my criticism of Thomson's argument and a more detailed critique of Rawls's treatment of abortion, see Robert P. George, 'Public Reason and Political Conflict: Abortion and Homosexuality,' *Yale Law Journal*, 106 (1997), 2475–2504, reprinted herein as Chapter 11.
7 Heidi Hurd, in an illuminating review of *Political Liberalism*, explains that 'Rawls is not premising his liberalism on skepticism; on the contrary, he is

seeking to premise his liberalism on [religious, philosophical, and moral] agnosticism and is therefore as loathe to embrace skeptical claims as to embrace
realist ones.' Heidi M. Hurd, 'The Levitation of Liberalism,' *Yale Law Journal*,
105 (1995), 795, 796, n. 6.

8 Rawls, *Political Liberalism*, 59.
9 Ibid., 145.
10 Ibid., 137–8. Rawls qualifies this prohibition somewhat by allowing that principles drawn from comprehensive doctrines may legitimately be invoked in
   political debate, even if that debate concerns constitutional essentials and
   matters of basic justice, when they are introduced in support of policies that
   could be successfully defended by appeal to a purely 'political' conception of
   justice: that is, a conception that is not derived from a comprehensive doctrine.
   See, ibid., 249–52; see also Rawls, *Political Liberalism*, (paperback ed., 1996),
   li–lii (detailing his further qualifications of the prohibition on the invocation
   of principles drawn from comprehensive views).
11 Rawls, *Political Liberalism*, (paperback ed., 1996), xlvi. For a detailed critique of
   Rawls's 'criterion of reciprocity' and his inferences about abortion, see George,
   'Public Reason and Political Conflict.'
12 See Rawls, *Political Liberalism*, 213–16.
13 Ibid., 137.
14 Ibid., 243, n. 32.
15 See Jean Hampton, 'The Common Faith of Liberalism,' *Pacific Philosophical
   Quarterly*, 75 (1994), 186, 208–9; Peter de Marneffe, 'Rawls's Idea of Public
   Reason,' *Pacific Philosophical Quarterly*, 75 (1994), 232, 235; Philip L. Quinn,
   'Political Liberalisms and Their Exclusions of the Religious,' in *Religion and
   Contemporary Liberalism*, Paul Weithman, ed. (Notre Dame, Ind.: University of
   Notre Dame Press, 1997).
16 Antonin Scalia, 'Of Democracy, Morality and the Majority, Address at
   Gregorian University' (May 2, 1996), in *Origins*, 26 (1996), 82, 88.
17 Gutmann and Thompson describe a 'deliberative disagreement' as: 'One in
   which citizens continue to differ about basic moral principles even though they
   seek a resolution that is mutually justifiable. The disagreement persists within
   the deliberative perspective itself. It is fundamental because citizens differ not
   only about the right resolution but also about the reasons on which the conflict
   should be resolved' (p. 73).
18 The most sophisticated version of the claim that laws prohibiting abortion
   constitute an imposition of a religious position is the one advanced in Ronald
   Dworkin, *Life's Dominion: An Argument About Abortion, Euthanasia, and Individual Freedom* (NY: A. A. Knopf, 1993). Gutmann and Thompson's rebuttal of
   Dworkin's argument (75–7) is, to my mind, entirely successful.
19 See Dworkin, *Life's Dominion*, 30–147.
20 See Cass R. Sunstein, *The Partial Constitution* (Cambridge, Mass.: Harvard
   University Press, 1993), 270–85.
21 It would be interesting to know what Gutmann and Thompson would say in
   response to the pro-life arguments advanced, for example, in Patrick Lee,
   Abortion and Unborn Human Life (Washington, DC: Catholic University of
   America Press, 1996); John Finnis, 'Abortion and Health Care Ethics II,' in
   Principles of Health Care Ethics, Raanan Gillon and Ann Lloyd, eds. (Chicester,
   NY: John Wiley and Sons, 1994), 547–57; and Germain Grisez, 'When Do
   People Begin?,' *Proceedings of the American Catholic Philosophical Association*, 63
   (1990), 27. Gutmann and Thompson also do not address directly arguments for
   the existence of moral personhood from the moment of conception, such as

those presented in Dianne Nutwell Irving, 'Scientific and Philosophical Expertise: An Evaluation of the Arguments of "Personhood,"' *Linacre Quarterly*, 60 (1993), 18, 21, and Helen Watt, 'Potential and the Early Human,' *Journal of Medical Ethics*, 22 (1996), 222, 223, 225.

22 In criticizing Ronald Dworkin's defense of the pro-choice position, Gutmann and Thompson correctly observe that the fetus 'is already a human being (as Dworkin acknowledges) and will naturally develop the sentience and consciousness of an infant if it is not killed' (p. 76). They suggest, however, that although pro-life advocates can reasonably believe that the right to life does not depend on the actual attainment of sentience and consciousness, such advocates are not able to provide an argument strong enough to dislodge the (also reasonable) belief of their pro-choice opponents that human beings who have not yet attained sentience and consciousness do not have a right to life— at least not of the sort that would entitle them to the status of 'constitutional [persons who] deserve the same protection that infants and women should enjoy' (p. 76). I think that such an argument has, in fact, been provided, for example, in Lee, *Abortion*, 50–4, and by the other authors cited above in n. 23.

23 John Finnis, 'Is Natural Law Theory Compatible with Limited Government?,' in *Natural Law, Liberalism, and Morality*, Robert P. George, ed. (NY: Oxford University Press, 1996), 1, 18. Gutmann and Thompson contend that certain hypothetical examples of justified killing that Judith Jarvis Thomson previously advanced should, by analogy, 'convince even people who perceive the fetus to be a full-fledged person that to permit abortion is not obviously wrong in the case of a woman who becomes pregnant through no fault of her own (for example, by rape)' (p. 85). These examples do show, I think, that abortion prior to fetal viability in the case of forcible rape need not be what traditional moralists condemn as 'direct killing,' that is the deliberate bringing about of (fetal) death as an end-in-itself or as a means to some other end, as opposed to 'indirect killing,' where death is foreseen and accepted as a side effect but is not, strictly speaking, intended. On this distinction and its significance for moral analysis, see John Finnis, 'Intention and Side-Effects,' in *Liability and Responsibility: Essays in Law and Morals*, R. G. Frey and Christopher W. Morris, eds. (NY: Cambridge University Press, 1991), 32, 44–64. In cases of 'indirect killing' (e.g., the foreseen but unintended killing of non-combatants in otherwise justified strikes against military targets in war), the moral norm, the sound application of which distinguishes justified from wrongful killing, is the requirement to treat others fairly. As to whether the indirect killing of an unborn human being conceived in an act of rape is unfair, I agree with Gutmann and Thompson that the answer is 'not obvious[ ].' Even people who recognize the humanity and equal dignity of the unborn might consider the question of abortion in this case a 'close call.' For an argument that abortion is unfair to its unborn victim even in the case of rape, see Lee, *Abortion*, 120–4. For an argument that administration of a postcoital birth control pill for the purpose of preventing conception after rape can be legitimate (that is, involve no injustice to the unborn), despite the risk that it will cause abortion (as a side effect) if it happens that conception has already occurred, see Finnis, 'Abortion,' 553–4.

24 Of course, not all of slavery's defenders were in good faith. Many saw perfectly clearly slavery's cruelty and wickedness and defended it out of malice, greed or some other ignoble motive.

25 See Nina Shea, *In the Lion's Den* (Nashville, Tenn.: Broadman and Holman Publishers, 1997), 33–4, 121, nn. 5–9; see also Joseph R. Gregory, 'African

Slavery 1996,' *First Things*, 63 (1996), 37, 38–9 (describing slavery in Mauritania and the Sudan).
26 It should sober anyone who thinks about the issue of abortion to remember that among the defenders of slavery were a far from insignificant number of otherwise generally decent people, including, let us not forget, some who strenuously objected to separating slave families and to other egregious forms of inhumane treatment.
27 Ronald Dworkin, *A Matter of Principle* (Cambridge, Mass.: Harvard University Press), 33.
28 It is worth observing here that, although Gutmann and Thompson argue compellingly for the capacity of citizens to engage in democratic deliberation about controversial moral issues, they are not centrally concerned, as Sunstein is, with the questions of when and why judges should defer (as he thinks they usually should) to democratic procedures.
29 See Dworkin, *A Matter of Principle*, 33–71.
30 The brevity of Sunstein's critique leaves unaddressed much that can be said in favor of originalism. For thoughtful recent expositions of theories of originalism, see Antonin Scalia, *A Matter of Interpretation* (Princeton, NJ: Princeton University Press, 1997); Christopher Wolfe, *The Rise of Modern Judicial Review* (Lanham, Md.: Rowman and Littlefield, 1994); and Gerard V. Bradley, 'The Bill of Rights and Originalism,' *University of Illinois Law Review* (1992), 417, 424–31.
31 Sunstein further develops the idea of 'incompletely theorized agreements,' and illustrates it by reference to recent decisions of the Supreme Court, in Cass R. Sunstein, 'The Supreme Court, 1995 Term-Foreword: Leaving Things Undecided,' *Harvard Law Review*, 110 (1996), 4, 20–28, 53–89.
32 See, ibid., 89–99; Cass R. Sunstein, 'The *Dred Scott* Case, Address at Princeton University' (Nov. 20, 1996) (on file with the Harvard Law School Library), in *Great Cases in Constitutional Law* (Robert P. George ed., forthcoming 1999).
33 *Adarand Constructors, Inc.* v. *Pena*, 115 S. Ct. 2097, 2111 (1995) (quoting *Winter Part Communications, Inc.* v. *FCC*, 873 F.2d 347, 366 (D.C. Cir. 1989) (Williams, J., concurring in part and dissenting in part)) (internal quotation marks omitted).
34 *Baehr* v. *Lewin*, 852 P.2d 44, 57 (Haw. 1993).
35 See Sunstein, *Partial Constitution*, 273.
36 410 U.S. 113 (1973).
37 505 U.S. 833 (1992).
38 See, e.g., *Cooper* v. *Aaron*, 358 U.S. 1, 18 (1958) (reasserting 'the basic principle that the federal judiciary is supreme in the exposition of the law of the Constitution' and holding that 'the interpretation of the Fourteenth Amendment enunciated by this Court in the *Brown* case is the supreme law of the land'); Larry Alexander and Frederick Schauer, 'On Extrajudicial Constitutional Interpretation,' *Harvard Law Review*, 110 (1997), 1359, 1362, n. 13 (defending *Cooper* and its assertion of judicial supremacy).
39 Jeremy Waldron, 'Remarks on Mark Tushnet, *Marbury* v. *Madison* and its Legacy,' Address at Princeton University, 6–7 (Oct. 4, 1996) (transcript available in the Harvard Law School Library).
40 347 U.S. 483 (1954).
41 *Dred Scott* v. *Sanford*, 60 U.S. (19 How.) 393 (1857).
42 In fact, Sunstein treats *Brown* as among the 'fixed points' that, he contends, the originalist interpretative method cannot account for or accommodate, 'despite the valiant, recent effort of Michael W. McConnell, "Originalism and

the Desegregation Decisions," *Virginia Law Review*, 81 (1995), 947, 1131–1140.'
Sunstein, 'The Supreme Court,' 50, n. 231.
43 In support of this point, Sunstein cites an important work by his University of
Chicago colleague Gerald Rosenberg, *The Hollow Hope: Can Courts Bring About
Social Change?* (Chicago: University of Chicago Press, 1991).

INDEX

Abortion
  anti-perfectionism principle 197
  Catholic doctrine 208
  human being, fetus as 209–11
  incompletely theorized agreements, idea
    of 326–7
  moral disagreement about 317–18, 320–2
  moral norm forbidding 44
  overlapping consensus 219, 221
  pro-life claims 208–9
  public policy, settling 196
  public reason, and 205–13
  right to life, balance against other
    rights 206
  women's liberty, constraints on 207
Adler, Mortimer 259–62
Anti-perfectionism
  critics of 197
  defense of 197
  principle 197
  strict, Rawls' defense of 198
Aquinas, St Thomas 31–2, 36–42, 60, 63,
  75, 108, 231, 236, 249, 251, 306
Aristotle 115, 234, 249–50
Authority
  need for 107–8
  reliance on 107
Autonomy
  personal, degree of 193
Aztec rituals
  intelligible acts, as 70

Blackburn, Simon 27–8
Bork, Robert 110–11
Boyle, Joseph M., Jr 17–21, 25–6, 83, 85,
  129–30, 229

Capital punishment
  morally permissible, whether 44
Causality
  empiricist theory of 41
  free choice not presupposing 57–8
Civil liberties
  liberal understanding of 7
Cloning
  nonzygotic cells, potential for
    development 212
Clor, Harry 187–8, 191
Collaboration
  political community, in 133
  religion as reason for 134–5

Common good
  central sense of 133
  human action, coordination of
    238
  individual or private good
    distinguished 129
  meaning 235
  religion as aspect of 133, 135
  territorial state, good of 234
Communities
  authority in 107–8
  choices by 107
  complete 234–6
  moral environment 192
Consequentialism
  comparison, standards of 270
  dispute about 269
  ethical theory, in 268–9
Constitution
  abortion laws, consistency of 327
  instrumental view of 327
  interpretation of 328
Contraception
  immorality of 151–2
Creation
  meaning and value 42
  parts, division into 41
Criminal law
  harmless wrongdoing, dealing with
    300–13
  liberal position on limits of 308
  minor evils, prohibiting 309
  offensive conduct, prohibiting 306
  permissive regime 305
  physical paternalism, based on 312
  punishment, justification of
    retributivist 11, 309–10
  traditional morality 311–12
Culture
  diversity 242–3

Democracy
  deliberative 11
    conception of 220–1
    constitution of 319
    moral 329
    reasonable disagreement, in face of
      319–24
  reciprocity 220
Desert
  entitlement, and 34–5

traditional law, in 215
validity, requirements for 143
May, William 83
MacCormick, Neil 113–15, 228
McDowell, John 31
McInerny, Ralph 84–5
MacIntyre, Alasdair 249–57
Mackie, John 2, 17, 24–5
Medicine
instrumental value 47
Metaphysics
ethics, preceding 84
Mill, John Stuart 193, 201
Money
instrumental good, as 103
instrumental value 47
reason for wanting 46
utility of 46
Moore, Michael S. 31
Moral harm
concept of 302
rejection of concept 310
Moral judgment
political decisionmaking, in 5
Moral knowledge
axial foundations of 259, 262, 264
Finnis's theory on foundations, critique
of 262–6
naturalist account of 259
Moral norms
abortion, forbidding 44
Aquinas, theories of 36–42
choice and action, guiding 125
choice as to 37–8
choices free of constraints of 71
feelings and desires, as projections of 17
first practical principles, from 49–54
free choice
as norms for 40, 118–19, 233
presupposing 55
fundamental principles of natural law
not being 102
human nature, derivation from 37, 40,
85
ideal of integral human fulfilment,
and 68
identification of 37
intention of evil, forbidding 96–7
knowledge, derivation of 87
political morality 127–31
practical principles, as 17
practical reasoning, role in 104
reasons for action, providing 118–19, 125
reasons not to choose action,
providing 229, 232
second order reasons, as 96
senses of good, confusion of 20

single correct answer, not generating 71
situations controlled by 95
specific 233
derivation of 44
Moral obligations
political action based on, refusal to
take 201
Moral principles
general, set of 49
intermediate 52
requirement of practical
reasonableness 49
Moral responsibility
causal determinacy, relations to 33
desert as implication of 34–5
free and determinate, act to be 32, 59
Morality
Catholic and natural law tradition 293–4
disagreement about
anti-perfectionism principle 197
fair procedures for resolution of 196
overlapping consensus 219
scope of rights, as to 219
stable political society, in 196
first principle of 44–5, 50–4, 103, 233
human flourishing as criterion of 9, 266
incompatible right options, choice
between 104
interpersonal conduct, of 304
Kantian theory 61
legislation, argument against 302
liberal understanding of 7
modes of responsibility, derivation of 52
nature, grounding in 84
nature, relationship with 86
ontology, separation of 33
political, norms of 127–31
principles 103–4
public, laws upholding 130
self-evidence 43
sexual, modern liberalism 214
traditional 309
Morals
legal enforcement 10
justification of 307
Motivation
Humean theory of 19
prescriptivity, link with 19
rational 19

Natural assets
entitlement to 35
Natural law
absolutist and doctrinaire, thinking as 8
cultural diversity, respecting 242–3
deontological understanding of 83
first principles 231